SCHOLARSHIP IN WOMEN'S HISTORY: REDISCOVERED AND NEW

Editor

GERDA LERNER

A CARLSON PUBLISHING SERIES

For a complete listing of the titles in this series,
please see the back of this book.

Working Women in Russia Under the Hunger Tsars

POLITICAL ACTIVISM AND DAILY LIFE

Anne Bobroff-Hajal

CARLSON
Publishing Inc

BROOKLYN, NEW YORK, 1994

Please see the end of this volume for a listing of all the titles in the Carlson Publishing Series *Scholarship in Women's History: Rediscovered and New*, edited by Gerda Lerner, of which this is Volume 3.

Library of Congress Cataloging-in-Publication Data

Bobroff-Hajal, Anne.
    Working women in Russian under the hunger tsars: political activism and daily life / by Anne Bobroff-Hajal.
       p.   cm. — (Scholarship in women's history ; 3)
    Revision of the author's thesis (Ph.D.)—University of Michigan.
    Includes bibliographical references (p.   ) and index.
    ISBN 0-926019-64-3
    1. Women—Employment—Russia—History—20th century. 2. Women—Russia-
-History—20th century. 3. Women—Russia—Social conditions.
4. Russia—Social conditions. I. Title   II. Series.
HD6167.B62   1994
331.4'0947—dc20   94-20199

Typographic design: Julian Waters

Typeface: Bitstream ITC Galliard

Jacket and Case design: Alison Lew

Index prepared by Scholars Editorial Services, Inc., Madison, Wisconsin.

Printed on acid-free, 250-year-life paper.

Manufactured in the United States of America.

Contents

List of Illustrations

Editor's Introduction
to the Series

An important aspect of the development of modern scholarship in Women's History has been the recovery of lost, forgotten or neglected sources. In the 1960s, when the practitioners of Women's History were so few as to be virtually invisible to the general profession, one of the commonly heard answers to the question, why is there nothing about women in your text? was that, unfortunately, women until the most recent past, had to be counted among the illiterate and had therefore not left many sources. It was common then to refer to women as among the "anonymous"—a group that included members of minority racial and ethnic groups of both sexes, most working-class people, colonials, Native Americans and women. In short, most of the populations of the past. These ignorant and erroneous answers satisfied only those who wished to stifle discussion, but they did make the issue of "sources" an urgent concern to practitioners of Women's History.

To historians who had done work in primary sources regarding women, it was obvious that the alleged dearth of sources did not exist, but it was true that the sources were not readily available. In archives and finding guides, women disappeared under the names of male family members. The voluminous records of their organizational work were disorganized, uncatalogued, and not infrequently rotting in file boxes in basement storage rooms. Since few if any researchers were interested in them, there seemed to be little purpose in making them accessible or even maintaining them. There were no archival projects to preserve the primary sources of American women comparable to the well-supported archival projects concerning Presidents and male political leaders. There were only a few and quite partial bibliographies of American women, while the encyclopedic reference works, such as the *DAB* (*Dictionary of American Biography*) or similar sources traditionally neglected to include all but a small number of women notables.

When the three-volume *Notable American Women: 1607–1950: A Biographical Dictionary* appeared in 1971, (to be followed by a fourth volume in 1980), it marked an important contribution to sources on women.[1] This comprehensive scholarly work consisted of 1,801 entries, with a biographical essay and a bibliography of works by and about each woman under discussion. It readily became obvious to even the casual user of these volumes how few modern biographies of these notable women existed, despite the availability of sources.

The real breakthrough regarding "sources" was made by a "grand manuscript search," begun in 1971, which aimed to survey historical archives in every state and identify their holdings pertaining to women. This project was started by a small committee—Clarke Chambers, Carl Degler, Janet James, Anne Firor Scott and myself. After a mail questionnaire survey of 11,000 repositories in every state, to which more than 7,000 repositories responded, it was clear that the sources on women were far wider and deeper than anyone had suspected. Ultimately, the survey resulted in a two-volume reference tool, Andrea Hinding, ed., *Women's History Sources: A Guide to Archives and Manuscript Collections in the United States.*[2]

The project proved that there were unused and neglected sources of Women's History to be found literally in every archive in the country. Participation in the survey convinced many archivists to reorganize and reclassify their holdings, so that materials about women could be more readily identified.

The arguments about "illiterate women" and absence of sources are no longer heard, but the problem of having accessible sources for Women's History continued. Even after archives and libraries reorganized and reclassified their source holding on the subject, most of the pertinent materials were not available in print. Many of the early developers of Women's History worked on source collections, reprint edition projects and, of course, bibliographies. The rapid and quite spectacular expansion of the field brought with it such great demand for sources that publishers at last responded. The past twenty years have seen a virtual flood of publications in Women's History, so that the previous dearth of material seems almost inconceivable to today's students.

For myself, having put a good many years of my professional life into the development of "source books" and bibliographies, it did not seem particularly urgent to continue the effort under the present conditions. But I was awakened to the fact that there might still be a problem of neglected and forgotten sources in Women's History as a result of a conference, which Kathryn Sklar and I organized in 1988. The Wingspread Conference "Graduate Training in U.S. Women's History" brought together 63 representatives of 57 institutions of higher education who each represented a graduate program in Women's History. As part of our preparation for the conference, we asked each person invited to list all the dissertations in Women's History she had directed or was then directing. The result was staggering: it appeared that there were 99 completed dissertations and 236 then underway. This was by no means the entire national output, since we surveyed only the 63 participants at the conference and did not survey the many faculty persons not represented, who had directed such dissertations. The questions arose—What happened to all these dissertations? Why did so many of them not get published?

When Ralph Carlson approached me at about that time with the idea of publishing "lost sources" in Women's History, I was more ready than I would have been without benefit of the Wingspread survey to believe that, indeed, there still were some such neglected sources out there, and to undertake such a project.

We used the dissertation list from the Wingspread Conference as a starting point. A researcher then went through all the reference works listing dissertations in history and other fields in the English language from 1870 to the present. Among these she identified 1,235 titles in what we now call Women's History. We then cross-checked these titles against the electronic catalog of the Library of Congress, which represents every book owned by the LC (or to define it differently, every book copyrighted and published in the U.S.). This cross-check revealed that of the 1,235 dissertations, 314 had been published, which is more than 25 percent. That represents an unusually high publication ratio, which may be a reflection of the growth and quality of the field.

A further selection based on abstracts of the 921 unpublished dissertations narrowed the field to 101. Of these we could not locate 33 authors or the authors were not interested in publication. Out of the 68 remaining dissertations we selected the eleven we considered best in both scholarship and writing. These are first-rate books that should have been published earlier and that for one reason or another fell between the cracks.

Why did they not get published earlier? In the case of the Boatwright manuscript, an unusually brilliant Master's thesis done in 1939, undoubtedly the neglect of Women's History at that time made the topic seem unsuitable for publication. Similar considerations may have worked against publication of several other earlier dissertations. In other cases, lack of mentorship and inexperience discouraged the writers from pursuing publication in the face of one or two rejections of their manuscripts. Several of the most valuable books in the series required considerable rewriting under editorial supervision, which, apparently, had not earlier been available to the authors. There are also several authors who became members of what we call "the lost generation," historians getting their degrees in the 1980s when there were few jobs available. This group of historians, which disproportionately consisted of women, retooled and went into different fields. Three of the books in this series are the work of these historians, who needed considerable persuasion to do the necessary revisions and editing. We are pleased to have found their works and to have persisted in the effort of making them available to a wider readership, since they have a distinct contribution to make.

The books in this series cover a wide range of topics. Two of them are detailed studies in the status of women, one in Georgia, 1783-1860, the other in Russia in the early 1900s. Two are valuable additions to the literature on the anti-woman's suffrage campaigns in the U.S. Of the four books dealing with the history of women's organizations, three are detailed regional studies and one is a comparative history of the British and American Women's Trade Union League. Finally, the three biographical studies of eighteenth- and nineteenth-century women offer either new information or new interpretations of their subjects.

Eleanor Miot Boatwright, *Status of Women in Georgia, 1783–1860*, was discovered by Professor Anne Firor Scott in the Duke University archives and represents, in her words "a buried treasure." An M.A. thesis written by a high school teacher in Augusta, Georgia, its level of scholarship and the depth of its research are of the quality expected of a dissertation. The author has drawn on a vast range of primary sources, including legal sources that were then commonly used for social history, to document and analyze the social customs, class differences, work and religion of white women in Georgia. While her treatment of race relations reflects the limitations of scholarship on that subject in the 1930s, she gives careful attention to the impact of race relations on white women. Her analysis of the linkage made by Southern male apologists for slavery between the subordination ("protection") of women and the subordination of slaves (also rationalized as their "protection") is particularly insightful. The work has much information to offer the contemporary scholar and can be compared in its scholarship and its general approach to the work of Julia Spruill and Elizabeth Massey. When it is evaluated in comparison with other social histories of its period, its research methodology and interpretative focus on women are truly remarkable.

Anne Bobroff-Hajal's, *Working Women in Russia Under the Hunger Tsars: Political Activism and Daily Life,* is a fascinating, excellently researched study of a topic on which there is virtually no material available in the English language. Focusing on women industrial workers in Russia's Central Industrial Region, most of them employed in textile production, Bobroff-Hajal studied their daily lives and family patterns, their gender socialization, their working and living conditions and their political activism during the Revolution: in political organizations, in food riots and in street fighting. The fact that these women and their families lived mostly in factory barracks will be of added interest to labor historians, who may wish to compare their lives and activities with other similarly situated groups in the U.S. and England. Drawing on a rich mixture of folkloric sources, local newspapers, oral histories, workers' memoirs and ethnographic material, Bobroff-Hajal presents a convincing and intimate picture of working-class life before the Russian Revolution. Bobroff-Hajal finds that the particularly strong mother-child bonding of Russian women workers, to which they were indoctrinated from childhood on, undermined their ability to form coherent political groups capable of maintaining their identity over a long period of time. Her thesis, excellently supported and well argued, may undermine some commonly held beliefs on this subject. It should prove of interest to all scholars working on gender socialization and to others working on labor culture, working-class activism, and class consciousness.

Rosemary Keller, *Patriotism and the Female Sex: Abigail Adams and the American Revolution,* is a sophisticated, well-documented interpretation of Abigail Adams's intellectual and political development, set firmly within the historical context. Compared with other Abigail Adams biographies, this work is outstanding in treating her seriously as an agent in history and as an independent intellectual. Abigail Adams emerges from this study as a woman going as far as it was possible to go within the limits of the gender conventions of her time and struggling valiantly, through influencing her husband, to extend these gender conventions. This is an accomplishment quite sufficient for one woman's life time. Professor Keller's sensitive biography makes a real contribution to colonial and women's history.

Elizabeth Ann Bartlett, *Liberty, Equality, Sorority: The Origins and Integrity of Feminist Thought: Frances Wright, Sarah Grimké and Margaret Fuller*, is another work of intellectual history. It attempts to define a common "feminism" emerging from the thought of these important nineteenth-century thinkers and concludes that feminism, in order to sustain itself, must balance the tensions between the concepts of liberty, equality, and sorority. The lucid, well-researched discussions of each woman's life and work should appeal to the general reader and make this book a valuable addition to courses in intellectual history and women's history and literature.

Mary Grant, *Private Woman, Public Person: An Account of the Life of Julia Ward Howe from 1819 to 1868*, is a sensitive, feminist study of Howe's life and thought up to the turning point in 1868, when she decided to dedicate her life to public activism in behalf of women. By carefully analyzing Howe's private letters and journals, the author uncovers a freer, more powerful and creative writer beneath the formal *persona* of the author of "The Battle Hymn of the Republic" than we have hitherto known. She also discusses in detail Howe's fascinating, never published, unfinished novel, "Eva and Raphael," which features a number of then taboo subjects, such as rape, madness and an androgynous character. This well-written biography reveals new aspects and dimensions of Julia Ward Howe's life and work.

Jane Jerome Camhi, *Women Against Women: American Anti-Suffragism, 1880-1920*, and Thomas J. Jablonsky, *The Home, Heaven, and Mother Party: Female Anti-Suffragists in America, 1868-1920*, are complementary studies that should be indispensable for any serious student or scholar of woman suffrage. They are, in fact, the only extant book-length studies of anti-suffragism. This important movement has until now been accessible to modern readers only through the somewhat biased lens of contemporary suffragists' observations. They consistently underestimated its scope and significance and did not engage with its basic paradox, that it was a movement by women against women.

Jane Camhi's comprehensive study of nationwide anti-woman's suffrage movements makes this paradox a central theme. Camhi analyses the "antis' " ideas and ideology and offers some thought-provoking theories about the competing and contradictory positions women took in regard to formal political power. Her insightful profile of a noted anti-suffragist, Ida Tarbell, is an additional contribution this fine book makes to the historical literature.

Thomas Jablonsky's study is focused more narrowly on the organizational history of the rise and fall of the movement. The book is based on extensive research in the organizational records of the anti-suffragists on a state and national level, the records of Congressional hearings, biographical works and the manuscripts of leaders. Jablonsky takes the "antis" seriously and disproves the suffragists' argument that they were merely pawns of male interest groups. He offers a sympathetic, but critical evaluation of their ideas. His detailed attention to organizational efforts in states other than the major battle-grounds—Massachusetts, New York and Illinois—make this book a valuable resource for scholars in history, political science and Women's History.

The four remaining books in the series all focus on aspects of women's organizational activities. Taken together, they reveal the amazing energy, creativity, and persistence of women's institution building on the community and local level. They sustain and highlight the thesis that women built the infrastructures of community life, while men held the positions of visible power. Based on research in four distinctly different regions, these studies should prove useful not only for the intrinsic worth of each, but for comparative purposes.

Darlene Roth, *Matronage: Patterns in Women's Organizations, Atlanta, Georgia, 1890-1940*, is a thoroughly researched, gracefully written study of the networks of women's organizations in that city. The author's focus on conservative women's organizations, such as the Daughters of the American Revolution, the Colonial Dames, and the African-American Chatauqua Circle, adds to the significance of the book. The author defines "matronage" as the functions and institutionalization of the networks of social association among women. By focusing on a Southern city in the Progressive era, Roth provides rich comparative material for the study of women's voluntarism. She challenges notions of the lack of organizational involvement by Southern women. She traces the development of women's activities from communal service orientation—the building of war memorials—to advocacy of the claims of women and children and, finally, to advocacy of women's rights. Her comparative approach, based on the study of the records of white and African-American women's organizations and leadership—she studied 508 white and 150 black women—is illuminating and offers new insights. The book should be of interest to readers in Urban and Community History, Southern History, and Women's History.

Robin Miller Jacoby, *The British and American Women's Trade Union Leagues, 1890-1925: A Case Study of Feminism and Class*, is a comparative study of working-class women in Britain and America in the Progressive period. Although parts of this work have appeared as articles in scholarly journals, the work has never before been accessible in its entirety. Jacoby traces the development of Women's Trade Union Leagues in Britain and America, exploring their different trajectories and settings. By focusing on the interaction of women's and labor movements, the author provides rich empirical material. Her analysis of the tensions and overlapping interests of feminism and class consciousness is important to feminist theory. Her discussion of protective labor legislation, as it was debated and acted upon in two different contexts, makes an important contribution to the existing literature. It also addressees issues still topical and hotly debated in the present day. The book will be of interest to labor historians, Women's History specialists, and the general public.

Janice Steinschneider, *An Improved Woman: The Wisconsin Federation of Women's Clubs, 1895-1920*, is a richly documented study based on a multitude of primary sources, which reveals the amazing range of women's activities as community builders and agents of change. Wisconsin clubwomen founded libraries, fostered changes in school curricula and worked to start kindergartens and playgrounds. They helped preserve historic and natural landmarks and organized to improve public health services. They built a sound political base—long before they had the right of suffrage—from which they trained women leaders for whom they then helped to secure public appointments. They worked to gain access for women to university education and employment and, in addition to many other good causes, they worked for world peace. Steinschneider's description and analysis of "women's public sphere" is highly sophisticated. Hers is one of the best studies on the subject and should prove indispensable to all concerned with understanding women's political activities, their construction of a public sphere for women, and their efforts and successes as builders of large coalitions.

Margit Misangyi Watts, *High Tea at Halekulani: Feminist Theory and American Clubwomen*, is a more narrowly focused study of clubwomen's work than are the other three, yet its significance ranges far above that of its subject matter. Watts tells the story of the Outdoor Circle, an upper-class white women's club in Hawaii, from its founding in 1911 on. Its main activities were to make Hawaii beautiful: to plant trees, clean up eyesores, preserve nature and rid the islands of billboards. To achieve these modest goals, the women had to become consummate politicians and lobbyists and learn how to run grassroots boycotts and publicity and educational campaigns, and how to form long-lasting coalitions. Above all, as Watts's fine theoretical analysis shows, they insisted that their female vision, their woman-centered view, become an accepted part of the public discourse. This case study is rich in theoretical implications. Together with the other three studies of women's club activities it offers not only a wealth of practical examples of women's work for social change, but it also shows that such work both resists patriarchal views and practices and redefines them in the interests of women.

Gerda Lerner
Madison, Wisconsin

Acknowledgements

This book began as a dissertation under the auspices of the Department of History at the University of Michigan in Ann Arbor. It could not have been completed without William G. Rosenberg's friendship, and his support and enthusiasm for my approach. My debt to him is great. Louise A. Tilly also devoted a great deal of time, and her friendly critical eye to my interpretation of the material, providing an invaluable contribution. Sherry Ortner of the University of Michigan Department of Anthropology confirmed my tentative diagnosis of male bonding in the behavior of Russian working men. Yvonne Lockwood early on supported my use of folklore in a historical work.

Timothy Mixter, Heather Hogan, and Scott Seregny gave me the myriad kinds of help only fellow researchers embarking on a year of research in the (then) Soviet Union could. Amy Saldinger and Donna Gabaccia read parts of the manuscript and provided comments of great help in making revisions.

I would also like to thank Serge Shishkoff of the University of Michigan Slavic Languages Department, who graciously gave many hours to helping me decipher the obscurities of folkloric dialect and poetic and grammatic license of Russian working-class folklore. Natalia Challis also gave willingly of her knowledge of the Russian language.

The staffs of the University of Michigan Library; the Hoover Institute in Palo Alto, California; the Slavonic Division of the New York Public Library; the Library of Congress; and the National Library of Medicine in Bethesda, Maryland helped me obtain some of the materials for this study. A number of scholars in the Soviet Union were of great help to me, above all A. M. Martynova of the Folklore Division at the Institute of Russian Literature (Pushkinskii Dom) in St. Petersburg. V. V. Mavrodin, A. I. Tishkin, R. F. Its, and B. N. Putov all helped smooth my way. I am very grateful to the staffs of all of the archives cited in this book, as well as that of the newspaper room in the Library of the Academy of Sciences in St. Petersburg, and the Lenin Library in Moscow.

Financial support for the years of work that went into this book came from a number of sources, and is gratefully acknowledged. The National Defense Foreign Language Fellowship program (through the University of Michigan's Center for Russian and East European Studies) and the UM Department of History supported preparation and research in the United States. The International Research and Exchanges Board and Fulbright-Hays dissertation fellowship program made my research trip to the Soviet Union possible. A Woodrow Wilson Women's Studies Research Grant and a UM Women's Studies Program fellowship allowed me to complete the writing.

Cynthia Merman edited the manuscript, doing salutary work in making it more concise. Kathleen Thompson provided a dramatist's viewpoint, suggesting important changes in the book's organization, as well as other invaluable contributions.

A very special acknowledgment must go to Gerda Lerner, who first introduced me to the Lowell mill girls when I was at Sarah Lawrence College. Lerner was the first history teacher I ever had who, with consummate sensitivity and support, helped me value my academic ideas, making me feel I had the capacity to embark on work in a field not traditional for women. She provided the editorial review which shaped this book in its final stages, but more importantly, the entire project would never have begun without her.

Finally, I would like to thank my family for their loving support over the years. My husband, Dr. Fady Hajal, and our two children, Nastassia and Nicholas, have provided the joy and stability needed to sustain this long project to completion.

Working Women in Russia Under the Hunger Tsars

Part One

A cloud like a canopy covered
The amber of the burning sun;
Everyone grew cold with terror,
This is the ferocious tsar coming,
The merciless Hunger-tsar.
Next to him sits
His wife, Bony Death,
She looks tenderly at her friend,
Her page, Horror, runs along
Burning incense.
Behind their fine chariot
Made of bones and skulls
Flies a flock of dismal black birds—
The faithful companion of dead dreams.
A terrible quivering seizes
All hearts—ever closer "He" comes!
            from "The Hunger Tsar" by Vera Poroshina,
            Gazeta-Kopeika, August 19, 1917[1]

ONE

Introduction:
The Shape of Action

Russia, 1917. Thousands of hungry working women fill the streets, taking food for themselves and their families from transport carts. Masses of women attend rallies and march in demonstrations, carrying red banners and wearing red kerchiefs. Significant numbers serve in first aid and reconnaissance positions during the Moscow October Revolution, at times taking up the guns of their fallen male comrades and going into battle themselves. A few individual women become highly visible political activists and later hold positions in the new government.

There can be no doubt that working women were an active and powerful force in the Russian Revolution. But despite their great activity, working women's position in Soviet society did not improve appreciably over that of tsarist times.[2] As one woman put it in the 1920s, "Our position in many respects remains difficult and unenviable. The kitchen, children, washtubs with laundry, work in the factory—this is our world, from which few have leapt to freedom."[3]

Why did this happen? Why was so much apparent activism—during a revolution which explicitly raised the issues of women's emancipation—ultimately ineffective? The February Revolution toppled the tsarist government and established the Provisional Government; the Bolsheviks did not take power until the October Revolution. Between these two revolutions, before reconsolidation of central power by the Bolsheviks, political life in Russia was relatively open to activity from below. Factory committees, provisioning committees, building committees, and other grassroots or democratically constituted organizations potentially held substantial influence. To begin with, we need to ask how women workers responded to these opportunities—albeit short-lived—to improve their lives.

In order to answer this question, I begin with a detailed examination of women's activism during 1917. Here are stories of tremendous individual heroism, and of great physical and moral courage on the part of women, who sacrificed wages and physical comforts, and risked bodily harm and even their lives. However, in the end, the examination reveals that women did not participate in or form the ongoing organizations necessary to change their life situations. Women workers were usually active sporadically. A small number of working women became very active, devoting virtually all their time to politics. But they did so as individuals, and exceptional ones at that, not as members of ongoing groups capable of wielding some power in their own interests. Without sustained organizational effort, women could make hardly a dent in the environment which shaped their lives and their grievances.

The question then becomes, why didn't they organize?

This question has been raised many times about other women in other situations. In the late 1960s and through the 1970s, historians of women asked why working women generally did not organize economically or politically to the extent that working men did. For example, Alice Kessler-Harris noted that in the United States, even at the peak of trade unionism among women in the teens of the twentieth century, one in every fifteen women in the industrial workforce belonged to a union, compared to one in every five men. She went on to observe, "Figures like this have led historians of the working class to join turn-of-the-century labor organizers in lamenting the difficulty of unionizing female workers. Typically, historians argue that the traditional place of women in families, as well as their position in the workforce, has inhibited trade unionism."[4]

Other historians have observed that the working women's double burden, of factory work and domestic work, has hindered labor organization. They note that the isolation of women in their individual homes after the factory shift has prevented the growth of the sort of community upon which men's organizations was frequently based. Men, they point out, typically gathered in group meeting places such as taverns after work, to relax with their fellow workers, forming the collective bonds from which economic or political action could develop. While women dispersed to their individual homes to work their second job as homemaker and childrearer, men had both the time and the material conditions—the group meeting places—which promoted union and other organizational activities.[5]

Awareness of the difficulty of organizing women who dispersed to separate homes after work has been seen especially in historians' fascination with the case of Lowell, Massachusetts, textile operatives in the first half of the nineteenth century. The earliest Lowell workers were unmarried women living together in dormitories provided by factory owners. Rather than dispersing after work, the Lowell women ate together in large dining rooms, and shared living space and many activities. Their highly active Female Reform Association led the struggle—of both men and women workers—for ten-hour workday legislation throughout New England in the 1840s. Their great activity has been attributed in part to the social contact facilitated by their communal living arrangements.[6]

Interestingly, many of the Russian textile workers who are the focus of this study also lived communally, in barracks similar to the dormitories which housed the Lowell women.[7] Most intriguing as a point of comparison for Lowell, many of the Russian working women who lived in barracks were married and had children; they continued to work throughtout their marriages, including during their child-bearing years.

These Russian women not only lived in barracks, they also had at least as much access as did men to large group meeting places, in the form of communal kitchens, bath houses (where women also did their laundry), and laundry drying rooms. During 1917 and earlier, these spaces were frequently sites for political meetings, because they were the largest rooms in the factory environment. At the Prokhorovka factory in Moscow, for example, political meetings typically took place in the huge communal kitchen, with whole families present. The kitchen tables were pushed together to form a podium, and little boys sat on top of the high Russian stove. "They rewarded our [Bolshevik] orators with furious applause and the shells of sunflower seeds, which spilled liberally from their tower onto our heads."[8] At a Kostroma factory, a working women's meeting was held "in the premises of the child care facility,"[9] presumably whatever poor excuse for a child care center the factory offered. During 1905, the Orekhovo-Zuevo workers' soviet was located in the factory barracks.[10]

In short, spaces where Russian working women typically spent much of their time together happened to be large, communal areas ideal as locations for meetings. Women gathered together in these areas each day, carrying out work which they all had in common. If married women workers anywhere might be expected to organize as had the unmarried Lowell women, it would be these.

In the months that led up to the revolution, a new meeting place for Russian women developed as well. It was the breadline, caused by the terrible wartime food shortages. Women of various occupations waited together on the same comfortless sidewalks in front of bread shops and shared their anguished concern over getting flour refined enough that it would not kill their babies and enough bread to keep their families alive for one more day. Close relationships developed among these women. What effect did they have on political participation? Did breadlines do for women what taverns—and, in Russia, men's outdoor meeting places such as factory yards and riverbanks—had done for men?

While starving women were very active in food actions designed to obtain food for their next few meals, they did not form ongoing organizations with which to influence the food situation overall. Russian women barracks residents, married or unmarried, did not form organizations similar to the Lowell Female Reform Association, to address the food crisis or any other grievance.

The real issue, then, seems to concern neither communal living quarters nor access to meeting places. It concerns the ways in which the culture socialized men and women to use these resources. Russian working-class culture encouraged men, as they met in taverns and factory yards, on riverbanks and soccer fields, to forge strong bonds among themselves which later translated easily into political action. Did Russian working class culture do the same for female bonding? If not, what did the culture encourage among women? And what was it about women's assigned daily life tasks which shaped their particular culture?

Since the early 1970s, some historians of women have emphasized the ways in which even women who did not live in communal situations had their own daily life networks, often delineated more by kinship ties than were men's.[11] At the same time, other historians have described women's activity in a range of types of protest: demonstrations, meetings, food riots, boycotts of offending merchants, and women's organizations.[12] These two strains of research are now coming together, albeit for middle-class women rather than women workers. Mary P. Ryan has shown that the middle-class New York Female Moral Reform Society had its origins in the participants' family, neighborhood, church, and benevolent associations.[13] Ellen Ross has speculated that the same connection held true for working-class women: women's "friendship and support networks have likely also provided the crucible in which acts of rebellion were formed."[14]

Here, the Russian material is also uniquely suited to provide a test case. Ethnographic sources—particularly Soviet field research among women textile workers regarding their lives before the revolution—detail the social structuring of groups of girls and women. As they grew up in working-class communities, Russian girls engaged regularly in a number of group rituals and activities which were central to their lives, and which, it might be supposed, would bond them together as a group capable of acting in their own interests. What was the nature of these groups? Might they have supported women's action in the public sphere?

In this book, I will use a synthesis of the various historical theories and approaches noted above to form a hypothesis regarding Russian working women. In the first chapters, I will look at the great activity of Russian working women during the Russian revolutions, paying particular attention to the forms it took and the evidence of long-term organization or the lack thereof. One problem with some historiography of women is that, while it has proven that women were active, it has intermixed tidbits of evidence about women's organization with descriptions of other, more sporadic, types of protest. The impression is sometimes given, therefore, that working women formed and sustained organizations over the long run, when actually little evidence is provided to that effect.[15] In order to avoid this pitfall, I will present a detailed description and analysis of working women's activism which asks at each turn: Did Russian working women form the ongoing organizations and alliances necessary for sustained improvement in their lives? Did they build on networks forged by their common work in factories and in barracks? Did they take advantage of resources available in their immediate environment?

In the second half of the book, I will present an overview of Russian working women's daily life activities and networks as they were shaped over the course of each woman's lifetime by the culture in which she grew up. How was the nature of women's networks effected by the daily responsibilities assigned to them by their culture? Did their networks support concerted action? Or was there something about these groups which, to the contrary, undermined organized efforts by women in the public sphere?

There were undoubtedly many factors which influenced Russian working women's political activity, some of which encouraged their activism and others of which inhibited it. These include men's opposition to women organizing, women's lesser literacy, and so on. I explore only some of the many potentially relevant factors, focusing on hindrances to women's preorganization posed by daily life responsibilities and culture. By focusing on these issues, I do not mean to imply that they alone explain the typology of women's political behavior in 1917. Rather, I suggest that these factors were important and complex and that they deserve in-depth study.

I also hope that the Russian evidence can provide a test case for some of the explanatory theories about women's political activities that have been put forward by other historians. Its distinctive features—from the communal living situation to the dramatic nature of the political events of 1917—may refocus our attention and provide the opportunity for significant new insights.

Delineation of Study

This study is limited to the light industries of some of the *guberniias* (provinces) of Russia's Central Industrial Region (CIR). The CIR is the industrialized area comprising Moscow and the surrounding provinces. Russia's textile industry, which employed more women than any other industry, was located predominantly in this area. I looked specifically at Moscow, Kostroma, Yaroslavl, and Vladimir *guberniias*[16] (the province of Ivanovo-Voznesensk, the capital city of which is called "the Russian Manchester," was created from parts of Kostroma and Vladimir *guberniias* after the 1917 revolution). While most of my material comes from textile factories, I also include other light industries where many women were typically employed.

I chose the CIR for my focus because of the high rate of married women who worked most of their adult lives in its mammoth[17] factories, long considered great cauldrons of working-class activism. It has sometimes been argued that women were historically less eager to organize because unlike men, they worked only before marriage, so factory labor was not a central, long-term aspect of their lives. Children and home were the primary jobs in such women's lives, it has been said; no wonder they did not organize. I wanted to control for this variable by researching women whose factory work continued throughout their married lives, and whose wages were as necessary to the support of their families as were their husbands'. I wanted to see whether even these women's factory-based preorganization would be outweighed by the tendency toward isolation caused by their second job in the home.

The factory work of women in Russia's CIR was a life-long occupation. A. Riazanova, in her classic study of women's work, noted that "marrying and becoming a mother, she [the textile worker] never even dreams about remaining at home to do housework and raise the children." Riazanova provided the age distribution of workers in textile factories employing 28,571 women and 11,687 men (Table 1). A. G. Rashin provided similar statistics for

TABLE 1

*1911-12 Age Distribution of Female
and Male Workers in Nineteen
Moscow Guberniia Textile Factories*

	Age	Men	Women
Cotton spinning,	15-19	24.6	20.0
weaving, and dyeing	20-39	51.6	61.0
	40-59	19.0	16.0
Wool spinning,	15-19	9.0	15.2
weaving, and dyeing	20-39	53.0	61.0
	40-59	35.4	23.0

Source: A. Riazanova, *Zhenskii trud* (Moscow: Moskovskii rabochii, 1926), p. 157.

TABLE 2

*1897 Age Distribution of Female and
Male Workers in Vladimir Guberniia*

Age	Men	Women	Total
12-15	2.3	1.6	2.0
15-17	6.0	7.7	6.7
17-20	13.6	20.4	16.3
20-25	17.0	21.5	18.7
25-30	16.3	16.2	16.3
30-40	25.3	21.9	24.0
40-50	12.9	8.1	11.0
50-60	4.6	2.2	3.7
60 and over	2.0	0.4	1.3

Source: A. G. Rashin, *Formirovanie rabochego klassa rossii; istoriko-ekonomicheskie ocherki* (Moscow: Izdatel'stvo Sotsial'no-ekonomicheskoi Literatury, 1958), p. 279.

Vladimirskaia *guberniia* for workers of all types, not only textile workers (Table 2). These tables demonstrate strikingly that roughly the same proportion of men and women workers were employed at each age in their life spans.[18]

Riazanova further estimated that 20 percent of women textile workers gave birth each year. "[E]ternally ill, burdened with anxiety about her family, and often about the unemployment of her husband, the Russian working woman must toil very hard all her life."[19] An ethnographer wrote, "Mothers work alongside fathers, especially in textiles."[20] The employment of mothers living in factory-owned housing (a very large proportion of all textile workers) was often ensured because employers frequently evicted families if one of the parents stopped working.[21] Ivanovo-Voznesensk was "densely populated with textile workers, emaciated women weavers and their ragged, rickety children."[22]

In addition, as we will see in detail below, mothers were often a more reliable source of support for the family than were fathers. Mothers' wages, then, were crucial to the survival of their families. Thus, married women in Russia's CIR might be expected to be as affected by the prospect of lifelong factory work as were men.

TWO

Food Riots:
Women's Militance

On March 15, 1917, a popular Moscow newspaper reported an event which, the reporter observed, had become commonplace in the city's streets. Its cause was the growing food shortage and the ubiquitous queues—nicknamed *khvosty*, literally "tails"—of lower-class people waiting outside food shops to get their share of the dwindling supply. In particular, the article noted that unground buckwheat groats, much beloved by Russians, "are hard to get in Moscow now," and that the price was very high when they were available, encouraging illegal speculation by unscrupulous merchants. The specific event described began while a long breadline of women stood outside Savost'ianov's bakery, next door to Kozlov's firm.

> . . . suddenly a cart came in through [Kozlov's] gate with eleven sacks loaded on it.
> The curious women felt the sacks and cried out with joy.
> "Women, they've brought buckwheat groats!"
> Many darted out of the breadline and started up a new line for the groats. But Kozlov did not even want to acknowledge their presence:
> "The groats aren't mine!" He drove the cart back out through the gates.
> "Where are you going, my friend?" shrieked the women.
> "Not here! I'm going to Kooperatsiia [presumably a cooperative society]."
> But he wasn't going to do anything of the sort. By now, women know the guile of tradespeople. They [the women] called a policeman, and he summoned the authorities from the commissariat.
> And they forced Kozlov to dump the eleven sacks of groats, 45 *pudy* [1,620 pounds] in weight, out of his cart and into a storage bin over which they posted a guard.
> What had Kozlov wanted to do with the groats? Sell them on the sly?

The article ended with the journalist's confident assurance that the new Provisional Government, in power since the February Revolution three weeks before, would soon give Kozlov and his type their just deserts.[1]

But as time went on, the Provisional Government proved unable to effect any improvement in the food situation. So lower-class women in the streets continued actively to make their own small-scale improvements from day to day (although only government-level policies could have dramatically affected the overall availability of food). Women focused their energies on individual merchants, especially those, like Kozlov, who tried their hand at speculating. One frequent action was stopping carts to search their contents for food being hoarded or transported out of the neighborhood to more lucrative markets. As the journalist wrote, "The people themselves have begun to check up on the 'honesty' of tradespeople, and the results are striking. Each day they open up secret stores of foodstuffs and unmask our thick-skinned merchants, who value profit above all else."[2]

This type of food activity was self-directed, had little connection with the factory, and produced no viable ongoing organizations. As a result, it has largely been ignored by historians, Soviet and Western, of the Russian Revolution, with the single exception of the often-mentioned Women's Day food riots, which began the February Revolution in St. Petersburg. Such "spontaneous" food activity was nevertheless pandemic throughout the year of the revolution, however disliked by contemporary proponents of more organized forms of political participation.[3]

The terms "spontaneous activism" and "riots," including "food riots," often connote mindless revolt without clear goals or strategies. Yet, although food activism may have appeared chaotic at times, in fact it had a clear purpose, utilized a range of strategies appropriate to differing situations, and was often successful in achieving its goal.[4] Thus, although food riots produced no ongoing organization, on a short-term basis they were much more organized than the term "riot" generally connotes.

This chapter examines three authentic characteristics of these "spontaneous" activities. First, food riots were not directed by members of the intelligentsia, but rather were engineered by the lower-class participants themselves. Second, their goals (and hence their strategies) were short-term and immediate, to provide food for the next day or two and not to affect the long-term availability of foodstuffs to Russia's cities. Third, the location and time of the actions were not planned and organized far in advance, although the repertoire of measures taken became well practiced. Women developed a range of actions frequently effective in securing a day or two's supply of food, and they used these actions repeatedly over the course of the year. But the particular occasions on which women initiated action were determined on a moment's notice and almost entirely by factors outside women's choosing: the availability of food in the neighborhood on any given day, a merchant driving by with a suspiciously full cart, rumors of hoarding by a wealthy family or monastery, and so on.

Food Shortages and Breadlines

Throughout 1917, the working-class population of the CIR suffered greatly, perhaps more than any other segment of the population, from food shortages—from the onslaught of the "Hunger Tsar." In May, a worker representative reported to a meeting of the *guberniia* provisioning congress that in the city of Kostroma, "the factory workers and city poor are starving, they do not have milk for their children and they feed them only tea and bread." *Povolzhskii vestnik* reported an unusually high death rate among Kostroma's children, "mainly in the factory district," due to the wretched quality of bread, which produced severe diarrhea and other stomach ailments.[5] In Moscow, the infant mortality rate was also growing "with each month" and was worst in the districts where factory workers predominated. "A year ago in January, 1,200 babies died. And now the number is up to 2000 each month."[6] By mid-August the situation had not improved. The entire factory population of all three major *uezds* of the Kostroma *guberniia* textile region did not have sufficient food.[7] The industrial area of Yaroslavl *guberniia* was no better off. "In several settlements where the factory population predominates, starvation has already begun. Of the 170,000 inhabitants of Yaroslavl *uezd*, 40,000 do not have enough bread."[8] On October 13, the same newspaper reported simply, "At present, it is difficult for our ordinary people to live, especially the workers."[9]

The result of such massive shortages was long lines of people waiting outside shops to obtain daily nourishment for themselves and their families. In the early weeks of January, a journalist recorded, "I was in the working-class outskirts of Moscow, in Dorogomilov and by the Semenovskie gates in Lefortovo. And everywhere before my eyes were long ribbons of people waiting by the doors of the bakeries. . . . The '*khvosty*' were especially great around the city-owned shops because the bread is cheaper there and better than in private stores."[10] In Ivanovo-Voznesensk in late January, in all the city's flour and groat shops "the bins and shelves are completely empty." As a result, "from early morning til late at night" queues had been seen of almost a third of a mile in length. On February 4, the same paper remarked that people had waited in line at the Kurazhev Brothers' shop up to four hours. By February 18, people in Ivanovo-Voznesensk were standing in queues "to get some crust of bread to appease their hunger, which many are actually experiencing, frighteningly in want of their daily bread, standing waiting for it in below zero temperatures for several hours, often having to leave without ever getting bread."[11] In the textile town of Shuia at the end of January, a girl, "Zina Zarezina . . . in line together with her mother, froze while lying in a sled."[12] (Small sleds are used in the wintertime even today as snow-worthy replacements for baby carriages.)

The problem was widespread enough that various individuals and groups proposed ideas for solving it. In an Ivanovo newspaper, a letter to the editor suggested that food lines could be substantially shortened if factory owners would undertake production of bread for their own laborers in factory artels (workers' communal food facilities), and distribute it to the workers at the workplace rather than through the city's shops.[13] A newspaper columnist in Moscow came up with a similar proposal.[14] Several months later, special ration cards for workers were one element of the Moscow city government's plan to shorten the breadlines.[15] Aleksandra Kollontai made an appeal to the women workers of Ivanovo-Voznesensk to vote Bolshevik as a step toward eliminating breadlines.[16]

In the first two months of 1917, the chore of waiting for hours each day in the breadlines was accomplished mainly by children and elderly women. In early January, a reporter wrote, "Since the holidays . . . we have observed a familiar picture in the streets of the capital: . . . little children shivering from the cold forming long lines near the bread shops and city bakeries." Another reporter later explained the reason for this: mothers who had to be at the factories each workday could not stand waiting in line all morning. Thus, children and elderly women were delegated to carry out this task for their families. As the reporter put it, "In this time of haste and bustle, who has more hours to spend waiting than children? Their fathers and mothers are busy—they're eking out kopeks, and the children—they're standing in line."[17]

However, by the end of February, the breadlines were no longer being described as dominated by children and elderly women. As food procurement became more difficult, working mothers themselves apparently had to take over the job, even when this meant being absent from factory work. My speculation is that this occurred whenever a long wait in line at one store might not result in bread, for the shopper then had to rush to other shops, hoping to arrive before all the supplies had run out there too. At this point, the task of food shopping became more complicated, requiring sharp strategic decision making about which shops were most likely to have a good supply of bread and in what order to try the various bakeries in order to ensure success by the end of the day. This type of strategizing became so necessary and widespread that a Moscow newspaper commented on it: "Among the simple people [*prostonarod*], 'khvosty' have so taken root that, even before women get out of bed [in the morning], they are discussing and planning out several bread shops for the 'attack.' "[18] It also seems likely that mounting such "attacks"—running from store to store to get in the next line as quickly as possible when the last shop ran out of bread—required more strength than children and elderly women possessed.

In short, as the food situation became desperate, women workers were compelled to sacrifice part of next week's paycheck in the immediate interests of getting food on the table that night. Newspapers commented on the widespread nature of this phenomenon and its harmful effects. For example, remarking on the need to try numerous shops before being able to obtain wheat flour in Kostroma, *Povolzhskii vestnik* complained that, "Many citizens must 'go fishing' for flour several days running, abandoning their usual work."[19] Five days later the newspaper reported that the provisioning board at the *guberniia* level, in response to an appeal by the Kostroma city government, urged that measures be taken to ensure that food distribution would occur "without the population having to lose work time in lines." A Moscow newspaper observed the same phenomenon.[20] Yaroslavl's *Golos* reported, in an article entitled "A Senseless and Harmful Phenomenon," that large numbers of workers, particularly women, from the neighboring Norskoe factory settlement were leaving work to come to Yaroslavl, the *uezd* capital, to appeal for bread to be diverted to Norskoe. The paper complained that on September 20, "not less than 500 workers of the Norskoe manufactory" had come. "Work time is being lost," clucked the newspaper, calling on the workers to delegate only two or three representatives to make their needs known in Yaroslavl.

Throughout the summer and fall, the food situation worsened. A new problem arose: since the only flour available was of the worst grade, the bread purchased in city bakeries was of very poor quality. Milk, too, was impure:

13

"Moscow milk—this is . . . a complicated chemical combination in which there is very little milk and very much of all sorts of muck."[21] This was potentially fatal for infants.

> [C]hildren's acute stomach diseases occur purely from bad food, from lack of milk and white bread. . . . A child's stomach is not yet strong and, being unformed, cannot tolerate either sour milk or mixtures of water and black and half white bread, so the children are dying like flies. In the new cemetery [in Kostroma], the little mounds of young victims are sprouting up out of the fresh mud.[22]

A poem that ran in *Gazeta-Kopeika* read in part,

> Marauders, speculators,
> Babies wail to you—
> Starving babies
> . . . barely living children
> Little arms, little legs like blades of grass.[23]

Adults, too, suffered from the poor quality of food. Doctors attributed a wave of stomach ailments among Moscow's population in part to "so-called white bread, though for a long time now it has not had anything in common with whiteness." The article also complained that the white bread on sale was only half-baked.

> [It is] some sort of putty which even a tin stomach could not digest.
> This "putty" is the cause not only of "obstruction of the stomach" [constipation], but also of complications to [those ill with] dysentery, which is extremely widespread in Moscow now.[24]

More and more frequently, deaths were attributed to the food crisis. The story of the mother of an infant who died at eight months was reported in a newspaper.

> I work in the factory. . . . My milk dried up a long time ago, and I had to feed the child with cow's milk. It's hard to get milk . . . [and] it turns sour. It was necessary to feed the child with bread soaked in water . . . black [bread]. . . . I carried the [infant] to the hospital. . . . Her stomach failed "from bad food," they say.[25]

On August 15, a local newspaper reporting on the severe food shortage among the textile factory population of Kostroma *guberniia* noted that a suicide victim had been found; she had hanged herself out of despair at not being able to find bread to feed her hungry family.

As food supplies became scarcer and scarcer in urban areas, some city people, "especially those having connections with the villages," began traveling into the nearby countryside to buy small quantities of flour at astronomically high prices. And by October, people living in towns directly on the Volga, the major river transport route of the region, had thought of yet another way to try to get bread.

> [I]t is not easy, but it guarantees obtaining several pounds of bread. Daily in the evening, and sometimes even in the morning, around the wharves of the steamboat lines, a rather sizable crowd of Yaroslavl citizens may be observed who, with sacks and baskets, have positioned themselves on the railings of the bridges. This crowd is waiting for the workmen from the lower Volga, who are bringing bread [to the upper Volga region]. Sometimes there are so many waiting that lines must form. This is going on in all the large Volga stations. . . . The crowds waiting here grow larger each day.[26]

Causes of the Food Shortage

The wartime food shortage in Russia did not result from an actual scarcity of food in the country as a whole,[27] according to Struve, Zaitsev, Dolinsky, and Demosthenov in their classic study, *Food Supply in Russia during the World War*. In regard to grain, the main ingredient in bread, "the Russian Empire unquestionably had an adequate supply of cereals throughout the period of the war," the amount of grain available for domestic consumption in 1917 being greater than in the pre-war years. And for foodstuffs in general, "The ratio between demand and supply in the foodstuffs market was far more favorable to demand in Russia than it was in the Central Powers and in the United States. . . . But the general economic backwardness of Russia prevented her from benefitting by this favorable ratio."[28] The food scarcity resulted from several factors: 1) the inadequacy of the Russian transport system, particularly the railroads, to meet the simultaneous needs of both the military effort and the civilian population; 2) certain government policies, especially the fixing of wholesale food prices; 3) widespread speculating by food merchants, who held back large quantities of foodstuffs from the market, hoping to reap higher

15

profits later; and 4) consumption demands of the army. Leon Trotsky, another contemporary observer with a very different political perspective, agreed with Struve et al.'s general analysis. "In the more fertile regions . . . there were still tens and hundreds of millions of *pudy* of surplus grain, but the purchasing operations at a fixed price [set by the government] gave extremely unsatisfactory results: and moreover it was difficult to deliver the ready grain to the [urban] centers owing to the breakdown of transport."[29]

Russia's northern industrial regions, including the CIR, relied heavily on the great grain-producing provinces of the South for food. Without continuous transport of agricultural products from the South, the cities of the CIR could not survive. During World War I, the Russian transport system proved insufficient to maintain a steady flow of food under the added demands of the military effort. The resulting uncertainty of food deliveries to the industrial areas led to successive price increases. This in turn set the stage for widespread speculation by merchants, who began massive hoarding.

Hoarding in turn caused an overall growth in demand. The lure of high profits, and the removal of large stocks of hoarded food from actual consumption, caused merchants to buy up more of rural food production than they did under peacetime conditions. In addition, the shortage of food in the retail market caused consumers to attempt to stockpile against future difficulties. Thus, the hoarding activities of both merchants and consumers (the former motivated by greed, the latter by hunger and fear) substantially increased the demand for food above the level of actual need. This in turn made the ground ever more fertile for speculators' activities.

In addition to these problems, at least two government policies greatly increased the difficulties. One was the fixing of differential food prices.[30] The price of food sold to the army was set much higher than that for food sold to the civilian population. This policy was a boon for speculators: the "possibility of disposing of their stocks at greatly inflated prices [by selling to the army] strengthened enormously the entire structure of speculative business."[31]

A second government policy reducing the CIR food supply was the embargoing of foodstuffs from those areas where the government purchased its supplies for the army. (The government did this in order to simplify its task of military food procurement.) This had numerous disruptive effects on the civilian food supply, the most obvious of which was that localities which had been dependent during peacetime on the embargoed areas lost their established means of food supply. And the interaction of embargoes with numerous other factors again provided fertile ground for speculators. Indeed, "an extensive use of embargoes is capable of encouraging speculation on an unprecedented scale."[32]

Finally, the army in wartime required a larger proportion of the country's overall food production to feed its soldiers than those same men consumed in peacetime. For the army provided a diet for its fighting men of a standard much higher in quality and quantity than that of the average peasant in peacetime. In addition, there were the needs of the army's horses, which received "special war-time rations far in excess of what they are given normally."[33]

Thus, the causes of the food shortage in wartime Russia were far-reaching. Women who attacked speculators for hoarding were directing themselves at one major source of the food problem, but they were not getting at its root. Similarly, women who demanded that local government food distribution agencies deliver more food immediately were not dealing with the major government policies that aggravated the civilian food shortage: price fixing and embargoes.

Food Activism

The Nets are Set

Merchant Pot-belly has supplies
Of bread, of cotton and various grains.
Merchant Pot-belly is of a special race—
Alien to the paunchy are the moans of the crowd.

He gets fatter and wider—he saves up not a little.
Swollen from hunger, the Russian people!
Merchant Pot-belly calculates wearily
Money, credit—these are not small concerns!

His children are fed because of big bribes
His wife goes around in sparkling jewels.
Enough outrages! The nets are set!
Reptiles! Your spring is over!

"Oskii" in *Gazeta-Kopeika*, July 1917[34]

From the beginning of 1917 through roughly mid-August or early September (the date varied from place to place within the CIR), almost all food actions undertaken by women involved some kind of appeal or demand made to government bodies, usually city councils (which were responsible for administering food rationing systems)[35] or provisioning committees. Provisioning committees, at the *raion* (city neighborhood), town, and *guberniia* levels, were the local branches of a hierarchical national bureaucracy which had been established during the war to deal with food supply for the army and the general population. The provisioning committee bureaucracy's principal purpose under the tsarist government was to supply the army at the front, but it was reorganized after the February Revolution to deal with the problem of "supplying the needs of the country at large." After February, the composition of the local committees was also changed to include representatives from local governments, peasants' and workers' organizations, societies of government employees, and trade and industry.[36]

Even though many food actions involved women's militant confrontations with these government agencies, the very fact that women turned to them for aid indicated that they accepted the Provisional Government as the supreme authority in Russian society, with all the attendant responsibilities for the population's well-being.[37] Women's trust in the Provisional Government must have been supported at first by the fact that the police routinely confiscated food from the carts of hoarders and speculators, sending it to the food commissariat or provisioning committee for public distribution. Since women could count on the police to perform these confiscations, they must have hoped that under the new revolutionary regime, the police would be reliable allies at all times. However, since the police were also the agency which almost always put down food actions, women eventually realized that the police, even those of the revolutionary government, were not a group they could count on. By mid-August, the newspapers reported that the crowds were beginning to beat up individual policemen who tried to put a stop to food actions.

Meanwhile, by late summer and early fall, new contenders for armed authority over food supply had appeared: rank-and-file soldiers, inadequately fed by their local garrisons and no longer completely loyal to Provisional Government orders; and workers' factory committees. These soldiers and workers were the constituencies of the local soviet of workers' and soldiers' deputies, and their contending with city councils for some measure of control over food supply was one manifestation of the dual power[38] which existed during 1917, resulting eventually in the October Revolution.

While the role of hungry soldiers and male-dominated factory committees on the food scene matured by August and September, women's role did not undergo major growth. Although women practiced a range of tactics to obtain food for the next few meals, they did not develop more sophisticated or organized methods of influencing the food situation.[39] Their own repertoire of actions remained much the same throughout the year. These points will be demonstrated below through an examination of food actions throughout 1917.

Descriptions of Some Typical Women's Food Actions

In early May, a group appealed to the Kostroma city council to enforce their demand for sugar from a particular shopkeeper, who saved his best sugar for chosen customers.

> Part of the crowd (about thirty women) went to the city council and there demanded a decree about the release of sugar, pointing out that "they allow some people a choice about the type of sugar they want, and they refuse it to others."[40]

In June, Kostroma soldiers' wives, many of whom were workers, were gathered at the city council to receive their government subsidy (resulting from their husbands' army service). Some of their number demanded that the city council increase their food ration.

> The [council] chief explained that additional credit had still not been allocated. These admonitions did not help. The soldiers' wives threatened violence. The police who were in the midst of the soldiers' wives hid, and the position of the cashier was critical. . . . Military deputies were called by telephone.

After this, and probably as a result of the arrival of the armed deputies, the "more reasonable of the soldiers' wives got the upper hand," apparently agreeing to accept the lesser ration, and the distribution then went on without further incident.[41]

By mid-July, the quality of the flour and bread sold in Yaroslavl had so deteriorated that it routinely produced severe stomach ailments, especially in children. At four o'clock on the afternoon of July 14, a crowd of enraged women gathered at the city food store, located in the same building as the city provisioning committee's offices, where they began to kick up a row and . . . even threatened to tear all the store managers to pieces; they tore off the door and began to drag out members of the provisioning commission by the arm . . . .With great difficulty [the provisioning committee members] managed to persuade the crowd [to listen] and they explained why and from where such poor flour had been obtained. Then the crowd began to demand a personal explanation from whoever had ordered such flour to be ground, and [for this] they were sent to the *guberniia* [provisioning] committee . . . but they did not find anyone there. On returning from the committee, the crowd gathered again at the shop and would not permit the sale of flour.[42]

The next day, still hungry for decent bread, the women returned to the *guberniia* provisioning committee.

The women raised a racket and demanded that the president of the provisioning committee . . . come out and talk to them. They conducted themselves threateningly toward the office employees. . . . A unit of police was ordered there. . . . Work at the committee was ended [for the day].

Several days later, the sale of bad flour continued, and the women's discontent had become more widespread.

Of late around the city food shops and also around the provisioning committees, large crowds have been observed, made up of excited and discontented citizens (in the majority of cases women), hurling accusations at the provisioning committees for the sale of bad white flour.

The next day, the newspaper noted the continued sale of "wheat flour, coarsely ground, with bran," and crowds of women protesting, "This isn't flour with bran, it's all bran; we're not cattle, our children are getting sick from such flour." On August 4, *Golos* reported, "Yesterday in the streets of Yaroslavl, a group of people gathered now at the provisioning committee, now at the shops, outraged over the food situation and calling for violence toward those meeting in the committee."[43]

In the first days of August in Kostroma, when the month's sugar ration was decreased from one and a half pounds to one pound, "a mass of citizens, primarily women of the factory and working class, gathered at the *guberniia* provisioning board with the demand that sugar be given out for August in the amount of 1½ pounds. The crowd awaited the results of the provisioning committee's session." When the committee did not begin its meeting, the "crowd continued to be agitated and decided not to disperse until it obtained a satisfactory answer." The crowd did not break up until a member of the provisioning committee had come out and given a "calm explanation" for why it could not meet at that time.[44]

August and early September also saw numerous food rioters' demands directed at Moscow provisioning committees. The city's newspapers for this period read like catalogs of the various *raions* of the city, with terse notations of disorders usually focused around the separate food commissariats which served each *raion*. The disorders were typically broken up with difficulty by the police. For example, on August 9,

> In Mar'inaia grove [a predominantly working-class *raion*] . . . local citizenesses, who could not obtain either flour or bread in the bakeries, surrounded the *raion's* commissariat and began to demand bread insistently. The women made disturbances until the small hours of the morning.

On August 27 and 28,

> in several parts of Moscow, very large crowds of citizens, primarily women, walked around. Surrounding Sushchevskii Commissariat No. 2, a crowd cried "Give us bread!" There were attempts to destroy the commissariat. The local militia tried to convince the crowd to disperse. The crowd asked them to suggest where it would be possible to get bread.[45]

In early September, in Alekseevskii *raion*,

> Women, surrounding the commissariat, demanded an increase in the ration, threatening otherwise to beat the members of the commissariat, the members of the provisioning department, and others unmercifully. On that day . . . there were no potatoes or other products of the first necessity in the local market [hence the need for a larger bread ration to make up the difference].[46]

On September 8, a "violently-mooded crowd" besieged the Mar'inskii Commissariat because supplementary bread ration cards had not been distributed on time.

> At the request of the district commissar, the provisioning department gave out ration coupons for three days. After this, the crowd quieted down. . . .
>
> After several hours another disturbance broke out: a new crowd appeared, which threatened the manager with taking the law into their own hands . . . but the distribution of coupons was set up, and the crowd quieted down.[47]

21

Of all such accounts of food activists appealing to provisioning committees and city councils, the story of Norskoe stands out. For Norskoe was an isolated factory settlement located outside the provincial capital, and as such it had no provisioning committee of its own. The hungry Norskoe food activists thus had to travel by steamboat down the Volga to the Yaroslavl *guberniia* provisioning committee.

In mid-September, after a long period of food shortage in Norskoe, there was suddenly no flour at all for three days. "Everyone, both in the settlement and in the [surrounding] villages [where many of the workers lived] are agitated and fear that they may drop dead." Each day the inhabitants hoped the situation would improve, "but there was no flour; all hopes were in vain. The citizens [mostly workers] decided to go themselves to the Yaroslavl provisioning committee."

This tactic of appealing to the Yaroslavl committee had been tried at least once before by the Norskoe workers, and their demands for flour and sugar had been satisfied.[48] Hoping to repeat this success, on September 13 at 11 o'clock in the morning, "eighty-eight of the starving" set off for Yaroslavl. The newspaper article did not give a breakdown by sex of these delegates, although from the rest of the report it is clear that both women and men were included, and that the majority were probably women. It is interesting to observe the different functions mentioned as having been performed by each sex. The men went to the mill and carried the heavy sacks of flour. The women accosted a provisioning official in their usual contentious manner and appealed to the committee based on their status as the mothers of starving children.

On the steamboat on the way, the group by chance met a member of the Yaroslavl provisioning committee, F. M. Plitin and, accosting him, began to demand the immediate delivery of bread. Plitin, stunned by the women's assault on him, began to try to calm them and to explain what the situation was, and that there was not enough flour. But the women insistently demanded bread. . . .

Getting off the steamboat in Yaroslavl, all eighty-eight people went together with Plitin to the provisioning committee. Here they made a statement about their hunger; many women cried, "We don't even have a crust of bread at home, our children are dying of hunger, this is our third day without bread!"

Those present were given baked bread, about half a *pud*, which they all undertook to divide among themselves, a quarter of a pound per person. The resulting picture was overpowering!

[T]he committee . . . declared to them that there was no flour, and they were advised to inquire at the Vakhromeevskaia mill. Several men went there. Flour was found there, and [the *guberniia* provisioning committee] ordered by telephone the release of 34 sacks to the Norskoe shop "Ob"edinenie," and twenty sacks to Norskaia factory. Then and there, the men began to carry the sacks of flour to the wharf themselves, in order to get it to Norskoe sooner.

[In Norskoe] on Thursday, September 14, people crowded around the shop almost all day waiting for the flour, but it arrived only at 11 o'clock at night. Many of the village inhabitants had spent two nights waiting at the shop.

Over the next weeks, the Norskoe workers continued repeatedly to travel to Yaroslavl to demand bread when there was none in their stores. The course of action was much the same each time, and the long-suffering Plitin apparently could never again count on peaceful passage along the Volga: he and another official were attacked on the steamboat again on the night of September 20, and barely escaped being thrown overboard by a group of workers.[49] The Norskoe events are particularly interesting because they indicate that, when necessary, women left their homes overnight and traveled substantial distances in the effort to obtain food.

Soldiers Join Food Actions

When rank-and-file soldiers from local garrisons first appeared on the food scene in the summer of 1917, they did so as consumers waiting in lines for bread alongside women shoppers.[50] These soldiers did not receive enough to eat in their garrisons, and were compelled to search for more food on their own. As they grew hungrier, they shifted from obeying orders to suppress food actions to joining in the rioting themselves.

When soldiers first participated in food disorders with women, the character of the actions as a whole remained much the same as before. For example, in Moscow on July 17, a crowd consisting mainly of women and soldiers gathered. "Throwing themselves at the shops, they had already snatched away some of the goods." Representatives of the socialist party organizations appealed unsuccessfully to the crowd; the militia finally dispersed them. Then the goods were taken in cars to the commissariat, for "the shop owners too are not without sin: they have bought up for speculation goods they are not supposed to have."[51]

A month later in Moscow, soldiers and women were still attacking speculators in an ad hoc manner. On August 19, mounted police in Solianka, near Khitrovka, were stymied by a crowd in which

23

There were quite a few soldiers from the company, which is hanging around doing nothing, and women with children in their arms and hanging from their skirts. There were old women with their canine teeth rattling in their sunken mouths as they talked, and many other people.

From the center of the crowd thrust out the shafts of a cart and from time to time someone's hand raised some sort of goods over the heads of the nearby people.[52]

The significance of soldiers soon began to reveal itself: soldiers were armed. As the Provisional Government proved unable to increase the overall amount of food coming into each area's shops, all shoppers began to demand widespread inspections of storerooms and especially the homes of merchants and other wealthy citizens, with confiscation of the food that speculators often hid in their dwellings. The Provisional Government resisted such searches, considering them illegal, because the government "protects the freedom and inviolability of the individual and the home above all."[53] Eventually soldiers' armed presence came to overrule the government's reluctance to search.

At first soldiers attempted to provide enforcement of women's small, ad hoc searches. However, this tactic did not always result in confiscation. The fact that ad hoc actions involving soldiers had greater strength than those of women alone was reflected only in that police were not usually sufficient to put down these disorders, and military units, often elite specialized units, had to be called in.

But within a relatively short time, the soldiers developed a more successful alliance than that with women. They formed ties with male-dominated workers' organizations from the local factories, creating a powerful, well-organized bloc in which women seem to have taken virtually no part.

Women, Soldiers, and Searches in Yaroslavl

The Yaroslavl newspapers provide the most complete record of this process in the CIR, as it took place in that city. While early in August, soldiers were still obeying orders to suppress women's food actions,[54] by mid-August soldiers were taking the women's side, attempting to provide the physical force necessary to carry out confiscations independently of the government.

A cart went down Myshkinskaia Street loaded with leather. A crowd of women, suspecting that the leather hid food, stopped it. With each minute, the crowd grew larger . . . consisting in the majority of soldiers and women. . . . A small group of soldiers was called to find the owner of the cart and they soon searched him out, beat him, and stole 5,000 rubles from him. . . . The crowd moved to loot Evetfeev's grocery store and others. In the shops, tea and other food products were found. The police standing nearby did nothing. It was necessary to call a military unit to suppress the disorders.[55]

This report gives a clear description of the division of labor between women and soldiers. The women initiated the action, stopping the cart by themselves. The soldiers exerted the physical force necessary to maintain the protest. They also stole a large sum of money from the cart's owner (something I found no indication of women ever having done).

Also in August, soldiers began volunteering physical authority to attempt to force searches of private homes. One large crowd gathered at the home of a citizen suspected of accumulating large quantities of food for speculation. "Shouts were heard of 'Make a search! . . .' The crowd broke into the yard and tried to make a search itself." But the militia arrived and quieted the crowd, while a soldier offered to make an inspection. He did so, uncovering some stockpiles of food. In another case, a crowd of women and soldiers forced the militia itself to carry out a search of a house. Large stockpiles of raisins, jam, and syrup were found, and a tense standoff continued for the rest of the day between the angry crowds and the militia, which insisted on locking up and protecting the goods from the rioters. There were "some dangerous-looking moments." An infantry regiment managed to disperse the crowds by evening.[56]

On September 8, at 3 p.m., a crowd began to gather near a shop whose owner lived in the same building. A rumor circulated that two hundred *pudy* (3.6 tons) of bagels and pretzels (*baranok sushki*) were hidden in the shed in the courtyard. The crowd began to demand a search of the shop and the owner's apartment, and requisition of all goods found. "The crowd began to grow. It was made up almost entirely of women and soldiers. . . . Some people from the crowd got into the shop and began to take whatever fell into their hands." When the owner appeared on the street, "soldiers and others began to give him a beating, and then led him to the police [station]." Meanwhile, back at the shop, the crowd was still demanding a search. They were finally dispersed by a special military unit.[57]

Soldiers in alliance only with women were thus unable fully to assert their will over the opposition of the government. By mid-September in Yaroslavl, soldiers formed a new alliance—with workers' factory-based organizations. This alliance was powerful enough to enforce an even more far-reaching demand:

25

systematic searches of the entire city, house by house, with confiscations of all major stockpiles of food.

The factory committee of the mammoth Iaroslavskaia Bol'shaia textile mill had taken some action in regard to the food crisis earlier in the year. In May, it had arrested the textile mill director for having raised food prices in the factory shop 200-500 percent.[58] In July, following the popular disorders over the high bran content of the flour being sold in the city, worker representatives from Iaroslavskaia Bol'shaia met with delegates from all other factories and plants in the city and from the local railroad to discuss the problem. A resolution was passed and a committee elected, with representatives from each constituency, to make an appeal to the *guberniia* provisioning committee to deliver better flour in order to protect the health of children.[59] In short, over the course of 1917, the Iaroslavskaia Bol'shaia factory committee had involved itself in organized initiatives regarding food, even as food riots were going on in the streets beyond the factory gates.

The citywide searches were initiated when, on September 20 at 2 p.m., work stopped at the Iaroslavskaia Bol'shaia textile mill, and the workers gathered in the factory school. Representatives from the soviet and other groups appeared, and a discussion of the food situation ensued. Ignoring the representative from the provisioning committee, the workers called for a search of a local monastery, and they elected delegates to carry out this search. The soviet tried to dissuade the workers. But, by the next day, threats and demonstrations by about five hundred workers compelled the soviet to call on soldiers to enforce three days of searches of two monasteries, many other religious establishments, food shops, trade firms, a consumers' cooperative, and ultimately private apartments and houses, the city council offices, an orphanage, and the fire station. The city was eventually divided into regions, each of which was assigned a search party consisting of representatives of workers, armed soldiers, and militia.[60]

Apparently no significant numbers of women workers were involved in these systematic searches, although they must have been present at the big meeting at the factory which initiated them. Newspaper reports made no mention of women participating. Rather, descriptions of the events of September 20-23 observed women elsewhere. Some were among the crowds milling about in the streets and outside the gates of buildings being searched, waiting to hear what food had been found.

The crowd is broken up into small groups and in each of them, naturally, discussions are going on. . . .

The women are worried—workers' wives and working women from the factory, who have come to the city [from the working-class suburbs] with their little children.

"It's all very well for these bourgeois," say these women with exhausted appearance and . . . gray faces. "They have everything: sugar and jam and flour. They've laid in stores of tea to last five years, and now they just sit at home. They're not likely to stand in line for bread!"

Cries of approval are heard.[61]

Only the official search party of workers and soldiers was permitted inside the yard, while guards forced the concerned onlookers back beyond the gates. Whenever one of the official search parties went in or out of buildings being searched, the crowds pounced on them, hungry for information about what the inspection had turned up. A newspaper reporter described the result.

Four sacks of flour were found in one of the houses . . . and by retelling and rumors [among the waiting crowd], this quantity grew threefold.

"Didn't you hear that at B.'s house, they found twelve sacks of flour, yes, and all of it wheat flour?" some woman tells a soldier standing near her.

"What do you mean twelve, they found only four at his house," I correct her, breaking into the conversation. But by now they don't believe me. "Probably they found four in the apartment and eight in the attic," the woman answers me. And it was not possible to dissuade her by any means. So on the basis of such hearsay, which gives birth to rumors, excesses are committed."[62]

The spreading of rumors, in which women played a major part during the searches, was not a typical aspect of everyday female working-class culture. It arose here as a result of the fact that women and others in the waiting crowds were not part of the official, organized action, but were on its periphery, with no guaranteed access to or responsibility for the facts. In the absence of reliable information, and given the level of hunger, wishful thinking came to the fore among the waiting crowds, and rumors spread exaggerating manyfold the actual amount of food discovered.

Newspaper reports located substantial numbers of women in one other place during the citywide searches. The searches had taken place in "two parts"—the official part and an unofficial part, performed by workers from the Iaroslavskaia Bol'shaia factory and other factories and plants. These unruly workers had taken even insignificant amounts of food which they discovered and "called forth against themselves the indignation and animosity, not only of towndwellers, but even of the [organized] workers."[63] Another report identified the "unorganized part" as "predominantly women," and indeed the few reports of specific "excesses"—which seem to have been simply unauthorized searches—mentioned that the groups involved were chiefly or partly made up of women.[64]

Actually, the official searchers were also often charged with excessive force, rudeness, destructive techniques, and theft.[65] Thus, it is probable that the difference between the official searches and the unofficial ones in which women took a greater part was not the unruliness of their techniques. It was that the unofficial searches were not performed on a systematic basis, as part of a single overall plan, and that they were not connected with any established social institution such as the soviet or factory committees.

In short, women seem to have remained on the periphery of the organized searches, despite their central role in food actions over many months before. One would assume that women's accumulated experience with speculators, privileged wealthy customers, and the food situation in general would have given them expertise that would thrust them into the forefront of the organized searches. Women had also participated alongside soldiers in many food actions. Yet they did not make the transition to working alongside soldiers during the organized inspections. Women made up more than half the adult work force at the Iaroslavskaia Bol'shaia textile mill (6,441 women to about 5,060 men)[66] where the searches were initiated. Yet this majority of the factory workers not only did not take this opportunity to utilize their factory's organizations, but in fact seems never to have used factory networks at any point during the long period of food actions.

Women, Workers, Soldiers, and Citywide Searches in Kostroma

Citywide searches by workers and soldiers' delegates were also made in Kostroma in mid-August. Here, the original demand for searches may have been generated more directly among women and individual soldiers in the streets (newspaper reports are not clear on this point), but the outcome seems to have been the same as in Yaroslavl: women did not take a significant part in carrying out the institutionalized searches.

On Saturday, August 19, a crowd of women appeared at the Kostroma city council, protesting the fact that wheat and rye flours were not available anywhere in the city. "The women pointed out that their children are in a difficult position, not having even a crust of black bread." The women were promised that wheat flour, the most easily digestible by children, would be available the following Monday or Tuesday. On Monday, the women came to the city council, again demanding wheat flour, and this time they

> began insistently to demand inspection of zemstvo and city storerooms and the storerooms of private merchants. Soldiers joined the crowd of women and the crowd moved off [to search a milk storeroom]. Then the soldiers began to inspect the storerooms belonging to the city and zemstvo.

Two members of the local soviet of workers' and soldiers' deputies who came to the scene to try to calm the crowd were beaten. The crowd discovered that the city storerooms held "sugar for September, salt for a year, and fifty-six sacks of the highest quality flour for the churches"[67]—and this while workers' children were starving.

These revelations developed ultimately into systematic searches of and confiscations in all shops and the homes of well-to-do citizens in the city, carried out by representatives from workers and soldiers. These searches were demanded by a crowd made up mainly of factory workers. Unfortunately the newspaper did not describe the relationship between this crowd and the one dominated by women and soldiers which had carried out ad hoc searches of city and zemstvo storerooms.

At any rate, very much against its will, the city council was compelled to agree to the "illegal" searches.

> The searches were undertaken only in order to calm the workers. The city council authorized them to hurriedly organize commissions of deputies from workers, soldiers, and peasants to carry out the searches. At the head of each commission was a representative from the workers. Each committee was given an armed soldier for protection.

The city was divided into sections and each commission assigned to search one section. According to the city council investigation's figures, almost 550 *tons* of food were found, including wheat and rye flour, oats, groats, rice, sugar, and tea. The newspaper sniffed that, when divided up among the entire city population, it would be enough to last only four or five days.[68] This calculation may well be correct, but to starving people, the hoarding of even four or five days' food supply for an entire city was considered criminal. And the government which protected the hoarders was soon to be regarded as illegitimate.

The events in Kostroma demonstrate clearly the contrast between women's and men's strategies regarding food searches. In Kostroma, as in Yaroslavl, searches in which women took a major part remained ad hoc even when the women were supported by the armed strength of soldiers. Women did not develop a systematic plan, dividing the city into regions and assigning some of their number to cover each area. Perhaps most significantly, women did not integrate their actions into existing workers' and soldiers' institutions, as did the organized inspections. And women did not play a major role in such systematically organized searches when they were set up by other groups.

Patterns of Women's and Workers' Smaller-Scale Searches

Further research may reveal whether citywide inspections and confiscations occurred in other areas in the late summer and early fall of 1917. One newspaper report from the town of Romanovo in Yaroslavl *guberniia*, said that the example of Yaroslavl had been "infectious," and that "searches are happening everywhere, as if by plan."[69] Systematic, widespread searches were undertaken in Moscow in mid-August, in hotels and other furnished rooms where speculators were suspected of hiding their goods. Large stores of sugar, coffee, fabric, and other goods were found.[70]

Whether or not citywide searches were common throughout the CIR as Russia moved closer to the October Revolution, scattered reports of smaller-scale searches throughout the year demonstrate a pattern similar to the one we have examined for Kostroma and Yaroslavl: isolated searches undertaken by workers' deputies which did not involve women workers in any significant way, while women undertook other searches independently of their factory networks.[71] For example, in June, Nerekhta factory workers searched the home of the manager of the city cooperative after he refused to sell sugar and flour; the workers found over a ton of the highest quality wheat flour and over five hundred pounds of sugar.[72] In Ivanovo-Voznesensk, workers initiated searches of storehouses, carried out by the police just before the February Revolution. Well over thirty tons of flour, nine tons of groats, 5.5 tons of rice, and large quantities of sugar were discovered at six locations.[73] On June 21 in Kostroma, deputies of the factory workers searched one private dwelling and found almost a ton of wheat flour and "a whole store of rye, wheat, groats, raisins, etc."[74] A food action in the settlement of Lezhnevo, near Ivanovo-Voznesensk, began when "hungry workers abandoned the factory and went into the street where they discussed for a long time the question of what to do." The crowd divided into two parts, each of which headed for the house of a member of the local provisioning committee. Searches were undertaken with much violence and destruction.[75]

Women workers were virtually never mentioned as taking part in any of these factory-based actions. But women in the streets do seem to have instigated other small-scale searches with roughly the same frequency. In the town of Pozhekhon'e, in Yaroslavl *guberniia*, the "proletariat in skirts," became convinced that a shop assistant who worked in the city store was hoarding goods for himself and

> carried out a search in the [shop assistant's] home without permission of the authorities, in the presence of only rank-and-file policemen. . . . Fifteen jars of jam and flour already accounted for were found. Cucumbers and other items belonging to [the shop assistant] were stolen.
>
> In the process, complete havoc was created in the apartment, after which [the shop assistant's] wife took sick.

The next day, "a large crowd of women . . . everyone talking at once and with shrill cries," conducted searches in the home of a member of the city council and of his neighbor. The food the women had suspected was hidden there was not found.[76] And during Moscow disorders on August 26, women in one *raion* of the city stopped all loaded wagons they met and inspected them.[77] Ten days later, a crowd of women demanded a search of a private apartment, where manufactured goods were discovered and confiscated. The crowd also broke into the commissariat and severely beat the commissar's assistant, who had shot and wounded a woman in the crowd.[78]

Women Workers and Their Factory Organizations

I found only two instances of women attempting to use factory workers' institutions to affect food availability. One of these ended with the women failing to mobilize their fellow workers. In Ivanovo-Voznesensk, "on Oct. 2, several women appeared at the factory committee demanding bread. With tears in their eyes, they testified that they had not eaten for two days." Soon all the factory's workers stopped work and went into the yard demanding bread. Two

31

orators called for action against government agencies, but representatives from the soviet and the provisioning board were able, with difficulty, to convince the workers to return to work.[79] One wonders whether the "tearful" approach of the women may have contributed to their failure to mobilize their fellow workers. It also raises the question of why women, so used to using threats and militance toward government institutions and merchants, sometimes used tearful pleading when it came to their own factory organizations, dominated by men from their own working-class communities.

The other attempt by women to use factory networks was unfortunately very vague as to the success or failure of the outcome. It took place in Novaia Gol'chikha, Kostroma *guberniia*, which, like Norskoe, was an isolated factory settlement with no provisioning committee of its own; it came under the jurisdiction of the Kineshma provisioning committee. The working women of one factory there,

> referring to the fact that at [other] factories, flour and groats were being sold at lower than market prices, demanded the distribution of flour and groats instead of a money compensation for the high cost of living. The workers of two other factories . . . supported this demand of the working women. The textile workers of all three factories went into the streets and demanded representatives from the soviet. After a long and stormy meeting, a delegation was chosen to make a trip, together with representatives of the factory owners, to the Kineshma provisioning board and the union of cooperatives.[80]

In this instance, working women were successful in mobilizing the workers of their own and two other factories to make demands for aid from the soviet. Delegates were chosen to travel to the *uezd* capital of Kineshma to appeal to the provisioning board there, a strategy similar to that chosen by the Norskoe workers. I found no indication, however, that the working women of Novaia Gol'chikha developed their influence over their fellow workers into an ongoing organization or even into a strategy repeated whenever necessary over the subsequent months. The Novaia Gol'chikha working women's use of factory networks may have been a one-time-only event. If so, it suggests that there must have been other factors which mitigated against women's repeating it.

What might these factors have been? Why did women workers in general not take part in ongoing organizations to improve the food situation? Perhaps working women simply did not have access to material or other resources necessary for organizing. Many social historians of political activism stress the importance of examining the resources available to lower-class activists, because these resources effect the shape activism may take. In the next chapter, I will look at the resources available to Russian women workers trying to provide food for themselves and their families in 1917.

THREE

Food Riots:
Resources Available
to Women Activists

Food riots in general are not sophisticated, organized forms of political activity. However, the food activists in Russia during 1917 had available to them many resources necessary for more systematic ways of attempting to affect the food supply. These resources included preorganization into groups having frequent, regular contact and time to organize; the opportunity to hear opposing political views of various parties during street meetings; potential allies in the breadlines and in their factories; awareness of their menfolk's long history of collective activity regarding food (artels and later food cooperatives); their own militance and courage; and newly democratic government committees overseeing the food supply.

Breadlines Provide Preorganization of Women

One factor conducive to successful political activity is the forging of bonds among the participants prior to the activity itself. Ironically, breadlines provided an environment which to some degree fostered the forging of such bonds. Over the months of the food shortage, queues became a social institution, a meeting place where, tired and weary as they were, women could share their thoughts.

Certainly the queues did not improve women's lives overall, but the continuous waiting in line may have been a rare, perhaps the only, time in married working women's lives when they were with large numbers of other women, and at the same time compelled to be idle, away from factory work and housework alike. One woman, asked her opinion of a government proposal to eliminate breadlines by setting up committees for food distribution, rejected the proposal out of hand, asserting the need she felt for breadlines as a place to talk with other women. "Without queues, where can a woman really clarify her thoughts, where can she unburden her woman's heart in these hard days?"[1] The journalist Mariia Ancharova also observed that the queues were a place where "women's hubbub" reigned, and where women had plenty of uninterrupted time to discuss the issues most deeply concerning them. By May, the food situation in Moscow had become so critical that it was necessary for people to begin getting into line in the very early morning.

> Around 1 a.m., Moscow—which has been taking a nap since 11 p.m. when the streetlights are dimmed "because of the war situation"—revives again.
>
> It awakens strangely and secretly.
>
> From the lanes women's figures begin to emerge imperceptibly, muffled in kerchiefs, and they gather in little groups in defined places.
>
> Near some of the groups fires are lit. The nights up until now have been diabolically cold.
>
> The muffled figures shiver, and yawn lingeringly and deliciously. Some, leaning against a wall, doze, trying to return to their interrupted sleep; others, rousing themselves in the cold, exchange a few frosty words, lapse into silence for a time, then again another phrase is heard and you look—alongside the dry twigs [of the fires] crackles the sound of women's speech [*babii govor.*]
>
> Here there is "women's dominance." There are men, too, but they are lost in the women's hubbub. . . .
>
> "What are you doing here?" I asked once, running across such a night gathering by a bonfire.
>
> "What are we doing?" a tall, emaciated woman snarled at me. "We're out for a promenade."
>
> "We're standing in line for bread," mumbled an elderly woman next to her. I got into line too.
>
> The little group imperceptibly lengthened out into a "*khvost.*"
>
> My neighbors peacefully conversed about domestic affairs.
>
> Suddenly from somewhere at the end of the *khvost* came the disturbing news that in several days, the sale of bread will "be ended everywhere."[2]

Thus, as women shared their burdens standing in front of the same neighborhood shops day after day, month after month, they built up the contacts and friendships among themselves which are one of the necessary bases for purposeful group action. The importance of these networks of interrelationships for concerted protest cannot be overestimated.

Women also engaged in constant strategizing as to which shops to try, and in what order. Women planned their "attacks" on food shops before they were even out of bed in the morning. We might wonder why this individual plotting never coalesced into joint long-term decision making.

Women did develop one organizational technique which had potential to aid them in developing more systematic political strategies. A number of sources describe agreements among groups of shoppers whereby one person waited in line, freeing the others to do other things. A journalist with the pseudonym "Thrifty Citizen" reported on a group of domestic servants who had arranged that each in turn would stand in line for all of them while the others left.[3] A memoir described a group of workers living together in a Moscow apartment: "we had an arrangement among us in that hungry time to be on duty in shifts in the line at Filippov's bakery. The line was there day and night."[4] Another newspaper article observed a more far-reaching version of this technique. It noted the recent development of

> new-fangled queue earnings, which for some people produce very solid profits.
> In each "khvost," some clever woman turns up.
> This shrewd woman gets in line before anyone else, at 10 p.m., sits by the door of the bakery and, waiting, talks to herself: "Fish get caught, big and small. . . ."
> And in truth, the fish start to be caught.
> One after another, distraught citizenesses, who fear that they'll be left without bread the next day, come up to the queue.
> The woman waiting first in line announces, "What, women, dears, why should you stand in line all night? Go to sleep, that's better. I'll wait here alone. You see, I'll give you a number now and you come back here as soon as the store opens [in the morning] and get into line by number, and for this I'll sit here all night, and you'll pay me twenty kopeks. . . ."
> Everyone wants to sleep and all willingly agree to pay twenty kopeks each, if only they can go and get some sleep.
> At big bakeries, three to five hundred people usually wait each night, so that some thrifty old woman can earn sixty to a hundred rubles.[5]

This technique had potential for furthering more systematic political actions than ad hoc riots. A daytime version of this system, minus the profit taking, could have been devised to permit women from various different lines to go off to meetings together or to engage in other organizational work in the interests of affecting the overall food supply.

In fact, women could have simply formed meetings in foodlines as they waited, especially in those where they had to wait hours for the shop to open. Street meetings were extremely common throughout 1917, and the *khvosty* would seem to have been a potential spawning ground for them.[6]

The Streets Provide Political Education

Because most working women were illiterate, they could not learn about politics by reading the many newspapers available, including those distributed free in the streets by various political parties. But the streets offered even illiterate women many other opportunities for political education. This education had both a theoretical side—provided by the political street agitators and meetings which were so prevalent throughout 1917—and an empirical side—as lower-class women came into constant contact with the power and privileges of the upper classes. The food situation in itself offered a case study of exploitation by merchants, the ruling classes, and the political system which supported the status quo, a case study which dovetailed with the analyses put forth by orators from the various political parties. A poem in *Gazeta-Kopeika*, the penny newspaper widely read by workers, observed how women talked endlessly with each other, "tongues awagging," about these various elements of exploitation and their impact on the individual poor woman trying to keep her children from going hungry.

> Tongues awagging—before there were
> beautiful goods, but where can you get
> them now, thanks to the marauders?
> Tongues awagging—they've been moved to
> the open-air markets . . . where the
> plunderers rip you off. There's no cream—
> all the milk merchants sold it to
> the Kadets and gave the rest
> to the Ministers.
> Be moved!
> There's no bread and no potatoes,
> there's no butter nor carrots—
> the bourgeois have eaten everything,
> —there are no greens, no flour!
> And rocking her baby, a woman
> whispers: "There's no tea"—the

bourgeois have drunk it all—
chew on a crust of bread for a while!"
Be strengthened! . . .[7]

The first way women got firsthand experience about the forces affecting food supply was through the activities of food merchants and shopkeepers. Tradespeople were often observed carting goods away from their shops, hoping to receive a higher price by selling them elsewhere or to hoard them until prices rose still higher. Tradespeople had access to food for their families and often moved large supplies to their private residences, both for the family pantry and as another storage point for goods on which to speculate.

In addition to these practices, merchants took advantage of the crisis in other ways. For example, because milk was necessary to families with small children, rudeness and other maltreatment of customers became widespread. One journalist revealed the practices of large-scale milk merchants, who, despite their competitive stance vis-à-vis one another, could afford to treat their customers cavalierly because of their own power and the latter's desperate situation. Two milk merchants, Chichkin and Blandov, had large empires.

As soon as the Blandovs open their 1,001st branch somewhere, Chichkin invariably opens his own "establishment" in the near neighborhood.

In front of the milk shops of both firms, beginning in the morning, are large, substantial, motley lines. . . . [in which,] certainly, predominate not the "*burzhuvazy*," but the laboring public. . . .

They stand in line in good weather and get wet in the rain, rotting their outer clothing and boots. . . .

The milk kings—their milk and cream highnesses—know that they are indispensable. . . .

According to the rules, they open the milk shops at 8 a.m., but in fact the "old friends" always appear late. . . . [sometimes] by an hour or more.

The cashier arrives, the sales people appear, but the chief is peacefully enjoying himself somewhere, he's sleeping it off after some moonshine.[8]

Two weeks later, "a reader" wrote to the *Gazeta-Kopeika* column "Our Complaint Book" about another milk merchant, in front of whose shop,

beginning at 5 or 6 a.m., people gather. . . . They wait, but the owner. . . . only arrives at the store when he takes it into his head. The merchant knows that family people cannot do without milk. Well, so he gives them a hard time: let them wait, he says, it's time to go eat.

Finally the milk merchant . . . opens his "firm." The people are in line [but]. . . . the milk merchant knows only one form of equity: whoever pays most is first. His established price is 35 kopeks. This is for those in line. If someone will pay 40 or 50 kopeks, that person is taken out of turn.

The merchant sells everything at the higher price to those last in line, and so someone standing in line several hours [unable to move to the head of the line earlier because unable to afford the higher price] does not get any.[9]

A major offense was tradespeople's willingness to accommodate wealthy customers (and their servants purchasing food for them) out of turn, and to reserve food for them even when this meant that those who had stood in line for hours would not get their share. This practice clearly illustrated to those standing in line that there were two groups of people colluding to make the difficult food situation worse for the lower classes: merchants and the wealthy elite. One account written by the reporter "Gorik" describes women talking among themselves about such an incident.

Recently I happened to observe the following scene, highly characteristic of these times.

On the corner . . . of Tverskaia-Lamskaia and Lesnaia streets, near the city bread shop, a group of people are talking excitedly. They are primarily women and children.

One woman, gesticulating, recounts in an agitated tone:

"I go into this shop, ask for black bread, and they say there isn't any! And just as I get outside the door, some *sudaryn'ka* [fancily dressed lady] goes in. I glance through the window, and that same saleswoman who told me there's no bread gets a whole loaf out from under the counter and weighs it out for the *sudaryn'ka*. I go back in there: 'What's this,' I say. 'There's no bread for me, but for her you found it?' And the saleswoman, how she yelled at me! 'Maybe she's my mother,' she says. 'So beat it.' 'Look,' I say, 'watch out that you don't get fired for a trick like this!' But she still didn't give me any bread!"[10]

A July article described an incident in front of a tea and coffee shop. It was introduced with a statement that the tea shortage was largely due to merchants holding goods off the market for speculation. Merchants were attempting to take advantage of the inelasticity of demand for tea, which was considered by the lower classes an essential, life-giving source of nourishment and warmth. The description illustrates the growth of a sense of solidarity among those in line, as they verbally assaulted a well-dressed woman going into the store ahead of them. (Hats were worn only by upper-class women, kerchiefs by working-class women and peasants; hence headgear was a widely recognized indicator of class.) The feeling of solidarity resulted from months-long common suffering and the experience of the blatantly inequitable assumption of privilege by the wealthy.

Given the present high cost of living, poor people . . . "live" on hot tea. . . . There are "*khvosty*" in front of the tea stores—everyone is stocking up on the Chinese poison.
"What times these are!" sigh the kerchiefs, caps, and babushkas in line.
"The end of the world!" mumbles an old woman in a reddish-brown cape. . . .
"That's the way it was with tobacco, and now with tea, things have gotten desperate," sadly jokes some threadbare "*spinzhak*" [lower-class colloquial for "jacket"].
    "There's no sugar and no tea—
    There's no bread or milk!
    Look at the people—how they get angry—
    They won't spare the fist!"
finished the merry "*spinzhak*" with an improvisation.
"Madame," out of turn, makes her way into the store.
The *khvost* hoots:
"Get in line! Stand in line! Your hat isn't an admission ticket [*propusk*] into the store!"
"I'm going for coffee, not for tea!" snapped the lady.
"Get in line, get in line!" hoots the *khvost*.
    "Coffee, cream, biscuits
    Chicken, geese, sturgeon!
    The life of the bourgeois isn't torture,
    It's a bowl of cherries!"
again put in the indefatigable "*spinzhak*."
    In the line, laughter:
    "Don't grieve, people—"
    "Dance a round dance!"
"See here, we've danced long enough, and look where it's gotten us."[11]

The streets also offered an arena for political education, both practical and theoretical, which went beyond issues of food. In addition to the street meetings in which political agitators put forth their political analyses, events were constantly occurring which were observed and discussed by the women to whom they became a familiar aspect of daily life. For example, in early March, a suspected enemy of the revolution, disguised as a policeman, was found hiding in a barrel in a shed just off the street. A crowd formed as the suspect tried to convince his captors that he had just been pulled off a tram running board by someone in the crowd:

A line of women and children waiting to buy milk during the food shortage
leading to the revolution of 1917.

A breadline in Moscow, 1917, shows how long the queues often became.

As food grew more scarce during 1917, women had to get in line hours before shops opened. Away from both factory work and housework, these women formed close bonds as they talked while endlessly waiting on sidewalks.

This Moscow breadline contains both lower and upper class women, the kind of admixture of "hats" and "kerchiefs" which often generated class friction in breadlines (Bakhmetev Collection, Columbia University)

Women surround a milk merchant's cart, 1917 (merchant is standing in his cart behind women; his horse is to the left.) When merchants illegally withheld food for a higher profit elsewhere, such scenes were often the spawning ground of food riots. (Bakhmetev Collection, Columbia University)

A 1917 demonstration of women demanding an increase in government allowances to families of soldiers. (The Bettmann Archive)

"You see, that one with popeyes and a nose like a potato. . . ."

"He pulled you off the tram, and now we've pulled you out of a barrel—like a herring. . . ."

"How much a pound, uncle?" jokes a woman coming up with rolls sticking out from under her arm.

The crowd surrounds the arrested man and sends him off with a convoy. . . .

Boys, jumping up and down, accompany the "procession."

At the scene of the "incident," several people remain to satisfy the curiosity of the inquisitive bystanders, who are asking them what happened.

Women predominate. Someone shares their impressions about an analogous case, someone describes how they discovered the "policeman" hiding in the deserted storeroom.

Exactly so do mice scatter, running to hide in their holes! [I.e., counterrevolutionaries were fleeing into hiding like mice.]

The street discusses events and episodes.

And a light snow everywhere falls and falls.[12]

Thus, the streets formed a world in which events occurred and were discussed with great frequency during the year of the revolutions. Although these incidents taken singly were not as fateful as those with which historians are generally more familiar, they were nonetheless the daily manifestations of the major trends that shaped the political developments of 1917. Since working-class women spent so much time in the streets, it was the accumulation of these small events which, over time, helped to form women's political awareness.

One description of a September breadline shows women's awareness of the various political parties and summarizes several of the points made here. First, the long, idle waits in line provided an opportunity for discussion of political topics as people argued with each other to pass the time, arguing most of all about who was responsible for the long queues. (The numbers refer to various political parties' places on the election ballot: "three" was the Social Democrats.)

The *khvost* by the bakery stretches agonizingly far. Everyone is fed up with standing. They would all like to bite off each others noses from malice.

An argument gets underway . . . on a topical subject.

A lady in a hat: "So much for your great number three, look what they've done! Do you like standing here?"

As the argument heated up, the lower-class women in line displayed their propensity to combine their daily, empirical experience of class privilege (symbolized by the contrast between hat and kerchief) and their broader political knowledge, gleaned mainly from political agitators. The lower-class women also demonstrated their developing sense of solidarity vis-à-vis the wealthy woman as they all jumped in together to contradict her analysis of who was responsible for the breadlines:

> . . . everyone cried, "I'm for number three, I'm for number three!"
> And a woman in a kerchief: "Well, the same goes for your number one [the Popular Liberty Party], they're good too, there in the government they haven't done anything [*ni iz kuzova ni v kuzov*].
> "Well, at least they've gotten down to business better than yours! Tell me, please. They sit in the Duma for three months and everyone talks, but what they've gotten done isn't worth half a kopek. You stand here for a crust of bread, like some kind of a dog."
> "And you think because you've got a hat on, you can't stand in line. You sure can stand!"
> "What's my hat to you? It's half as expensive as your kerchief. . . . Your brain can't understand a thing."
> "And you're so smart, what kind of a show off do you think you are, you aristocratic swine!"

In the Ivanovo-Kineshma area in September, women workers in long lines outside polls, many carrying infants or "with tails of two or three children holding onto their skirts," discussed the various political parties as they waited to cast their votes. At a rally in Orekhovo, a Menshevik orator got up to speak, calling for support for the Provisional Government and its policy of carrying on the war until victory.

> For this, the working women pulled him down from the platform, setting up a real row against him. They shouted, "Here's your war until victory! Here's your Kerensky!" After this, [the orator] fled from Orekhovo.[13]

Clearly, in the turbulent political climate of 1917, even illiterate working-class women were developing at least a rudimentary sense of political issues, and were actively defending their political beliefs.

Potential Allies: Soldiers and Factory Organizations

There were two potential allies with whom working women could join to strengthen their position: the soldiers in the breadlines, and the factory networks and organizations at women's workplaces. While women were apparently intimidated at first by the armed soldiers, who cut ahead of them in breadlines, women lost their timidity over the months and became bolder in their stance toward their uniformed fellow shoppers.

> Formerly, soldiers used to go into the bakeries and milk shops out of turn, but now more and more often the Moscow "amazons" energetically send these out-of-turn customers packing:
> "That's enough of that! Stand in line! You showed off your courage when you were running from your positions like dogs with their tails between their legs! And you call yourselves heroes!" [The women were referring to the fact that these soldiers were no longer at the front, but at the garrison in the rear, with little to do, performing no service to the population and appearing parasitic.]
> And the confused soldiers either slink away from these shouts, or shamefacedly get into line.
> And the tamers crow [over their victory].
> "That's the way it should be. Warriors indeed! These days even we women are soldiers!"[14]

Like upper-class shop customers, soldiers often felt they had the right to go to the head of the queue. And, as with the elegantly dressed cutters-in-line, the women who waited patiently eventually began to shout down the soldiers, telling them to get back in line and wait their turn like everyone else. But unlike the upper-class shoppers, the soldiers often submitted to the women's scoldings, perhaps because soldiers shared the same lower-class origins as the waiting women and thus were psychologically unable to maintain their claim to privileged status. They slunk back to their places like boys scolded by their mothers.

It was no small victory for women to convince soldiers to relinquish their privilege of avoiding hours-long waits in line. However, women did not carry this influence over soldiers into their food actions. Women were generally aware that in order to carry out their attacks on hoarders and shopkeepers, they needed the backing of groups which had authority and control over arms. Women routinely made bids for such aid to governmental authorities, demanding that they search for and confiscate hoarded food, even after those authorities proved unresponsive in helping them to obtain food. Yet women almost never appealed to soldiers for aid, even though, when soldiers themselves chose to join food disorders, they usually took over the role of providing the force necessary to achieve the same goals as did provisioning committees and city councils.

Women ultimately came to identify Provisional Government bodies as enemies, making threats and taking violent action against legal food authorities. But from there they did not turn to the soldiers, who would probably have proven more reliable allies. There is almost no indication that women were ever responsible for bringing soldiers into an action when the latter were not already on the scene by their own choice. That is, women in food actions where soldiers were absent almost never sent some of their number to bring soldiers from their barracks, gathering places, neighboring bread lines, or wherever, to their aid.

This was true despite the fact that working-class women were well known during 1917 to have a great capacity to influence soldiers to abandon the government and join the women's side. Women's ability to influence soldiers was manifested at the very inception of the February Revolution, when the insurgents faced armed forces ordered to suppress them. "A great role is played by women workers in the relation between workers and soldiers. They go up to the cordons more boldly than men, take hold of their rifles, beseech, almost command, "Put down your bayonets—join us!"[15] In St. Petersburg, these soldiers had come over to the revolution, and in the CIR, women's influence over soldiers was known as well.[16] Women's effectiveness was widely enough recognized that when the Orekhovo-Zuevo Bolsheviks learned that a trainload of soldiers would be stopping briefly in Orekhovo on the way to the front, the Bolsheviks called a mass meeting of working women, asking them to convince the soldiers not to get back on the train when it left town. "As was standard at the time, a racket was made in all the barracks and artels with the cry 'Come out to a meeting at the Winter Theater to meet the soldiers!' People gathered quickly, as always." Several thousand workers came to the theater, most of them women. The Bolsheviks told them,

"Our task is to tell the soldiers the truth about this war. You, comrade women, can tell the soldiers the truth about this war especially well, because the burden of the war lies on you." There were cries of "Down with the war! . . . Long live the Soviet of Workers' Deputies!"

Proceeding to the train station, "all the railroad lines were occupied by several rows of women." When the train stopped, it was immediately surrounded by the crowds. The officers in charge were furious, but they were far outnumbered. Fraternization began:

The women called the soldiers "sons" and "comrades."

"Where are you being taken?" they said fervently. "To your deaths! And for what? For the capitalists!"

The conversations were truthful and convincing, and the soldiers understood this. . . .

All the cars were empty. People were scattered in groups, arguing, debating.

The soldiers listened especially attentively to the women. Their stories about their lives without their husbands, without sons, about their poverty and hunger convinced the soldiers. Several, recalling their own families, wept.

Another observer's account recalled that, "All the soldiers dispersed throughout the city—there was singing and dancing; they went to the barracks, to homes, to taverns. The echelon stood for several hours, blocking the normal movement of two important railroad lines." According to this account, barely 50 percent of the soldiers returned to the train."[17]

In this setting, women's influence over soldiers was based on arousing family feelings. One might imagine that in the setting of food actions, women could also rouse soldiers' sympathies and aid with accounts of their starving children, but I found no evidence that they ever did so.

For their part, soldiers were ready to take part in food actions, participating in many alongside women when they happened to be already at the scene. Soldiers also formed alliances with factory committees and other workers' organizations to carry out organized and planned food actions. Soldiers and working women, too, would seem to have been logical allies. Yet although women often bossed soldiers around in the bread queues, and although they convinced soldiers to join them in other situations, in food protests they did not move to develop their relationship into one of an organized alliance or even one of frequent but not consciously planned joint action.

Women workers who undertook food actions also seem to have only very rarely used their factory organizations and networks in any way to advance their food-related goals. Women trying to obtain food took action in the streets, not in their factories. Women workers became involved in food actions as individuals attempting to do the day's shopping for their families, not as workers. Close relationships were established among women who spent a great deal of time waiting together day after day, but these relationships were not necessarily among workers from the same factory. In fact, when soldiers' and workers' organizations allied to carry out systematic searches, women abdicated the position of leadership (or at the very least participation) which their long months of experience should have conferred on them. It is as if women denied or repressed their capacity to act based on the knowledge, skills, and experience they had gained over a long period of intense activity.[18]

Working women's failure to use their factory networks might seem doubly puzzling given the tradition of artels among Russian workers and also the precedent of factory-based workers' food cooperatives. Artels were work crews and/or collective food purchasing, preparation, and consumption arrangements which had a centuries-old history among the working class. Food cooperatives were a later phenomenon, first occurring in the late nineteenth century and developing further during the interrevolutionary period. Workers' food cooperatives seem to have been dominated by men and to have been generated as a result of high food prices, not during times of food shortage.[19] However, given the cooperative effort among men, one might wonder why women did not at least experiment with such institutions, either by creating their own cooperatives or by taking part in existing ones.

A last type of workers' factory-based organization which existed in working women's environment in 1917 focused on efforts to obtain needed fuel and raw materials to run their factories. Transport and supply of these items had become disorganized during 1917, just as food had, and workers often took over responsibility for obtaining them for their own factories. For example, when Ivanovo-Voznesensk factory owners began to hold up shipments of fuel and raw materials to their factories (in order to subvert the revolutionary process among workers), the Soviet of Workers' Deputies sent delegates to the faraway southern cities of Samara and Astrakhan to get the barges containing the raw materials moving up the Volga again.[20]

The parallel with the food situation is instructive. Substantial supplies of food were also being held up in southern Russia, and women, too, might have traveled south (just as they traveled shorter distances to *uezd* provisioning committees) in an attempt to make sure that food supplies for their cities got their share of railway transport northward.[21] Had women developed a systematic strategy of going to the source of supply, rather than depending on middlemen who stood to profit by hoarding, they might have been much more successful over the long run. Such an effort at consumers' control over food supply would have paralleled workers' attempts to establish democratic control over industry prior to consolidation of central power by the Bolshevik government.

Popular Representation on Provisioning Committees

Provisioning committees were a potential resource for women. After the February Revolution, they were charged with providing food for the entire population, not just for the army. At the same time, their composition was altered to include representatives of all segments of the population, including workers, in order to be responsive to the needs of the people. Throughout 1917, women constantly appealed to provisioning committees during food actions, voicing specific measures they felt the committees should undertake. Yet women themselves were not represented on the committees. Why did women not protest their lack of representation on the committees, and why did they not demand that this oversight be rectified?

Women were not generally timid or self-effacing in interactions with these committees, nor did they lack self-confidence in formulating and expressing their ideas for measures the committees should undertake. Women asserted their ideas with a great deal of insistence, and it seems strange that it did not occur to them that, if they were members of the committees, they could have ensured that their proposals would be carried out.

In particular, a number of spectacular cases of government bungling in regard to spoilage of huge food stores should have made it clear to everyone that, if those most concerned with food—women—had had major official control over food supply, provisioning committees might have done a better job. One case occurred in Moscow, where the Union of Cities (to whom the provisioning committees were accountable) had been "conserving" stores of food for future use, and had negligently allowed it to rot before it was made available to the population. The union then disposed of the huge quantities of putrid food by dumping it into the Moscow River.

> The all-Russian Union of Cities has distinguished itself again.
> This time, the Union "marinated" four wagons of eggs and 240 *pudy* [4.3 tons] of coconut oil.
> Millions of eggs have been marinated up to now, while in the neighboring homes they have not begun to smell the noble fragrance of orange blossoms [i.e., they have been smelling rotting eggs]. . . .
> The eggs, you understand, are now in direct communication with the Moscow river, and the coconut oil will also be sent to improve the soil. . . .
> Tens of thousands of famished people vainly upholster the thresholds of food shops.
> Tens of thousands stand in lines and *khvosty* in order to obtain a quarter pound of oil and just one—do you understand—one egg!

How many trembling hands convulsively reach out to these eggs, perhaps necessary to save some child's life!"[22]

Such incidents might have aroused an outcry and demands that women, who were more immediately involved with food than anyone else, and hence more likely not to be negligent about government stores of it, be represented on provisioning committees. Yet nothing of the sort was ever demanded or considered by these women.

Russian women food activists had a number of resources available which they did not take advantage of. If they had utilized all their options, they might have been able to undertake much more far-reaching strategies than food riots: influencing government policy on the war and the priority the Provisional Government gave to military transport needs as opposed to civilian consumers' needs; changing the government's fixed price policy, which encouraged speculation; tracking down the food supplies in rural areas of the country and making sure they got to consumers without the unchecked intervention of profiteering middlemen. An alliance with rank-and-file soldiers' and workers' organizations might well have provided the strength for such far-reaching goals, in the face of Provisional Government opposition.

That women did not utilize resources in their environment was not due to carelessness, stupidity, or neglect. It had its roots in the constraints of daily life. Some of these constraints will be explored in Part Two.

Militance

Although the strategies undertaken by women food rioters did not develop into ongoing organizations, women were certainly not passive or dependent in their attempts to obtain food. They were, on the contrary, militant and courageous, constantly demanding immediate results rather than adopting a gradualist stance.[23] Perhaps the main fuel igniting women's militance was their responsibility for feeding their children, who got hungry every day, who could not wait for food or develop patience through an intellectual understanding of the food shortage, and who got sick and often died from impure food. Women's commitment to the needs of children, greater and more immediate than those of adults, inflamed mothers' anger toward the government which could not deliver food, and caused their implacable demands for immediate concessions.

49

Batya Weinbaum and Amy Bridges have discussed the extreme disjuncture between the values and priorities of women within their households and the values and priorities of the social world beyond the family.

> Women are responsible for "nurturance," . . . and it is the housewife's responsibility for nurturance which conditions her confrontation with capital in the form of commodities. . . . It is the housewife's responsibility for "nurturance" on the one hand, and the impossibilities of helping other human beings be healthy and creative within the constraints of the present system on the other, that create the incredible tensions of the practice of consumption work. . . . [H]ousehold-based demands insist that production and provision of services be oriented to social needs and in this way embody values antithetical to capitalist production.[24]

In other words, the nature of the interchange between mother and child is closer to the notion of "from each according to his abilities; to each according to his needs" than is any other system of human interaction in the world beyond the home. Thus, women's responsibility for childrearing has the potential to prime them for radical action against the status quo when it cannot meet basic human needs.

This disjuncture between family and capitalist values generated women's radicalism during the Russian Revolution, perhaps most clearly in women's contention that they had a right to appropriate for their children any food available in their locality, as against the merchants' contention that they had a right to keep any food they had paid for. One of the primary characteristics of women's activism was their impatient insistence on the primary importance of satisfying the human needs of the people they loved, particularly their children. While the agencies of the Provisional Government, and sometimes even the soviets, sought to placate the starving and protect the property rights of the wealthy who hoarded food, women shrilly and totally rejected any view which did not value human needs above all else.

Russian women's food riots were thus somewhat analogous to millenarian movements, as Eric Hobsbawm discusses them. Hobsbawm notes the spirit of millenarianists, their clarity of conviction that they had an incontrovertible right to immediate justice and equality. This spirit, argues Hobsbawm, is a positive quality, but by itself it cannot be effective. For without being joined with "the right kind of ideas about political organization, strategy, and tactics," it cannot survive. Millenarianism can be, indeed it always will be, intensely moving for anyone who cares for the fate of [human beings]: but . . . it will certainly be perennially defeated. However, when harnessed to a modern movement, millenarianism can not only become politically effective, but it may do so without the loss of that zeal, that burning confidence in a new world, and that generosity of emotion which characterizes it. . . . And no one can read the testimony of [millenarianists] without hoping that their spirit can be preserved.[25]

Surely one can say the same of Russia's women food activists during the upheavals of 1917.

FOUR

Street Fighting:
The Moscow Revolution

While the Bolshevik revolution in St. Petersburg was almost bloodless, its victory in Moscow was achieved only after a week of fighting in city streets between Red Guard units under the Soviet's Military Revolutionary Committee and their opponents led by the city duma's Committee of Public Safety. This fighting began October 27, the day after reliable news of the St. Petersburg Bolsheviks' victory reached Moscow. Diane Koenker's account of the October events in Moscow observes, "Moscow did not rise in order to seize power for the soviets, but to defend the soviets from the counterrevolution." Probably one half of the soviet defenders were Bolsheviks, the other half nonparty.[1]

Many of the workers who took part in Moscow street fighting were from heavy industrial plants (which I have excluded because they did not typically employ large numbers of women and hence would not provide a legitimate basis for comparison of male and female workers). However, light industry factories in which many women worked were among those which armed and sent Red Guard units into battle. This included the Tsindel' textile plant, Khishin's textile dyeing and printing factory, the Mars clothing factory, the Postavshchik military clothing supply factory, the Gabai tobacco factory, the Karavan tea plant, Einem's candy and biscuit factory, the Kauchuk rubber plant, the Zhiro (Giraud) silk plant, and the Vtorov chemical plant.[2]

Two accounts have noted the small percentage of Moscow's total working-class population which joined Red Guard units and the even smaller number which actually took part in the fighting (although Koenker also argues that the majority of even nonparticipating workers favored soviet power).[3] Thus, in this chapter I am looking at a relatively small group of workers, highly active, and willing to lay down their lives for their political convictions. This was as true of the working women who took part in the fighting as it was of the men. Yet in spite of the elite character of this group, and of the high level of militance, courage, and commitment of women equally with men, a gendered pattern of participation can easily be discerned.

The overwhelming majority of Red Guards who actually fought during Moscow's October days were men. Women performed support services such as first aid for the wounded, reconnaissance, food preparation, guarding factories, and other miscellaneous tasks. While the revolutionary leadership was partly responsible for establishing this gendered division of labor, few working women objected to it. The great majority seem to have considered it perfectly acceptable, if they thought about it at all. Most of the jobs performed by women were extensions of their role in everyday life. This was true not only in terms of tasks, such as food preparation, which women were skilled at from long experience, but also in terms of social relationships: women followed the cultural expectation that they would lovingly perform daily "support services" for husbands, boyfriends, and sons.[4] Reconnaissance was the one job performed by women which, at least at first blush, does not appear to be an outgrowth of women's daily-life role.[5]

Food Provisioning

Food provisioning was the clearest example of women adjusting an aspect of their daily life role to accommodate circumstances during the street fighting. Sometimes this was literally a case of wives bringing food to their husbands. Said one male worker, a Red Guard fighter, "There were many cases when working women [living near an area where fighting was taking place], the wives of workers, brought hot potatoes, bread, and boiling water to us at the front lines."[6] But food provisioning often became a well-organized operation. In Butyrskii *raion*, "Women were designated to organize food provisioning; they were headed by the middle-aged working woman Comrade Ushakova. The women seized an appropriate kitchen somewhere and began to prepare hot food for the fighters who were battling against the junkers."[7]

Several working women provided descriptions of their own work in provisioning. As these memoirs indicate, organizing large dining rooms often entailed women taking measures to obtain supplies that went beyond their daily repertoire of behaviors. E. Vantorina, who worked in a knitted goods factory and was a member of the War Revolutionary Committee of Dorogomilovskii *subraion*, told how she became involved in food provisioning.

54

On October 30, one of the Red Guard detachment chiefs in the *raion* came running into the *raion* headquarters, saying that the men in his unit wanted to leave their posts because they were hungry. Vantorina went to investigate the situation and discovered that the hungry men had staged a small mutiny. They had locked their commanders in a room and were threatening to beat them unless they were fed.

> Talking with the fighters, I promised that I would try to deliver bread, sugar, and tobacco; the railroad cooperative helped in this.
>
> The workers of Dorogomilov [*raion*] and some of the railroad workers, despite the fact that they were not working at that time, gathered 5,000 rubles to support the wounded and the soldiers.
>
> The wives of workers were also on our side. When I arrived [at a shop] to get groceries for the fighters, they [women customers] raised a cry . . . declaring that the soviet was taking food and there was not enough for them and no one knew when the food would be given back. But after negotiations, the women agreed to give up the groceries.
>
> In addition to this, we managed to get tinned food in the Miuskii tram park, which [two male supporters] went to get in a car.[8]

In the city center, the provisioning system was better organized, and the women who ran its dining room developed sources of supplies other than the shops in which women workers bought food for their families. P. Sakharova, a working woman from a sewing factory, described the organization of the Red Guards in Gorodskoi *raion*.

> . . . it was not only necessary to organize the fighters. It was also necessary to feed them. And so we opened a dining room in the People's house on Sukharevskaia square. . . . But where to get groceries? The shops were all closed, all the trade storehouses were locked. . . . Our comrade women, party and nonparty, found a way out. They took some Red Guards with rifles with them and began to requisition food from the Sukharevskii speculators, whose cellars were full of all sorts of food. The women—simple working women—were not frightened by any kind of danger, they were convinced of victory. They gave out receipts to the merchants: "We took such and such food. We will pay after victory."
>
> The dining room worked around the clock. It pulled everyone closer. In the dining room it was possible to get hot tea, *kasha*-gruel, a can of tinned food. The working women, young and old, did not turn anyone away without feeding them and giving them something to drink. The dining room even served the headquarters of the Red Guard sometimes.[9]

These two accounts were written by women who were involved in a number of different types of activity during the October days. Their contact with the food provisioning operation was peripheral. Neither of them became deeply involved in the day-to-day tasks of food provisioning. We may wonder whether, for the other working women who did take daily responsibility for food provisioning, the dining room developed sustained ties among the female participants.[10] Unfortunately, I found no memoirs of these women. The lack of evidence in other sources suggests that major participation in the dining rooms did not lead to further involvement in ongoing organizations beyond the October days. Those working women who immersed themselves in running the dining rooms may well have done so purely to feed their fighting menfolk, with very little change in their assessments of their role and goals in life.

First Aid Work

Perhaps the largest number of working women who took part in the October Revolution in Moscow did first aid work. Women who performed first aid did so in small groups usually organized at *raion* headquarters and attached to or sent out with particular detachments of fighters. "Our first aid nurses," wrote one Red Guard fighter, "who came from among the workers, were very few, and they drove with us or walked wherever we carried on the struggle."[11] Another memoirist described in detail the organization of the first aid detachments. They were

> . . . very primitive: they consisted of a group of three comrades; they received several individual packets of dressing, bandages, cotton, and bottles of iodine; they registered their surnames, were given short instructions, and then left for the designated point. In Zamoskvorech'e, there was not a single important battle point without such a first aid detachment.[12]

In this *raion*, Zamoskvorech'e, a woman Bolshevik was charged by the Red Guards with setting up a first aid station, to which the wounded could be transported, in the Frantsiia café in Serpukhovskaia Square. (This was necessary because regular hospitals refused to treat the insurgents.) The woman Bolshevik "got a lot of women, including some working women from the factories," to help her organize the station.[13] In some areas, first aid units were organized in particular factories and attached to their factories' Red Guard units.[14] Detachments of worker-Red Guards from outside the city who came to Moscow's aid were sometimes accompanied by women first aid workers. From Podolsk, for example, "a detachment of volunteers was sent with a first aid detachment of twenty women and men."[15]

Women first aid workers displayed great bravery under fire, a fact attested to by numerous male participants in the fighting. One man recalled walking past a bridge when shooting suddenly broke out. "At this shooting, our first aid workers ran from all sides. . . . [T]hey were not afraid, and, hearing about danger, they threw themselves wherever their help could be used."[16] A working woman memoirist, P. Zamogil'naia, gave an account of her struggle to overcome her fear under fire, a struggle which many first aid workers may have undergone in order to carry out their tasks successfully. Zamogil'naia had been given orders to join one of the outlying medical points.

> They gave me a band with a red cross on it and a bag of medicines, told me the password, and I headed toward Krymskii bridge.
> The night was dark, it was drizzling, and a cold wind penetrated to the bones. Somewhere right beside me occasional shots sounded. Shooting swept the bridge the whole time, and it became terrifying. You see, this was the first time I had to walk on a pitch black night under fire. Later, I had to do this a number of times, and I grew accustomed to it.[17]

As the fighting went on, the women first aid workers manifested their courage under fire by performing many military support tasks in addition to their medical work. For example, a male metal worker of the military-artillery plant in Butyrskii *raion* recalled:

> It is necessary to note the exceptional heroism of the working women [who worked in] the military-artillery plant, in particular that of the director of the first aid detachment, the nonparty Tsetsum, who, crawling under crossfire near the Nikitskie gates, supplied the Red Guards with cartridges, bandaged wounds, and carried wounded Red Guards out of a . . . burning house on stretchers. She also dragged arms and a machine gun out of this house.
> . . . Young working women also crawled to junkers who had been killed, took their guns and cartridges and supplied the Red Guards with them.[18]

Zamogil'naia recalled her own participation and that of other women in the first aid brigades.

> We all performed the most varied assignments: we bandaged the wounded, walked to the revolutionary committee to get reinforcements and cartridges, gave out arms and cartridges, packed machine-gun ribbons with cartridges, organized short relaxation for the Red Guards who were coming in from their positions, and took new detachments to the front lines.

All through one night, Zamogil'naia helped to drag dirt to build a protective wall from the courtyard to the third floor of a building where the Red Guards had set up a bomb thrower. One evening she was asked to go to headquarters to get reinforcements and cartridges, which were running dangerously low. Arriving at headquarters, she was informed that they had neither reinforcements nor cartridges to spare.

> I asked [the commander] to give me just one case of cartridges since we had no more. [He agreed.] Since the case was not big, I did not suppose that it was heavy. Rashly, I put it on my shoulder and left. I carried it through Kaluzhskaia square, but it became heavy and I transferred it with difficulty to my other shoulder and walked another short distance. When I set the case down in order to rest, I could not get it back up on my shoulder.

Struggling with the heavy case, Zamogil'naia finally managed to deliver the all-important cartridges to her staff.[19]

Several accounts indicate that women of the first aid units even moved into actual combat when the need arose. For example, a male memoirist said of one first aid unit:

> It fell to me to direct this detachment, and to observe a characteristic phenomenon. The comrade workers who joined this detachment [most of whom were women] at the very first possibility went to the center, where the fighting was taking place at that time. On the way, seeing stray guns left by one or another of the comrades during the fighting, they [the women] would run from the unit, seize the gun, and run into battle. There were many such cases.[20]

Thus, although the first aid detachments continued to be designated as medical units by the Red Guards and by the women themselves, in fact they performed whatever support or errand work was needed by the male fighters. One man in charge of a first aid unit described a particular battle.

> Women from my detachment began to drag cartridges to the fighting comrades. . . . The women threw aside their usual tasks and dragged cases of

cartridges [where they were needed]. The comrade women rendered great help to the comrade men.[21]

The wording of this man's account suggests that first aid women's military support tasks were seen as a form of aid given by women to the men, who continued to be viewed as the center of military action no matter what tasks women actually carried out. This memoirist did not mention women again in his recollections after the point when the male fighters had obtained enough arms and ammunition and no longer had to turn to women for aid in getting them. Thus, the women of the "first aid" detachments were in essence a "reserve army" which was relied on when shortages arose, but was never given official recognition for the sometimes military role it played.

Reconnaissance and Communications

A very large proportion of the reconnaissance needs of the Red Guards was met by women, as well as by children and by youths who could not go into combat because of lack of arms. A similar task was the performance by individual women of carrying messages to maintain communication among Red Guard units battling in various parts of the city, many of whom became cut off from one another during the fighting. (Telephone connections were unreliable, because of the ease with which the enemy sabotaged them.)[22]

Interestingly, most descriptions of women's reconnaissance work were provided by male participants in the October fighting. One male worker said, "it is necessary to note the fearless and skillful performance of reconnaissance work by the comrade-women of our plant; moving stealthily behind enemy lines, obtaining the necessary information, they made their way back with reports which helped military headquarters to determine their military tasks more exactly."[23] Another male worker wrote that "reconnaissance was organized in the enemy's rear in order to ascertain its position, strength, and firing points. In this, the female Red Guards of our plant rendered us great assistance—Iudina, Rodionova, and others, and even children and youths."[24] And a man from Butyrskii *raion* noted, "Our reconnaissance consisted of women. It worked very well. We sent the women into all the little corners to find out and eavesdrop on what was going on. They brought us correct information and fulfilled all tasks well. Of them I remember Comrades Izvest'eva, Soboleva, Berzina, and Kazakova. Most of them were working women from Gabai [tobacco factory], Ralle [perfume factory], and the clothing workshops."[25]

Women workers were extremely militant in the sense that they were willing to face great danger in pursuing their goals. A soldier recalled:

> Some working women were used, at the instruction of the revolutionary committee, as reconnaissance scouts and for connections with central revolutionary headquarters. . . . [The women did this work successfully] despite the fact that in the majority of cases it involved risking their lives. Some of these working women did not come back, slain by the junkers' bullets. But this did not disturb the other working women revolutionaries: those wanting to go into dangerous places were always more than were needed.[26]

This militant willingness to confront the most dangerous of situations was a characteristic of female behavior in other types of revolutionary activity as well. Whatever differences there were between men's and women's activity, bravery in face of death was not one of them.

Despite these male memoirists' tributes to the heroism and accomplishments of working women reconnaissance workers, women memoirists themselves had little to say about their experiences and about precisely how they went about achieving their objectives. Their accounts of their scouting work were telegraphic and contained almost no description of their activities behind enemy lines. This contrasts with men's memoirs, which are full of boasting about their confrontations with the enemy. The only detailed account I found by a woman worker of her information-gathering techniques turned out not to have occurred within enemy territory. On the fifth or sixth day of battle, she recalled, she was sent along with several other women to find out what had become of a Red Guard detachment which had left to try to liberate the telegraph station and had not been heard from since.

> It was midnight. It was raining buckets. We arrived at the telegraph. We saw soldiers sitting there in their greatcoats. . . . We pretended to be housemaids sent by our master. We put stupid expressions on our faces and asked, "Are they receiving telegrams?"
> "What kind of telegram are you expecting?"
> We saw that their faces were not wicked. We began to talk to them carefully and it turned out that these were not White soldiers, but ours. They had locked the junkers up in the basement.[27]

The most detailed woman's account of her activity in hostile territory was by a woman worker of the Brokar factory: "Besides giving first aid, it fell to me to perform reconnaissance tasks. I had to make my way stealthily onto Red Square, where the Whites stood by the very gates."[28] This was the sum total of this woman's description of her reconnaissance work. The brevity of her account cannot be attributed to a lack of political sophistication, for most of her memoir was taken up by a description of her close, sustained contacts with Bolshevik organizers from 1914-17.

Another important characteristic of many working women's descriptions of their activities is that most women who moved beyond their factories to take part in events directed by the military-revolutionary committees did not do so as members of factory-based groups of working women.[29] Rather, they participated as relatively isolated individuals, drawn into the action by political agitators or by male members of their families who were already involved. While male worker memoirists often boasted about the accomplishments of their factory or region as a whole, women rarely referred to such ongoing collectivities. Women's memoirs are much more focused on themselves as individuals, performing whatever tasks were needed by the revolutionary committees or by the fighting men at any given moment.

This isolated mode of functioning by most women did not change during the civil war. In contrast to male workers, those few women who went off to the fronts did not do so as part of solidarity groups established at home. A recent Soviet article claims that women textile workers from Ivanovo-Voznesensk "struggled on the fronts of the civil war, and went shoulder to shoulder beside men workers with whom they had stood at the machines." However, the evidence the author uses to support her point is brief individual life histories of four working women (and it is unclear whether the fourth was actually a worker) who were exceptional. Two ended up working for the All-Russia Central Executive Committee of Soviets, one became a deputy of the commissariat of light industry, and one was a member of the board of the commissariat of health.[30] These were stories of great individual achievement by a handful of women, but they reveal nothing about whether women were able, on a mass scale, to form large solidarity groups and maintain their cohesiveness over time. There is in fact no evidence that detachments of first aid workers, for example, maintained strong cohesiveness throughout the October fighting in Moscow, let alone over various fronts of the civil war, as was the case with some men's Red Guard detachments.

A related phenomenon in women's activity was the multiplicity of tasks which women performed during the Moscow uprising. "I worked in the *raion* military headquarters as a reconnaissance worker," said the working woman P. Sakharova.

> But the old division of labor did not exist. As soon as you returned with reconnaissance information, you would go to bandage the wounded, then it was necessary to rush off for groceries.
> One time it was bad for us. The junkers approached First Meshchanskaia Street, on the corner of which our headquarters was located in Romanov's tavern. We began to dig trenches and build barricades around headquarters. . . .
> And we were all like this. From early morning to night—in the revolutionary committee, in the dining room, in the street, on a reconnaissance mission.[31]

(Sakharova was also the woman quoted above who organized a dining room for Red Guards.) The "we" and "us" to which Sakharova referred here were not a factory-based solidarity group. Indeed, she never mentioned her factory or fellow workers throughout her entire memoir. Rather, she used "we" in a vague manner, possibly referring to different groups of people at different points, never defining specific solidarity groups.

That each working woman was relatively isolated, and that each performed a multitude of tasks, were closely related factors. Most men arrived at revolutionary headquarters with groups of co-workers from their factories, groups which had long histories of solidarity. These groups were logically assigned to form Red Guard units. Women workers, in contrast, tended to become active in revolutionary activity singly or at most along with one or two close friends. It was thus logical to assign these volunteers to tasks which generally required individual or sporadic endeavor, not to jobs which needed long-term, teamlike behavior. This is one more indication of the way in which, however heroic and advanced particular women's feats appeared, their overall pattern can perhaps be described as a "reserve army" of errand runners and Jills-of-all-trades, including highly dangerous "trades."

The isolated quality of women's reconnaissance and communications tasks can be seen in the following description.

> When we had to send one of the women workers to communicate with the center, we dressed her as an upper-class lady, fastened a red cross on her, and sent her on reconnaissance: she could carry whatever she wanted, packages, even arms—the White Guards did not touch her. From the other side, they sent their

reconnaissance workers among us dressed in the simple clothes of a working woman or one of our Red Guards.[32]

Thus, as practiced during the October days in Moscow, reconnaissance (and communications) work was not based on highly sophisticated techniques, nor did it involve careful coordination among skilled military groups. It was ad hoc and primitive. Women were often especially well suited to perform it because small numbers of women walking through the streets were less suspicious to the enemy than were men. They could easily be disguised as maids or upper-class Red Cross workers for the Whites. It was precisely the assumed innocence of women which the insurgents capitalized on when they chose women to carry out reconnaissance. And women had all the knowledge needed for such ad hoc, local reconnaissance work during the guerrilla-like city rebellion. Later, during the civil war, fought on many distant fronts, women did not possess the qualifications needed for more sophisticated reconnaissance, and it ceased to be a task dominated by women.

During the October days, reconnaissance could not be carried out by sizable groups. It required people who were self-reliant and worked well alone. Many working women fit this job description well. But at the same time, such isolated activity did not give women the leverage they would need in the long run to push for their own interests in the new postrevolutionary society.

Women's Friendships During Street Fighting

The types of ties to female peers which women activists talked about in their political memoirs were often friendships with one or two other women seen periodically throughout the fighting when the friends' paths crossed. One woman, for example, described a moment of activity shared with her girlfriend. They were walking through the streets at the beginning of the uprising when they came upon groups of armed soldiers. "Going up to the soldiers who were standing near Iverskie, my girlfriend—a member of the party, Lena Tsarik—and I began to agitate." Suddenly, firing began from another direction, and "Lena and I ran around the corner of the city duma building. . . . Arriving at the Moscow Soviet," they received news of the Petersburg revolution.[33] Beyond this, the memoir contained no description of activities shared with Lena, suggesting that this was a purely personal friendship, not one which formed a basis for ongoing joint political work.

Another woman worker's memoir shows the same pattern. Its author, Zamogil'naia, said she had "formed a strong friendship" with other "young comrades" whom she met at a Bolshevik party gathering place early in 1917. Yet she worked in a more or less isolated fashion throughout the October uprising, doing various different tasks which did not involve her friendship group as a basis for collective political activity. At one point during the fighting, she ran into some of these friends at headquarters, but they had no time for her. "They were all busy, hurrying somewhere, and they had other things to worry about besides me. After a while [a Bolshevik organizer] arrived. Greeting me, he said, 'Go to [headquarters located in] the Frantsiia café, you'll find Kalinin, Karmanov, or Afanas'ev there, and they'll find something for you to do.' " Alone, Zamogil'naia made her way to the café, where she was ordered to go to one of the battle stations as a first aid worker. Still alone, she set out through the dark embattled streets. When she finally reached her destination, she identified herself and then, through the darkness, "I heard a familiar, friendly voice: 'Ah, Polinka [affectionate nickname for Zamogil'naia], come here. We're over here!' It was Lelia Kravchuk. The night was dark, it was pitch black. The friendly voice of Lelia and Valia Kravchuk heartened me right away."[34] Zamogil'naia continued to perform various jobs throughout the rest of the fighting, but her memoir made no further mention of these friends.

Zamogil'naia, and perhaps many other women as well, formed personal relationships in the course of their political activity, friendships which had the capacity to "hearten me right away" after a long, frightening trek through the pitch black, threatening city. The intimacy of such friendships differed strikingly from men's social behavior during street fighting.

Male Workers' Role in Street Fighting

In contrast to women workers, male workers joined Moscow revolutionary fighting in groups based in the factories where they worked. The coherence of these groups was based not on their potential for personal intimacy, but on their common workplace. Men in each such factory formed themselves in a proto-military unit, which was later armed.

Throughout the summer [of 1917], individual factories had organized armed or semi-armed units of young men, usually for the defense of their own factories.

After the Kornilov mutiny, these units were augmented by fighting squads, formally Red Guards, organized under the aegis of factory committees, *raion* soviets, or Bolshevik party committees.[35]

William Rosenberg has observed that, even before 1917, male workers throughout Russia manifested "a strong element of occupational sectarianism, a tendency . . . to see themselves primarily as members of a given shop, factory, or trade, rather than a broader collectivity. . . . Russian labor leaders called this phenomenon *tsekhovshchina*, a term difficult to translate (itself suggesting the particularities of Russian labor in this regard), but which might best be rendered as 'shop orientation' or even 'shopism.' "[36] This *tsekhovshchina* was the formative element of male workers' activity in Moscow October fighting as well.

In their memoirs, working men who took part in the Moscow October days virtually always identified themselves and other men as members of particular factories or other solidarity groups. Take, for example, a male worker of the Mars clothing factory, which produced military uniforms and employed a majority of women in its work force. Even though he had stopped work there in mid-September to become a full-time Bolshevik agitator, he still took pride in noting the presence of workers from his old factory among those who arrived first at headquarters on the eve of the uprising to prepare for the fighting the next day.[37]

As word of the impending fighting began to spread, many Red Guard units hurried to their local branch of the Soviet's Military Revolutionary Committee to ask for arms, as did other groups of working men not yet formally organized into guard units. By the evening of October 26, said a male worker memoirist active in the Zamoskvorech'e district south of the city's center, "workers' detachments began to arrive at [the district headquarters] from the Mikel'son [mechanical plant], the Telephone [station], the Bromlei [mechanical plant], Postavshchik, the transport workshops, the Tsindel' [textile factory], and many others."[38] Another recalled that on the night of October 26, "Workers came to us from various plants and asked for arms, but we had none."[39] To the north of the city's center, in Butyrskii district, said another man, "Workers came by the score from all the plants, declaring that they had [selected their] platoon commanders and asking only that we give them arms and orders. These were workers from the Duks [bicycle factory], the Ustrits [machine building factory], the Gabai [tobacco factory; many women worked here], saddlers' workshops, Tsimerman's, the crystal plant, and various small workshops."[40]

Several memoirists observed intense competition among the workers of various factories as they rushed to see which factory's workers would be the first to obtain guns, the ultimate macho status symbol among male workers. "Each plant competed with the others as to who could arrive more quickly at the Soviet to get arms."[41] Another male observer recalled, "The first to arrive was the detachment from Zolotorozhskii yard. After them ran, racing each other, the Guzhonov workers, the workers of Podobedov, Dangauer, the Mars [clothing] factory, the Karavan [tea factory], and others."[42]

Just as Rosenberg observed for trade unionism, throughout the Moscow fighting, the working men of various factories did not melt into one large collective, beginning to consider themselves above all members of a single army. Rather, they continued to take pride in their identity as members of particular factories or at most as members of city districts which achieved certain objectives during battle. For example, a male worker of Moscow's Kauchuk rubber factory (which, like many large rubber plants, employed many women as well as men) said that, although they had arms for less than half their number,

> Almost all of the 450 Red Guards [of Kauchuk] took part in combat. . . . The Kauchuk detachments participated in the taking of the commissariat depot on Krymskaia square, in the taking of the headquarters of the Moscow military district, of the fifth school of ensigns, and of the Aleksandrovskii military college [the last being the most important, final battle of the Moscow revolution].[43]

This statement demonstrates the pride men typically took in the accomplishments of their own factory group even as they fought alongside Red Guard units from other factories. Another example was that of a male worker of the Postavshchik plant.

> Some of the Red Guards of our plant participated in the liquidation of separate attacks by White Guards on [many different] streets of Zamoskvorech'e. The Red Guard forces of the Mikhel'son [plant], Postavshchik, and others, and also the revolutionary soldiers of the 55th infantry regiment, liquidated all the main hotbeds of White Guards in Zamoskvorech'e in the course of two days.
>
> The majority of Red Guards of our plant were thrown in the main line of advance . . . where hard fighting broke out. Here the junkers stubbornly defended the approaches to the bridge. . . . However, the united forces of the Red Guards of Mikhel'son's, Postavshchik, the Varshavskii armatur and the

soldiers of the 55th regiment persistently broke the enemy . . . and then . . . took the Lycee and Krymskaia square.[44]

This memoir continued in the same vein, as did many others by male workers.[45]

As men from various factories fought side by side, the competitiveness they had demonstrated in arming before battle was somewhat tempered by cooperation. They began at times to identify with a unit larger than the factory: their region of the city.[46] As one worker said of his area, the Rogozhsko-Simonovskii *raion*, four years after the battle,

> We can still see depressions in the street on Alekseevskaia street now, after four years. . . . These are the remains of the former trenches, which were covered with wire entanglements. This is how our Rogozhskii *raion* prepared for war. The military significance of this *raion* was very great. Our *raion* was a pathway through which the White Guards and junkers could obtain military supplies. [The *raion* was assigned the task of preventing such resupply by the enemy.] This task was accomplished by the Rogozhsko-Simonovskii *raion*. And that wasn't the only thing we did. . . . The first large action in which Rogozhskii *raion* participated together with Lefortovskii and Basmannyi [*raions*], and with the 85th regiment, was the taking of the Alekseevskoe military college. Then the Rogozhskii *raion* forces took the Krutitskie barracks.

The worker's identity with the accomplishments of his region was maintained even when the Rogozhskii *raion* fighters were sent to another region of the city to fight there.

> After this, when the rear was secured, when nothing threatened internally here, the whole Rogozhskii *raion* [unit] was transferred to the center [of Moscow] and . . . our detachments freed the part of Moscow between the Moscow river, Iazaia, and Soliankaia, Varshavskaia square; [and] Varvarka.[47]

During the civil war, male workers from the Rogozhsko-Simonovskii *raion* were sent to distant parts of Russia and they remained together as a unit and retained their pride in their region over time and great geographic distance. Six male workers of this *raion*, in a joint memoir, recalled that "Rogozhskii *raion* sent more than a few fighters to various fronts which developed at all ends of Soviet Russia." Then, in words which could have been inspired by some of their daily-life army songs, these workers said, "Not a few of our dear friends perished, bold fighters. Only our memory of them has not perished. It lives among us—workers of the Rogozhsko-Simonovskii *raion*."[48]

The same type of factory or regional solidarity is evident among men of Red Guard detachments which formed in workers' towns and settlements at a distance from Moscow. For example, a workers' detachment began with five members in the Iakhromskaia factory in Moscow *guberniia*; by October it had thirty members. Another group formed in the Ikshinskaia factory.[49] These male groups often seized the institutions of power in their localities, usually encountering little resistance.

Some of these outlying units traveled to Moscow to support the Red Guards during fighting there. For example, the working men at the Likino textile factory near Orekhovo-Zuevo, having taken over the factory from its owners, formed a Red Guard detachment, which received a request from Moscow for reinforcements.

> On the next day, a detachment of three or four platoons (one hundred fighters) arrived in good time at the command of the Moscow headquarters of the Red Guard. . . .
> In fighting, the Orekhovo Red Guards did not lose their self-respect. They fought well—in combat from the Borodinskii bridge to the Kremlin; then they protected the Moscow Soviet: they fulfilled the operative-military tasks of headquarters, participating in the liquidation of terrorist groups and counterrevolutionary outbreaks.

The Orekhovo detachment was sent to the southern front during the civil war. Then, returning to Moscow, the Orekhovo-Zuevo working men formed their own company within the new Red Army.[50]

Podolsk also received a request from Moscow for reinforcements. The next morning, meetings were held in factories throughout the area, and seven hundred workers volunteered to go to Moscow by train. Recalled a male memoirist, "The Podolsk worker-volunteers participated . . . in military operations . . . at Triumfal'naia square, near the Nikitskie gates, near the Metropol' hotel, and in other parts of the city, until full destruction of the White Guards was achieved."[51]

A crucial element of the success of the workers' Red Guard units was their alliance with soldiers of the tsarist army who had turned against the old regime. In contrast to food-rioting women, who did not take advantage of their influence over hungry soldiers to build an ongoing alliance with them, groups of male Red Guards readily formed ties with groups of soldiers.

The ease with which working men utilized contacts with soldiers is seen in numerous memoirs, as soldiers aided in the clandestine arming and military training of factory workers. As one memoirist said, "The Red Guard, securing the sympathies of soldiers of the old army, and then moving to organizational ties with them, began to act more decisively against the Provisional Government."[52] For example, Kauchuk rubber factory workmen who could not obtain arms were given combat engineering implements by the 193rd regiment, and they began to build the barricades for their area.[53] Another memoirist, I. Ia. Ledov, a former worker at the Mars clothing factory, recalled that the 85th reservist regiment supplied eighty-five rifles for male workers of various factories in his area. And he described a case where he had turned to a friendly soldier for aid. Ledov had been put in charge of trench digging along Alekseevskaia Street, and the soldier responded to Ledov's appeal for help, demonstrating "how best to dig trenches." Later, at Ledov's request, the soldier took "the people and shovels to begin digging trenches at the opposite end of Alekseevskaia Street."[54] Such incidents were part of an ongoing alliance, in which soldiers routinely responded to male workers' appeals for expert instruction and help in acquiring arms and other tools for combat. A Bolshevik participant in the October events wrote that the soldiers "willingly went to the workers, gave advice, making numerous corrections when Red Guard instruction was not carried out completely correctly."[55]

A party activist described the free, constant contact between workers and soldiers in the various regional party headquarters, which "were like armed camps: they were full of Red Guards and soldiers; there were especially many worker youths."[56] Another memoirist recalled Romanov's tavern, which was turned into the Gorodskii *raion* war revolutionary committee headquarters. It "was turned into a war camp, not recognizable as the jolly tavern belonging to Romanov: . . . in the corridors, on the stairs, in all the rooms were the gray greatcoats of soldiers and the plain black figures of workers."[57] Such contacts and mutual aid between male workers and soldiers seem to have occurred in the provinces beyond Moscow as well. One memoirist recalled working men's contacts with soldiers and their explorations of how they could help each other.[58]

Social Relationships within Groups of Men

While men usually described their activities during street fighting in rather impersonal terms, we have a small amount of evidence about the quality of men's relationships with each other. Koenker describes the behavior of groups of Red Guardists as the October battles became imminent.

> . . . most Red Guardists mustered their units in their factory courtyards and waited for something to happen. . . . A bizarre sense of holiday prevailed. Some workers gathered at their plants in order to hear the latest political news; others arrived to drink with their fellows. A Red Guard courier recalled arriving wounded at a plant whose workers were drinking and playing cards. They laughed at first at her appeal for help, but when they saw she was bleeding, they volunteered to form a squad and fight the opposition.[59]

Koenker also states that the "overwhelming impression" given by her sources is that the "Red Guards were very young, undisciplined, and radical but not doctrinaire; for them the October revolution was the great adventure in their lives, as going to war in 1914 had been for a generation in western Europe."[60] Was the mixture of politics with card-playing and drinking a chance occurrence among a few young, unruly Red Guardists? Or was the group drinking and game-playing more basic to the group cohesion of male workers? This question will be taken up more fully in Part Two.

Another intriguing piece of evidence is a newspaper description of one aspect of the developing political awareness of youths by the spring of 1917.

> On the boulevards and squares may often be seen a group of teenagers, mainly boys, who . . . having bought a newspaper, argue about the fate of Russia, about politics and war.
> Arguments break out which sometimes have a hot-tempered and even cruel character. Two cases have been registered in which political arguments ended in bloodshed.
> On one of the boulevards . . . some teenagers began to argue about politics so fervently that they broke into hand-to-hand combat. . . .
> [In] the other case . . . four youthful politicos, not having managed to persuade one another, grappled with knives. Two were seriously wounded and sent to the hospital.[61]

Again we may wonder whether such combative behavior was typical only of the unruly fringe, or whether it was more basic to the development of political behavior by youthful working-class males. Might the competitiveness and

70

combativeness of male Red Guardists have been prefigured by combativeness among themselves in defense of their political beliefs? This question will be taken up in Part Two.

Who Determined the Sexual Division of Labor in October Street Fighting?

The question of whether the participants themselves or the male leadership of the rebellion decided the work to which women (and men) were assigned involves the issue of whether material reality or cultural prescriptions about women's behavior constrained their actions during the revolution. My view is that both types of constraints were operating, via a complex process. Some women did, more or less insistently, express a desire to be given arms and to be assigned to actual combat positions. The male leadership generally seems to have reacted negatively. I suspect that, at this point in the interaction, the reminder from men that in Russian working-class culture womanly women did not formally take up arms was sufficient to set into motion most women's internalized sense of what was considered appropriate and rewarding. Then almost all women retreated to accepting assignments to first aid and other support work. My sense is that the majority of women did not object to the gendered form of work assignments to begin with.

Unfortunately, the memoirs I have used are not detailed enough to provide clear evidence of exactly how the desire of those women who did wish to enter combat was defused.[62] In one case, working women assigned to food provisioning and first aid points "watched with envy those [men] who were being sent to the front—they [the women] declared their wish to participate in battle." The memoir mentioned two individual women. One became involved with forcefully taking food supplies into the hands of the revolutionaries and patrolling suspicious homes (probably the homes of merchants suspected of hoarding food). The other, preserving throughout the fighting "her characteristic calmness—work[ed] equally with men in the most serious work."[63] Aside from the activity of these two women, this memoirist gave no indication that groups of women demanded to be allowed to fight.

Another memoir seems to suggest that in Khamovniki, "the majority of working women [who] demanded arms and to be permitted to use them in military actions" were in fact put to work in reconnaissance and communications under extremely dangerous military conditions.[64] These tasks seem to have satisfied their willingness to risk their lives to protect Soviet

71

power, hence defusing their insistence on an actual combat role. In the Kauchuk rubber plant, 450 workers appeared to volunteer for Red Guard service on October 26. Of these, thirty were women. "Most of the women were sent to be at the command of the *raion* headquarters, where they carried out first aid service. . . . The rest of the women were included in the *desiatki*," military units of ten people each. This author, however, noted that they had forty-two *desiatki* in all, or 420 people, which is the exact number of men who had volunteered.[65] Presumably, then, only a very small number of women were included in the fighting units, certainly not enough to reflect a solidarity group among women workers of the scope of men's.

The most detailed account of action taken by women who wanted to fight described the situation in Orekhovo-Zuevo, where Red Guards were organized to travel to Moscow to aid in the revolution. This group of women also appears to have been the most insistent of all those described in memoirs.

The women persistently demanded that they be joined to the detachment. Their insistence grew to extreme measures when Nazarov [a male organizer] tried, not completely tactfully, to point out the impracticality of the female organism in war. Baryshnikov calmed the women: he pointed out that experienced fighters were necessary for victory over the junkers, and that those women who would go through military training, however hurriedly, could go with another detachment (so it happened: In the first Orekhovo-Zuevo Red Guard detachment there were women—Podviaznova and others).[66]

But another account, written by seven women who lived in Orekhovo-Zuevo, said that Podviaznova had been a member of this detachment, but not as a fighter: "from the women, Tania Podviaznova was in this detachment in the capacity of a first aid worker."[67]

Clearly, the male revolutionary leadership actively tried to exclude women from combat positions. The question is whether most women also acted partly in accordance with an internalized image of women's proper role, thus undermining their own capacity to push their claim to a new role over men's objections to it.

In addition to cultural prescriptions about "feminine" behavior, another important factor was that men came to street fighting already preorganized in cohesive groups which formed a ready basis for Red Guard units. These units in turn could easily develop relationships with revolutionary-minded soldiers. Women, in contrast, came to street fighting alone or at most with a close friend or two. Had women been part of cohesive groups—which had in turn formed alliances with soldiers—they might have been strong enough to insist they be given a central role in the fighting, rather than a peripheral one. Because women were active alone or with a few friends, they did not have the long-term group cohesion which would have been necessary to revolutionize men's—and their own—conceptions of which activities were appropriate for women. Nor had they the collective strength needed to question whether women had the right to claim a place at the center of the action rather than supporting it ad hoc in whatever way they could.

It might be supposed that, because working-class males did military service themselves, they could form ties with soldiers more easily than could women. Male workers could bond naturally with soldiers because they had recently been soldiers, or would be in the future. However, women also had a special tie to soldiers. We have seen that, both in breadlines when soldiers tried to go to the head of the line and in agitating soldiers to come over to the side of the revolution, women at times wielded great influence over men in uniform. Women often wielded this influence by invoking family metaphors: You are our sons, our brothers, don't hurt us, come over to our side. Had large groups of women chosen to unite and exert their power as mothers and sisters, I believe they could have wielded substantial power over men. But in working-class culture, other female roles, as wives and daughters—roles in which women were raised not to act collectively vis-à-vis their men—came to the fore, reducing women's will to exert the power they did have. We will examine the underlying reasons for this in Part Two.

The relationships among women active in street battles, as we have seen, were highly personal and intimate. The strong yet less personal nature of male friendships permitted men to form sizable groups whose bonding was based on such impersonal factors as common employment in a particular workshop or factory. Men worked in large groups regardless of whether individual members were emotionally compatible on an intimate level. While women's choosing friends based on compatibility probably made their friendships more personally satisfying than men's, it may also have tended to limit the size of the groups women worked comfortably with, as well as the type of activity the group could take on. While we might hope that emotional openness and supportiveness will become more dominant features of public-sphere behavior in the future, in the meantime, small friendship circles are not necessarily adaptive to the tasks of creating major social change, which requires unified activity by large groups of people.

FIVE

Attraction
to Political Work

This chapter examines the initiation into political work of a small number of working women who became political activists involved with the Bolshevik party over a number of years. Even among this relatively educated, elite group of women, a gendered pattern of behavior is seen, similar to that of their less educated sisters active only a short time. (Memoirs of Bolshevik women are much more readily available than those active with other political parties. It will be interesting to see whether further research reveals similar patterns among women of other parties.)

Among the memoirists who described their initial attraction to political work, one of the most common ways women came to politics was through male members of their families. For young, unmarried women, this male family member was often their fathers. For example, Zamogil'naia described her initiation into the Bolshevik effort. She had heard stories of the Bolsheviks' leadership of the proletariat from her childhood.

My father, Georgii Petrovich . . . worked in Ganzen's wood-finishing plant and was connected with the underground organization of social democrats (Bolsheviks) of Zamoskvorech'e. *He participated actively in the revolutionary movement*, organized strikes in the plant, participated in demonstrations and disarmed the police together with the workers of Zamoskvorech'e in the February days. He was killed in 1918 in the ranks of the Red Army.

The day January 9, 1917, is clearly impressed upon my memory. My father went out of the house early and did not return until evening. His overcoat was dirty, his sleeves torn, his face was pale, he was strangely agitated. My mother, throwing up her hands, asked, "What's happened to you? Where have you been loafing around? You look awful! Is it another strike?" Father turned away angrily and began to undress. *After dinner I asked: "Why are you so upset? Was the strike broken?" Then father told me that the workers of Zamoskvorech'e had gone to the demonstration* that day in memory of the massacre of the workers by the tsar on January 9, 1905, in St. Petersburg. But the police blocked the path of the demonstrators and opened fire. Now arrests would begin again. "But they'll have to pay for it!" said father.

After the February revolution, *I participated in a demonstration for the first time, together with my father.* This demonstration was organized by the Zamoskvorech'e raikom of the Bolshevik party. We were demanding the eight-hour day. Many people gathered, with red bows on their chests. We sang the "Marseillaise" and other revolutionary songs. . . . *My father introduced me to his comrades,* and I soon felt like an adult, although I was only sixteen.

After the demonstration, father began to take me in the evenings to the student dining room [where Bolshevik organizers gathered informally every day]. There I recognized many Bolsheviks. . . . Under their influence, I joined the [Bolshevik party] on May 5, 1917.[1]

Despite her father's introducing her into advanced political circles, and despite the fact that she formed friends among them, those friends did not become a peer solidarity group with whom she carried out joint political activity. Zamogil'naia worked in an isolated way on various different tasks during the October street fighting.

Valentina Petrova, who was a twenty-five-year-old widow in Likino in 1917, described her initiation into political awareness as being much more involved with her father than with the fellow working women who eventually elected her as their delegate to their workshop committee. Her first contact with radical politics was in 1905, when she was fourteen years old. "My father took no part in the revolution, but the active participants came to visit him constantly, and I became friendly with them." Petrova described the trauma that occurred in her family several years later when her father criticized the tsar. Although her father was not yet political—the remarks had been made when he was drunk—he was fired from his job, and he wandered for three years with no means of support while awaiting his day in court. He was pardoned in 1913.[2] By 1916, Petrova's father, living in Moscow, had become involved in revolutionary activity. He came to visit his daughter in Likino, where she was working in the textile factory to support her infant son. Her father told her,

"Here you're a downtrodden person, you'll come to nought here. Let's go to Moscow, among us in Moscow the people are different, the community is completely different. Things will be better for you there: we'll all live together." But I had already grown accustomed [to Likino], while there [in Moscow], life was unknown to me, frightening. *Then my father said there would be a revolution soon;* I little understood his words, so I imagined something, but in Moscow he had developed a completely different frame of mind. *When he met with his friends, he talked to them about revolution.* The next day I was going into the weft workshop, and there they told me, *"Your father's talking about revolution all the time."* I got scared and said, "He's shooting the breeze, he never talked about that with me"—I was so afraid that they would fire me.

We still did not know anything about the February revolution, when *my father wrote me a letter, "Long live the revolution," and described the whole thing. The letter was pleasant, merry, festive, and I read it with delight.* Two days later we had an organizational meeting for elections to the shop committee. They cried out for me to be the delegate. They elected me because I was literate. Suddenly I got a telegram: *my father had died. Everything fell apart for me: I missed my father terribly.* He had gone for a walk, had a good time, gotten drunk, and had gotten membranous pneumonia. He died two days later in the hospital. It was necessary for me to go [to Moscow]. I buried my father. . . .

Then I began to work actively.

Petrova went on to describe her successful struggle to develop the skills to be an effective political activist and her joining the Bolshevik party. She talked about her interactions with her male Bolshevik superiors, about trying to convince her brother of the Bolshevik position, and about her selection as a trade union organizer, secretary of the factory committee. She was later sent as a member of a food-provisioning detachment during the civil war and she worked with the *Zhenotdel* (the Women's Department). In 1929 she became assistant to the director of the huge Trekhgornaia textile factory in Moscow. She ended her memoir with a statement: "Woman in the Soviet Union is equal to man; . . . woman actually runs our government and builds socialism together and equally with the men."[3]

Petrova is a fascinating case partly because of her personal success within the Soviet system. What is striking about her initiation into political activism is her description of it within the context of her relationship with her father, *not* within the context of a solidarity group of the women workers who elected her to her first political position. No interaction with those women was recounted; none of them was described.

The single brief exception to this was Petrova's description of a demonstration which the working women joined, but even this was organized by a male Bolshevik agitator and did not manifest any real group solidarity among the women. When the Bolshevik proposed the demonstration, "the working women sobbed violently and decided to walk to Orekhovo-Zuevo in a demonstration" to plead for help from the workers there.

These women's stance was not to form a unified group which actively supported its elected leaders. Instead, the women as a group remained fragmented and largely passive, electing Petrova to every post that arose during 1917 because she was literate.[4] Petrova was far less a genuine member and representative of her constituency than she was an agent of the Bolshevik organizers, most of them men, whose respect she strove so hard to win. As she moved up in the Soviet system over the course of her career, she remained an exceptional, successful woman, not a member and leader of an active grassroots women's movement. The result was that she easily became convinced of the claim that women ran the government equally with men. Without unified groups of women telling her otherwise, isolated from her constituency, she lost sight of the realities of the lives of the women of that constituency.

In the case of married women, the family member drawing a woman into political activism was sometimes her husband.[5] Such was the situation for P. Sleptsovaia, a textile worker who eventually became a women's delegate attached to child care centers in 1920 and a member of the Moscow Soviet. She recalled her first contact with politics during the 1905 revolution.

> Both I and my husband often went to mass meetings and distributed leaflets. My husband was arrested by the Semenovskii regiment, suppressors of the Presnia workers [one of the most important battles of the 1905 Moscow armed uprising]. He barely managed to break free, so as not to be killed. I myself also gave help [during the uprising], however I could, to the people on the barricades, and I went to defend the factory from the black hundreds.
>
> I experienced much grief during the world war. My husband was taken into the army. I was left alone with little children. It's true that my husband returned from the war alive, but this time left a deep impression on me.

Sleptsovaia did not describe any further political activity until after her husband's return from the front, which suggests that without him to share in her political participation, she may not have been able to maintain her interest in it (her sole responsibility for their small children must also have been a factor). After the revolution, she worked in the plant production committee of her factory, as well as in the posts mentioned above. Her position in the Moscow Soviet was in the health department, where she worked for the protection of mothers and children. She described these very briefly, noting also that "My husband became a member of the [Bolshevik] party in 1918; I also joined, but only in 1930." She ended her memoir with the statement that her children were happy: "they do not have the griefs and anxieties which I had before the revolution. Lucky children—Soviet children! And as a mother

I am lucky that I am building a new society."[6] Sleptsovaia thus defined the building of the new society as relevant to her as a mother, but not in any other way.

Male memoirists mentioned their wives and children far less frequently in describing their initial attraction to political activity than did women. They never mentioned mothers or sisters. Men never attributed their introduction to politics to their mothers or wives, as women did to their fathers and husbands, nor did men cite even *male* family members as having been instrumental in this process. Two excerpts of male workers' memoirs illustrate the sense of peer solidarity in political effort which I believe was common among men workers. The first is from an Ivanovo-Voznesensk worker.

> I began work at Griaznov's factory in May 1913. . . . Within the walls of the factory I found for the first time *a group of advanced workers*, comrades Morozov, Vorob'ev, and others, who worked in the underground Ivanovo-Voznesensk Bolshevik organization. Several months of *our joint work* followed. In the autumn of that same year arrests tore the experienced party workers *from our ranks*. . . . By spring of 1914, *we had managed to restore connections* with the city's active party members [four names listed, all men]. I remember how, *all together, we organized* a May 1 celebration in 1914. . . . More than *thirty people gathered*, conducted a small meeting, and the comrades vowed to give all their energies to the noble cause of struggle for the liberation of the working class.[7]

Another memoirist described the agitational techniques of the political organizer active in his factory between the revolutions.

> *We [politically minded] workers usually gathered* in taverns on holidays. We got a table somewhere on the side, in a corner, and tried not to attract the tavern customers' attention to ourselves. We ordered tea with rolls. . . . At the beginning of the conversation, Viktor Alekseevich [a Bolshevik agitator] asked us about the conditions of work among the factory owners, about the workers' mood, and then told us about politics, about the causes of the 1905 revolution's defeat, about the significance of the Communist Manifesto, about the party minimal program and the maximal program.
>
> . . . In the summertime, *we gathered* most often in Izmailovskii forest: *fifty or sixty advanced workers* usually came here from the factories and plants of the *raion. We were taught* how to assemble and use revolvers, and to fill sacks quickly with dirt and build barricades from them. *We even learned* to sing revolutionary songs. In such meetings, *we got to know each other better and to establish friendly relationships*.[8]

Each of these memoirs describes groups of male workers being initiated into political activity by one or more political agitators. One memoir gives the figure of fifty to sixty men gathered in the forest to learn Bolshevik fighting techniques. Thus, in contrast to women's being drawn into activity individually, often by family members, men were initiated in groups, by agitators not related to them.

One last way women were drawn into political activity was described in E. S. Goriacheva's memoir. Goriacheva was the daughter of skilled velvet makers, and at the age of twelve she began to work in the same factory as they did. She had hoped instead to go to school, but those hopes were dashed by her family's need for additional income.

> Working in Savva Morozov's weaving factory No. 1 as a weaver, I became acquainted in 1903 with the Social-Democrat (Bolshevik) Stepan Andreevich Terent'ev, who was also a weaver. Comrade Terent'ev was already an advanced worker at this time, . . . a professional revolutionary, a member of the Communist party since 1903. . . .
> Having become acquainted with me and with my brother Grigori (who was a year older than me), he [Terent'ev] began to visit us often in the barrack. . . .
> *He told me* about the existence of the tsarist order, about the situation of the working class, about the cruel exploitation of workers in factories and plants, about the need for workers to struggle against the tsarist autocracy. *He revealed to me* all the dark sides of the people's lives in Russia at that time. *He showed me* how to read literature—you see, I read a lot, but with no system. . . . In general, *comrade Terent'ev had a great influence on my* intellectual development. *He attracted me* into the ranks of the party. . . .
> [Terent'ev organized and led a workers' study circle, of which she was a member.]
> Then *Terent'ev began to take me* to underground mass meetings. They happened in the spring, summer, and fall in Zuevo, near Isakievskii lake.[9]

Terent'ev became Goriacheva's devoted mentor in intellectual and political development. The contrasts between the italicized phrases of this excerpt and those of the previous man's excerpt are striking. The man was one of a group of men coming into contact with an agitator, while Goriacheva did not have a peer group. The closest she came was a small women's political education group organized by Terent'ev. However, this lasted only a brief time, disintegrating once its male leader was arrested. This contrasts again with the previous male memoir, in which the male group stayed together and reestablished ties with the Bolshevik party even after its original party contact people had been arrested.

Goriacheva was passionately interested in self-education. As a young girl, she had wished to attend school, but had to work in the factory instead; her Bolshevik mentor provided an opportunity for education missed in her earlier years. While the attraction of opportunities for education through activity in the Social Democratic Party has been noted as one of the factors which drew some aspiring male workers into radical circles,[10] what is important in Goriacheva's case is the closeness and exclusivity of the relationship between her and her mentor. Her description of her relationship with him suggests that it was very personal. It contrasts with the male memoirist's recollections of his contact with a Bolshevik agitator. The man gave a strong sense that he was one of a group of men present in the tavern listening to the agitator and in the forest learning to use guns. Goriacheva's stance vis-à-vis her organizer was highly individualized, Terent'ev tailoring his nurturance of Goriacheva's intellect to fit her needs (for example, her need to learn to read systematically) and his own.

I suspect that among particularly talented, aspiring working women, Goriacheva's pattern may have been relatively common. The outcome of her case was also suggestive. She was active during the 1905 revolution, and in 1907 she was elected as a delegate to the fifth party congress in London. Arrested in 1909, she spent almost three years in prison. She devoted this time to reading extensively in her cell. She also formed intimate friendships with some of the other women prisoners, friendships which outlasted their prison terms. The major break in Goriacheva's life resulted from her marriage, when she was twenty-five, to a skilled textile worker at Savva Morozov's factory, a revolutionary activist himself. Her husband had severe rheumatism in one leg, for which he had to move to a faraway city to be treated with mudbaths. He required painstaking care, and Goriacheva soon went to live with her husband. This was apparently the end of her political activity, and she ended her memoir at this point.

I went to Piatigorsk [to be with her husband] in June 1915.

I returned to Orekhovo-Zuevo from Piatigorsk only in 1922, when my friends O. I. Maksimova, S. A. Terent'ev, and others helped me to get out of there, sending me money for the trip.[11]

The terseness of this statement contrasts sharply with the optimistic, excited, and inspired tone of the bulk of the memoir, suggesting that marriage became for Goriacheva a literally unspeakable experience, the end of her reaching out for new contacts with political activists and greater learning.

This evidence is far from conclusive, but it is suggestive. Whereas Sleptsovaia's husband's enthusiasm for political activity drew her into political work, Goriacheva's husband's medical needs removed her from it. For each of these women, the influence and needs of her family were paramount in shaping her political career.

Chastushki (a type of working-class song, usually four lines long, the last lines being improvised by the singer) from the early 1920s suggest that even after the revolution, women continued to be drawn into political activity individually, often through men. Sokolov wrote in his commentary to these *chastushki* that, in them, a young woman typically described herself as entering the Komsomol (the youth organization of the Communist party) "only after her sweetheart—he shows her the new path, he influences her world view." Two examples are:

> They say that I'm a Komsomolka [female member of Komsomol.]
> I wasn't a Komsomolka.
> Then I began going out with a Komsomol boy:
> And I became a Komsomolka.

> My dear girlfriend,
> We're both cute Komsomolkas
> We didn't register ourselves [in the Komsomol]
> Our boyfriends registered us.

Women in these *chastushki* were encouraged to adopt the correct political viewpoint, but the main reason was in order to win the party man as her husband.

> My husband is a Communist,
> But I'm non-party
> Because of this, our love
> Isn't getting anywhere.

And

> To love a Communist man,

You have to change yourself—
You can't carry a cross,
You can't pray to God.

Sometimes the woman's efforts to achieve her sweetheart's standards for political purity were successful. Then the girl could exult,

My sweetheart is a Communist,
And I'm a Communistka,
He comes to talk with me
We're a [politically] advanced couple.[12]

In these songs, girls in working-class communities even after the revolution were still proudly declaring that they did not form social and political bonds themselves, but left this task to the men in their lives.

The result of this pattern of activism was that even those exceptional women workers who remained active over a long period of time were hampered in pursuing women's interests: they became largely cut off from their constituencies, closer to the interests of the male Soviet leadership than to their peers. And most women, having never broken out of their daily life bonding pattern to their nuclear families to establish strong peer bonding capable of sustaining political activity, soon returned to political inactivity.

SIX

Ongoing Organizations

Some Bolshevik memoirs appear to indicate that during revolutionary activity of 1917, substantial portions of the female working class were well on their way to becoming longstanding active members of ongoing political organizations. These memoirs describe masses of women attending meetings, substantial numbers of women being elected to factory committees,[1] and some local soviets.

However, when the evidence is examined carefully, the picture seems less clear. Working women were elected to factory committees in considerable numbers (often in factories employing an overwhelming majority of women, especially during the wartime absence of many men). However, the memoirs give little evidence of what groups of women actually did on these committees. Virtually all detailed accounts of women workers' participation in these and other organizations reveal one or more of the following patterns: 1) one or two individual women became highly active in working with the (overwhelmingly male) local Bolshevik organization; 2) working women came to factory committees, soviets, and other organizations to seek help for family problems, but did not become members of, or work for any period of time with, these committees; 3) women retreated from their positions on factory committees; 4) women in groups participated sporadically, at the request of the local party leadership, in demonstrations, agitation, and other tasks, but did not participate in ongoing organizations.

For example, one working woman began her memoir with the statement, "I remember the first workers' meetings in our factory after the February Revolution, when the soviet of workers' deputies, the factory committee, and then the shop delegates were elected. This was a large group of active people [*aktiv*], up to three hundred people, the majority of whom were women." Yet of the many descriptions of female activism given in the rest of this memoir, there is no material on the presumed ongoing daily activities of this very large group of women.[2] Rather, each of the events described fits into one of the patterns enumerated above. While such lack of evidence cannot be considered conclusive, it is highly suggestive, especially given the abundance of evidence for the patterns I have noted.[3]

Individual, Exceptional Women Workers

There is no question that small numbers of women became extremely active, first as agitators for the Bolshevik cause and later, after the consolidation of the new government, in various posts of the revolutionary regime. These women do not seem to have been supported by substantial numbers of other women who, if somewhat less active, at least formed cohesive groups committed to improving women's lives. Thus, this handful of highly active women must be considered exceptional, not representative of either the behavior or the interests of average working women.

For example, in the textile settlement of Likino, where a majority of the labor force in 1917 was female, four working women were elected to the soviet. Two of these women traveled as far as Moscow to arrange fuel and food supplies for the factory. But there was no sense of their working with substantial groups of active women—rather, they appear to have been exceptional individual women.[4]

Even the one possible exception to this rule, the Union of Soldiers' Wives in Ivanovo-Voznesensk, had only a handful of activists out of the city's pool of twenty thousand women workers. The union was formed "under the Bolshevik banner" shortly before April 21, 1917, and after the October Revolution it was used and later disbanded by the new government, two years after it had formed. Only the executive committee of the union was active on an ongoing basis. The executive committee comprised twenty-seven woman representatives elected from each of the city's factories, and it was attended (perhaps dominated) by four or more members of the local presidium, all of whom were Bolsheviks. Of the twenty-seven women, "many worked very actively during the entire course of the existence of the union"; thus presumably some dropped out. The five-member "presidium," which included one male Bolshevik party member, may well have been the most active group.

While the executive committee of the union organized two mass meetings (the first to establish the union, and the second to come out in support of the Bolshevik call for "All Power to the Soviets") and a demonstration during 1917, ongoing mobilization of the main body of members did not occur. Meetings in each factory were held only twice, the first time to elect delegates and the second time to agree to a dues system proposed by the executive committee. During 1917, the union used these dues, and whatever other meager resources it could gather, to distribute to the neediest among them.

Another activity of the executive committee was to encourage individual women to come to the committee with any questions they had and to obtain help with reading or writing, since most were illiterate. Above all, this involved writing letters for the women to their husbands at the front. "In the letters to the husbands, we tried to communicate not only what was going on in their families, but also what was happening in their home towns. Thus, the soldiers were informed about the situation with food supply, work, wages, the mood of the workers, and so on."[5] We might wonder whether the purpose of this organization, from its Bolshevik organizers' point of view, was more to gain a point of access for agitation among soldiers at the front than to mobilize the women to pursue their own grievances.

Thus, the Union of Soldiers' Wives seems to have been the work of a small number of exceptional women, possibly in a pupil-mentor relationship with the male Bolshevik party members who always attended their meetings. There is no indication of committed activity among large groups of women. In fact, the activities of the union—such as handouts to those in need, and writing letters for illiterate women—served not to mobilize the great mass of women workers but rather to eliminate the need for such mobilization.[6]

Even the exceptional women who became active on factory committees and in other revolutionary organizations continued some behavior patterns typical of the culturally prescribed women's role. One male memoirist recalled a woman weaver who had actively supported the revolutionary movement "long before the fall of the autocracy." After the February Revolution, she was elected to the Kovrov local soviet. "Tania always voted for the Bolshevik proposals, but she herself never spoke. She sat modestly in the back rows."[7] We may wonder how many other women elected to factory committees and soviets, like Tania, held themselves back from speaking out to help shape the decisions made.

S. Brodskaia, elected as one of three people (the other two were men) to run the Sokolnicheskii *raion* military effort during the October Revolution in Moscow, stressed her confusion and lack of confidence in her ability to handle difficult situations. Giving a speech years later, in which she described her revolutionary activity, she began, "I'm a bad orator, I do not know how to speak well—I will tell you only what I remember as an eye-witness." One evening in October 1917, "there was no one in the revolutionary committee [office]" when an urgent telegram arrived. That is, there was no one except herself, but apparently to Brodskaia, her capacity to deal with the telegram was nonexistent, so she considered herself unworthy of mention. As she went on with her account—in which she displayed a sound ability to handle the demands made on her—she continued to claim that she did not know what to do. The telegram said

> that it was necessary to send three hundred people to the Moscow soviet because the junkers were coming. I was lost: there was no one in the [office]—what to do? Nevertheless, I managed to call around to all the plants and by five o'clock around five hundred people had gathered.

Brodskaia had managed to find two hundred more volunteers than had been requested. A scanty supply of rifles was delivered to the office

> and everyone threw themselves on them. . . . But we wanted first to distribute them to the people who knew how to fight. I was alone again in the committee. And I did not know what I should do: everyone was demanding rifles. . . . I . . . sat on all those rifles and said: "I won't give anything to anyone, as long as the rifles are not divided among those who know how to shoot." One of the comrades, Savel'ev . . . from the Shtabe plant, said to me: "You must certainly give me a rifle." And I said, no, I will not give it to you.[8]

Despite—perhaps because of—Brodskaia's demonstrated ability to run the office, including standing up to male workers hungry for rifles, she felt compelled by cultural norms, even years later, to undermine her effectiveness by constantly saying she felt lost and did not know what to do. This contrasts with the memoirs of male workers, who constantly boasted of their many successes.

Coming to Revolutionary and Other Organizations for Aid

A number of sources indicate that women workers approached factory committees, soviets, and other organizations for aid in resolving important issues in their lives, particularly problems with their husbands' drinking and other irresponsible behavior. One memoirist described a typical example of a working woman appealing to her factory committee for help.

"Comrade president! Why won't you tell me how to sober up my husband, for goodness' sake. He doesn't give us any peace, either me or the children. Put him in the clink, even if just for a day."

"Take your husband and get the heck out of here! Big deal, he gets drunk. When he runs out of money, he'll wake up. We've been standing here for half an hour, we're making arrangements about work, and you bother us about your husband."[9]

Another male memoirist, writing about a small silk factory settlement, said that in 1917, even before the local soviet had taken power in October, "already the poor, especially wives and soldiers' widows stretched in long lines, coming to it for information, and with their needs and questions on which the soviet workers had to spend a great deal of time [providing] explanations and solutions." And another memoirist in Orekhovo-Zuevo recalled the same phenomenon: "The workers went to the soviet with their needs and complaints, even for opinions on family misunderstandings."[10]

Women also turned to certain voluntary associations for aid. A Moscow newspaper printed a letter to the president of the local temperance society from a group of women in Mar'inaia grove, a workers' suburb.

Respected doctor,

We, the women of Mar'inaia grove—wives, sisters, and daughters—ask you to report in some kind of meeting, or wherever possible, about drunkenness among us in the grove. Mar'inskii district, along Stremiannaia and Novotikhvinskaia streets, and in all Tserkovnye thoroughfares, has a great number of tea shops, and all of them sell wine and spirits. . . .

They drink . . . and in some of the tea rooms there are even girls, and card games are played. . . .

Wine and spirits are hauled to the tea rooms on wagons. Our foreman saw the landlady of the tea shop on Stremiannaia Street paying nine hundred rubles for spirits. She does not sell to people she does not know, but among us in the grove, everyone knows each other, and if our husbands do not drink in the tea room, then they send to her with their own containers [to bring liquor home in] and they drink at home.[11]

There was no further information about whether the doctor came to the women's aid. And there was no indication that the women joined the temperance society as a means of trying to improve their situation.

Although all these working women reached out for aid to various organizations and societies of which they were not members, the effect of such strategies was limited. To begin with, following cultural expectations, women adopted a stance of helplessness in making these appeals. Like the women food activists who did not act upon their ability to form alliances with soldiers and factory organizations, these women had been socialized not to assert their own collective power to form ongoing alliances with the bodies to whom they appealed. In many cases—such as the ones involving soviets and factory committees—the women did not even approach the organization in question as a group, but as individuals who had run out of ideas themselves for how to control their husbands' behavior. Even in the case of the letter to the doctor-president of the temperance society, which women had apparently joined together to write, they were appealing to the doctor to use some of the society's resources (e.g., access to publicity) for their benefit. But they were not acting in the manner of potential allies. They did not offer to devote some of their own resources—for example, the strength of their very large numbers, their determination and fighting spirit (as evidenced in food actions), their skills in sewing banners and making posters for demonstrations, and so on—to support the temperance society in return. They behaved as if they were entirely helpless, having no strengths of their own to bargain with.

Because of such culturally mandated self-defeating behavior, these women could be brushed off and ignored. The factory committee president considered the woman seeking his aid a nuisance who interfered with the real, important work of the committee. Another memoirist defined the position such appeals put the soviets in as having to spend "a great deal of time" on them. If the soviets had considered these women's problems important political issues—if women had been able to *make* them political—the soviets would not have felt put upon by "women's complaints."

As we will see in Part Two, these intrafamilial problems were paramount issues in women's lives, as important as receiving better wages and being treated better on the job. Men's alcoholism, for example, was a critical cause of misery and poverty for wives and children. But the political leadership never came to define women's "complaints" as political issues. This problem leads back to the issue of women being drawn into political activity as individuals rather than in unified groups. When people are drawn into ongoing organizations as individuals, they must adopt the goals and ideology of the organization. In contrast, when solidarity groups approach an organization with a clear sense of their own resources usable as bargaining chips, they may have leverage to change some of the goals and ideology of the organization in their own interests.

Newspapers provide some additional information about women workers hoping for aid from outside groups. These accounts, from several towns and cities in the CIR, reveal an intriguing pattern of upper-class women reaching out to working-class women. Soon after the February Revolution, there was a flurry of such activity. The issues taken up were child care facilities and literacy classes for women. Yet by the end of July (and earlier in some places), this activity seems largely to have petered out. There was no further participation reported on the part of working women, and only one account (in October) of continued work by upper-class women, in Kostroma.

The developments in Yaroslavl and Kostroma were especially similar. In each town, between late March and early May, an organization had begun which attempted to unite women of all classes. (The Kostroma organization was called the "democratic union of women"; the Yaroslavl one united a local branch of the All-Russia League of Equal Rights for Women and the local Union of Democratic Women.) The early meetings of both organizations had a high attendance of working women from their areas. The April 12 meeting of the Yaroslavl League of Equal Rights was attended by about "one hundred members, of whom more than half were factory women";[12] at the May 5 meeting of the Kostroma group, "many working women and employees of the local enterprises gathered."[13]

The initial issue which seemed to attract the working women to both groups was the hope of learning to read and to understand the course of the political and social events occurring around them. When the Yaroslavl women's group was forming, two women workers addressed them, saying that "they wanted with all their hearts and souls to learn, to partake of education, but the difficult conditions of their lives fettered their lives like strong bonds."[14] During April, the Yaroslavl group worked on plans for a women's democratic club containing a library and reading room, having noted "the fervent aspiration of women workers to education—a wish to understand what is occurring at the present time in the political life of the country." The league also sent delegates to the Soviet of Workers' Deputies.[15] By early May,

the Democratic Women's Union, together with members of the League of Equal Rights, had united several regional unions in the city and in the factories. . . .

In each district, schools of literacy were designated and a registration was conducted for those who wished to attend. The results of the registration were staggering: in [Iaroslavskaia Bol'shaia textile mill] alone, over five hundred adult women were registered [over six thousand women were employed there]. The thirst for education among all [the working women] is tremendous; they thank each action of the League and the Democratic Union touchingly, they earnestly request the [league and the union] not to leave them in the lurch, and to help them understand the great events rushing around them.

The union in turn appealed to

intelligentsia women with a fervent call to help in the hugely important cause of educating the masses of women. Our sisters, thirsting for knowledge, look on us with great hope. . . . Let us not betray their trust, and let us help them![16]

Despite these dramatic developments, this was the last that was heard of the project in the newspaper. The last few articles said nothing about working women or about the literacy classes.[17]

This might seem accidental, except for the fact that the same pattern occurred in the Kostroma newspaper. By mid-May, the women's union had hung announcements in all the city's factories, inviting workers of both sexes to register for free classes to be held "in various places, primarily around the factories." In addition, students of the Kostroma middle schools had been asked to provide free private lessons for workers in their homes. "Working women, suffering greatly from illiteracy, go with great eagerness to register themselves." Yet the next meeting of the union was described as poorly attended, despite the fact that it included the people's classes on its agenda. This was the last newspaper coverage of the union until October, when the union was beginning to set up a Montessori preschool for thirty to forty children of workers, a minute fraction of the total in the city. They received five thousand rubles from the city duma to aid the project.[18]

In Moscow, a similar situation occurred, this time concerning the issue of child care. A meeting about establishing children's playgrounds was set up by various non-working-class groups (the society for the protection of children, a cooperative society, representatives of the Khamovnicheskii *raion*, and the "7th health trusteeship"). The audience was "democratic in constitution," and one "woman in a kerchief" asked those running the meeting "to establish a place for our children." She was told, "I won't establish anything for you, but you yourself can arrange tens of such playgrounds if you want." The meeting worked out plans for two playgrounds and appealed to the city government for material aid. In the group's second meeting, there was "discord. . . . Complicated organizational questions did not find sufficiently experienced directors." However, the group was awarded 175,000 rubles shortly thereafter by the city government.[19] But over the course of the year, the newspaper said nothing further about the role of working women or about whether the organization survived, with or without its "democratic constituency," beyond its first few meetings.[20]

What explains, in each of these cases, the early reports of enthusiastic activity by large numbers of working women, followed by the absence of reports about their activity? If the eventual absence of newspaper accounts reflected a sharp decline in participation by working women (as seems likely, at least in part), this may parallel the pattern I have observed in women's activity: women were active, but sporadically or with initial enthusiasm followed by retreat. In fact, the newspaper accounts follow a pattern similar to that observed in memoirs for women workers on factory committees. There are substantial reports of women workers being elected to factory committees (initial enthusiasm), but virtually no descriptions of their activism on those committees, except for the cases of a very few individuals.

Another possibility is that these large groups of women workers shifted their arena of activity to an organization of different political views, perhaps following the general trend toward radicalization among the working class over the course of 1917. It might well have been difficult for women workers who were becoming increasingly antiwar to take literacy classes from women who advocated war until victory (middle-class women likewise may have withdrawn from working women whose growing radicalism threatened the middle class's relatively privileged position in Russian society). On the other hand, no newspapers of any political hue reported the defection of large groups of working women from the liberal all-class unions to the radical parties, even though such a defection would have been a noteworthy coup on the part of those parties, and hence some coverage of it might have been expected. Thus, it seems likely that, wherever these women workers moved politically, they did not move en masse but rather as a fragmented constituency, their political clout dissipated.

Another possible partial explanation for the drop-off in reportage of working women's activity involves some general newspaper policy, whether conscious or not, to clamp down on such reporting after women's groups had reached a certain point of success. It is also possible that upper-class women failed to fulfill the promises they had made to working women. Especially given the numbers of women workers who registered to learn to read, it is very possible that the upper-class women were simply overwhelmed and unable to provide the corresponding number of teachers needed.

The memoir of a Bolshevik who was a teenager and member of a mostly student youth union during 1917 provides some evidence here. A group of five Bolshevik women students attempted to set up a reading class in the dining room of a Moscow silk factory. Six working women attended, but, wrote the memoirist, "Our 'pedagogues' ' lack of sufficient knowledge and experience doomed our arrangement to failure in the pedagogical sense" (although the writer said it had agitational success).[21] If upper-class women's inability to provide certain resources for women workers was indeed a cause of a decline of such efforts, it seems that working women had again become too dependent on groups outside themselves, without offering enough of their own resources in return. We might then ask what circumstances in the daily lives of working women constrained their capacity to commit their energies and resources in an ongoing way to institutions which might have improved their lives.

Retreating from Factory Committees

Far from containing evidence about women's groups' successes after being elected to factory organizations, the small amount of detailed description I found portrayed women's group retreat from their elected posts. One Bolshevik organizer walked all over Bogorodsk *uezd* in the summer of 1917, helping to set up factory committee elections in each factory. In one factory,

> The elections were a novelty for the workers, and when the candidates were elected, and a majority of those elected turned out to be women, the old working men got upset:
> "How can this be, a majority of women will order us men around? This can't happen."
> Despite all our oratory about the equal rights of the sexes, and that we are going through a difficult war and hunger not because the tsar listens to his wife, but because the ruling class which existed until the revolution could not lead to anything else—nothing helped: we had to yield and reelect the factory committee with such a calculation as to elect a majority of men, although a majority of workers in the factory were women.[22]

One wonders how the men managed to insist on getting their own way in this case and why women did not insist as adamantly on their right to be a majority of the committee. The men cannot have had much more to hold over the women than the women had over the men, for the women were a majority of those working in the factory, their husbands did not provide their families' total income, they were already abused by their husbands long before factory committees were even thought of (as we will see in Part Two), and many if not most of their husbands were away in the army in any case. Again, we may wonder what other constraints were operating to prevent women from seizing an opportunity to improve their lives.

Groups Participate Sporadically

Some memoirists and historians have used working women's conspicuous presence in demonstrations, meetings, and other political settings to portray women as active in an ongoing way. There is no question that large numbers of women indeed marched in demonstrations and attended meetings.[23]

Women workers wanted the end of the war so that their husbands, sons, and fathers would return home and so they could obtain enough food for their children. As a result, they were often eager to heed Soviet, Bolshevik, or other political groups' calls for demonstrations of their political sentiments. For example, the Moscow Soviet of Workers' Deputies organized a citywide demonstration on Sunday, May 14, to protest the death sentence for the Austrian Social Democrat-Internationalist Adler. Workers and soldiers from all parts of the city gathered "with music and red banners" on the square in front of the Bol'shoi Theater. Many of the slogans were antiwar. According to a newspaper article, there were more women than men among the demonstrators.[24] The same issue also served as the occasion for a "protest demonstration" in Ivanovo-Voznesensk. The orators included speakers from the local soviet, the Social Democrats, a member of the second government duma, and a soldier recently returned from the front. An especially strong impression was made by the last,

> standing on the platform on crutches, with no legs and a bandaged, wounded head; the heart of each of those present shuddered looking at such a picture.
> The women especially cried, remembering their husbands, brothers, and fathers perishing even now at the front.
> "Down with the war" sounded from the platform.[25]

Another demonstration occurred in Norskoe in honor of May Day.

. . . at twelve noon, workers of the Norskoe factory began to gather on the square near the barracks. There were around four hundred people, workers with songs and three red banners. Both adults and children took part. The children went at the head and the adults, men and women behind. Everyone had red ribbons on their chests.

This group marched toward the Volga, meeting another group marching from Norskoe. The demonstration continued until six o'clock that evening, moving back through the streets of the town, with speeches near the fire depot.[26]

One of the largest and best-known demonstrations was that of five thousand starving Likino textile workers, who walked to Orekhovo to seek aid.

Five thousand working men and women, the women with little children in their arms, set out from the courtyard of the factory with banners, singing revolutionary songs. On the banners was written: "Down with the War!" "We are starving, our children are starving!" "Whoever is not for us is against us!" "We demand participation in public affairs!"

Stopping off at the grave of a revolutionary killed in 1905, the huge crowd walked to a central square in Orekhovo, where they were met by twenty thousand of the latter's workers. An Orekhovo working woman got up before them and spoke:

Comrades! The Likino working men and women have come to us for help—this is our younger brother who has fallen in our embrace. They are starving; look, they have little children in their arms. We extend our brotherly hand to them and we must give them our brotherly help. Let's give the starving Likino working men and women and their children one day's wage.

This proposal was accepted unanimously, and the Likino demonstrators were taken to the Orekhovo barracks, where they "fed us and gave to each of us what they could of their food," as one Likino supplicant described. "I personally carried home a four-hundred-gram piece of bread and five cucumbers. . . . [T]he Orekhovo workers shared their last crust with us."[27]

Like many other demonstrations, this one was organized by the Bolshevik party, not by the participants themselves. A working woman member of the Likino Bolshevik party wrote,

In September, the Orekhovo-Zuevo committee of the RSDRP(b) passed a resolution about supporting the Likino workers materially; Bugrov communicated this to us in our closed party meeting. In the party meeting of the Likino factory, a decision was made to call the workers to a demonstration and to set off for Orekhovo, to the workers, to ask for their help in the ranks of solidarity.[28]

Working women who participated in rallies and demonstrations sometimes displayed their usual militance and propensity for direct action, attacking speakers they did not agree with.[29] They also helped in some of the nitty-gritty work of preparing for demonstrations and other major events. People had to "dilute paste to glue posters in squares and streets, [write] cards announcing [the demonstration] for plants and factories, etc. Before demonstrations and rallies, working women and working men themselves made flags and painted them. . . . Very often it was necessary to spend the whole night, especially before some elections to a committee to the soviet, etc."[30] On the eve of a demonstration and mass "Red Burial" for the Red Guards killed during the October Revolution in Moscow, "all night long, women and girls were sewing miles and miles of red cloth, cutting and trimming and fashioning it into banners for the procession."[31] John Reed wrote that these women "worked now sternly, many of them with eyes red from weeping. . . . The losses of the Red Army had been heavy."[32]

Women attended at least some factory meetings.[33] Their presence was probably facilitated by the fact that many meetings were held during the regular workday, the workers leaving their machines idle while they met.[34] Newspapers provide some descriptive material about various types of meetings.[35] One article about a mass meeting of female laundry workers illustrates what I suspect was a common pattern for female workers. In the meeting, one "middle-aged working woman" got up to speak, presenting clearly formulated demands for improvements in their work and domestic lives. She called

> for a fifty-kopek increase in wages, to be fed with meat, and given an eight-hour workday. There were cries of bravo as she [finished speaking]. The crowd was agitated and discussed further steps. But nothing was decided practically, and the laundresses scattered in various directions.[36]

Women also got involved in the ad hoc meetings which occurred so typically during 1917 in streets and factory yards. For example, when a man was sent to Orekhovo, charged with working alongside the city soviet to set up elections to the Constituent Assembly, the local working women, their eye caught no doubt by the visitor's hat and silk suit,

surrounded him and bombarded him with questions. . . .
"Who are you," asked the working women, "Menshevik, Social Revolutionary, or Kadet?"
"I'm an independent, don't you see? . . ."
"Get out of here! We don't have any of those around here!"
[He] tried to protest, but this just irritated the women more: in the turmoil they tore the sleeves and pockets off his jacket.

At the same time, the Orekhovo women showed their support for political organizers whom they admired by contributing their particular skills when the need arose. One agitator, for example, told how the women workers had made some shirts for him: "They found out that I'm single and hadn't changed my shirt for a long time. So they sewed four shirts for me." The women had also supported agitators in another way before the February Revolution: "Sometimes, if the police were chasing a worker [for participating in illegal political activities], all he had to do was to run into the nearest barrack—they would not extradite him from there!"[37] *Golos*, an anti-Bolshevik newspaper, carried an account of a political conversation between two women "of the simple folk" who had heard Bolshevik agitators. The women had misunderstood the Bolshevik position, believing their anti-Provisional Government stance meant that they were in favor of returning to the tsarist system.[38]

Other ways women participated in political life from time to time included donations arranged through the factory.

Yesterday working men and women in the factories willingly made a deduction for the benefit of our prisoners [of war]. In the factory region, workers carried out flour, sugar, tobacco, and tea on wagons. Many of the factory working women have husbands languishing in captivity and thus the call for sacrifices for the benefit of the prisoners met a fervent response among the factory poor.[39]

Working women also participated in voting of various kinds, ranging from national elections to deciding local issues. An Ivanovo-Kineshma area Bolshevik newspaper described conversations among women workers waiting in long lines outside the polls in early September.[40] In Kostroma, some working women lost out when all the workers of the city decided to work on a women's holiday (*Zhen mironosits*), in order to make up for an extra day taken on the eve of May Day. The women had objected to this, but the "men insisted on their way" of arranging the holiday.[41]

All of this activity indicates that women were not only interested in, but committed to, political change. They were active in many different ways; they were capable of effective tactics and strong stands. Working women—partly because of their tremendous numbers in working-class areas—were neither resourceless nor helpless. Yet to a large degree, they held their potential power in check. In their lengthy catalog of political activity, we again see that one puzzling lacuna. In the space labeled "Ongoing Organization," there is a distressing blank. And the question again arises, why?

Part Two

Dearest mama gave me to be married
Dearest mama wanted to come often
To come often, as a guest, to my house
Summer passed, but no mama
Three went by—mama comes.
Already mama does not recogize me.
"Who is this woman? Who is this old woman?"
"Poor me, I'm not a woman, I'm not an old woman,
I'm your child, dear mama."
"Where, where has your white body disappeared?
Where has your rosy glow gone?"
"My white body is on a silken lash.
My rosy glow is on a right hand.
Hit with a lash, the body will lose parts of itself,
Hit on the cheek, the glow will disappear."
                    —*song sung by young women to prepare for marriage*[1]

SEVEN

The Shaping
of the Activist

Both working men and working women fought and risked their lives during the Russian Revolution. Both showed courage in their struggle for a better life. There were many and significant similarities between the two sexes, but there were also, as we have seen, great differences. What caused those differences to be so marked? Why did men organize so readily and women so seldom? Why did the political action of working women remain sporadic even when it was at its peak of urgency and intensity?

The reasons for the absence of long-term, systematic organization among women were certainly complex. Most of the women involved were illiterate, poor, and hungry. They confronted the greater experience of men in organizations, as well as the determination of men to keep women out of positions of authority in the public sphere. Yet these factors are not sufficient to explain fully the failure of women to attempt to participate in ongoing organization.

Historians and sociologists studying a range of countries have recently elaborated the idea that the patterns of activism during times of political upheaval grow out of the patterns of daily relationships during routine times. This theory suggests that men who work in factories are "preorganized" by virtue of their daily contact, making the leap to organized political or economic action a natural step. Similarly, women's domestic work, because it occurs in individual homes, isolates women from one another, making effective political organization difficult.

Russia's CIR forms a highly unusual test case of the theory of preorganization because so many of its women worked in factories their entire lives. In addition, many of these women lived in huge factory dormitories, even after they married and had children. Thus, in their factory work and communal living arrangements, married women in the CIR had the advantages of close contact and shared work that historians have theorized is conducive to political organization. If married women anywhere could become organized effectively, surely these women could.

And yet, they didn't.

Even their breadline rebellions were sporadic, spontaneous, and lacking in long-term organization. And the breadlines had given them a parallel to men's assemblies. True, a cold street corner is hardly as congenial as a warm tavern, but as we will see below, male workers often forged their daily-life solidarity in outdoor meeting places, in fields and on riverbanks. And as Ancharova's and other descriptions indicate, women in breadlines found themselves deep in "women's talk" and discussion of street events even when they were cold and tired. Also, women were compelled to neglect a portion of both components of their usual double burden—work and family—to stand in the lines. This enforced idle time could have been used for organizing. Street meetings were extremely common throughout 1917. What better place for them to be convened than the breadlines?

And yet, they weren't.

A clue to the reasons for this negative stance toward organizations dealing with the food problem may be gleaned from the following interview conducted by a Moscow woman reporter. The interview followed the establishment of building committees in Moscow in September and October. The goal of the committees was to shorten breadlines throughout the city. In large apartment houses, one committee was established per building, while small buildings were grouped together and elected joint committees. Residents elected their own committee members. Ration cards were distributed not to individuals, but to the committee, which was then charged with obtaining the food for all of the building's residents from an assigned bakery. In the districts of Moscow where building committees were successfully established, they were often effective in sharply reducing queues, getting bread delivered to individual homes without the womenfolk having to stand in line for hours.[2]

A Moscow woman reporter, "Thrifty Citizen," investigated women's responses to the building committees. She conducted an interview with a lower-class woman, one Mar'ia Sidorovna. The reporter began by asking the interviewee whether the residents of her building had formed their committee yet.

"My God, no! . . . [I]n our building no one can understand a thing about this business."

[The reporter began to explain the system of electing delegates to manage the building's food supply.]

"But these elected delegates [*vybornye*], are they horses?"

"What?"

"Just so. These delegates, if they're given food for a hundred people, they'd have to be stallions, excuse the expression, in order to carry it."

"Hmmm . . . Yes . . . I didn't think of that! But you could hire a waggoner, a carter, after all."

"Akh, my dear, with such prices? For poor tenants, in poor housing, you see, a waggoner or a carter would be a millstone around the neck."

"Every day."

"There you are! Exactly! And then, dear, I have still another question: Let's say my ration is four pounds of bread for my family, yours is three pounds, someone else gets two pounds, and another eight or ten pounds. Then, you see, how would they buy it—would they weigh out the bread separately [in the shop], or take whole loaves and divide it up in the buildings?"

"Oh, well. I guess the tenants would have to have special bread shop assistants."

"And what about pouring out kerosene for each tenant?"

"And measuring out sugar by the pound?"

"And really, this just doesn't make sense, they want to put an end to the queues, they make up a law, but how can you do it—it's impossible to see your way through it. It'll turn out, if you please, that the *khvosty* will get even longer."[3]

Reading Mar'ia Sidorovna's remarks, we are likely at first to be drawn into her clever defense of the small-scale family economy as superior to any plan involving economies of scale. The building committees suddenly seem to be an example of a too hastily conceived bureaucratic program. But on second look, the conservative direction of her perspective becomes apparent. She was contending that the only sensible way to obtain food was for each family (or rather, its womenfolk) to continue to stand in line for hours. Different analyses of the same flaws in the building committee system were possible. Improvements might have been proposed in the committee system, rather than declaring the whole concept untenable. For example, given women's general propensity for appropriating food from hoarding merchants when they needed it, it would not have been surprising if they had advocated that merchants be responsible for delivering food to apartment houses. Mar'ia Sidorovna's second objection, that the division of goods into family-sized portions could be done more efficiently by individual family shoppers, seems flimsier still. Shopkeepers could still have been responsible for preparing individual orders, as they always had, perhaps with help from committee members. Considering the amount of time each of thousands of women stood in line, surely a more rationally organized plan would have been more efficient for everyone. And in fact, the building committee system did save women countless hours of waiting in lines where it was put into practice.

In short, the perspective through which Mar'ia Sidorovna viewed building committees reaffirmed the self-reliance and isolation of the nuclear family. She glorified the family's "superior" capacity for carrying out a task which had long been an aspect of women's socially designated role, even when wartime conditions made that task dramatically more difficult for women.

Mar'ia Sidorovna was not the only woman who viewed the committees negatively. Another interviewee responded, "Why are you thrusting all these committees on me? . . . Without queues, where can a woman . . . unburden [her] heart in these hard days?" This woman did not perceive of committees as tools with which women might alleviate many of the grievances of "these hard days" in addition to talking about them. Her response suggests a general suspicion of committees, despite the fact that the building committees were selected by the building's residents, presumably including the women themselves. Perhaps women's daily life experience with organized groups made them expect that such groups would undermine women's interests, rather than serving them. At any rate, this woman's assumption that committees would destroy women's sociability makes clear the disjuncture she felt between women's friendships and organized activity to improve their lives—suggesting in turn that women's friendships may not have been suitable as bases for political activism, as some historians have anticipated.

Women's fragmented, anti-organizational approach was also evident in the system, described above, whereby one woman sat in line all night, reserving places for all the other women who were then free to go home to sleep. This is the only instance I found of women generating a systematized division of labor, the closest they came to establishing any ongoing organization. Intriguingly, however, the purpose of this system was not to facilitate concerted action by a group of women, but rather to enable women to disperse to their individual dwellings. Women thus utilized organizational methods to *fragment* social bonds rather than to strengthen and make them more effective. Had women applied the same method of reserving places in line to engage in concerted political action, they might have been able to bring the food crisis under some sort of rational control, thereby in the long run satisfying their hunger as well as their need for sleep. Thus, the notion of using their organizational skills to create ongoing institutions seems to have been alien to women. Instead, their perspective focused on the individual nuclear family as the only locus of relief from the physical hardships of their lives.

Women's solutions for grievances had a distinguishing temporal aspect. Even though women appreciated and wanted their contacts with other women in the queues during the day, those commitments were dissolved each night when the women returned to their families.[4] One of the imperatives which caused the nightly dissolution of commitments to peers can be seen in the case of the starving Norskoe working women who *did* leave their families overnight, forced to travel by boat down the Volga to the Yaroslavl provisioning committee to obtain food. As women made the overnight journey, problems arose in caring for their children: "Not only those who come and go to Yaroslavl suffer, but also their families, their children, who are often left without anyone to look after them and because of this, they are . . . often the unwitting culprits in the fires which are occurring in the [factory] villages on every side because of children being left unattended."[5]

Fires set accidentally by untended children were only the most obvious and immediate problem which occurred when adult caretakers were absent overnight. Children also needed other forms of caretaking: to be fed, washed, put to sleep, awakened, clothed, and fed again.

The late-twentieth-century observer might envision these women organizing shared child care, either in their home towns or on the boat down the Volga. Certainly, one can envision sharing child care to enable some of their number to attend meetings in their own towns or factory barracks. Making such arrangements would have been difficult, but no more so than standing in line for hours, attacking merchants, and watching their children die from impure food. Yet these women did not share child care to facilitate political activism. Therefore it seems likely that food-rioting women's reluctance to take on commitments to organizations and institutions beyond their families was in part a result of their belief that the best way to care for their children was always within the confines of the individual nuclear family, never varying this through political involvement.

In short, it was not isolation in the home or the double burden which in and of themselves inhibited women's political organizing. The daily needs of children—and women's sense of how best to meet those needs—were a more basic cause.

Women's constancy in placing the immediate needs of their children before those of the peer solidarity and political organization which might have helped starving children more in the long run, was not purely instinctual. (After all, women left their children inadequately tended for long hours each day to work in the factory.) Nor were women's attitudes toward their family responsibilities simply a question of consciously calculating the actual needs of various family members at any given moment and weighing them against the demands of organizational involvement. In fact, the attitudes which prompted women's rejection of sustained organization were probably largely unconscious, never rationally considered. Women's commitment to their families was the centerpiece of an entire life perspective typified by Mar'ia Sidorovna's unwillingness to consider that taking part in "committees" might help her family rather than hurting it. Let us now turn to women's daily lives, to discover some of the roots of these attitudes.

As I began my research in the Soviet Union, I quickly found newspaper and memoirist descriptions of a common pattern of public interaction between women and men. One example occurred in Kineshma, outside one of the large textile factories as men were leaving work. A woman holding a baby stood waiting in vain for her husband to come out of the factory. Finally, she asked one of the other workers if he had seen her husband.

> The fellow burst into loud laughter. "Search for the wind in a field! Brothers, she's been watching for her Mitrii there, but he's long been in the Tulon [a tavern] if not in the Meeting of Friends [another tavern]. . . . You're late, Pelageia Karpovna. Mitrii Vasil'ich . . . felt in his bones his mate would pay him a visit so, after picking up his pay, he evaporated. . . ."
> "Ach, he's a monster . . ." screamed the woman. "There isn't even a half kopek in the house, the children are hungry, I myself haven't eaten a thing since morning, but he's drinking up his wages again, I'll bet!" [Then she directed her thoughts toward her husband.] "No-o-o, I'll catch up to you, you lost cause of a drunkard, I'll tear the money from your throat."

Her baby in her arms, Pelageia began a search. In the Tulon tavern, she learned that her husband had been there earlier, but had left, after sarcastically instructing the bartender to "pass along my humblest, loving respects to my lawful wedded spouse." The bartender reported this to her, laughing and jeering along with the other male customers.

> "I only ask you," cried Pelageia, "not to make jokes about somebody else's grief."

At that, *even worse laughter inundated* the unfortunate woman. . . . "Tell me [where he went], for God's sake," she implored. "He'll drink up everything . . . if I don't find him in time."

Pelageia checked the other local taverns, but Mitrii had left each one before she arrived.

Night came on, starless and dark. . . . The baby awoke and began to cry loudly, numb with the cold.

And ahead still more vain searches and the terrible, implacable specter of the next hungry day.[6]

This was not an isolated interaction. In Yaroslavl, where Russia's largest textile factory was located, a newspaper article reported:

Very often around the beer houses you see a pitiful picture: a woman, apparently worn out with suffering, with an emaciated, anguished face, stands by the door of the beer hall and begs plaintively:

"Vania, come home! It's the third day that we haven't eaten a thing."

And in answer is heard the drunken husband's vile abuse *and the appreciative laughter of the other [male] customers.*

The major part of the [male] worker's pay is invariably left at the beer hall.[7]

The wives, factory workers themselves, routinely tried to prevent their husbands from drinking up their pay not because the man was the sole support of the family, but because the women's wages alone were not sufficient to support it. In short, long before the food shortages of 1917, Russian working women struggled to cope with daily life hunger tsars who threatened their children as well as themselves.

Why was Pelageia so devoted to her children while her husband was so unmindful of them? Why was Pelageia alone in her struggle, while her husband drank and laughed together with a whole group of like-minded pals? Where were Pelageia's women friends when she needed them?

Journalists who covered working-class towns noted that Russian workers spent a lot of time drinking in taverns as an escape from the terrible conditions in which they lived. Russian workers in the late nineteenth and early twentieth centuries endured long hours in the factory, constant harassment by foremen, frequent fines for petty offenses, low wages, extreme heat or cold, and dampness (to reduce the likelihood of threads drying and breaking in textile factories), absence of ventilation, textile lint clogging the air, and terrible stenches in rubber and other chemical factories. At home, workers were crowded two families to each small room in factory barracks, with no place for children to play except filthy hallways and dusty streets, and no room for adults to relax after work. Men went to taverns in part because there was literally no room for them at home and in part to escape constant noise and turmoil.

But while all of this helps to explain why men sought escape in alcohol and camaraderie, it does not explain why women—who lived and worked under the same conditions as men—did not seek similar escapes. Nor does it explain why men so often went drinking in same-sex groups, why they were antagonistic toward their wives, or why Pelageia had no support group of her own in her time of need.

Various historians have dealt with some of these questions.[8] However, none of these historians provides a theoretical framework that explains the differences between female and male workers' interests and commitments. Anthropologists' work on social bonding is of use here, in spite of their more extensive work on male bonding than female. While my primary interest is female social ties, a brief look at the literature on male bonding is informative. For Pelageia faced a *group* of jeering men, not her husband alone, and the men's laughter resembled a male solidarity group's rejection of a competing claim made on the time and devotion of one of its members.[9]

Anthropologists offer differing theories as to why male solidarity has so frequently been an aspect of human culture.[10] Lionel Tiger argues that men have been genetically selected for the capacity to form bonds with other men,[11] but this theory contributes little to an understanding of why bonding is so strong in some cultures and less manifest in others. Frank Young has advanced a far more useful and convincing position. Taking a broad, representative sampling of the world's communities, he demonstrates a correlation between the presence of male solidarity on the one hand, and on the other, subsistence bases and warfare that require close, cooperative activity among the community's men. In these societies, everyone's survival depends on each man's willingness to contribute reliably and enthusiastically to the group effort. Because a man who feels an emotional bond to his group is much more likely to do his share than is a man who has no such feeling, these societies devote a portion of their material resources to forging a deeply felt solidarity by means of regular male ceremonies and ritual practices, including initiation rites.[12]

What is most useful in understanding the Russian working-class situation, for both men and women, is the anthropologists' awareness of the importance of *emotional* bonding. When some type of activity is central to a community yet difficult to achieve, emotional bonding to arouse the interest and commitment of the participants is important to ensuring that each person will carry out the prescribed tasks. Linking this idea to the approach of social historians, I hypothesize that work and other basic responsibilities generate not only the social ties historians have observed, but also networks of profoundly felt emotional commitments (bonding) as well. This has important implications for political activism because patterns of loyalty shaped, often unconsciously, through emotions prescribed by the prerevolutionary order, may not be accessible to rationally considered change in revolutionary times.

In working-class Russia, there were various activities that were crucial to the survival of the community and each of its members. Workers lived on the brink of poverty. They were subject to arbitrary firing, large fines, and a very high rate of job-related injuries, illness, and death. At any time, a worker might suddenly be unemployed, be fined such an exorbitant amount as to leave little for living expenses, lose a finger, or have a hand crushed in a machine.

Under these circumstances, and in the absence of government social welfare programs, workers could survive only by means of an active, ongoing commitment to mutual aid. Robert Johnson and Diane Koenker have written about consumers' cooperatives and insurance funds, the institutionalized forms of mutual aid among Moscow workers. However, only a small number of Russian workers belonged to such organizations, largely because of the barriers placed in their way by the tsarist government. In the absence of the legal freedom to easily establish formal mutual-aid organizations, it seems likely that Russian workers engaged in mutual aid informally by means of traditional networks. Johnson and Koenker have both noted the strong ties among *zemliaki* (workers originally from the same village, county, or province) in determining urban residence patterns and in helping one another to find employment. It also seems likely that the same *zemliak* networks were utilized for other forms of mutual aid as well. Indeed, Johnson found evidence of clusters of *zemliaki* in formal cooperatives and mutual aid societies.[13]

It seems likely, then, that working-class male bonding served the purpose of strengthening each individual man's commitment, informal but nonetheless strong, to aid others in the *zemliak* group. Men's collective card-playing, drinking, and other activities may have played the same role as did initiation rites and other ritual practices in societies studied by anthropologists.[14]

All of this establishes a convincing rationale for solidarity in Russian working-class communities. But it still does not explain why women did not take part along with men in maintaining the bonds of mutual aid with regard to wage labor and financial crisis. After all, women of the textile-producing region worked in the factories, too, and they were often a more reliable source of immediate support for the family than were men.

Anthropologists have noted that women's bonding patterns are typically different from men's, that they are usually bounded by family and kinship even in societies where men are not.[15] Among the Russian working class, women—and not men—bore the responsibility for rearing children under the age of seven or eight years old. I hypothesize that women's work of rearing children played an even more critical role in shaping women's patterns of loyalty than did their factory work.

My research into women's everyday networks reveals that the solidarity which might have developed among women because of their proximity at work and in barracks was actively inhibited through socialization, in order to make family commitments women's first priority. This was accomplished through the social engineering of women's emotional lives.

I suspect that men took on by themselves the tasks of maintaining the social bonds necessary to provide longer-range financial security (such as it was) in case of unemployment or financial or medical crisis. While women attended to the immediate, everyday physical and emotional needs of their children, men often ignored *immediate* needs in order to channel resources instead into the all-male group, which dealt with long-range security. Earnings were insufficient to support both short-term needs and insurance against catastrophe over the long run. Thus, wives and husbands battled over the family income, each attempting to finance that aspect of family need for which he or she was responsible.[16]

Why should the bond between the Russian mother and her children have led to partial inhibition of ongoing ties with other women? What was the nature of the mother-child bond? Some historians have argued that maternal love is a recent phenomenon that did not exist in premodern societies. For example, Edward Shorter, building on the work of Philippe Ariès (*Centuries of Childhood*), has argued that, among the lower classes, maternal indifference toward children was not replaced by maternal love and caring until recent times.[17]

Because Shorter could find no direct evidence for his hypothesis, he used indirect evidence (maternal abandonment of children and mothers leaving their children inadequately supervised when they went to work). At first blush, his evidence might seem to support his view for Russian women. However, I found substantial direct evidence that Russian working mothers (and peasant mothers before them) did love their children and that they engaged in behavior toward their offspring similar to what today we think of as maternal love. Memoirs and life histories of working women make clear their tremendous love for and commitment to their children. Lullabies and other forms of folklore used daily by Russian workers express women's exquisite tenderness toward their infants. Endless proverbs comment on mothers' tendency to adore even the most unlovable of their offspring.

While Shorter's claim of "maternal indifference" is erroneous, at least for the Russian working class, he and other historians have raised an important issue. Historians have never made a detailed analysis of precisely what the essential aspects of childrearing are and in turn what effect this job has on caregivers' patterns of social ties and loyalties to other adults. Refining the general theory of preorganization through factory work, social historians have examined the work process of various types of jobs in order to explain the differing patterns of social ties among their workers. For example, Joan Scott and Michael Hanagan have examined the work of glassmakers, metal and textile workers, and bolt and file makers, respectively, showing how the work process of each influences the social ties formed among coworkers.[18] In the same vein, it is important to examine the work process of child rearing to find out whether it was likely to have produced patterns of social ties or emotional bonding specific to women responsible for it.

(Of course, recognizing that women have historically been the primary caretakers of children does not mean they always should or will be in the future. As men in Western societies today have begun to take more responsibility for child rearing, they have begun to adopt some of the nurturant behaviors toward children previously considered innately maternal.)

There has been a pervasive awareness among contemporary feminists that women are nurturant to their children (and that this nurturance at times carries over into women's relationships with other people). Thus, we might suppose that nurturance is part of the work process of childrearing. But in seeking to understand the impact of children's needs on social structure, historians have not asked precisely what nurturance is or exactly why children need it.

To get a better understanding of these issues, historians must turn to the work of psychologists, who have studied the interactions and bonding between parents and their children.[19] Although psychological studies may seem an unusual type of evidence for historians, I would argue that the social organization of women's work cannot be fully understood without making use of psychologists' data about the developmental needs of young children.

Many scholars of the family in history have assumed that the interaction between mother and child known as "mother love" is a purely emotional phenomenon, a luxury enjoyed only by the middle and upper classes.[20] However, careful perusal of psychologists' work indicates that for infants and very young children, parental behaviors typically seen as gratuitous expressions of love are in fact important to basic cognitive, motor, and verbal development.[21]

But are data gathered by psychologists in the West today applicable to other cultures and other time periods? Cross-cultural work done by psychologists for Jamaican Blacks, a Latin American Indian village, and most extensively for various African groups indicates that on the whole, children in these premodern societies go through the same developmental sequences as they do in the United States and Europe today, and that their mothers engage in a highly similar repertoire of interaction with them.[22] Aside from this cross-cultural research, a number of Western psychologists have studied the mother-infant relationship in working-class and various racially diverse populations and have found them to be, on the *basic level* I am discussing here, identical to the middle-class data.[23]

Furthermore, my evidence from Russian working-class communities reveals the same types of mother-child interactions as have been shown in regard to the United States and Africa today. Although detailed observational data on Russian working-class infants of the early twentieth century are not available, the evidence that does exist, together with the indications that on the most *basic* level, mother-child interaction is highly similar across class, race, and culture today, suggests that the same types of mothering behaviors served the same needs in Russian children as psychologists have shown them to serve elsewhere.

Therefore, I posit that the "work process" of the job of parenting involves meeting the developmental needs of children as they grow and change throughout childhood. This entails a highly personal commitment to one's own children, above all others, over a period of many years. Children's needs require consistent, daily attention. If only one parent is responsible for child rearing—as was the case among Russian workers—in the absence of alternative child care, and given the very long factory workday, there will be a strong tendency toward this parent having to curtail ongoing loyalty to any institution beyond the family.[24]

But if basic mothering has been omnipresent through history, how can Shorter and other historians have failed to observe it? The confusion may result partly from the awareness of the extraordinary time- and energy-consuming nature of lower-class women's economic and domestic chores as compared with those of middle-class women in modern societies. Shorter, for example, assumed that working women's leaving their children to go off and work all day in the factory meant they did not love their children. He and other recent family historians have leapt from the knowledge that women had a heavy work burden in addition to child rearing, to the assumption that these women therefore had no conception of the specific needs of young children, did not care much about their children, and made virtually no effort to meet their needs aside from, at best, the most obvious physical ones (food, clothing, shelter).

Although parents in recent decades have had more time to devote to child care, it is not conversely true that the parents of earlier periods devoted no time at all to meeting the emotional and developmental needs of their children. Routine child care offers opportunities for playful, affectionate, and nurturant interaction. Feeding and bathing are two of the most obvious; lullabies are another classic example of combining gentle sensory stimulus with routine child care. A parent doing household chores may break off periodically for brief but nurturant interaction with a child. An example of this is the nursery rhymes that Russian working-class mothers sang to comfort their children when they hurt themselves.

Balancing all of these tasks along with a ten- or eleven-hour workday was difficult for Russian women and it resulted in less than ideal care for children (fathers' lack of involvement probably did even more so). But this does not mean that mothers did not strive to give their children the attention they needed. Whatever shortage of attention children received was not due to lack of maternal love, but rather to the extraordinary material hardships that all workers faced.

While childrearing posed similar demands on adult caretakers in Russia as elsewhere, I believe particular circumstances among Russian workers exacerbated women's isolation within the realm of childrearing, and helped strengthen their reluctance to view women's organizations as a potential aid to their children's well-being. We noted that, because men were so preoccupied with their solidarity groups, women were left with tremendous responsibility not only for child care, but for financial child support as well. A further consequence of the emphasis placed on strong male bonding among both Russian workers and peasants was the tradition of patrilocal marriage. While many working women living in cities and large factory towns may have married local men and did not have to actually change residence, their cultural heritage was the peasant one in which each woman moved to the village of her new husband's family (peasant women in small villages were more likely than urban dwellers to have to marry someone who lived at a distance). Sustaining ties among men necessitated their remaining living among their *zemliaki*. Therefore, when marriages took place between men and women who lived far apart, it was the wife who had to move. Her ties were considered expendable.

For the peasant woman, patrilocal marriage meant the loss of all the caring human ties with her friends and family that she had developed over the course of her life until that time. The wife-beating which was so much a part of Russian peasant and working-class life was the most obvious manifestation of married women's isolation—whether imposed by actual patrilocality or simply by tradition—from the protection of those who loved her in childhood, and her resulting vulnerability to her husband's abuse.

Even the working-class bride who remained living physically close to her parents must shift her loyalties from her own extended family to her husband's. However much her own parents might wish to go on protecting her, they were obliged to give her up to whatever fate lay in store for her. Note the urban song printed at the beginning of Part Two, in which—as was typical in these songs—the bride's mother wanted to visit her newly married daughter often, but instead did not make her first visit for years—by which time her daughter had been beaten into premature old age.

However much a mother longed to maintain close ties with her married daughter, cultural mores required parents not to act on that wish. Parents must give up their daughters to their new husbands' families. In beating his wife—and in being able to keep his in-laws from protecting her, even though they knew he was hurting her—a husband demonstrated that she belonged to his solidarity group, no longer to theirs.

Although women were expected to shift loyalties to their families of marriage, among the peasantry the bride could not in return count on absolute loyalty from her husband's extended family, because she had only recently married into it. She would be seen as something of an outsider for years to come. Meanwhile, her husband and his parents continued their loyalties to each other as they always had.[25] (One working-class courtship song had the protagonist, a young bride, pleading with her in-laws to stop her husband's beating her. Each in turn unblinkingly took their son's side in the dispute: "Dear daughter-in-law . . ./ It's up to my son/ If he wants to, he can beat you."[26])

Even among workers who married within their home town or city, patrilocal heritage encouraged brides' giving up reliance on premarital peer and family-of-origin support networks. Cut off from her family of origin, without reliable new adult loyalties, a woman's only potential allies, she might expect, would be her own children. Thus, within the patrilocal setting, women themselves may have wanted to be highly invested in their own children. For they were her one remaining hope for help in achieving a better life. Here we may have located one of the reasons for Mar'ia Sidorovna's glorification of women's role within the nuclear family. Cut off from alliance with her peers, each woman's nuclear family—more specifically her children—became her only possible kingdom, the only realm in which her will might, at least sometimes, prevail.

Inducing the bride to leave her childhood protectors for an uncertain future with her husband required some incentive, some irresistible lure that made the shift look attractive despite its terrible difficulties. This lure, in Russian working-class culture, was the tremendous emphasis placed on the centrality of romantic love in women's lives. Each woman was to feel that her husband—however disloyal he might be to her—was the one true love of her life: exquisitely, deliriously, sexily wonderful despite his flaws—or perhaps because of them. Without him, her life had no meaning. This cultural hyperintensification of romantic feelings helped bind women to husbands who in reality frequently acted unlovably. (In contrast, although romantic love for one special woman played a limited role in men's lives during courtship, the macho male ideal discouraged men from continuing this attitude toward their wives much beyond their wedding.)

This cultural encouragement of women's adoration of their husbands may also have been an additional source of mothers' love for their children. Mothers did not view their children instrumentally, simply as their allies against a harsh world. Mothers often gave lovingly and unreservedly to their offspring, feeling that the children of the unions with their beloved husbands were likewise exquisitely unique and precious. This commitment was not purely a result of a biological tie, for they were her husband's biological children, too, and he did not display the same attitude toward them that she did. Rather, the mother's attitude was in part a byproduct of her romantic attachment to her husband. As he spent less and less time with her after marriage, she began to turn her inextinguishable loving attention instead toward their children.

The exciting promise of the romantic bond with her husband fueled women's expectations that pleasure, comfort, and life satisfaction were to be found within the family, not through organization in the public sphere. And because these attitudes were shaped at an unconscious emotional, not a rational level, they were not questioned when romance turned ugly, or when children began to starve during 1917. Thus, primary commitment to a deeply felt, highly personal bond with her husband and children formed the core of each woman's patterns of loyalties with other human beings in her world.

Women participated in daily home-centered activities, friendships, and holiday celebrations alongside other women. But in order to maintain women's family-centered commitments, women's networks were not structured and elaborated by the community for the purpose of supporting group activity in the public sphere, as were men's. As we will see in detail below, unlike men, women were taught to act only as individuals in the public sphere, and to inhibit any impulse to join in daily-life group behavior to alleviate their grievances. Women's networks were in effect structured to self-destruct continuously as women returned to their families after each work day. Thus, the culture of women's groups served as much to fragment women periodically as to bring them together.

But why could the division of labor not have been shared, at least somewhat more equally, by men and women? Why could men not have shared child care, at least sometimes, while women sometimes took joint action in the public sphere? We have seen that, while women chose friends based on intimate compatibility, male bonding entailed large groups of men working together even when they were not personally compatible. As we will see below, in order to suppress their intragroup disagreements and dislikes, men turned their aggression outward instead, against other solidarity groups, battling them on a regular basis and blaming them for many of the daily griefs they encountered. Women's friendships, in contrast, involved the same intimacy skills that childrearing did. In short, it seems that not only did the *people* bonded to differ for men and women, but also the *quality* of the bonds themselves differed, each to accommodate the work for which men and women were responsible. In order for men to acquire the necessary callousness (in the words of one of their songs, "It's all the same to me, to love or to hate/ Love was forgotten by me long ago") and the capacity to deny the true sources of their emotions, men had to be removed from the sphere of nurturance they had lived in as children. They had to reject the world of childhood, however appealing its nurturance might have felt. To be able to sustain the solidarity of large, impersonally selected groups, men had to suppress their capacity and longing for intimacy. Women, in contrast, remained within the realm of childhood nurturance and intimacy to care for their own children.

Thus, we come full circle back to the issue of emotional ties as part of the work processes of childrearing and solidarity groups. Childrearing requires a nurturant attitude toward other human beings, while, in the poverty-stricken conditions of Russian workers, large-group bonding to support action in the public sphere required a denial of the need to nurture and be nurtured. Women had to be attuned to human emotions and all their nuances; men had to tune them out. To accomplish their respective assignments successfully, women and men had to develop very different emotional skills. Under the very difficult conditions in which they lived, any given man or woman could hardly develop both sets of skills for, like athletes skilled in different sports requiring the development of different muscle groups, one set of skills would undermine the other in anyone who tried to develop both.

A Note on Sources

Because the activities of men's solidarity groups were loudly displayed in public spaces, men's behavior was often described in working-class newspaper articles. Women's networks, however, tended to be more hidden, behind closed barracks, kitchen, and bath house doors. Traditional historical evidence regarding women's daily relationships is very sparse. One of the best sources is working women's memoirs and life histories (told orally to ethnographers and deposited in Soviet archives). But there are only a few such life histories.

Another type of source, which happens to exist extensively for Russian working-class women, is folklore, recorded by a range of scholars and amateur collectors, and deposited in archives.[27] Folklore was collected in performance before the revolution; in addition, during the Soviet period, ethnographers interviewed elderly workers about their lives and folklore before 1917.

While using folklore as evidence involves different methodology than historians typically use, it is a rich source for understanding the social engineering of working women's networks over the course of their life cycle. This is because in the largely nonliterate, pre-electronic age communities of the

119

CIR, socialization occurred largely through yearly rituals, songs sung every day, and other forms of folklore. For most Russian working-class women, hearing and performing folklore took the place of the range of modes by which we convey mass culture today: magazines, newspapers, television, radio, rock and roll, and so on. Most genres of folklore were specific to the sex and age group that performed them and hence they make excellent material for the study of prescribed sex roles. As we will see in more detail below, women's group rituals—in contrast to men's—were designed to strengthen not the women's group performing them, but rather the intimate bond between each woman and her husband.

What is working-class folklore? Certain genres of folklore—lullabies, wedding and other ritual songs, and lyric songs, for example—were virtually the same among workers as among peasants. Other genres—the *chastushka*, for example—originated in the working-class or city milieu, and disseminated from there back into the countryside.[28]

In this book, I have included only enough examples of folklore to give support to my conclusions. The dissertation which inspired this book deals in great detail with the folkloric aspects of Russian workers' lives. The interested reader is encouraged to look at the dissertation for texts and textual analysis of more songs and other forms of folklore, as well as for additional material regarding folklore and other issues that could not be included here.[29]

Other sources consulted include published worker memoirs and memoir fragments, and local newspapers from working-class areas. A question might be raised as to the reliability of these sources, particularly regarding such negative working-class behaviors as men's irresponsibility to their families, their drinking, gambling, brawling, and wife beating. Both middle- and working-class observers, it may be suspected, exaggerated the extent of such behavior because they disapproved of it and wished to see it changed. We might suspect that it was precisely the literate workers, those capable of writing memoirs, who might be most guilty of this bias in their wish to "rise above their class."

However, the life histories dictated to ethnographers in two major studies of working-class folklore in CIR textile centers seem relatively free of such bias. The primary purpose of these ethnographic studies was the collection of early twentieth-century working-class folklore, as recalled by workers in the 1920s and 1930s. The informants were interviewed as part of their performance of everyday, nonpolitical folklore. Yet these oral histories provide the same picture of prerevolutionary working-class life as do memoirs of workers chosen for publication in Soviet anthologies because of the memoirists' "advanced" political views. Both types of sources also correlate with the extensive evidence provided by newspapers, as well as by folklore located in archival collections. All of these sources give evidence of a way of life in which abuse, violence, drunkenness, and other negative types of behavior were common. While the historian must always consider the possible bias of evidence of such negative traits, the fact remains that all available sources, including those most likely to be unbiased on these issues, seem to corroborate it for the Russian working class.

Throughout this section, I rely heavily on local newspaper stories that often appeared in regular columns with such titles as "Pictures from Factory Life." In addition to corroboration from other types of sources, the reliability of these descriptions is attested to by the fact that the newspaper accounts themselves were consistent in all the newspapers, of varying political perspectives, that I read, across a large part of the Central Industrial Region.

In addition, the newspapers on which I rely most heavily are known to have been widely read by workers, and some, like *Gazeta-Kopeika* (costing only one kopek, hence "The Penny Newspaper"), were produced specifically for low-income readers. That *Gazeta-Kopeika* was widely read by workers was revealed in several surveys of journal and newspaper readership among workers.[30]

Furthermore, *Kineshemets* frequently printed reports and letters to the editor from workers in the local factories, clearly indicating that this newspaper was being read and commented on by workers. The fact that letters would sometimes complain about the inaccuracy of a story (usually when a specific worker had been blamed for some misdeed) indicates that if workers had disagreed with newspaper accounts of factory life in general, they would have complained about them. Yet letters to the editor from workers never denied the descriptions of working-class daily life. In fact, reports and letters confirmed the stories.[31] For example, one letter came from a small factory in the area, protesting that the newspaper always wrote stories about the largest factories, never about them.

Here in Pokrovskaia factory we have [only] 70 working men and working women, but we're not second to the large factories in any respect. . . . Drinking, cards, and fights happen among all of us. . . . But however much we raise Cain, it's insulting—not once have you printed a scorching criticism of us in the newspaper. You write this about Sevriugov's factory, and that about the Tomna factory, but about us, nothing. But you see, wine, cards, and the urge to raise hell eats into our workers, too.

Here we have testimony from "less advanced" workers confirming the accuracy of descriptions of drinking and brawling written by "advanced" worker and middle class reporters; the Pokrovskaia workers complained only that their *own* dissolute behavior didn't attract "scorching criticism" in the paper. Thus, while a few more educated workers did deprecate fighting and drinking, apparently they did not exaggerate its extent. Most working men admired and aspired to extreme capacity for drinking and fighting. As the newspaper noted:

> Worst of all is that our worker boasts of his wildness. To him, it's insulting that nothing is written about him, how he fools around and brawls, because in badness he is accustomed to seeing himself as a hero. If he gets drunk until he loses consciousness, people talk about this—he already feels himself a hero.[32]

Working-class male culture was what we would today describe as "macho"; from this viewpoint, workers' pride in their drinking and brawling is understandable.

EIGHT

Housing and Living Arrangements: The Nuclear Family in a Communal Setting

In the Russian textile industry of the turn of the century, few workers had the luxury of single-family housing. For the most part, they lived in grossly overcrowded communal conditions, often in barracks provided by factory owners. Yet, against all odds, they clearly constituted themselves as nuclear families. Though two or three families shared a single, small room, and used communal kitchens and bathhouses, each family arranged their minimal possessions in such a way as to define their separateness. Workers seldom abandoned this pattern, in spite of the well-established Russian working-class tradition of forming communal groups called *artels*, often for the purchase and cooking of food. The artel was most common among workers who lived apart from their families, such as male construction workers and unmarried textile workers. The fact that the artel did not usually occur among families suggests that the absence or presence of children and child care made an all-important difference in the way Russian workers chose to organize their living situations.

Although the Russian working class is often assumed to have been dominated by workers whose families still lived separately in peasant villages, by the twentieth century, many workers in the textile industry lived in families. It was possible—indeed desirable—for male workers employed in or near textile factories to bring their wives, and often their children, to settle at the workplace, because the industry also hired many women.[1] Thus, by 1899 in Ivanovo-Voznesensk—the "Russian Manchester"—79 percent of the workers

123

lived with their families, and 21 percent lived without them. Of women living in the factory area, 96 percent worked in local factories.[2] In Kineshma, another major textile settlement, by 1913 the majority of weavers lived with their families.[3] Although in 1897 only 7 percent of Moscow workers lived with their families, by 1923, 66 percent did.[4]

Families in Factory Barracks

Many working-class families lived in barracks-like dormitories (called *kazarmy*, "barracks") built by factory owners to provide housing near the workplace. This was necessary because most factories were located in the countryside or the outskirts of a city, where there was insufficient housing in nearby villages for the workers. In the late 1890s, for example, 57 percent of Moscow *guberniia* workers in all industries lived in factory housing.[5] In the major textile region around Kineshma, the majority of workers lived in barracks.[6] The giant Glukhovskaia textile plant in Bogorodsk housed 14,000 workers and family members in barracks, while at the neighboring Balashikha factory, 5,500 were barracks residents.[7] In Moscow's Trekhgorka factory, about 80 percent of the workers lived in barracks.[8]

Factory barracks were usually multistory buildings of cheap construction. The Balashikha factory barracks were nine floors high; the Morozov factory barracks in Orekhovo-Zuevo ranged from three to four stories.[9] Inside, there were mass dormitory rooms for unmarried workers of each sex, with tens of people sleeping shoulder to shoulder in each vast room. Married workers and their children were housed in small rooms, two or three families to a room so cramped and ill-suited to normal living that they were called *kamorki*, literally "closets." Long, dark corridors usually ran the length of the building, with tens of doors to the rooms off either side. In the Trekhgorka factory in Moscow, for example, long corridors with asphalt floors stretched the full length of each building, dimly lit by one window at each end. There were forty to fifty rooms off each side of the corridor.[10]

The rooms themselves, each of which housed two families, were approximately 200 to 250 square feet. One working woman described the barracks room in which she lived in 1914: two families, fourteen people, "lived in a *kamorka*; among both families there were eight children and us, the adults. There was no room to stand up or lie down. . . . It was unbelievably stuffy. There was no place to put the furniture."[11]

A description of the inside of a *kamorka*, by a working woman who lived in the Orekhovo-Zuevo barracks for fifty years, is typical. It shows that each family had its own table and stools, cabinet, dishes, cleaning supplies, and so on, despite the crowded communal living situation:

> In the entrance to the room, near the door, stood a slop-pail and one or two brushes. Under the beds, footwear, potatoes, and dirty laundry were stored in baskets. . . .
> On each side [of the room] was a long narrow shelf for icons. . . . Along the wall stood trunks or chests—wooden, plain, or trimmed with tin. Sometimes there was a cloth covering the top of the trunk, sewn together from many-colored scraps. . . . Each family had a table . . . and two or three wooden stools. Along the wall stood large wooden cabinets, decorated in yellow paint. . . . The dishes were kept on shelves and in the windows: earthenware pots, cast-iron kettles, glazed dishes, and wooden spoons.[12]

The factory inspector P. A. Peskov, in his 1884 report on factory life in Vladimir *guberniia*, described *kamorki* in which two families lived:

> Each *kamorka* is lighted by one large or two medium-sized windows. . . . In the entranceway, on either side of the door, stand beds belonging to the two families; the children . . . usually sleep on the floor. . . . Finally, on either side of the window each family has its table, at which they eat. In the corners, several icons usually hang, always with an icon lamp at each; and on the walls hang cheap popular prints, almost always including pictures of members of the Tsarist Family. . . . In some *kamorki* there are even flowers in the windows, and curtains.[13]

Sometimes, in an effort to fit three families into a room, factory owners built platforms partway up the walls and installed a third family there. A stairway up to the platform was built along one wall. In some factories, single workers not living with their own families lived on these platforms.[14] An observer noted that "all this gives rise to many unhealthy phenomena in workers' lives." Crowding and lack of privacy created friction among barracks inhabitants, with arguments flaring frequently. "During these arguments, those living on the platforms are in a genuine state of siege, fearing to come down to the floor. Those who live in the space below divide the area by counting floorboards, and they cry to each other, 'Don't walk on my half!' "[15] Thus, each family defined its own space within the common room, sometimes even counting floorboards to delineate their own family's territory precisely.

When all of a *kamorka*'s inhabitants were at home, bustle and confusion reigned. A local newspaper reporter described the scene in a *kamorka* at ten o'clock at night, as the last workers returned home from the factory at the end of the evening shift.

> Then such turmoil arises that "save me from my misery!" . . . Positively every little corner is occupied. You have to eat in the same place that you sleep, that is on the bed, since the table is occupied, usually either with the tenants, or with family lodgers, and the single people huddle together in the garret [i.e., the platform] and wherever they can in the corners. When dinner is finished, the room takes on the appearance of a wood shed: people lie everywhere [to sleep], like logs cut from trees.[16]

Usually only the parents had beds. A measure of privacy was achieved by hanging curtains around the bed. These curtains were often made out of the calico produced by the workers and bought in the factory store.[17] Most of the children slept on the floor or on top of the trunks, for lack of other space, lined up so closely that "at night, there was nowhere to step."[18] In the Kineshma barracks, heating was unreliable—the factory owners claimed that the barracks were kept warm by steam heat, but most of the time "in winter, nothing resembling steam heat appears except the steam from people's breath that you can see in the *kamorki*." This, together with the fact that the floors, on which the children slept, were often made of asphalt, led to a high rate of illness among factory children.[19]

Nursing infants, however, slept in a more protected place: carved wooden cradles were hung over the parents' beds, on springs or poles to permit rocking. This was such a distinctive feature of working-class living arrangements that it was noted in almost all descriptions of workers' rooms.[20] Hanging the cradle inside the curtains above the parents' bed both protected the infant from the cold and made the child accessible for rocking and night feedings. Thus, babies occupied a privileged position compared to older children: warm, protected, and within arm's reach of soothing, feeding, and other attention.

Each family in the *kamorka* had its own table for eating and its own cupboards for storing dishes. Food was bought separately by each family and stored in its cupboards and under the bed, and, for staples such as jam, sometimes in large sheds in back of the barracks building.[21] The preparation of hot food was a complicated matter because kitchens were located at a distance from the *kamorki*. Women had to carry the food to the kitchen in order to cook it, and then carry it back to the *kamorka* to serve it. One factory inspector wrote, "the kitchens are located downstairs in the same building, or in separate structures. . . . The ovens in the kitchens are either simple Russian ones, or communal ones with niches (*gnezdy*) in which each family places its own pots." The Trekhgorka barracks kitchens had huge stoves divided into small ovens to accommodate separate cooking by each family. Long tables were provided for food preparation.[22] Ermilov described the general evening routine: "Here, by the stove, the inhabitants of the barracks usually gather and busy themselves each with their own tasks: women look after the children, wash the laundry, cook, check each other for lice, gossip, etc.; men play cards or recount indecent anecdotes."[23]

Despite common food-preparation facilities, cooking was done separately by the women of each family. In most factories in Vladimir *guberniia*, workers prepared food and ate as families, forming artels—the traditional Russian communal cooking arrangement—only very rarely.[24] Apparently something resembling an artel existed in the late nineteenth century in the Trekhgorka factory; but even this had a dominant element of family-based food preparation and consumption: "In the family barracks communal Russian stoves were provided. At the expense of the inhabitants, a cook was hired, who was paid fifty kopeks a month by each family. The inhabitants gave the cook pots filled with already-prepared food, and she watched over them as they cooked."[25] Unlike the traditional artel for single workers, in which food purchasing, preparation, and consumption were all done collectively, this family artel collectivized only the heating of the food. All food purchasing, preparation, and eating were done separately by each family. Thus, while single workers living apart from their families, including those in the textile industry, found collective food preparation and eating an efficient way of handling meals, once they married and had children, these workers cooked and ate as separate nuclear families.

Laundry was often done in the communal bathhouses established in many factory barracks—again by each woman separately for her own family, in spite of the communal washing facilities. Factory owners sometimes set up certain hours during the week when the women were permitted to use the bathhouse for laundry. Large rooms for drying clean laundry were sometimes provided in the attics of the barracks.

Laundry and bathing facilities together were among the least satisfactorily arranged aspects of factory life and were the subject of many demands for better conditions in workers' strikes. A letter to the editor of *Kineshemets* from

127

The Bol'shaia Kineshemskaia textile factory in Kineshma was typical of modern (1913) Russian factories of the CIR. Most worker families lived in housing such as the multi-storied barracks in the left background. This painting was commissioned by the factory and proudly displayed in a trade show.

Newly built barracks for workers at the Tsindel' silk factory in Moscow. Even in this model barrack, each window represents a single room in which two to three *families* were housed.

A typical workers' settlement on the outskirts of Moscow, housing workers who did not live in barracks. Note the "streets drowning in mud" in the foreground.

Women doing their laundry in the Moscow River. While the factory's public bathhouse was the more common location for women workers to do their laundry, women's housework often brought them together, rather than isolating them in separate homes, as it typically does in the West today. (The Bettmann Archive)

Lenin gives a revolutionary speech while standing on a table in the kitchen of the Trekhgorka factory in Moscow. This painting shows how amenable the communal spaces of factory barracks (where women gathered everyday to do their housework) were to political activity.

The interior of a typical CIR factory barracks room housing two or three families. The ubiquitous curtains are hung around the adults' beds for privacy. Children beyond infancy usually slept on the floor.

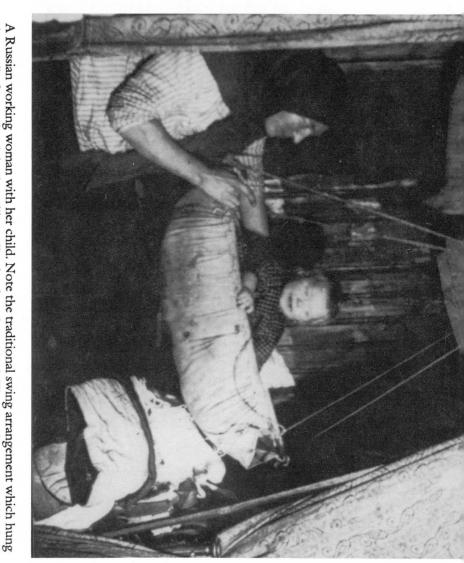

A Russian working woman with her child. Note the traditional swing arrangement which hung the cradle from a hook in the ceiling, allowing it to be rocked. The curtains surround the bed of the parents.

Women textile workers leaving their Orekhovo-Zuevo factory at the end of the workday. Small children often came to meet their mothers at the factory gates at the end of the workshift.

a worker at the Tomna factory listed a number of grievances relating to the bathhouses and laundry: it was heated by burning "some kind of rubbish," which filled the bath with bad fumes; there was not enough hot water; there was water on the floor in the dressing area, and "during the washing of laundry (which occurs three times a week) the women are not permitted to walk through the factory yard" directly to the bathhouse, but had to walk around the factory wall by a path dangerously icy in winter.[26]

Another series of problems arose when the Tomna factory administration made changes in the bathhouse routine: "A great deal of inconvenience threatens our wives: before they were permitted to go to the bath when they needed to, even around three times a week, and could wash out their laundry there little by little, if a lot of it had piled up. But now [they can only go once a week], so they have to remain in the damp steam for 6-7 hours.[27]

In addition to carrying their laundry to the bathhouse to wash it, women probably had to carry cleaning supplies as well: basins and other supplies were stored underneath the beds in the *kamorki*, again owned, transported, and utilized by each woman for her own family in spite of the communal laundry facilities. Although I found little material regarding the bathing of children, one newspaper description suggests that children probably accompanied their mothers into the women's section of the bathhouse.[28]

Families in Private Housing

Workers sometimes rented or owned their own houses and apartments. Conditions in private housing, however, did not differ greatly from those in the barracks. Overcrowding existed here, too, with several families squeezed together in tiny *izby* of a few rooms or into mass dormitory-style arrangements. In Ivanovo-Voznesensk, many workers lived in "squalid hovels with their tiny windows—hovels which, in some amazing manner, housed several families where there was hardly room for one."[29] The textile settlement of Iam, where most workers' families lived in private housing rather than barracks, had "small, literally toy houses" set along streets "drowning in mud. . . . In the entire expanse of [workers'] quarters, not a single birch tree or green bush could be seen. Dust or mud in the streets, rubbish in the yards, the endless roar of the factories, and smoke and soot in the air."[30] In Orekhovo-Zuevo, privately owned homes were built of "various types of junk-lumber," and were damp and very small, with just enough room for a bed, small table, and stool.[31]

If a factory was located in the countryside and workers lived in the surrounding villages, they often had to walk to and from work each day. At a factory in Shuia *uezd*, for example, there was a daily commute of up to two miles through the countryside. And even here, workers and their families could not find enough living space: "in a typical *izba* about thirty people huddle together."[32]

In Moscow, a range of mercenary characters exploited the housing needs of workers in various types of urban buildings. One "Citizeness Bobrova" rented out twenty-five rooms to working people, "and she only heats the stoves twice a week . . . with splinters and slivers. . . . Everyone freezes: men, women, and children. Requests and threats do no good."[33] In another lodging house,

Imagine a large room, along the walls of which are arranged rows of beds. Each "bed" is rented out separately. . . . The landlady herself squeezes in somewhere in the kitchen and dreams only of how she can rent "corners" for such a price that she can live free. . . . [S]he doesn't care who rents the "bunks," as long as they pay their money.

The result is the following: in one room, next to the bunk of a worker, is the bunk of a recidivist, further is a prostitute or even an honorable working woman, whom need has driven here. . . . Very often families live in such corners next to single people; in this case the parents surround their beds with curtains for decency's sake.

In Moscow . . . at every step one finds [such housing]. . . . For an endless distance along the streets and courts appear many-colored signs advertising "corners" and "bunks."[34]

A local Yaroslavl newspaper described daily life in a neighborhood of private shanty housing, in an article entitled "Grimaces of the City."

In the streets adjacent to the factory are extremely densely populated houses, "*Batumy*," as the working people call them. In them are a huge number of apartments, corners, and nooks [i.e. additional tenants would often rent a corner of a single room shared by a number of families]. . . .

Colossal overpopulation and constant close contact among the inhabitants give rise to fights and farces to which, like everything, people have grown accustomed. Noise and wild cries are heard.

"The joiner is beating his wife again."

A child squeals at the top of its lungs. . . .

The sounds of a harmonica and drunken choral singing are heard.

"Mitryi won at cards!"

129

"Vasilii got paid!"
Everything is known to everyone.
Consumption . . . is the scourge of "Batum."
It's natural! Poisoned air, a hard life, a life full of privation—these are conditions favorable to the development of tuberculosis and other city diseases.[35]

This, then, was the environment in which the married textile worker found herself. She confronted crowding, dirt, and lack of privacy to a degree almost unimaginable to most of us. Her lot in life might have been eased through cooperative activity—sharing of meal preparation, laundry, and so forth. And yet, this kind of activity did not take place. Every effort was made, in fact, to do exactly the opposite. All possible boundaries, physical and social, between nuclear families were emphasized.

Women's noncommunal utilization of communal barracks facilities in daily life seems a striking precursor of their behavior during revolutionary times, when women did not utilize resources available in their immediate environment to organize to improve their lives. It also contrasts with the daily-life activities of the Lowell, Massachusetts, dormitory-dwellers, who formed self-improvement circles in their dormitories, "debated religious and social questions," studied and sewed together. One Lowell woman worker said, "There was a certain class feeling among these [dormitory] households; any advantage secured to one of the number was usually shared by others belonging to her . . . group."[36]

Why did Russian women (both married and unmarried), in contrast, consistently, during revolution and in daily life, choose an approach so tightly focused around the nuclear family? Over the next chapters I will look at women's daily-life activities and bonding patterns to explore this question.

NINE

Childhood:
Who Took Care
of the Children?

Russian working-class mothers strove hard to meet the needs of their children, but the factory environment was, by our standards today, an impossible one in which to rear children. Even before birth, the demands of factory work interfered with the mother-child relationship. Maternity leaves were generally not permitted, and in their poverty, women had to continue working up until the moment of birth. The working woman V. N. Tiurina remembered "Many women gave birth right by their machines. . . . Often . . . pregnant women worked right up to the last day, well, they gave birth at the factory." Another working woman, Batovaia, said, "I myself worked until the last day of pregnancy. I left the factory only two hours before the birth. I had my child . . . at home; a midwife delivered the child." And P. Sleptsovaia: "I gave birth, like everyone then, practically by the machine. I barely made it home."[1]

Mothers were unable to remain at home to care for the infants for very long.[2] Tiurina recalled, "no one was paid during childbirth, and there were no leaves."[3] An investigation by the Pirogov Society on the effects of women's factory work on their children revealed that, in one textile factory, an above-average one with regard to living conditions, women were usually able to stay home with their children for only the first month after the child was born.[4] After this, women were compelled to return to work; they needed to help support the family, and employers did not permit longer leaves of absence.

At this point child care was usually taken over by girls of roughly seven to ten years of age, called *nian'ki*. These girls were the older sisters of the infants, or other workers' daughters who were too young to begin factory work.

Sometimes families that still had ties with the countryside sent to the village for a *nian'ka* from among their relatives or friends.[5] But the help such a young caretaker could provide was often not sufficient. One working woman remembered, "we brought an eight-year-old girl from the village to work as a *nian'ka* for two rubles. But what of it? She was such a young girl, she needed to be looked after as much as the baby."[6] A local newspaper in Ivanovo-Voznesensk noted that many of the working women "are awaited in their lodgings by infants, often left almost completely unattended."[7] Infants in their cradles were kept quiet with pacifiers made of chewed bread mixed with saliva. Many children sickened from these pacifiers; some died from them.[8]

Older children roamed as they wished. One working woman said, "I grew up without any supervision. My mother was at work the whole day, and my brother and I were free; we either sat in Kliaz'ma [the town], or ran in the dusty, dirty street, often hungry. When she got home from work, my mother couldn't always find us, and when she did, she came up to us in horror—our dresses were dirty and torn, our faces smudged."[9] And another working woman, referring to herself and her siblings, said, "we brought ourselves up, from morning to night, in the streets."[10]

The situation of toddlers was worst, for at this age, children could move about on their own but were too young to distinguish dangerous situations.[11] Local newspapers frequently contained items about small children who had been left with insufficient supervision while their mothers were at work.

> One [child—probably a *nian'ka*] kindled a fire in a little iron stove, and then went outdoors. . . . The other child, left alone, began the usual children's pranks, the result of which was that firewood and coal fell out of the oven and burned the floor. The fire spread to the little girl, whose clothes burst into flames.[12]

> On October 15, 1909, after noon in the family dormitory, a four-year-old boy fell through the seat opening of the fourth-floor privy. At the time of the incident, the adults were at work. When the father returned from work and rushed to help, half an hour had already passed, and the little boy was pulled out dead.[13]

Two little boys playing on a sandy slope in the backyard of the barracks were smothered by a small landslide.[14]

Working-class families had great difficulty obtaining food pure enough for infants' delicate digestive systems, since pasteurized milk and refrigeration were not available to provide an alternative to breast-feeding. Only a very small number of factories permitted nursing mothers breaks to return home to feed their babies.[15] The Pirogov Society stressed this factor as a major cause of deaths among working-class children, as did Dr. I. S. Veger of the Society of Moscow Factory Doctors.

Nadezhda Kolesnikova, the daughter of a white-collar employee at a large textile plant, was a continual witness of working-class life as she grew up at the factory. She noted that by the end of each work shift, infants would be famished.

> I used to see the mothers, weavers, when they came out of the shops of the factories in throngs after the whistle blew. Old women and children [nian'ki] with babies in their arms would already be waiting by the gates; the mothers would hurriedly take the babies and begin to breast-feed them as they walked along, while children two and three years old clung to their skirts.[16]

Dr. Veger reported that the reason for the "horrifying" death rate of factory children was "the peculiar conditions of workers' daily life, thanks to which children are deprived of proper feeding at the breast, and are often left completely without milk, fed with whatever comes their way."[17] A Kineshma newspaper report of factory life in the area noted that even feeding with cows' milk was done only until the baby was six to nine months old because of the difficulty of obtaining milk. "Beyond that, the children must become accustomed to the same food adult workers eat."[18]

Inadequate child care and the lack of reliably wholesome food led to an infant and child mortality rate much higher among factory workers than among any other segment of the Russian population in that period.[19] The Pirogov Society study of one textile factory produced the figures in Table 3. It should be kept in mind that this factory had unusually good conditions, permitting women to stay home with their newborn infants for one month after delivery and to take breaks each shift to return home for feedings throughout the first year of the child's life. Thus, the survival rates at this factory were undoubtedly higher than the average among working mothers in the CIR.

TABLE 3

Pregnancies, Miscarriages, Stillbirths, and Infant Mortality

	Mothers Working in Factory				Mothers Not Working in Factory			
	Working more than half their married lives		Working less than half their married lives		Living in factory housing		Peasants living in village	
	Number	% of total pregnancies	Number	% of total pregnancies	Number	% of total pregnancies	Number	% of total pregnancies
Number of women	895	—	196	—	193	—	168	—
Total pregnancies	4,231	100	1,062	100	1,177	100	1,255	100
Miscarriages	116	2.7	16	1.5	27	2.3	24	1.9
Stillbirths	78	1.8	9	0.8	18	1.5	5	0.4
Live births	4,037	95.4	1,037	97.6	1,132	96.2	1,226	97.7
Died before 1 mo. old	296	7.0	83	7.8	64	5.4	60	4.8
Died between 1 mo. and 1 yr.	1,136	27.0	266	25.0	271	23.0	217	17.3
Died between 1 yr. and 3 yrs.	744	18.0	172	16.2	137	11.6	193	15.4
Died beyond 3 yrs.	246	6.0	91	8.6	123	10.5	119	9.5
Still living	1,615	38.2	425	40.0	537	45.6	637	50.8

Source: Pismennyi, "O vliianii fabrichnykh," p. 40.

Among mothers who worked more than half their lives in the factory, only 38.17 percent of the children conceived survived through childhood, as compared with 50.8 percent of children conceived by peasant women. This includes a higher rate of miscarriage and stillbirth, as well as a higher rate of death among the children in every age category given in this survey, except that beyond the age of three.[20]

Thus, the average working woman gave birth to more than twice as many children as survived to adulthood. The working woman E. S. Goriacheva wrote in her memoir, "While I was growing up, I remember, our family was five or six people, there always being two or three little ones. The little ones often died, not living to be a year old. My mother had thirteen children, and only three lived."[21] Another working woman recalled, "I had twelve children, but only two survived."[22] Thus, despite the large number of births, workers' families tended to be rather small. In Moscow in 1897, the average number of people in workers' families was 4.4.[23] Worker-memoirists and informants in other cities also usually gave a figure of two or three children for their own families.[24]

Maternal Responsibility for Children

Among Russian workers, mothers took ultimate responsibility for both the emotional well-being and the financial support of their children. Fathers frequently undermined their families' ability to survive by squandering their wages and free time on drink. Meanwhile, mothers routinely contributed virtually all their earnings to the family, and after work they went home to care for their children, to do the housework, cooking, and laundry, and to develop schemes to obtain their husbands' pay before it was all spent in the local tavern.

Under the best of circumstances, both parents probably contributed all they could to the support of their children. The point is that fathers were not consistent in their contributions to the family's well-being—it was in fact not uncommon for men to go off to find work in another city and then to disappear entirely or to return home only infrequently. Meanwhile, mothers, with virtually no exceptions in my evidence, took responsibility for the support and care of their children even under circumstances when they themselves could not provide that care.

Newspaper stories about local factory life frequently evidenced this pattern of acceptance of responsibility among family members. For example, a piece about a Maslenitsa holiday celebration at the Tomna factory described male workers' group drinking (a standard aspect of every holiday celebration). On their return home, they were met at the factory gate by their furious wives, who berated their spouses with such accusations as "you drunkard, you should fear God—you took the last money, and there's no milk for the baby."[25]

The very different emotional orientations of women and men to their children can be seen in a woman worker's explanation of why she did *not* drink. She had gotten drunk at a party once in the barracks and began dancing wildly. Suddenly her little son "darted out of our *kamorka* and cried, 'Ai, Mama's gone out of her mind!' Then I passed out, though I don't remember it, and when I came to, I was lying on the floor and my children were crying. Well, from that time on, that was enough drinking for me."[26] Since drinking interfered with this woman's ability to take care of her children, she did not need to debate what was the priority.

In short, women's perspective on life, their decisions and actions, were based on the needs of their children. While men often avoided their wives and children, women's lives were focused and shaped around their offspring. A number of memoirs describe mothers' lifetime commitment to their progeny despite their husbands' abandonment, infrequent presence, or other abdication of responsibility. S. N. Rodionova told field ethnographers:

> My father was a metalworker and my mother a weaver. . . . My father was a terrible alcoholic. [He went to St. Petersburg to work] and mostly from that time on he lived in Piter and helped my mother very little. In 1879, once when my father was drunk, he froze outside a tavern. My mother was left a widow with three little children. . . .
>
> Our mother brought us up with great difficulty. . . . [She] worked [at the factory] one shift and then a second shift as a field laborer; she took in laundry, and she washed not only linens, but any kind of rubbish. She washed floors, not just in warm apartments, but also in cold hallways. Our supervisors and foremen depended on her cleaning work, especially on holidays.[27]

The weaver M. A. Khitrovaia had wished as a child to go to the local priest's daughter for schooling. But this would have cost a ruble a month, and "my mother didn't have even one ruble. My father, a worker at the Ozerskaia factory, drank up everything."[28]

Another case, distinguished only by its greater brutality, was reported in *Iaroslavets*. A local factory worker, Mariia Pavlova Maslova, was the mother of four children aged eleven to sixteen.

> Maslova's husband is an inveterate drunkard—for around twenty years he has had no occupation, he goes around barefoot and visits his wife from time to time in order to drink at her expense and at the same time to dispense to her a quantity of hostilities.
>
> Maslova, working in the factory and supporting the whole family, devotes her free time to the upbringing of her children.

Maslova's husband began to suspect her of infidelity, although her children attested to her faithfulness, and he eventually stabbed her to death.[29] This case was more extreme than the average, but its basic vocabulary of male and female responsibility for the family was typical.

This pattern of parental relations with children may have been experienced by many workers who grew up in the countryside as well as those who lived their entire lives near the factory. The working woman Praskov'ia Stepanovna Komarova was born into a peasant family in the village of Starye Bobrovniki in Riazan *guberniia*. When she was seven or eight, her father went to work in Moscow,

> and we were left alone. My father went from place to place, he worked in the calico factories, he went to all the factories. . . . He was a hard drinker. He got into fights, and his legs were dislocated. Our little *izba* [in the village] crumbled, but he didn't send us any money.
>
> My mother bought ten wheelbarrows of bricks [to repair the house] and sent my father a telegram telling him to send some money. He came, bringing ten rubles, but he drank it all that same day.

Komarova's mother then decided she herself would have to go to Moscow to earn money for the family, so she arranged for the children to live with their grandparents.[30] Thus, while neither parent was able to carry out full financial and child care responsibilities, the mother did what she could to arrange for the best alternative possible.

How typical were these cases? Did the majority of men avoid parental obligations to one degree or another? The evidence does not permit a definitive answer. On the one hand, a great bulk of evidence (not limited to any one type of source or political perspective) describes Russian working-class men as drinking to excess, wasting needed family resources, and engaging in wife abuse, often including wifebeating. A 1917 Ivanovo-Voznesensk newspaper article criticizing widespread working-class alcoholism noted that "because of drunkenness, our wives, mothers, and children are left in the streets, barefoot and naked, cold and hungry."[31] A Kostroma newspaper article observed that almost the entire male population of the northwest *uezds* of the *guberniia* went to work in the capital city in the summers. The article was particularly concerned about the bad effect of this practice on family life, for many of the men "completely forget their families, not rendering them any financial support."[32] (This article was referring specifically to trades other than factory work; it is quoted here to indicate how widespread this phenomenon became in some areas.)

On the other hand, a small number of worker memoirists and informants described their fathers as hard-working or having other positive qualities. For example, E. S. Goriacheva described her father, "By himself, he wasn't a bad person—he worked willingly, he tried, he loved truth, and hated tell-tales who reported everything to the boss's assistants, he was cheerful and hospitable." Yet Goriacheva's statement that her father worked willingly was contradicted in her very next sentence:

> He was often fired from the factory for absenteeism—and then my mother would prostrate herself before the old timekeeper Osip Zakharovich Medvedev, begging him to rehire my father at the factory.
>
> My mother, Tat'iana Nikitichna, lived a hard, bitter life with her drunkard-husband. A twelve-hour workday at the factory, the whole day on her feet, wore out all her strength, even though she was a very energetic woman.[33]

Valentina Ivanovna Petrovna recalled her father as

> a good worker. . . . My father was a very good person, kind and simple, but he drank terribly, especially after my mother died. . . . My father was very strict. . . . He was a conscientious worker and taught his son to work—my brother is now a good mechanic. My brother would complain that when my father was teaching him, he [the father] yelled and swore at him [the son] all the time. But on the other hand, he spoiled his children, and loved them so that his children were content.[34]

Rodionova described her husband, the father of their four children, as "conscientious and hard-working, only he drank vodka often and got into fights when he was drunk," and he frequently beat his wife. He also eventually decided he no longer wanted to work, after which Rodionova took over complete support of the children.[35]

Another woman recalled her mother critically; she and her siblings "loved my father more, he didn't yell at us and didn't beat us but my mother beat us half dead."[36] Komissarova recalled her grandfather, who brought her up from the time her parents had to go to work in Moscow. "My grandfather was literate and religious. . . . My grandfather loved me very much and spoiled me. He would to go a tavern and take me with him, and we would drink tea with *baranki*. And he began to wash me and comb my hair. He didn't force me to go to church, only to read prayers. I loved my grandfather more than my mother and father. He never drank and didn't smoke tobacco. We lived very poorly."[37]

It is interesting that even among accounts that attributed positive and lovable qualities to fathers, three of the women also stated that these men drank and were violent and/or irresponsible at times. Thus, it does seem to have been normative for men to drink and often to be irresponsible toward their wives and children. However, the partial deviations from this general rule, and the positive qualities attributed by some women to their fathers, make it clear that many variations on the culturally dominant theme existed, as did exceptions to it. Although men on the whole tended to be less involved and less caring toward young children than were women, some men were as much or more so than some women. Yet this did not negate the general pervasiveness of the predominant culturally defined sex roles.

The example of the mother who beat her children "half dead" may also represent one extreme of the range of female personalities: mothers whose determination to ensure the survival of their families (and perhaps their own aggression and anger) made them overly severe taskmasters. The working woman Praskov'ia Komarova remembered her mother—who had been effectively abandoned to poverty by her alcoholic husband—as just such a demanding overseer of the family's work and earnings. Each day after Komarova had finished her other chores, her mother "forced me to spin, I wanted to sleep, but Mother forced me to work."[38]

However, it apparently was not a cultural norm for mothers to mistreat their children: I found only these two examples. Most mothers were intensely involved with and committed to their children, but the precise nature of individual relationships, whether strict or affectionately lenient, varied according to particular personalities and life circumstances.

Female Abandonment of Children

One historian who argues that lower-class women did not love their children until recent times uses as a major piece of evidence the abandonment of children by lower-class women.[39] The evidence on Russian working-class women's abandonment of their children is intriguingly contradictory. On the one hand, none of the workers' memoirs or oral histories I found described a mother leaving her children except when she had to go to the city to earn money for the family and therefore arranged for the children to be brought up by relatives. On the other hand, newspapers from time to time carried stories about abandoned infants who were left anonymously at orphanages, churches, and less promising locations. A Yaroslavl newspaper noted, "It has recently been noticed that the abandonment of children within the city limits has increased"; the city's zemstvo-run orphanage was becoming overcrowded as a result.[40] In Kineshma, private citizens established an orphanage to aid "unfortunate children abandoned by their mothers and mothers who do not know what to do with their children (whether as a result of difficult conditions of life or other reasons)."[41]

How can we explain the differences between workers' recollections and newspaper reports? Newspapers of course covered all of the area's inhabitants, including the most destitute and ill-fated. Workers' recollections of their parents, on the other hand, could be written or recounted only by those who had survived relatively unscathed to adulthood. Russian orphanages and foundling homes were institutions, after all, probably similar to or worse than the ones studied by Rene Spitz and other twentieth-century psychologists, who found that children who had lived in orphanages *beginning in infancy* were at high risk for severe retardation in their social, linguistic, and motor development.[42] Many or most babies abandoned by their mothers at Russian institutions undoubtedly had no better prognosis. Thus, it appears that the kind of care mothers gave their infants in Russian working-class communities was for most people almost a prerequisite for survival into normal adulthood. In contrast, many worker-memoirists and informants recorded that their fathers abandoned them or behaved irresponsibly toward them. Hence it seems very likely that the type of care mothers typically provided in Russian working-class culture was indispensable to normal development of most children, but that provided by fathers was not.

The newspaper accounts do not record the marital status of women who abandoned their children. However, because most of the abandoned children were infants, I suspect that the overwhelming majority of their mothers had become pregnant out of wedlock. I also suspect that the small proportion of married women who abandoned their children had fallen into such extreme poverty that they could not provide financial support, and had no other extended family members to turn to for help; they left their children only in cases of extraordinary desperation.[43] Men, on the other hand, abdicated responsibility for their children much more casually and frequently and, the evidence suggests, sometimes when they were able but simply unwilling to render financial support.

The circumstances of abandonment or irresponsible behavior also differed by sex: when married men abdicated their obligations, they knew their children were still receiving attention from their mothers. They withdrew their aid openly, often with rancor and without shame.

Most married women, on the other hand, do not seem to have left their children to others' care when they could provide it themselves. Married or unmarried, women often took their babies to a place, such as an orphanage or church, where they hoped decent care might be provided. The mother almost always acted in secrecy, undoubtedly partly because the law was much more likely to hold mothers than fathers accountable for child abandonment. But it also suggests that most women who abandoned infants did so only with a tremendous sense of shame, a feeling that they were violating profound maternal responsibilities and thus had to hide their actions from those around them, and perhaps from themselves as well.

The only life history I found by a working woman who had given up her infant to a foundling home expresses the tremendous grief, rage, and regret she felt even years afterward. This woman, Golubeva, became pregnant out of wedlock. Unable to support the baby, she was advised to give it up to a foundling home,[44] which she did.

> The system there was an atrocity: they took the baby from the mother and gave her a receipt with the condition that the mother could not return for it earlier than ten years later. . . . [A] working woman had to wait ten years before she could find out what became of her son or daughter. You can imagine how this tore a mother's heart: she didn't have the means to keep her child at home, and it was also forbidden for her to ask after the child.

As soon as the February Revolution occurred, although there was yet another year to go of the ten-year waiting period, Golubeva went to find her child at the foundling home: her most deeply felt wish and expectation of the new revolutionary regime was that she would be able to recover her child.

> I went to the home. I showed them my receipt and they looked in their records and told me "your baby lived only three months and then died."
> So you see what kind of monsters they were, they didn't even notify the child's own mother about her baby's death for nine years.[45]

Golubeva's testimony hardly squares with Shorter's assumption that the mother who gave up her children was callous and unloving. There may have been some small minority of working women who had the material capacity to care for their children but abandoned them nonetheless, for whatever reasons. If so, such women were not behaving according to the norms of their culture, as the historians of maternal indifference portray women who abandoned children. Rather, they were deviants from the typical role of mothers in Russian working-class communities.

Emotional Relationships Between Parents and Children

Russian working women's involvement with their children went beyond taking responsibility for the difficult job of child rearing. That they loved their children is demonstrated in working women's memoirs and in the songs (lullabies, etc.) they sang to their children as they cared for them.

That mothers formed a loving bond with their children is an important aspect of my argument. The profound emotional cast of this bond—so much a part of women's socialized identity from their own childhood onward—focused their lives so unquestioningly on their children's immediate daily needs that women's capacity to form peer bonds, which in the long run might have served to improve their own and their children's lives more, atrophied. Commitments deeply felt as a central focus of one's identity are often unavailable for rational reassessment when conditions change, including during revolutionary upheaval. Ironically, the purely instrumental approach to child care which some recent historians claim existed might have led to a more rational assessment of the benefits of organizing—if it had actually existed. But, at least for Russian workers, the mother's bond to her children was formed over a lifetime of rituals and other folklore, making that bond the profoundly felt center of her sense of identity.

Some historians of the family believe that parents did not love their children before child mortality rates were reduced by modern medicine, because young children were so likely to die that emotional investment in any particular child would have been risky.[46] As we have seen, the mortality rate among working-class children in the CIR was very high. Yet, although I agree that the likely possibility of death may have had some deleterious effect on parents' emotional relationships with their children, the evidence for the Russian working class does not support the view that parents therefore did not love their children. Mothers in particular did not react to their offspring's difficulties with indifference, but rather with compassion and sometimes desperation. A working woman, Kiseleva, recalled, "I had eleven children, but only three grew up. You'd go off to the factory, but there was anxiety in your soul, your heart always ached for your children."[47]

We saw the fury with which food-rioting women responded when their children went hungry. We saw also the passionate sense of loss experienced by Golubeva, who had to give up her child to a foundling home. Occasional newspaper stories also provide evidence regarding working women's emotional orientation toward their children. For example, the emotional, rather than purely task-oriented, involvement of mothers in caring for their infants' physical needs is evidenced in a *Kineshemets* article. Very few of the local inhabitants had cows. As a result, so many workers tried to buy milk from those owning cows that some had to be turned away despite their frequent "tearful entreaties." Working women "appear for milk a day or more in advance with the request that some be set aside for them, if even just a tiny bit, and even offering money in advance. The owner of the cow is sometimes left without milk himself if he doesn't have the strength to refuse a crying mother who has a nursing child and offers to pay any amount of money if only he will give her some milk."[48] Such stories indicate that mothers did not react to the tremendous difficulties of child rearing with an absence of feeling, but quite the contrary, with heartache and a strong, often deeply felt, commitment to do all they could to meet their children's needs.

Proverbs also testify to mothers' emotional involvement with their children. For example,

[When] the child's finger hurts, the mother's heart hurts.

A mother weeps for her child by the bucket, not by the cup.

Your own fool is dearer than another's smart child.

143

To everyone else, [her child is like] a swamp, but to a mother, [her child is like] gold.

Your children are bad, but all the same they're dear.[49]

Folklore forms an important type of evidence regarding the intimate relationships between parents and children among largely illiterate populations such as the Russian working class.[50] This is true partly because other forms of evidence relating to workers' behavior cannot always give an accurate picture of the emotional coloring of such relationships. Much of Russian workers' *behavior* was dictated by the harsh conditions of their lives. If we look only at behavior—such as women leaving their children inadequately cared for when they went to work—we may tend to assume that workers did not love their children. But a quick glance at a sampling of the over one hundred lullabies and other songs I found recorded (half collected before the revolution, the rest afterward from elderly workers recalling their prerevolutionary lives) immediately makes it clear that mothers cherished their children. Mothers rocking their babies in cradles sang with tremendous tenderness: there was no other interpersonal relationship portrayed in all of Russian working-class folklore as more exquisitely sweet or devoted than this.

I put my little son down to sleep
In a cozy bed, in a cozy bed
In a feathery comforter
On a downy pillow.
I myself will go out to walk
To gather flowers for you [i.e., the son she's singing to]
And weave garlands
I'll weave garlands for your head.[51]

Mothers nurtured their children, wishing for physical growth:

Sleep, dear little son, by night
And grow by the hour.[52]

Mothers lovingly indulged their children:

Sleep baby, until noon,
And after noon we'll have a good time.
[Then] sleep til evening—
Little children don't have to do anything.

And how you'll sleep til morning
I'll awaken you myself.[53]

When the physical needs of the children in lullabies were met, the interchange was never purely functional. There was always a strong element of pleasure delightedly shared with the child as well. Food rarely appeared in children's folklore as everyday fare, but rather as special delicacies.

Ah, rockabye, rockabye
We ate our fill of *kalach* [a fancy bread],
If only we had a little piece of gingerbread
For Vasia to feast on.[54]

Cradles in lullabies were not made of plain everyday materials, but were almost always described as gold and velvet. Clothing was "red calico," "velveteen," "Moroccan boots," "a new fur coat," and so on. Mothers' awareness of and delight in their children's feelings is conveyed in these songs; for example, the pride felt by a toddler wearing "grown-up" clothing:

My little son is barely bigger than a felt boot
When he dresses in his felt boots, he swells up
    with pride.[55]

Mothers also sang a special type of song to their children when they had fallen down or hurt themselves in some other way. That mothers had such songs to comfort their children makes it clear that mothers attended to their children's emotional as well as their physical needs. For example,

How our Little Ninka has new boots
Ninaka knows how to put them on
And run and skip
And catch up to her brother.
There's a hole in the road,
Nina fell right in it very hard.
She fell and cried a lot.
But all the child's tears passed
In an instant there were dreams again
She runs and skips and catches up to her brother.[56]

Because the Russian working-class mother was singing about herself and her child, she was using her songs to express her feelings to her child. Unlike other

145

forms of literary evidence, these are not just *characters* claiming to love children, but an actual *act* of love by the real-life mother singing the comforting song or the lullaby. As such, these songs are windows through which we may look into an intimate emotional relationship between two real people, a type of evidence rarely available to social historians. Lullabies and comfort songs are direct evidence of a loving, caring emotional communication between mother and child. That mothers continued to cherish their children as they grew up is demonstrated by their loving portrayal of their older offspring in other types of songs, which are examined in a subsequent chapter.

Of course, Russian working women could not provide loving care for their children during those hours when they were away at the factory. But folklore gives strong evidence that mothers did provide love when they could be physically close to their children. It also presents a clue to understanding how these women, burdened with a double work day, found time to nurture their children. Via folklore such as lullabies, mothers often combined a utilitarian task with communication of caring and concern. Since folklore is verbal, a mother could convey love to her child through singing, while her hands were engaged in other tasks.

Historians who assume that women who left their children for work did not love them have been blind to the fact that in other cultures women have more often worked than not, and thus have developed different arrangements that more or less satisfactorily permitted them to express their love and serve their children's developmental needs. Folklore was probably an important—though certainly not the only—aspect of the arrangements made by Russian working women to do this. It was precisely the strength of Russian working-class mothers' love for and commitment to their children that fired their resistance to unfavorable conditions during the 1917 revolution.

What made women so steadfast in their commitment to their children? Why did women not follow their husband's example and ignore their children's daily needs? To begin to answer this question, let us turn to the subject of sex role socialization, which began to differ markedly for girls and boys around the age of seven or eight.

TEN

Late Childhood and Adolescence: Girls' and Boys' Paths Diverge

The basic bond of the early childhood years was between the mother and child of either sex. As girls and boys reached the age of seven or eight, they began to take on new social ties assigned to them by sex. As girls moved through adolescence, they remained in a social environment that permitted them to retain access to the nurturing, empathic, highly personal modes of interaction that they experienced in their early childhoods. As early as age six or seven, girls were given responsibility for taking care of younger children while their mothers were away at the factory. Soon they also began taking part in rituals that focused each girl's attention on her future role as wife and mother.

Boys, on the other hand, were raised to deny their memory of nurturant, empathic modes of interaction. At the age of seven or eight, boys began to be drawn out of the female domain. Their fathers began to take them along to card games, introducing them to the male world, whose concerns and mores were very different from those of early childhood. Boys were initiated into the social pursuits of drinking and fighting as well. While girls were encouraged to retain the values of nurturance from their childhood, male social organization inhibited men's longing for nurturance by proclaiming a male ideal of aggression and violence, particularly toward women and the loving intimacy they represented.

From childhood through married life, this intricate and by no means natural passage into adult social and psychological relationships was engineered by community customs. One of the major tools of this community engineering was folklore—yearly rituals as well as various types of songs—that were usually gender- and age-specific. Another such tool was the assignment of sex-segregated tasks to girls and boys.

Girls

Late Childhood

Although Russian working-class girls and boys began to engage in gender-specific activities similar to those of adult women and men, the child was by no means considered an adult at this point. His or her new tasks constituted training for adult roles, full responsibility for which would not be adopted for many years. This training period was transitional, and there is evidence that it was not always smooth or easy.

For girls, this period entailed learning adult women's household work by, in effect, serving as their mothers' apprentices. From seven or eight years of age, the girl learned to sew and knit; she was trained to do housework.[1] The most important aspect of a girl's apprenticeship at this age was taking care of younger children, either her own siblings or the children of other working women whom she was paid to look after. A girl performing this job was called a *nian'ka* or *niania*. The working woman E. S. Goriacheva recalled, "from the age of eight or nine years, my parents gave me out to be a *nian'ka* to neighbors. They only paid me a few half-kopeks, but even this was a help to my family." Goriacheva wanted her parents to send her to school instead, but her "father and mother said: 'girls have no reason to go to school. You're going to work in a factory, not an office.' " She continued to work as a *nian'ka* until the age of twelve, when she entered the local weaving factory. "I don't remember my childhood," she said. "I guess I didn't have one."[2]

The working woman Rodionova said that her older sister began to work as a *nian'ka* at the age of six. As a little girl, Rodionova herself, along with her mother, had aspired to school, but when her sister began work at the factory, only Rodionova was left to look after their younger brother, so she too became a *nian'ka*.[3] P. Sleptsovaia had also hoped for schooling, but when she was eight years old, her mother "broke her leg and she was in bed all winter," so Sleptsovaia became *niania* to her five-year-old sister and ten-month-old brother.[4]

Working women who spent all or part of their childhood in peasant villages also typically worked as *nian'ki*. K. S. Ovsiannikova, a factory spinner, grew up in a village in Riazan *guberniia*. "Mother had to go to Moscow and she lived there for a long time in domestic service. I moved from one aunt to another, and I took care of [*nian'chila*] children, washed floors, and helped in the fields."[5] A description of child care in a rural area of the Central Industrial Region (CIR) stated, "children and youths are left to their own devices a large part of the time. An old woman or an older daughter in the family usually looks after them; the daughter is therefore called '*niania*' by her younger brothers and sisters. Often this *niania* is older than the other children by only two or three years."[6]

Need for additional family income, or for someone to take care of the youngest children while the adults earned a living, often forced girls to embark on their child care careers before they were old enough to handle the job. This left a residue of anger and guilt in some of them even after they had reached adulthood. Rodionova, unable to obtain hoped-for schooling when she alone was left at home to take care of her younger brother while her older sister went to work in the factory, remarked with ill-concealed hostility years later that her older sister hadn't been much of a *niania* anyway: "You see what kind of a *niania* she was, she twisted the child's leg. . . . [H]e didn't walk until he was seven years old, his legs were like rubber. . . . He was lame his whole life."[7] A. S. Mozzhenkovaia as an adult still felt responsible for the death of her toddler sister, Mania, for whom she became *niania* at age five. The emotions engendered by it affected her powerfully:

[Mania] died because of me; I wasn't looking, and Mania put her head into a cast-iron tub and fell into the water. Before they dragged her out she had choked. I remember she lay in the house for twelve days, and a terrible smell hung in the air. And all because the police officer didn't come to register the death for a long time. . . .[8]

Some girls were hired to help with domestic chores other than child care. Valentina Ivanovna Petrovna took care of her infant half-brother, but "after six months, the baby died. I was twelve then, and I began to help the charwoman who was hired by the workers to clean the barracks; from her I earned one ruble, fifty kopeks a month."[9] At the age of six, V. N. Tiurina began to do the food shopping for an elderly woman, and to carry water to her house from the river.[10]

Thus, at a very young age, girls were (sometimes reluctantly) beginning to make a service and/or financial contribution to the well-being of their families. The work girls did at this age was almost always centered around families, children, and domestic tasks. Although girls were in training for their future roles as adults, they had not departed from the sphere in which they had always been located physically and emotionally. They remained in the home, their own or one belonging to someone else very much like their own mother. And they remained within the caretaker-infant dyad, having simply switched roles. It was this phenomenon of remaining within the home, concerned with domestic tasks, especially child rearing, that above all distinguished girls' activities at this age from boys'.

Adolescence

The work life of working-class adolescents in the Central Industrial Region's textile and other light industry factories was much the same for girls and for boys: both were expected to work in the factories, and to begin work at roughly the same age. Table 4 shows that in Moscow *guberniia*, for example, almost identical percentages of male and female textile workers began work in each age category, most between twelve and seventeen. A number of working women's memoirs and oral histories recount how they falsified birth certificates and used other techniques in order to be hired before they reached the legal minimum age. Klavdiia Ukolova, for example, recalled that when she was fourteen, "They added a year to my real age, and I worked at the factory like an adult."[11] Thus, it is likely children began to work at a younger age than official statistics indicate.

TABLE 4

Age of Beginning Work, Female and Male Workers of Cotton-Spinning and Weaving Factories, Moscow Guberniia (1908)
(24,884 women and 19,495 men)

Age	Men (%)	Women (%)	Total (%)
To age 10	3.5	1.7	2.6
10-12	5.8	3.2	4.3
12-15	28.0	25.7	26.7
15-17	37.2	41.8	39.8
17-20	10.8	10.8	10.8
20-25	6.3	8.0	7.3
25-30	4.3	3.9	4.1
30 and over	4.1	4.9	4.5

Source: Rashin, *Formirovanie rabochego klass Rossii*, p. 275.

Factory work played a minimal role in creating the very different gendered behavior patterns of girl and boy adolescents. We must avoid a "vulgar Marxist" concentration on income-earning work alone as the basis for consciousness if we are to understand the differences between male and female bonding patterns in everyday life and through the political activity of 1917. Married women had a second, equally demanding job, after all: childrearing and housework. And unmarried women prepared psychologically for this future second job in their after-work hours. In fact, it was leisure-time activities, not factory work, which differed greatly for adolescent girls and boys and which were largely responsible for structuring the different bonding patterns and commitments of each sex.

Leisure-Time Activities of Teenage Girls

Throughout the year there were a number of holiday rituals that young unmarried women celebrated together.[12] These rituals played an important role in socializing female adolescents' mindsets and bonding commitments. They were very similar to rituals which had been celebrated among the peasantry for centuries. They focused on each participant's future husband and, sometimes, on her future children as well. Thus, although the rituals were performed by groups of girls together, they did not elaborate and strengthen the girls' sense of group solidarity with one another. Rather, the group celebration served the dual purpose of strengthening *each young woman's* commitment to her own future nuclear family, and clarifying *the group's* understanding that each woman's husband and children were a higher priority than was any female friendship group. These rituals were celebrated in groups (as opposed to by individual girls within their own families, for example) to establish in all the girls' minds an understanding of their *lack* of claim to first place in their friends' priorities. Had each girl's commitment to her future family been reinforced privately rather than in groups, the *group* would not have learned the appropriate respect for other women's commitments to husbands and children.

In fact, because marriage was patrilocal the group of adolescent friends may have at least partly dispersed within a few years, as each young woman and/or some of her friends followed their husbands to live elsewhere after marriage. Whether or not a given group dispersed, their adolescent rituals prepared them to (metaphorically or literally) say goodbye to each other upon marriage, rather than preparing them to bond for life.

Fortune-telling

The yearly round of rituals began with New Year fortune-telling. Starting on the New Year and ending on Epiphany (January 6), groups of unmarried girls got together to engage in fortune-telling of many kinds, the primary purpose of which was to make predictions about the identity and character of each woman's future husband. Such fortune-telling occurred throughout the year as well. One source documents unmarried women telling their fortunes nightly in Vladimir textile factory dormitories through the 1920s.[13]

Girls used many different methods of fortune-telling (I found seventeen described by participants).[14] For example, at night a group of girls would look into mirrors lit only by a candle and would "see" their future husbands; girls would write names of boys on pieces of paper, which they placed under their pillows, and whomever each dreamed about would be her husband; groups of girls would eavesdrop under windows or call into bathhouses at midnight to get clues interpreted as information about future husbands; each girl put her finger through the looped handle of a sieve. If she would be married soon, the sieve would turn on her finger.

Working women believed that fortune-telling was an accurate predictor of a woman's future. Tiurina said, "On the New Year, we were coming home from work, and I went up to a guy and asked him, 'What's your name?' I asked him at a crossroads [a standard way of telling fortunes]. He answered accurately, giving my [future] husband's name."[15]

Rodionova's aunt told her fortune at night using a mirror and candles. She was in a room where men were sleeping on the platform near the ceiling. "I had just sat down to tell my fortune . . . when all the chimney flues started to clang." The girl took this as a sign that the future held danger for her and, terrified, "I leapt behind the men on the platform as fast as I could, and left the mirror behind." In the words of one song girls sang while pouring melted wax into water (another method of fortune-telling), "For whom we pour the wax,/ Her fate will be revealed/ And she cannot escape it."[16]

In addition to responding to young women's curiosity about their future spouses, I suspect that fortune-telling also helped *cause* that curiosity. As younger girls watched their older sisters engage in the excitement and mystery of fortune-telling—and as they themselves grew up to enter the magically enticing, slightly dangerous realm of mirrors, candles, midnight appeals to bathhouses, and sanctioned eavesdropping—their emotional attention gradually became more and more focused on the object of all this razzle-dazzle. Fortune-telling contained many references to sexuality,[17] intensifying girls' excitement about their future husbands. Thus, the emotional bonding commitment of women to their husbands was underwritten by the most powerful element of human bonding, sexuality.

The very notion of fortune-telling—an activity designed to predict the identity and character of one particular person—focused teenage girls' developing sexuality not toward men in general, but toward one specific man. This is in sharp contrast to the channeling of male sexuality, which was toward women, but—with a minimal exception during actual courtship—not toward their future wives in particular. Young men were also to be married soon, and yet they did not indulge either in fortune-telling about their future brides, or any other equivalent practice. Indeed, in comparison, young men were quite incurious about the particular women in their marital futures.

Fortune-telling was done by groups of women together. But because the focus of each woman's attention was far less on her girlfriends than on her future husband, fortune-telling did less to strengthen women's solidarity than it did to strengthen each participant's commitment to a bond outside the group. As each woman's commitment to her future husband was supported and particularized, the importance of the all-female group receded: it existed only to facilitate each woman's search for her own man.

Annunciation

The next yearly ritual for young unmarried women was on March 25, Annunciation. According to Rodionova, it "was considered more important than Easter."[18] For girls, the main element of this holiday was that they were forbidden to braid their hair. The working woman Kokushkina described the ritual: "On Annunciation day, all the girls didn't braid their hair, because, it was said, 'The little bird doesn't weave its nest, and the girl doesn't plait her hair.' This was a sad holiday: it was forbidden to have fun or dance or sing. Only the guys had freedom [razdol'e]. The guys set birds free. They kept the birds in a cage for several days before Annunciation day: they held them, and then they let them go."[19]

The long single braid worn by unmarried Russian women workers and peasants was called her "maiden freedom"; married women traditionally wore their hair parted, half pinned up on each side of the head over the ears. Brides parting their hair for the first time, doing away with their single braid forever, sang ritual wedding laments mourning the loss of their freedom.[20] Thus, Annunciation may have been in essence a rehearsal for the wedding ceremony and the loss of freedom that marriage implied for women.

Annunciation is the day on which angels were said to have brought Mary the news that she would give birth to Jesus. It seems likely that the full implication of the Annunciation day observance among Russian working-class women was the surrender of "maiden freedom" in order to take on the demanding responsibility of child bearing and rearing. There were both responsibility and reward implied in the ritual: the Russian word for the Annunciation holiday is Blagoveshchenie, literally "prophesy of blessing," the blessing being, of course, the news of the birth of the baby Jesus. For boys, in contrast, this holiday encouraged a carefree attitude rather than responsibility as they "had freedom" and freed caged birds.

Semik

Perhaps the most important young women's ritual occurred in the seventh week after Easter, on Semik Thursday (*sem'* is "seven" in Russian) and the following Sunday, Trinity Day. Among both peasants and workers, the Semik-Trinity Sunday holiday was a girls' ritual centered around cutting, decorating, and parading with a young birch tree. The decorations were ribbons and wreathes made of grass and flowers by the young women, and placed over the birch branches. In factory areas, young women brought decorated birch trees into their factories and barracks, and danced with them in the streets. Rodionova recalled setting birches on the frames of textile machines and dancing during work in the factory. Kokushkina said that in the barracks, "in the rooms and corridors—everywhere we stuck birch trees." At the end of the celebration, the girls took the wreathes from the tree and threw them into a lake or river to tell their fortunes. If the wreath sank, it meant the girl would die or not get married that year; if the wreath floated, the year would be fortunate or she would get married. Little girls had their own separate, somewhat abbreviated Semik celebration.[21]

Young women ate traditional foods on Semik-Trinity. Rodionova reported, "On Semik we made fried eggs, baked unleavened *kozul'ki* [a local type of bread], and made fancy pastry."[22] Tiurina recalled, "[On Semik] we . . . collected about thirty or forty kopeks from each person. . . . We got together about ten people. 'How much should we each chip in?' 'A ruble.' 'What should we buy?' 'Wine.' "[23]

Throughout the Semik celebration, the young women sang traditional songs. The content of these songs made almost no reference to the group of girlfriends. Rather, couched in terms of the enduring beauties of nature, the songs helped each young woman prepare for her own marriage.

Although this was a merry holiday, many of the songs the young women sang and danced to were about very painful realities of married women's lives. Addressing these realities in an atmosphere of fun and celebration helped the young women begin to confront and develop their capacity to cope with them.

On the one hand, marriage was made to seem enticing and exciting because many of the Semik-Trinity songs dealt poetically with sex and fertility. Common images were of green gardens, raspberry bushes, meadows, rivers, flowers, and handsome young men enticing unmarried women out of *terems* (the women's quarters in ancient Russia). The most characteristic Semik image was of garlands placed around or hops growing up and around support poles, the word for which in Russian comes from the verb "to poke."[24] The girls sang about hops encircling support poles as they themselves did a round dance around the birch tree. This, as well as the girls' placing their wreathes around the birch, were all symbols of sexual intercourse.

On the other hand, women were told to expect pain in marriage. A number of the Semik songs dealt with men's unreliability in love. A song sung as the girls paraded with the birch tree, for example, begins with what appears to be a standard romantic story:

A maiden garlanded hops—
A young man paid court to her.

[Refrain]:
  See the cranberry bush, see the raspberry bush!

A merchant from the valley below,
A dashing, fine lad.

He lifted the girl in his arms, . . .

He seated her in his ship,
He unfurled the fine sail, . . .

He set the ship toward the sea.

The ship . . . cuts through the water toward the shore. . . .

Toward a green meadow.

Here, the romantic fantasy was suddenly shattered, for

On that meadow
A[nother] girlfriend has waited three years.

"I have waited with difficulty
To throw my arms around his dear neck. . . .

Alone, I cried rivers of tears.

Akh, you, my dearest,
Why are you walking with another? . . ."

Although women must not expect men to be faithful, women were not to allow themselves equivalent latitude. As the young women garlanded the birch tree, they sang another song which instructed them not to fall in love with married men:

The young little (female) nightingale
Flew out of the garden; . . .

She cursed her fate. . . .

"Accursed is the fate,
Of one who loves a married man, . . .

A single fellow is a good man,
But a married one is like a beast."[25]

Yet other Semik songs made it clear women should not expect their husbands to be faithful to them in return.

As the girls garlanded the birch tree, they sang a song very similar to married women's laments (examined below) over the loss of their husbands' love:

. . . My little canary!

. . . free little bird,
Chase away my grief.

My grief is known to everyone
My darling left me. . . .

He didn't say goodbye,
That means he forgot about me. . . .

I'll say a few words
To the free little bird in flight

A few little words in secret:
"Fly to my darling!

Alight on a leafy apple tree
On a green branch

Sing to him [the departed beloved] . . .,

157

All about my fate. . . ."

Bitter fate of mine! . . .

What have you brought me to! . . .

To disgrace, to shame.

There was a dear time—
When I used to pick berries with my darling.

But now what has happened,
How did I come to be left alone?[26]

Another painful issue confronted in Semik songs was the loss at marriage, mandated by patrilocal tradition, of the young woman's close bond to her family of origin. This loss of her childhood protectors was recognized as a terrible, painful time of transition for brides, and was also dealt with in depth during the marriage rituals. The shift of patrilocal residence at marriage was often expressed as the bride's crossing a river to her new home. In the following Semik song, a new bride eagerly makes beer in preparation for her father's visit to her new home across the river.

How the hops twine beyond the river. . . . [the bride's childhood home]

On our side [of the river: her home of marriage]. . . .

What a big farmstead there is,
A silver support-pole . . .,

Gar-garlands of gold. . . .

I, a bride, will walk to the green garden. . . .

I, a bride, will pick a batch of hops. . . .

I, a bride, will boil beer
Heady beer,

I will invite a guest to visit me
A dear guest . . .,

My own father.

Yet despite her excited preparations for her father's visit, the young wife could never keep him on her side of the river for long—for, like many other songs (including the one at the beginning of Part Two), this one conveyed the culturally mandated prescription that parents curtail their emotional attachments to their daughters after the daughters' marriages.

"Really, father mine,
You visit rarely
[And] you don't visit for long!

You stay only one night
And you pine [for home] the whole time!

In the chamber you lie down to sleep,
Close-close to the window!

You open the window,
You wish for dawn!"

[Father speaking] "But why is there no light so long,
For so long it doesn't—doesn't grow light!"[27]

Thus, the young woman celebrating Semik rehearsed her father's culturally prescribed eagerness to return to his own side of the river, where he was the patriarch, and his unwillingness to spend time with his daughter after her marriage. This loss of parental investment was a traumatic transition for real-life working-class women, and confronting it during the adolescent ritual of Semik helped women begin to develop the capacity to tolerate it.

Countering all the negative aspects of marriage for women were the portrayals of its exciting aspects, above all the sexy young man the girl hoped to marry. For example, as the young women danced in a circle around the birch tree, untwining the ribbons, they sang,

Twine, climb, dear little hops,
To the top, along the support pole! . . .

To the very tippy top . . .

In my garden
Wide expanse . . .

There walks and dances

A dashing, good young man. . . .

Another song the young women sang as they danced together was

You major, my major
My young major!

From the Hussars' Regiment
A sharp saber at your side

Shiakifer [probably a helmet] with a feather,
A golden eagle upon it,

Your attire is all costly,
Your epaulets golden

Epaulets with portraits,
Boots with spurs.

The major walks along the street,
With his spurs shining smartly.

This gorgeous young major whispered a proposal to the maiden Masha, who quickly slipped out of her *terem* to get water at the river—the only way a young woman could traditionally escape her parents' watchful eyes to meet her boyfriend. The song then shifted to a poetic portrayal of the girls' desire for sex, as the water has been muddied by (a symbolic representation of) the Hussar major. Masha sang

Come, mud, come, mire,
Come, muddied water. . . .

Go away, fresh water, from here!

She swung wide,
She drew deeply.

Having "drawn deeply" of the Hussar's "muddied water," Masha metaphorically shouldered responsibility for the concomitants of sex (marriage and children).

She raised [her yoke] onto her shoulders

And walked to the mountain.[28]

(Rivers were often used to indicate marriage in Russian folklore, while mountains represented difficult life obstacles.[29]) Thus, Masha took on the heavy burdens of marriage by herself.

In summary, although young women celebrated Semik together as a group, the ritual did not work to forge the women into a solidarity group capable of taking collective action in its own interest. Rather, the group rehearsal of the painful experiences each woman would later suffer on her own (perhaps far away from these childhood friends) seems designed to make women expect solitary suffering: not to react by taking concerted action to alleviate their grievances, but to accept them without outrage. Each woman was taught to accept her own *and her friends'* suffering. Thus, Semik did not unite its participants. It prepared each to divide off from the company of her peers to cleave to her future family and her own, private grief.

The trappings of all adolescent girls' rituals—the mystery and hocus-pocus surrounding fortune-telling, the beauty of the celebrations, and the symbolism of songs and rites—worked to shape women's bonding commitments at a very deep and enduring emotional level. The associations, for example, between wreathes of flowers and women's sexuality, or between women's fertility and the fertility of all of nature's growing things, may have made women feel part of the grand drama of nature and its eternal cycles, with a sense of enduring and continuing whatever the surrounding practical difficulties.

That much of the socialization which took place in these rituals occurred via metaphoric communication rather than direct instruction aided women's development of prescribed adult emotions and of nurturing skills. But it did not encourage or assist their rational understanding of their situation as married women, or their ability to analyze and change it when necessary. Thus, women's commitment to their most important (as defined by their culture) role in life, that of wife and mother, was made and strengthened through rituals that had a purely emotional cast, rather than in a setting which also encouraged rational consideration and decision-making. Herein lay a barrier to women's liberation when the issue was raised during the revolutionary period.

Girls Perform Chastushki

Teenage girls who worked in factories spent part of their leisure time performing *chastushki*. Girls sang these songs "at work, in the street, at outdoor fetes, at gatherings, at evening parties."[30] One folklore collector described a factory settlement in the first years of the twentieth century: "all the factory youth had poured out into the street. Some strolled around in groups; others, gathering in small groups . . . sang songs. And these songs were special factory songs. . . . The factory has produced a particular form of song, the *chastushka*."[31]

Chastushki were short, usually four-line, songs performed by unmarried youths before informal audiences of their peers. The group typically formed a circle, with individual youths moving by turns into the center to dance and sing, displaying their virtuosity at producing on-the-spot entertainment.

Sometimes two or more performers would compete against one another, trying to outdo the others in "amazing the audience with some new dance step or with new *chastushki*."[32] The *chastushka* had a standard form and usually some standard introductory lines, often regarding culturally prescribed sex roles, but the performer composed the all-important punch lines: that is, the resolution of the problem raised in the introduction. I suspect that, on one level, *chastushki* served as a test of mastery of culturally appropriate sex roles, a sort of "complete the sentence" quiz of each participant's absorption of the "proper" attitudes.

Both boys and girls performed *chastushki* in a similar fashion, but the content differed dramatically by gender. Girls' *chastushki* were preoccupied with "love, jealousy, fights with her boyfriend, separation [of lovers] with all shades of associated feelings."[33] For example, in one *chastushka*, a young woman describes very specifically the young man of her dreams. She has already narrowed her romantic longings to one boy whose distinguishing characteristics are a beautiful voice and heavenly taste in clothes.

My sweetheart wears a white shirt
Just like an angel from the heavens,
He'll begin to sing "Golden Hills"
No one has a better voice.

Girls' *chastushki* were often concerned with differentiating the beloved from all other men. This singer advertises her fancy for a boy who is the proud possessor of curly hair and a watch chain.

I loved in a yellow house
He has a watch chain
We had a happy conversation
He has curly hair.[34]

Because the choice of love object was so specific, and the chosen one supposedly so uniquely worthy of love, loss of a boyfriend was seen as a devastating blow, one from which the girl could not recover. In this "testing" song, the second girl passes with flying colors when she describes a culturally accepted response to losing her romantic partner.

First girl: Dear friend Katia
                Tell me your secret:
                When you parted with your sweetheart
                Did your heart beat or not?

Second girl: Dear friend Zhenia,
                I'll tell only you
                When I parted with my sweetheart
                My heart beat painfully.

Another *chastushka* shows what the culture considered an appropriate response on the part of a woman whose boyfriend was unfaithful. The first young woman presents a statement having the quality of a "True or False" quiz. The second girl gives a "False" response to gain the approval of the judges, her peers.

First girl: Akh, dear girlfriend,
                What are you upset about?
                So what if he was unfaithful to you,
                You'll fall in love with someone else.

Second girl: Akh, dear girlfriend,
                How can I not be upset?
                He's so wonderful
                I can't leave him.[35]

The culture required that a girl's sexual-object choice be so highly personalized that no one else would do except the original love object. This was another manifestation of the same tendency noted in fortune-telling.

The tenor of boys' *chastushki* was very different. Though the boys sometimes expressed tender feelings toward their girlfriends, their songs frequently dealt with topics other than love: fighting, drinking, military service, and male solidarity groups. And many of the *chastushki* that were sung about girlfriends made rude, hostile, and even violent jokes or comments about them. As *Kineshemets* remarked, "Factory girls are portrayed in [male factory youths'] songs in far from flattering terms."[36]

> On the table stands a bottle
> A half of white wine
> I'll give it to my sweetheart on the back of her head
> So she'll wise up.

And,

> I have a sweetheart
> It's frightening to walk with her in the street
> The horses are startled
> The peasants yell at me. . . .[37]

Another example goes even further.

> My sweetheart (female) washed a dress.
> And I watched her with pleasure.
> My sweetheart drowned,
> And I cracked up with laughter.[38]

It seems likely that boys balanced their tender sentiments by rude verbal assaults on the very objects of their love in order to reassure themselves that their girlfriends' hold over them would never be so strong as to threaten the cohesiveness of the male solidarity group. Rivalries among boys over girls they loved were considered anathema.

Girls, however, never expressed such hostility in their *chastushki*. The intense rivalry among girls for a particular boy was recognized, sometimes even emphasized and played up, rather than muted. For girls, same-sex friendships were secondary to love for a boyfriend.

Methods of fortune-telling used by unmarried working girls were similar to those used traditionally among peasants. Here young women "predict" their futures by taking objects (interpreted as clues) from a bowl covered by a handkerchief, and by "seeing" their future husbands in a mirror illuminated only by candlelight. If a chicken pecked out a ring hidden in a bowl of grain, the girl would be married soon.

Young working women would gather to eavesdrop outside the door of bathhouses as another form of fortune-telling. Certain words and phrases they overheard were interpreted as clues about their future marriages.

The celebration of Semik (Trinity Sunday) was one of the most important yearly rituals of young, unmarried Russian working women. Here, girls dance with a birch tree decorated with ribbons (center) and weave wreathes later placed over birch branches and used to tell their fortunes (right). In working class settlements, decorated birch trees were brought into the factories and workers' dormitories.

From an early age, Russian working class and peasant girls alike spent time with their girlfriends doing round dances and singing traditional songs. The songs transmitted socialization about expected women's roles in Russian lower class society. Note the single braid, the hairstyle of unmarried women.

Groups of men from the same factory, workshops, or other solidarity group, frequently wandered, singing, through the streets of villages and factory settlements, sometimes to the accompaniment of an accordionist. Their songs, often obscene, were very different from the songs women sang.

A rare photo of a mainstay of Russian working class and peasant culture: the courtship dance (*gulian'e*). In factory settlements these dances were often very large, with up to three hundred couples dancing and many onlookers.

The young, unmarried women workers we have looked at here were of the same age and marital status as the women textile operatives of Lowell, Massachusetts, who were so active in organizing to improve their lives, leading the entire New England movement, of both men and women, for the ten-hour workday during the 1840s. The folkloric material makes clear the tremendous cultural differences between these two sets of women. While the Lowell operatives were the daughters of New England farmers, and the Russian women also lived in a culture still largely dominated by peasant traditions, the rural cultures which influenced each differed markedly. Russian girls' adolescence seems to have been largely focused on the task of struggling to integrate, on the one hand, their culture's emphasis on the excitement of romantic love for women, and on the other, tolerance of the solitary suffering marriage would bring. The round of adolescent girls' yearly rituals conveyed to them, as a group, that their husbands' attention would soon be elsewhere, while brides must also break their bonds to their families of origin. Because the suffering of marriage was foreseen and portrayed as normative for all women, their capacity to unite among themselves to improve their lives was undercut. As we try to picture young Russian women passing repeatedly through the series of yearly rituals which taught them they would have no long-term adult allies through the hardships of their lives, we may begin to get some sense of why these young women did not organize as their Lowell counterparts did.

Boys

The leisure activities and rituals of boys in the late childhood and adolescent years were very different from those of girls. Boys' activities involved some components—most obviously solidarity groups, especially the more organized ones created by the development of soccer teams—which laid the groundwork for collective action in 1917. (Boys' activities also involved many negative components, which will become apparent below.)

Beginning at about age seven or eight, boys were removed from the almost exclusive care of mothers and *nian'ki* and transferred to the world of "manly" pursuits.[39] They imitated their fathers in learning to play lotto and cards, brawl, and drink. They formed youth gangs and, with the aid of rituals, formed a bonding orientation of loyalty to the all-male solidarity group coupled with an aggressive, unromantic attitude toward women and sexuality.

Late Childhood

I found no evidence that working-class boys aged seven to twelve were typically expected to engage in wage-earning tasks or to take responsibility for major domestic chores similar to girls' working as *nian'ki* and helpers at home. Further research must be done to determine how typical it was for boys of this age to attend school; if it was typical, school attendance may have been boys' responsibility equivalent to girls' babysitting and domestic work. If most boys did not attend school or have other duties toward their families, this suggests that from an early age, boys were being permitted, perhaps even encouraged, to adopt their fathers' attitude of financial and emotional irresponsibility toward their families.

In contrast to girls, who remained within the sphere of domestic concerns, boys of seven to twelve began actively to be drawn out of the home and into the public sphere of adult men. Boys' point of entry into the outside world was largely recreational, as they began to accompany their fathers to taverns and card games. This process was described in a *Kineshemets* report written by one of its worker-correspondents at the Tomna factory:

> Beginning in spring and ending in late fall, the workers of Tomna spend all their days playing lotto. . . . The children—youths *beginning with seven-year-old boys*, all to a man, are there. Among them have developed such specialists at playing the game that their papas refuse to play cards with them. Whenever possible, the boys cheat; otherwise they curse so loudly—not even "Vtorovskaia Loshad" [apparently a reference to a local place where swearing was heard constantly] hears such foul language.
> Often you hear a father who is losing at cards ask his *ten- or twelve-year-old son* to lend him money, and then send him "to the devil." Drunkenness, fights, and all kinds of outrages are there in abundance, especially on holidays. . . .[40]

An eyewitness newspaper reporter recorded a male worker's description of an eleven-year-old boy. "I saw him last night. He was hanging around the card games. Down the hill they had five games going all night—well, he did everything there: he ran off to get one guy some wine, and another one some tobacco. He probably earned twenty kopeks running errands. So now he's playing lotto [with the twenty kopeks]."[41] In Moscow, "the children of workers . . . were included at a very young age in the drunken life of the Prokhorovka dormitories. Youths imitated their fathers: they got drunk, used bad language, participated in fights. . . ."[42]

Other evidence demonstrates that working-class culture recognized the need to draw sons away from their mothers' sphere in order to prepare boys for their future roles. One study of proverbs of Vladimir *guberniia* noted that "Maternal upbringing [of older sons] is not approved in proverbs; mothers' upbringing is often said to give deplorable results. Having a gentle nature, the mother is not able to forge the child into a stoic fighter in the struggle for existence." (It was of course not "nature" alone that caused the gentleness of women's personality.) Thus, in the words of the proverbs:

A pampered son doesn't live all his life with his
   mother,
And afterward he takes on stupid habits.

A mother's son has an empty mind.

Referring to mothers who remained the primary caretakers of their sons for too long, one proverb put it:

An egg sat on too long is always an addled-egg [*boltun*, the other, figurative, meaning of which is "a failure"].

The problem with mothers, according to the proverbs, was that they were too soft on their children. When punishing her child with a beating,

One's own mother raises her hand high
But doesn't hit hard.

If the mother is beating, it's not really a beating.[43]

It took exposure to the violence of the father's world to produce in the son the more hardened personality considered "manly" among the Russian working class.

Leisure-Time Activities of Teenage Boys: Rituals

Unlike pre-courtship-age girls' activities, the rituals of boys in the corresponding age group did not encourage the participants to focus their attention on their future wives. Rather, they continued to develop and consolidate their ability to relate to groups of males.

Maslenitsa: Relationships to Women

We saw above the boys' role in the Annunciation celebration, which stressed boys' freedom through their setting birds free, while the girls' Annunciation celebration stressed their future responsibility for children. In addition to Annunciation, there were two other yearly rituals in which boys played a role assigned specifically to them because of their age and/or gender. The first was Maslenitsa (or Maslianitsa), corresponding to the European carnival of Mardi Gras or Shrovetide. This holiday preceded the long Easter fast and was a time of gluttony, drunkenness, revelry, and dissipation. (A 1912 Kostroma newspaper, following Maslenitsa of that year, recorded the deaths of three men, all from too much drinking over the holiday.[44])

The boys' role was to collect scrap wood, trash, and other combustibles, and then to set bonfires on the last day of Maslenitsa, as a farewell to the holiday. This was called the burning or "sending off" of Maslenitsa, the climax of this holiday of licentiousness, followed the next day by the onset of the great pre-Easter fast.[45] A 1913 newspaper described "the 'sending off of Maslenitsa' by the boys" that year: "Maslenitsa was burned on the Kineshemka [river] in 8 or 10 places. . . . The glow from the bonfires was of huge proportions. . . . The district beyond the Volga represented the same beautiful picture. Here, there, and everywhere were seen large bonfires in the darkness."[46]

The burning of the Maslenitsa was traditionally accompanied by crude sexual jokes, sayings, and songs. Straw dummies, addressed as females, were burned in the bonfires.[47] One song, for example, addressed the straw dummy as "Bitch, bitch," and called on "her" to overindulge and to defile herself.

> Bitch, bitch, Maslianitsa,
> Semeon's niece!
> Tomorrow is a fast day [i.e. the beginning of the Lenten fast]
> Be gluttonous, *obmolosnis'se*,*
> Defile yourself![48]
>> *I was unable to determine the meaning of this word, possibly because it was a slang sexual term. Sokolov wrote that the songs boys sang as they burned the fires were characterized by "a license which cannot be reproduced in print."[49]

Thus, the burning of the Maslenitsa bonfires encouraged in young men a perspective on sexuality very different from that of young women. The male perspective had an active, aggressive tone, beginning with the physical exertion of collecting the material needed to fuel the bonfires, and climaxed by the explosion of that material into fire.

In contrast to the much more passive, romantic view of love and sexuality in young women's rituals, this bonfire-symbol of male sexuality was the climax of a holiday which emphasized licentiousness rather than fidelity and stable, married love. In contrast to each young woman's focus on learning more about her own future husband's identity, young men engaged in group burning of a single straw "female" who had no particular characteristics defining her as an individual, but represented all women. The fiery destruction of the dummy by the male group celebrated the participants' power over women, and encouraged men to feel they could and should use that power to annihilate the individual attachments to wives which might undermine the solidarity of the male group.

Ritual Fighting: Male Solidarity Groups

The other yearly ritual in which young unmarried men took part as a group occurred every August, and it stressed aggressive group solidarity through fistfights. The occasion for these fights was the church holiday of the commemoration of the death of John the Baptist, which was celebrated August 29 through 31. Each evening at twilight, violent fistfights took place among all the men of the community, young and old. The fights took place in a specific location; for example, in Yaroslavl they occurred near the Ziminskii bridge on the opposite riverbank from the church. According to one worker informant:

The worst fights were on the 29th of August and the next day.
The fistfights continued almost the whole night. Sometimes the police broke them up. Both youths and old men were in the fights. They even threw stones at each other. Once you were in a *"stenka"* [slang for "fight"], teeth and lips and eyes all got smashed up.[50]

The fights were so violent in Yaroslavl that they were finally banned by the local authorities around 1914. "The fights reached the point of murder, the factory workers against the town dwellers, and the town dwellers against the factory workers. One time a policeman was killed and from that time on they stopped the fights—about three years before the revolution, from that time on they were forbidden."[51]

169

The purpose of this ritual was to strengthen each male's commitment to his own solidarity group as against others. Fighting and other rivalries among working-class males were always organized by solidarity groups: factory workers against town dwellers as in this example;[52] workers of one factory or trade against another; or workers of one subsection of a factory against another. These solidarity groups were the central point of identity for all working-class males. Loyalty to their own solidarity group shaped all youth's and men's daily activities. The fact that both young and old men took part in the John the Baptist fights suggests that this event formalized the transmission of this aspect of male culture from one generation to the next.

Youth Bands

The combative spirit fostered by this male rite was continued with gusto throughout the year, without need for further special holidays. Young men often formed "hooligan" bands that seem to have been something of a universal youth section of adult male culture.[53] These youth bands fought against other bands and also hung out together, playing cards, loafing, singing, and picking on women. Participating in these groups did not preclude similar activities with adult men; rather, the "hooligan" collectives seem to have resembled the initiation groups studied by anthropologists, groups which dealt explicitly with the initiation of teenage boys into the activities of grown men.

Ermilov's study of factory life stressed the typicalness of "hooligan" activities. Living conditions in workers' settlements

> produce a certain kind of factory youth. In the evenings, these fellows loiter around the factory settlement and engage in hooligan activities . . . and during the day they loaf in the kitchen or in the corridors [of the barracks], playing nonstop card games, "*kozel*," "*trynka*," and "*ochko*" [slang names for card games popular at the time].
> Each workers' settlement has its place for "hanging out," "lounging around," "loitering," or "screwing off," where the youth aimlessly idle away hours at a time.[54]

An account in an Ivanovo-Voznesensk newspaper also gives evidence of daily fistfights: "behind the station, on [the factory owner] N. Garelin's land, every day in the evening, fistfights occur. Two sides ["*stenki*"] gather: one railroad [workers] and the other factory [workers], and they fight. These fights attract masses of the curious and idlers, who cheer on the fighters."[55]

A man who had come to Moscow to work in the Trekhgorka textile factory when he was a youth recounted that in addition to drinking and playing cards in their spare time:

> The youth gathered, played pitch and toss, and organized fights. On Sundays, on the bank of the Moscow River, we used to have fistfights with the Sugar plant workers with huge numbers of people taking part. We broke one another's bones, broke one another's noses. . . . We teased one another, we quarrelled with one another. We teased the [textile] dyers by calling them "Mamais" and they did the same to us weavers by calling us "*rogali*" and other insulting nicknames.[56]

Note that this account mentions two types of solidarity groups: the workers of one factory (Trekhgorka) against those of another (the Sugar plant), and those of various jobs within the textile factory against one another (the dyers against the weavers). The solidarity youth felt with workers from their own factories and workshops formed the basis for *tsekhovshchina* in the trade union movement, and later for the Red Guard units which developed in many factories in 1917.[57]

Young men's *chastushki* give a sense of how teenage boys in these "hooligan" groups thought about themselves:

> We boys, crew cuts,
> Have knives in the tops of our boots;
> Two dumbbells apiece at the ready,
> A revolver in our belts.
> Our knives are steel, our dumbbells are forged
> We're boys, bullies with a lot of practice.[58]

There is bragging.

> They wanted to beat us up
> They wanted to pummel us,
> But we ourselves are Cossack chieftains
> And we can defend ourselves.[59]

There is boasting of war wounds.

> They beat me, they pummelled me,

In an open field on the sand—
They punched holes in my turbulent head
In seventeen places.[60]

There are threats.

I go out for a good time at the factory,
I'm not afraid of anyone.
If someone just bumps into me
I'll fight them with a knife.[61]

One can easily see in these sentiments the precursors of the factory-based Red Guard units racing with each other to Bolshevik headquarters, competing to see which factory could obtain weapons first. In daily life, youth had always fought in groups based within their factories. In becoming Red Guard units, young men simply added a new kind of weapon—guns—and a new common foe which tended to unite the competing factories more than they had been in everyday life.

Youth bands also participated in other types of activity. They exercised their drinking capacity in order to work it up to that of adult men. One young worker who didn't want to drink told of the peer pressure brought to bear on him, ultimately successfully; another told of being beaten when he didn't want to drink, by the workers to whom he was apprenticed.[62] Teenage boys also got together to sing "either bawdy or hooligan songs." One source observed how typical it was for boys, playing an accordion, to "walk along and bawl songs."[63]

Another common activity of the youth bands was hanging around the streets, harassing passersby, and addressing obscene remarks to women. This pastime undoubtedly helped to reinforce the sense of unity among the group as against others. "Adults—not only women, but men as well—pass by gangs of youths, and if they don't want to be cursed at, it's dangerous."[64] Near the Bol'shaia textile factory in Yaroslavl, the local youth staked out a part of the road nearest the factory as their territory by giving it a name, "Calves Boulevard," and began to badger the people who relaxed there after work in the evenings. One evening in another Yaroslavl youth haunt, when the street emptied of people, the boys' "hands itched. Having hit one person, and not finding anyone else they could pick on, this rowdy company began to destroy the bridge, even dragging away several logs. Such cases aren't rare. . .—they occur almost every Saturday."[65]

172

Countless newspaper reports of crimes committed by youth revealed the high frequency of violence;[66] accident reports told the same story.[67] A *Kineshemets* article described the outcome of a sexual attack on a young woman by a youth.

> The police booked V-v, who confessed and asked the girl's father to settle for fifty rubles. The father refused, wanting to see V-v punished. So V-v rounded up his hooligan friends and on June 30 they surrounded him and jeered at him. . . . "Congratulations on the bride [the implication was that she'd 'been around']."
> . . . The matter ended with beer bottles flying through the air, and the girl's father was beaten bloody.[68]

While it is unclear how typical sexual assault was, an important feature of this incident is the peer group that "V-v" could rely on to aggressively defend his action.

Thus, young men underwent, in essence, a period of training in order to develop the commitment and skills necessary to being a member of adult all-male solidarity groups. This "training" involved both participation in adult groups and the formation of all-youth bands.[69]

Although the socialization of male youth often gave them the upper hand over their female peers, boys' daily lives were not necessarily happier than girls'. Some male youths' songs expressed a kind of deep despair that may well have been caused in part by the culturally required norm of denying the "feminine" aspects of their personalities, and the need to be constantly aggressive and "tough." In songs such as the following three *chastushki*, boys likened themselves to prisoners, to dogs, and to inanimate objects such as logs.

I was born despairing
And I will die despairing.
If they chop off my head,
I'll fasten on a log.

I walk like a dog,
Only without a collar
Police record after police record
[Is written] on me, a swindler.

Winter is passing, summer approaches,
In the fields flowers blossom,
But I, a poor kid

173

—They're holding me in iron fetters.[70]

Such feelings of utter meaninglessness are not found in young women's songs, suggesting that their lives may have held some kind of reward which men's did not, despite the many terrible aspects of women's lives.

Development of Youth Solidarity, 1912-14

The general pattern of male behavior had a dual aspect: on the positive side it involved group cohesion, support, and unified action; on the negative side, the stance of the group was often self-destructive, as well as hostile and violent toward other men and women in the community. The positive qualities in youth bonding grew and developed as, by 1912-13, working-class youths became involved in group sports, especially soccer. This development channeled group solidarities, aggression, and competitiveness in a more organized fashion than had the brawls of one factory, workshop, or neighborhood against another, providing a more sophisticated basis for unified group action during the revolution.[71] (The development of youth activities was not unidirectional: its negative tendencies also intensified by 1917.[72])

By 1912, soccer—*futbol* in Russian—was flourishing, with substantial audiences attending matches between a number of different teams. In the early summer of 1913, *Kineshemets* reported, "Soccer is suddenly becoming very popular. It progresses rapidly in Kineshma *uezd*, developing even in the villages." Most of the local teams were from the area's large textile factories.[73] A month later, a reporter was complaining about the fact that rough-playing soccer enthusiasts had taken over all the public outdoor spaces where workers usually went to relax: the grove, the field, and the city's outskirts. The reporter grumbled that only the cemetery had not yet been appropriated by the *futbolisty*.[74]

Like the solidarity groups of the fistfights, *futbol* teams were often based on the factory of employment (or on workshop or profession, in those cases where one factory supported two teams), or on living areas (towns, settlements, or particular neighborhoods or streets in cities). The difference was that in *futbol*, the competitiveness between male groups was set within a much more organized structure. Extensive practice was followed by games planned well in advance and often culminating in areawide championships which brought together teams from towns substantial distances away from each other. Teams marked their solidarity by naming themselves, for example the "Falcons," the "Realists," and the "Doves" from Kineshma, the Konovolov factory "Stars," and "Shot" from "beyond the Volga."

A newspaper report described the meeting of two teams about to start a game at the Annenskaia factory: "The greetings, as usual, were lively: thanks are expressed by both the visitors and the home team: the first for having been invited, the second for the visit."[75] This mutual courtesy and shared goodwill between teams, despite their competitive relationship during the games themselves, was a far cry from the near-total antagonism between contending sides in the more traditional fistfights—where insults were used to goad the other side into fighting, as contrasted to the cooperative, long-term planning by which soccer matches were set up. Although the violent physical competition remained during the *futbol* game itself, it was now placed within a context that also encouraged cooperative behavior among the teams.

In a number of other ways as well, *futbol* represented a higher level of organization than did brawling. The teams were, at least sometimes, well organized. For example, a report from Navoloki noted a meeting of one team to elect its directors.[76] Soccer also produced structure beyond the individual teams as championships were organized. For example, in the final competition of a championship between the Tomna factory team and the Kineshma Falcons, the grand prize was a silver cup.[77] The final match of this championship even involved calling in a special referee from another city a substantial distance away.[78]

Soccer also involved learning techniques and rules which were probably more extensive and sophisticated than those of fistfights. Team play had to be developed in order to win. The competitive aspect of soccer thus encouraged the gradual mastery of various skills and concerted group action, by individuals and teams.

In addition, the need for a financial base—to purchase a ball at least, and later perhaps uniforms and other equipment, as well as prizes for the winners of championships—encouraged the formation of stable team groupings that sometimes assessed dues on their members and/or worked with other, often non-working-class groups, to raise funds. Outstanding among these were local theater groups, which contributed the proceeds of certain performances to the teams.[79]

In addition to contact with theater groups, the teams themselves sometimes had a varied class composition. General information suggests that some of the teams were made up partly or entirely of people other than industrial workers:

students, white-collar employees, and so on. The Half-Moon team, for example, formed when the workers and the white-collar employees of the Vetka and Konovolov factories "bought a ball and began playing peacefully."[80] In these instances, soccer broke down traditional antagonism among solidarity groups, facilitating the development of more sophisticated networks among workers and males of other social groups.

These contacts among workers and other groups eventually generated several sports societies, which involved various sports and activities in addition to soccer. One of the most successful societies was located in the Navoloki factory settlement. The grand opening of this society involved people from various organizations and occupations:

> On Sunday, May 25 [1914] the opening of the sport circle "Navoloki" took place. The weather was good. Before the beginning of the opening, there was a public prayer service with the participation of the local chorus.
> The brass band of the 183rd Pultusskii infantry regiment played three hymns. Among those present were people of all the factories in the vicinity of Kineshma, many from Kineshma, and also some arriving from Ples.
> Then the entertainment began. For the amusement of those attending there was croquet, swinging, *gigany*, *prokhozhdenie*, and climbing up poles.
> At 6 pm there was a soccer match on the sport field between the [Navoloki] team "Sport" and the "Stars" from Konovalov's factory, which ended four to two in favor of Navoloki.
> At 9 pm the local amateur players put on a show. They performed "A Day in the Life of the Deceased," a farce in three acts, and "From the Altar to the Police-Station," an original jest in one act.
> The plays were very successful, and were met by the general applause of the audience. The theater was full. . . . During the show, there were fireworks.
> At the end of the performance, the theater hall was opened for a dance. Music was played during the play's intermissions and the dance.
> The dance ended at 4 am and then there was an outing on the launching along the Volga, which belongs to the society. At this time, there was a specially arranged sale of fruit, waters, tea, ice cream, and cold snacks.[81]

Similar societies were organized in various towns.[82] Referring to one in Yaroslavl, the newspaper *Iaroslavskie novosti* noted its "highly important role. Hundreds of young factory workers spend their holidays and Sundays in the garden of the society, watching the shows with pleasure, rather than going to the beer halls." The nascent connection between such youth organizations and political activity is seen here: "among the number of members of the society is one who is something of a celebrity—the worker Ermolin, an elector to the Government Duma, arrested [and imprisoned] in 1905 for striking."[83]

Thus, the male bonding groups of soccer teams had a proclivity for expanding outward to form ties with new groups: other teams from distant towns, white-collar employees, students, even members of the intelligentsia (such as Dr. Lebedev, secretary of Kineshma's Sport Society), theater groups, and so on. The anthropologist Rayna Rapp Reiter noticed a similar characteristic among men's networks in Colpied, in the Southern French Alps. She observed that male newcomers to the village, even though they were still recognized as outsiders, were able to insert themselves into the existing male networks, but the newcomers' wives could not likewise become part of village women's networks. For men's pastimes—the game of *boules* and conversation in cafés—were "public rather than familial": men all over Provence played *boules* and thus shared this interest.[84]

The same quality of interchangeability of men playing games can be seen in Russia, even in less highly organized pursuits than soccer: "On Sennaia Square recently, various games of chance have developed to a strong degree, including *biko* and roulette. The players are mainly soldiers, workers, artisans, and little boys." In Kostroma, a fight begun by drunken soldiers was joined by local factory workers.[85]

This quality of male networks seems likely to have given Russian working men experience in relating in groups to men of other classes, and hence to have made male workers' groups conducive to organization by political parties, which were made up largely of people of other social groups, above all the intelligentsia. Workers taking part alongside soldiers in daily-life soccer matches and games of chance also undoubtedly facilitated these two groups' joint efforts in systematic, citywide food searches and in street fighting during 1917. While groups of male workers grew accustomed to interacting publicly with other social groups, women workers did not have a similar experience. Their networks and rituals predisposed them to a concern above all with their husbands and children.

Other aspects of soccer also probably gave working-class men experience and skills that would later be valuable in political activity. Internal organization of teams (having captains or a committee that directed, assigning players to the various positions) and the acquisition, in a self-disciplined manner, of knowledge of the rules, techniques, team play, and the ability to integrate competitive and sportspersonlike modes of behavior within a differentiated organizational setting were skills similar to those necessary for political organization. Practicing and developing these skills during the years before 1917 undoubtedly prepared working men for political functioning in a way that women were not prepared.

Men's organizational activity in soccer was probably valuable in yet another way in aiding them to form and maintain politically active groups in 1917. Men had fistfights only with the local solidarity groups with whom they had daily contact. Soccer matches, in contrast, brought together teams from much greater distances apart. The cooperation in 1917 among Red Guard units which forged solidarity with a wider group, the city district, was prefigured in daily life by cooperation among soccer teams forging a wider solidarity.

Thus, as ongoing, stable *futbol* teams traveled to other cities and factory settlements to meet various area teams, the basis was laid for unified activity of other types of workers' groups across substantial distances. The Bolsheviks themselves were aware of the political usefulness of the regionwide organizational structure inherent in soccer: they used the matches for clandestine agitational purposes. For example, in 1913,

> It was decided [by the local Bolshevik committee] to take advantage of the game of *futbol* as a means of camouflage. For this, a *futbol* team, "Thunderstorm," was organized. This was a [Bolshevik] party team, not registered [with the authorities], but "wildcat." But it traveled to play in Usad, Dulevo, Likino, Pokrov, Dresna, and Pavlovo-Posad, and also played in Zuevo. Each practice session was used as a meeting or discussion. When the Cossacks or mounted guards came up to us, we explained, "We've been practicing, and now we're resting." Seeing our soccer ball, which we would set in an obvious place, the Cossacks or mounted guards would be convinced that we weren't doing any harm. Since we didn't have a playing field, our "practice" had to take place everywhere—so they [the police] didn't pursue us.[86]

In 1917, male workers traveled through these same areas to establish ties among various revolutionary groups in the region. It seems very likely that working men's experience traveling to soccer meets gave them valuable experience in arranging and carrying out such ties. In fact, use of soccer by political agitators may well have been widespread.

> Given the unusual growth of *futbol*, it is not surprising that old men and old women shake their heads in distress, prophesying widespread sedition.
> "Disorder is beginning," say these grizzled folk. "Provocateurs have appeared who, under cover of the game, are stirring up the waters."[87]

Even the fact that soccer terms were direct transliterations from English may have made Russian workers aware of cultures far beyond their own localities. "Along a city boulevard walks a group of youth, fervently arguing among themselves and gesticulating . . . with their legs [kicking techniques]. You hear 'khafteim,' 'gol,' and 'golkiper' and other complicated futbol terms."[88] A crowd going to a soccer game at the Annenskaia factory carried on "a noisy conversation in which, scattered like peas, are the words, 'gol,' 'aut,' 'korner,' 'pas,' . . . and so on."[89] The strange foreign words must have been conversation pieces in and of themselves, making male workers conscious that they shared a favorite pastime—and maybe other interests as well—with workers of countries beyond their own.

All of this is in striking contrast to the situation of working-class women, whose adolescence continued throughout the interrevolutionary period to be shaped by the same rituals peasant women had engaged in for centuries. While young men's activities encouraged them to form enduring ties with many of their peers, including those beyond their immediate surroundings, young women's activities narrowed their concerns to a tremendous preoccupation with their future families.[90]

These differences between teenage boys' and girls' concerns formed the basic bonding patterns that continued throughout their lives. It was one of the important life tasks during the teen years for each individual to develop the bonding orientation "appropriate" for his or her sex.

ELEVEN

Courtship and Wedding

Courtship

The period of courtship held great importance in Russian working-class culture. The public setting for much courtship activity was the social dance, above all the large public outdoor dances and fetes known as *gulian'ia*, in which the entire working-class population of the community took part. The young people danced round dances, quadrilles (square dances for four couples), polkas, and the like,[1] while the rest of the community looked on and made merry. The musical accompaniment for the dancing was songs, typically sung by factory workers who were skilled at performing. Sometimes the singers had an accordion to accompany them.

The ultimate purpose of the dances, as far as marriage-aged men and women were concerned, was courtship: they could meet and get to know each other in a situation where mingling of the sexes was encouraged—and guided—by their elders. Working-class *gulian'ia* were a continuation of the same type of courtship revelry among the Russian peasantry. One rural folklore collector noted, "The fundamental principle in round dances [the most common type of dance] is the selection of groom and bride. Here future weddings are contemplated, there is match-making, acquaintances are begun. The round dances were surrounded by a huge crowd of onlookers."[2]

A. P. Golitsynskii, a doctor who made frequent medical visits to factories in the Moscow area, described the typical working-class *gulian'e*:

if the weather was propitious . . . on the big square in front of the two . . . entertainment establishments, that is the tavern and the vegetable shop . . . a kind of *gulian'e* was arranged. The factory lads, adult women, and young girls, dressed up like outlandish birds, the most flirtatious of whom were perfumed with, I think, *finder-bal'zanchik* and mint drops, flowed together there from the factory. Songs, dances, and round dances were started among them; accordions and balalaikas were heard; and the people caroused and made merry all day and often all night until early morning.[3]

A woman worker described the romantic pairing-off of courting couples by the end of the *gulian'e*: "After the evening dances, everyone walked in couples under the linden trees up to the factory to enjoy themselves there, and then returned by another path, and everyone parted for home."[4]

The *gulian'ia* often included entertainment in addition to dancing. There might be bands and fireworks, and in the largest cities, jugglers, tightrope walkers, dwarves and giants, buffoons (*balagany*, a type of performance by old men who conversed from the stage with the audience, often on political and social themes), panoramas, and so on.[5]

The factory administration at the huge Iaroslavskaia Bol'shaia textile mill in Yaroslavl, where roughly 10,000 workers were employed, helped pay for a brass band to accompany the dancing.[6] Because thousands of workers lived in Yaroslavl, the *gulian'ia* there were massive events. During two summer months of 1912 alone, *Iaroslavets* noted eight of them. Seven to eleven thousand people of all ages took part in each *gulian'e*, among them 380 to 500 young couples.[7]

Not all CIR textile workers had such sophisticated *gulian'ia* as the Iaroslavskaia Bol'shaia workers. The workers' accordion was a more typical accompaniment to the dance songs than a brass band. But whether sophisticated or rudimentary, the tradition of *gulian'ia* continued through the revolution.[8]

In the wintertime, various types of indoor spaces were found to permit courting parties to continue. Kokushkina recalled that, at the Norskoe textile plant where she worked, for the Christmas parties

> we danced in the dining room in the red barrack. There was such a big room there, where the *bezdorozhtsy* [people temporarily unable to travel because of impassable roads, such as when roads became enmired in the springtime] from beyond the Volga stayed. [The workers living in] each barrack got together by themselves. In the spring, all the barracks held round dances together near the bridge by the flour shop.[9]

At Savva Morozov's textile factory in Orekhovo-Zuevo, the factory administration authorized the attic laundry-drying rooms to be used as dance floors (and the local underground Bolshevik agitators suspected them of attempting to absorb the young workers' energies with dancing to prevent them from becoming politically active.)[10] Other locations were sometimes found beyond the factory itself. For example, there was an evening of dancing for Iaroslavskaia's Bol'shaia workers at the fire station of the Volunteer

Firemen of the nearby village of Zverinets. Another party took place the day before in the nearby tobacco factory.[11]

Winter or summer, church and other holidays were often the occasions for dancing: Christmas, All Souls', and the day of Peter and Paul (following Semik-Trinity).[12] There was also a factory holiday the Monday after Easter, when textile operatives were freed from work as their machines and materials were being readied for the next year's assignments. On this day, refreshments were prepared and brought by each participant, and they danced to accordion accompaniment.[13]

One of the most important elements of the *gulian'ia* was the singers, young women workers who had developed a large repertoire of songs, usually partly handed down from older members of their families. Ekaterina Vorob'eva, for example, described how songs were passed on among various of her female family members and friends, including her mother, her grandmother, her grandmother's older sister, a female neighbor, and several of her aunts.[14] Another working woman informant, Lobova, told ethnographers, "We were poor, but we loved songs. My father, my mother, and my sisters—we were all singers."[15]

But singing for dances was apparently not open only to those whose families taught them to sing. Anyone with a good memory, a loud voice, and self-confidence could become a respected singer.[16] Good singers were sought after and highly esteemed because they were the centerpiece and driving force of *gulian'ia*, and thus could make the difference between a lackluster dancing party and a rousing one.

Dance Songs

The songs to which the young people danced were lively, and often humorous and sexy, but at the same time they provided important instruction as to how heterosexual couples were to relate. Successful negotiation of the courtship period was a tricky business in Russian working-class culture, because it involved potentially contradictory elements. Young men had to establish heterosexual unions and at the same time maintain male bonding that required denial of the pleasures of home and family. Each woman had to break ties with her parents and girlfriends, forming an unbreakable alliance with her husband—even though her husband would not devote the same allegiance to her.

These contradictory elements of courtship and marriage required working resolutions. Each individual's achievement of such a resolution was as important an outcome of the courtship period as was her or his wedding itself. The dance songs of the *gulian'e* were a major tool by which the culture's typical modes of resolution were conveyed. As with any type of contradiction in a social structure, the conflict was never completely nullified. Rather, most individuals achieved a working integration of the opposing demands made on them. One way folklore aided this achievement was by providing a pleasurable context for the working-through of contradictions: music, dance, rhythm, rhyme, joking, and laughter camouflaged the difficult psychological work that took place during the *gulian'e*, and hence made that work easier.

One common type of song involved a cute animal coming to a young woman's window at night.

"Oh, you, Vaniushka, Vania [diminutives of "Ivan"] sweetheart,
Come, Vania, to me. . . .
Don't knock, don't knock . . .
. . . and don't make clatter!
[Stand] under my window sill, and just scratch a little."
Soon Katia heard scratching, and she let in a smoke-colored cat
A smoke-colored cat, undecided.[17]
The cat was wearing a rose-colored shirt, the cat was wearing velvet pants.
The cat walked . . . the floor boards creaked.
The floor boards creaked, and its boots squeaked.
Dear papa was sleeping on the platform . . .
He began to wake up.
. . . now Katen'ka had trouble on her hands.
"I'm going to get in trouble, where can I get rid of this cat?
I'll tuck the cat in my skirt, I'll carry him to the yard.
I'll carry him to the yard, I'll set him on the fence."
But the cat jumped away, and broke the whole fence.
In the morning, it began to get light, and they [her parents] began to investigate
the tracks:
Not cat's prints—a young man's boot prints.[18]

In another such song, a boy disguised as a goat came to the girl's window. She asked her parents to invite him in,

to me, a young girl, in my bed.
I won't be sleeping, I won't be dozing.

I won't be sleeping, I won't be dozing,

I'll be kissing the gray goat.[19]

Sometimes it was a dove who appeared at her window. Underneath, the animal was always really an exciting young man. Such disguised depiction of girls' excitement about sex on the one hand encouraged that excitement, and on the other hand portrayed sex as something about which girls must be coy and indirect, saving actual fulfillment until marriage.[20]

Other songs dealt with how a woman should prioritize her relationship to her female friends as against her husband. Every song I found which began with a focus on a group of girlfriends shifted focus, often abruptly, to one young woman and her boyfriend, never returning to the girlfriends. One example plays on the double meaning of *liubeznyi* (as noted) and of *golub'* (dove), which is also a term of endearment in Russian.

Shouldn't we go down, girlfriends,
  to an earthly grove?
Shouldn't we invite, girlfriends, an
  amiable (*liubeznyi*) guest?
My sweetheart (*liubeznyi*) returned late
  at night
Late night—as a warm-gray (male) dove.
The dove came through the window to wake up
  his sweetheart:
"Get up, my darling. Open the door!"
The (female) dove got up and she opened
  the door, opened the door,
She let the (male) dove in, and embraced him
  passionately,
She embraced him passionately, and kissed
  his face.[21]

And another:

. . . The maidens sat in a meadow
Where there are grass and flowers,
Where we gambolled from early evening
And made merry in a round dance
In the pleasant peacefulness
Alone under the birch tree here
Where are you, my Cossack captain,
Without you, my boyfriend, I'll die. . . .
On my window,

Lay a dear little thing . . .
A shoot from the grapevine
A grapevine ripe and mature—
A curly-headed blond-haired fellow!
A curly-headed blond-haired boy
Has made the maiden wild over him!
The ice breaks up [in springtime]
The water splashes.

In this song, the phallic grapevine shoot lying at the girl's "window" seems a clear metaphor for the exciting promise of marital sexual intercourse, which was to draw women away from each other. In another song, a group of girls frolicked, gathering cranberry branches. But when an officer appeared on the road, the group of girls dropped from the song, which turned to focus on one girl proposing, "Dear young officer,/ Unmarried, single,/ Take me with you. . . ." She then volunteered to harness two horses to drive the couple "into the green garden."[22] In all these songs, the girl completely forgot her group of girlfriends as soon as a sexy young man captured her excited attention. (Interestingly, the songs of married women—examined below—never mentioned female friends, focusing only on husbands and children. This supports the idea that girlfriends were an expected part of unmarried women's lives, but were supposed to be relegated to second priority as soon as the future husband appeared.)

Romantic attachments tend to undermine same-sex friendships in many cultures. Russian courtship songs condoned and exaggerated this tendency in women, and encouraged them, when a conflict arose between friendship bonds and bonds to husband and children, to neglect the former, not the latter. (Men's songs encouraged them to do just the opposite.) Women's songs conveyed their message in part by describing all of life's meaning and excitement as residing, for women, in their boyfriends and husbands: "Where are you, my Cossack captain,/ Without you, my boyfriend, I'll die."[23]

Many courtship songs dealt with men's violence and drunkenness, encouraging women to love their men regardless of these flaws. In one, a young woman whose husband was away missed him so much that she cried "rivers of tears." Despite her torment, she did not reproach her husband when he returned.

My husband came home drunken . . .
I put him to bed.

"Sleep, comely one, sleep, handsome,
I won't say another word."[24]

In another song,

I, a young girl, a maiden,
Plucked little stars from the sky.

The first little star fell—
And I fell for a drunkard

They say he's a drunkard
I, a beautiful girl will go [with him]!

They say that he drinks wine—
I'll go willingly to marry him![25]

Other songs subtly or not so subtly taught women to expect abuse from their husbands. In one of the less subtle, a young wife appealed to her mother- and father-in-law to stop her husband's lashing her when she disobeyed him. Each in turn—amidst a merry refrain about leafy birch trees—told her,

"Dear daughter-in-law!
Beloved daughter-in-law!

This is not my affair,
It's up to my son.

If he wants to, he can beat you,
If he wants to, he'll show mercy!"[26]

The song ended with the wife apologizing to her husband for her stupidity in disobeying him; he then dropped his lash.

Many songs had specific dance steps and formations made by the dancing couples; these enacted the crux of the plot. As in American square dances, the song was repeated until each couple had a turn to perform the key steps while their fellow dancers watched.[27] I suspect this opportunity for each participant to "rehearse" culturally prescribed sex roles via dance movements helped socialize young people.

Some songs had each girl act out indifference to another woman's fate when she was being beaten. In one such song, each girl took her turn going into the center of the round-dance circle to act out the part of a swan.

. . . How on the sea, the blue sea . . .
A swan was swimming with her baby swans. . . .

Now, the girl's male partner joined her in the circle and danced steps which acted out hitting her, as the song continued:

Under her the water swelled. . . .
He appeared, the shining young falcon . . .
He slayed, he struck the white swan. . . .
And her little feathers [scattered] all along the shore. . . .

Now a second girl danced into the circle and enacted picking up the feathers.

She appeared, the beautiful, sweet maiden. . . .
She collected the feathers and repeated . . .
"For my father . . .
I'll put feathers in his pillow
For my mother . . .
I'll put feathers in her pillow
For my darling boyfriend . . .
I'll put feathers in his quilt.[28]

In many Russian songs, swans represented married women with their children, while falcons represented men.[29] And each dancing boy and girl acted out the parts of the swan and falcon, identifying their own life situations with those of the birds as the boy "struck" the girl. Thus, in this song, each woman, as she danced the part of the maiden, rehearsed indifference to the fact that the feathers she was so purposefully collecting were obtained at the expense of another "woman," (the swan) who had suffered terribly. Rather than questioning the evidence of another woman's being attacked, the maiden was instead expected to use that evidence (the feathers) to help her own kinfolk, giving the largest share to her boyfriend, whose body she would warm with them.

The physical violence described in this song, along with its enactment in the dance formations, represented the violence toward women which was common in working-class Russia.[30] This song conveyed to young Russian working women the following message: you will frequently see evidence of other women being abused by men. This is not your business. Don't ask questions about it or even wonder to yourself about it. You must misinterpret this evidence and render it invisible to yourself. And as each woman danced the part of the swan, she rehearsed the experience of being beaten and expecting no help or even acknowledgement of her suffering from another woman who saw the evidence of the beating.

Such messages were often conveyed metaphorically, as in this song about the swan and the falcon. My sense is that the most painful aspects of socialization were often conveyed metaphorically or humorously in order to get the message across to young people without arousing the resistance and rational rejection that might have occurred with a more straightforward, serious presentation. That the message was in fact successfully conveyed to women will be shown later, in memoir evidence which indicates that married women felt unable to even talk to each other about their husbands' physical abuse, let alone take steps to stop it.

Another courtship dance song was sung back and forth between two "teams," one of girls, the other of boys, lined up in two long rows facing each other. The girls began as a spirited unified team, but ended quite differently.

Boys: We sowed . . . millet. . . .
Girls: We will trample it down. . . .
Boys: With what will you trample it down . . . ?
Girls: We'll let the horses out. . . .
Boys: But we'll capture the horses. . . .
Girls: But we'll ransom the horses. . . .
Boys: And with what will you . . . ransom?
Girls: We'll give you a hundred rubles. . . .
Boys: We don't need a hundred rubles. . . .
Girls: Then we'll give you a thousand. . . .
Boys: We don't need a thousand. . . .
Girls: What do you . . . need?
Boys: We need a girl. . . .
Girls: And which girl do you . . . need?
Boys: We need the one at the end [of the girl's line]. . . .
Girls: She's the fool among us. . . .
Boys: But we'll teach her. . . .
Girls: And with what will you teach her . . . ?
Boys: We'll give her some silk to sew. . . .
Girls: She'll tangle up the silk. . . .
Boys: But we'll hit her with a lash. . . .

Girls: She'll obey a lash. . . .
(Here the boys took the girl on the end of the girls' line over to their side, and the singing continued:)
Boys: Our side has gotten bigger. . . .
Girls: Our side has gotten smaller. . . .
Boys: On our side, dancing is going on. . . .
Girls: On our side, weeping is going on. . . .
Boys: And we wear bast sandals, bast sandals [i.e. heavy peasant footgear].
Girls: And we wear shoes, shoes [i.e. delicate footwear].
Boys: And we walk stamp, stamp, stamp, stamp. . . .
Girls: And we walk click, click, click, click. . . .
Boys: We drink from buckets. . . .
Girls: And we drink from wine glasses. . . .
Boys: For this you're fools. . . .[31]

The song was repeated over and over, until the girls' side had been completely dismantled and integrated into the boys'. Thus, the courting couples rehearsed the cultural prescription that girls must not stand, united and strong, among themselves, but must join with the boys. The girls began the song with feisty boasting about their own resources (horses and a thousand rubles). But they changed radically when the boys threatened the lash, ending by listing the artifices (clicking shoes and delicate glasses) by which their culture exaggerated their delicacy and weakness relative to boys. The song had the girls collude with the boys' boasting claim of greater strength than males actually possessed, through their macho affectation of heavy bast shoes, drinking out of buckets, and walking with a thumping step.

Above all, the destruction of the girls' "team" as the boys absorbed them one by one taught young women that they should not bond together in solidarity, but instead should cleave to men. Marriage did not simply involve coupling. It also required a breaking down of women's solidarity, and the absorption of cowed wives into patrilocal male solidarity groups. The fact that it was specifically the threat of a beating which finally convinced the girls to begin dismantling their solidarity group suggests that the institution of wife-beating in Russia did not simply serve the purpose of enforcing each man's domination of his own wife. It also helped men keep women isolated from each other.

Dance songs are important not because they described *reality*, but because they conveyed patterns of loyalty sanctioned by the culture. In reality, women had feelings other than those described in these songs. But folklore for the most part did not encourage women to recognize and act on those feelings, because it did not name them or talk about them.

Courtship songs encouraged women, as individuals, to go right on loving husbands who abused them. Beyond this, they also taught women *collectively* not to join together to prevent that abuse. For sex role socialization did not only occur for individual women in *private* (e.g. each mother socializing her daughter at home). It also took place with the whole *community* present, all of its young women together learning how they should behave as a group—which is to say, *not* to act as a group. Women's folklore served the purpose of breaking apart a natural solidarity group, rather than fortifying it. This contrasts sharply with the powerful cultural support given to male solidarity groups, which fought ferociously against even small slights to one of their members ("If some one just bumps into me/ I'll fight them with a knife"). I suspect this cultural inhibition of women's impulse to help each other rectify to their most deeply felt daily grievances formed one basis for their inability to organize together in large groups to redress their grievances during the revolution of 1917. As in the courtship song, their "team" had long since been dismantled.

Wedding

The weeks-long series of wedding events and rituals among textile workers in the Central Industrial Region[32] was similar to the elaborate Russian peasant wedding,[33] though somewhat simplified. Most of the wedding activities focused on the bride. Thus marriage was portrayed as involving a much more elaborated and hence significant role for women than for men. The bride's family and girlfriends played a major role in the weeks before the wedding, helping her to achieve an enduring and deep-rooted transition from her family of origin to her new family of marriage.

The groom, meanwhile, had minimal obligations besides appearing at the specified festivities at the proper time and visiting his fiancée regularly before the wedding. The groom's friends and family did not play a substantive role in preparing him for marriage during the weeks before the wedding: his task was simply to achieve the formal state of marriage without disturbing too greatly the other important loyalties in his life.

According to Moscow *guberniia* statistics, 34.4 percent of working women married by age twenty and 42.6 percent married between twenty and twenty-four. Men married, "depending on circumstances, either at 18-19 years or, more frequently, after their military service at 25-26 years."[34]

The entire series of wedding events in textile factory settlements lasted about three weeks or a month. The process began with a matchmaker, sent by the prospective groom, making overtures to the family of the young woman. If her parents agreed, the boy and girl and both sets of parents met for the *smotrenie*, the "looking over," where the prospective bride and groom could look at each other silently while their parents conversed. The young woman and the young man were then each asked, out of the hearing of the other, whether they wanted to marry the proposed person.[35] If they agreed to the marriage, the couple was betrothed. A number of activities and rituals took place over the next two weeks,[36] leading up to the church wedding ceremony.

The Bride's Role During the Wedding

As a woman moved from single to married status, her life underwent a profound transition that had no parallel in the groom's. This sharp change in women's lives derived partly from the patrilocal residency customs of the Russian peasantry, by which the peasant bride left her family of origin to live permanently with her husband's extended family, often in a distant village. This meant an almost overnight shift in the bride's loyalties, interests, and friendships.

Thus for the young peasant woman, the world was divided into two halves: her family of origin called "our *storona*" (our "side" or "region"; the Russian word *storona* has a broader range of meaning than either of the English words, with both a geographic connotation and a connotation of an interest group or team); and "the strangers' *storona*," her family of marriage. "Our *storona*" contained all that was familiar to the woman from birth until her marriage, all the networks and bonds she had established in her own village. Her transition to "the strangers' *storona*" meant the culturally mandated loss of her closest human bonds and the pain of moving far away into another tightly knit alliance group, where she would be considered something of an outsider for many years. She traveled a long distance at marriage, metaphorically as well as literally, beyond the protection and caring of her family of origin.[37]

In textile workers' settlements, the wedding activities also utilized the concepts of two different *storony* and the image of the bride traveling a long distance between the two at marriage. These concepts expressed an emotional reality in working women's lives that resulted from factors other than location of residence alone.[38] For the working-class woman, too, was to shift her loyalties entirely to her new family (in this case, the nuclear family formed with her husband) and relegate to secondary status ties to any other network formed before marriage. Her parents must let go of her; they had no business trying to protect her any longer.

That marriage entailed a difficult and painful transition for working-class women was recognized in many of the songs sung during the prewedding events. But the very existence of songs and rituals designed to help a woman traverse this difficult emotional territory indicates how crucial women's successful accomplishment of this transition was. During the working-class betrothal ceremony, for example, the bride sang a long song back and forth with her mother, grieving over and working through the bride's confusion, anguish, and sense of loss at leaving her mother and being sent to a distant *storona*. The bride sang that she had been betrothed to a man who lived "beyond the Urdaia River."

Bride sings:
. . . That *storona* is not where I want to go.
The dear matchmaker
Arranged my marriage.
He who fed me [through childhood],
My dear father,
Pledged me in marriage.
But my . . . dear mother,
Gave me a long talking-to.
I surely lived the first year [of marriage] . . .
I lived, but I didn't cry.
In the second year . . .
I began to cry.
Having cried for a while,
I went into the forest.
In open country
I will throw myself down on the damp earth [symbol of mother] . . .
I will listen to the earth.
Isn't that the sound
Of my dear . . . mother's voice . . .

Bride's Mother sings:
My own . . . dear little child,
Wasn't it in the forest,

193

That you lost your way!
Wasn't it the grass that entangled you.
Wasn't it in the dew that you got wet?

Bride sings:
I got lost among strangers [her husband's family]
I was entangled by empty words [that said marriage would bring her happiness].
I got wet with bitter tears.

Bride's Mother sings:
You, my darling,
My little child! . . .
Endure grief silently,
Don't talk about grief! . . .
Enduring grief silently,
Grief will be known.[39]

In this song, the mother helped her daughter rehearse how she must "hear" her mother's voice in the damp earth after they separated at marriage: the bride must remember her mother telling her to endure grievances without talking to anyone about them. In fact, the mother herself refused to hear her daughter's grief, systematically reinterpreting each fact the young bride presented: the mother claimed she was lost in the forest, not among her new husband's family; and had gotten wet with dew, not with bitter tears. Thus, the mother suppressed the true meaning of her daughter's communication by "rewriting" her history. That a woman's communication with her own mother—presumably the model for her relationships with all other women—could be so distorted sent a powerful message to the bride. Her mother, after all, had once suffered the same dislocation at her own marriage—she in fact had once sung the *bride's* part in this song—yet the words provided in the wedding ritual did not encourage her to share sympathy with her daughter's plight. This cultural prescription of silence among women about their most deeply felt pain continued that of the courtship songs, which instructed women to deny their awareness of other women's suffering.

It might be argued that, outside of these rituals, mothers must have shared private communications with their daughters in which they did listen fully and respond sympathetically to their fears. This may well have happened. The point is that the rituals presented the publicly condoned responses, and as such, they had a powerful, if not monolithic, influence on women's behavior—especially their *public* behavior.

During the two weeks after her betrothal, the bride's girlfriends helped her make her transition to marriage. Although they all gathered together, the focus of their activities was not on the friendship group itself—which she would soon be leaving—but rather on helping the bride adjust to her coming departure from her childhood *storona*. Once the marriage had been agreed on, the girlfriends gathered every day during the two-week interval to help the bride sew her trousseau.[40] As they sat sewing, they sang songs which recognized and helped ease the fears the bride was experiencing, including her fear of losing her mother as her protector and being sent (metaphorically if not always literally) far away to an unfamiliar, unhappy place.[41] One song they sang was about a young woman who was weeping as she sat sewing a gift for her fiancée.

Her own dear mother came to her;
She tried to persuade her:
"Don't cry, my dear little child.
I will give you a dowry
And with the dowry a guide:
The guide, your own brother. [A reference to the fact that male relatives, such as
    brothers—not her parents—escorted the bride to the groom's local church to be
    married.]
So that he can accompany you
Through three dark forests,
Across three quick rivers,
Through three green gardens."
The guide returns home; . . .
But I am left [in the distant land] with grief.[42]

Another song sung by the bride and her girlfriends concerned the bride's single braid, the traditional hairdo of the unmarried Russian woman, called her "maiden freedom," symbolizing the relatively carefree existence of the young woman before she took on the heavy responsibilities of marriage and motherhood. The girlfriends sang all together in the bride's voice; that is, they identified with her, the closest form of sympathy:

Really, mother mine, dear mother!
Climb up, climb up, dear mother,
To my high *terem* [women's quarters in ancient Russia].
Look at my Russian braid,
At my maiden beauty!
My maiden beauty is a thing of the past,

195

It's besmirched with black dirt,
With black dirt from the road.[43]

Thus the girlfriends empathized with the bride's impulse to call her mother to recognize her fears and foreboding.

Another central task of the girlfriends occurred the night before the wedding, when, with flowers and wine, singing and dancing, they took the bride to the bathhouse. They ceremoniously undid her single braid, her "maiden freedom," and replaced it with the married woman's hairstyle.[44] The girlfriends then often spent the whole night with the bride before the wedding ceremony.[45] One of the songs they sang at this party helped the bride through the transition from loving her father to loving her husband. The song began with descriptions of the wind blowing through open country and the oars of a boat pulling through blue waves, both symbols of movement and hence of a period of transition and of traveling over long distances. Then the song focused on the bride-to-be:

Flowed, flowed,
Tears from Mashen'ka's eyes. . . .
Whom, Mashen'ka, are you brooding about
Whom, Andreevna, are you brooding about?
I was brooding . . .
My thoughts were with my dear father.

But then Masha caught herself and, recalling the attitude she should now properly hold toward her father, she rehearsed it:

The thought of him didn't enter my head, . . .
His words weren't pleasing [to me].

The questioner obligingly repeated the original query, giving Masha the opportunity to answer correctly this time:

Whom, Mashen'ka, are you brooding about
Whom, Andreevna, are you brooding about?
I was thinking, . . .
My thoughts were with my dear sweetheart . . .
Thoughts of him all crowded my head . . .
His words were pleasing to me.[46]

This song was psychologically very helpful. It provided the bride an outlet for her "inappropriate" feelings by giving her the opportunity to answer "incorrectly" and then channeled those feelings back to where they "properly" belonged: focused on her soon-to-be husband.

On the morning of the wedding, the girlfriends dressed the bride in her bridal clothes, an elaborate dress with silken ribbons, lace, flounces, and flowers. This expensive dress among poor workers conveyed the great importance of the wedding for women.[47]

The last event in which the girlfriends had a specific role to play as a group was the church wedding ceremony itself, where they simply stood next to the bride.[48] The girlfriends' part in the wedding ceremony was minimal; they had accomplished all of their real work before the ceremony. As significant as the girlfriends' part prior to the wedding was their total lack of role as a group during the festivities and feasting after it. Once the wedding ceremony was completed, there were no more rituals sympathetic to the bride's difficult situation in marriage. And married women's folklore never mentioned groups of friends. From this point on, the bride stood alone behind her new husband.

The trauma of the moment of final transition was recognized. When two of the bride's unmarried male relatives arrived to take her to the church to be married, she sang:

My own dear brother!
Come to me slowly,
Take very little steps!
My frisky legs won't walk,
They won't walk, they buckle
My white hands have grown ugly,
My turbulent head rolls from my shoulders.[49]

Yet sing all she might, her "brothers" carried her off to her wedding. One working woman said that in Sed'maia Tysiach', the bride's parents did not go to the church for the wedding.

After the wedding ceremony, the couple and the guests went to the groom's house for feasting, dancing, and singing. On the wedding night, the bride and groom were ceremoniously put to bed there by the matchmakers.[50] The bride was required to make ritualistic gestures of submission to her husband, such as taking off his boots and asking him which side of the bed he would permit her to lie on.[51] The next morning, the matchmakers and all the wedding guests reassembled outside the bedroom to check the bride's bedclothes. If the bedclothes proved virginity,

> then everyone beats plates and dishes. Meanwhile, the matchmakers pass the bride's chemise and bed sheet to the father-in-law in a dish. If all is not well, then they make a wry face. But this happens very rarely. Then everyone walks . . . and all of them beat dishes with rolling pins. . . . They make a lot of noise and laugh, and everyone makes funny comments [*pribavki*: stock one-liners]. Many of the expressions weren't too nice [i.e. were obscene]. Then everyone asks the father-in-law . . .: "Mishen'ka, how did the newlyweds pass the night?" And one of the guests is dressed up as a bear. He shows everyone how the newlyweds passed the night.

Then the bride had to go to fetch water; next she made pancakes for all the assembled guests. If the bride's premarital chastity had been proven, the first pancake was left whole; if not, the guests cut a circular hole in it (presumably to symbolize her breeched hymen).[52] Either way, this pancake was saved to present to the bride's mother during a later ritual visit to her home.

The beating of dishes, pots, and pans, accompanied by obscene banter and songs, continued into the streets, as the guests went to the bathhouse for a ritual that took place there. One newspaper reported that in Ivanovo-Voznesensk, the "Russian Manchester,"

> The present *Miasoed* [the period between Christmas and Shrovetide] has distinguished itself among us by an unusual abundance of weddings: there were days when in several churches they wedded from morning to night, uniting thirty couples.
> These weddings once again demonstrated the disgusting custom which has existed in our city to the present. On the day after the wedding, a long procession of "feasters" appears, who "accompany" the newlyweds to the bathhouse. . . . The "feasters," walking around in the streets, dance, beat on frying pans and lids and, for some reason, without fail they sing indecent songs.[53]

This sexual joking and singing, accompanied by the symbolic banging of phallic objects against dishes symbolizing the bride's hymen, conveyed the social sanctioning of sex now that the couple was married. This was relevant for the bride especially, because her virginity had been such an important issue, and now she had to make a sharp about-face, allowing full expression of her sexuality on the wedding night.

The public test of virginity, along with the girl's fear of the shame of having to present a punctured pancake to her mother, and the guests' hoopla of beating dishes, must have conveyed to every adolescent girl in the community the cultural expectation that she narrow her sexual attention and involvement to one man, her future husband. From the point of view of bonding patterns, this ran parallel to and reinforced the notion that a woman must be exclusively committed on every level to her husband and to the children produced through union with him and only him.

During the post-wedding night festivities, the bride had to perform— intentionally badly—a number of household tasks, serving all the guests by herself.

[T]he bride goes to fetch water. All the guests follow the newlyweds, walking and dancing. The bride gets the water and carries it home. . . . The bride must bake pancakes for everyone. . . . Then everyone goes to the bathhouse. They . . . force the bride to do everything: comb the guests' hair, sweep the [bathhouse] floor, carry the water, but she does everything backward [i.e., incorrectly]. Then they thrash the matchmaker [for arranging a marriage with such a bad housekeeper]. Then the bride brings water for real. Everyone washes themselves.[54]

Another informant recalled that the bride was required to sweep the floor incorrectly while the guests made fun of her, interfering to make her sweeping more difficult.[55]

While these rituals were undoubtedly done in a joking, merry manner, the underlying message was clear. Throughout all this work, the bride was no longer helped by her girlfriends, as she had been in sewing her trousseau before the wedding. She served all family members and friends present under humiliating circumstances (required to perform the tasks badly and to be made fun of for it), never allowed to ask help from anyone.

The bride's single-handed responsibility in all these domestic tasks, her enforced subservience (however "joking") to everyone present, and the absence of any equivalent actions by the groom, communicated to the bride what her position was to be throughout her marriage. Carrying most of the responsibility for the future family, the wife was to endure humiliation without turning to anyone else for help. This was one manifestation of women's being socialized into isolated activity even when there were other family members and friends present to whom she might in theory appeal for aid. Such socialization was part of the reason working-class women did not develop ongoing political organizations.

The emphasis placed during the wedding on establishing the interest and loyalty unit between husband and wife, as against among female family and friendship groups, may have resulted partly from the fact that women had daily domestic work in common. Whether or not they actually helped one another with these tasks, they often worked side by side: in the same workshops in the factories, in communal kitchens as they cooked, in the public bathhouses as they spent long hours doing laundry. This was far more time than any of the women typically spent with their husbands. Yet because it was women who shouldered the responsibility for holding nuclear families together, they had to develop a primary commitment to their husbands and children. The very trickiness of negotiating an absolutely adhered-to primacy of interests with a husband she did not spend much time or share many activities with, while reducing to secondary status those female friends with whom she did both, may have been one reason these issues of establishing to whom the new wife's unequivocal loyalty belonged took on such importance during the wedding ceremony.

The Matchmaker

The role of matchmakers was unusual in Russian working-class culture in that it involved women acting in an official, public capacity to form alliances among families. Might this role therefore have provided some basis for public alliance-building by women in revolutionary times?

The matchmaker, according to Tolstov, was an elderly relative living in the same city as the bride and groom, or else someone from work, usually an elderly woman who was hired as a professional matchmaker. The matchmaker was an essential part of the wedding in spite of the fact that working-class youths to a large degree chose their own marriage partners. For "the official arrangement of the marriage was considered necessary for the conclusion of the marriage," even in urban Moscow.[56] The matchmaker was responsible for performing or overseeing many of the rituals and customs carried out during the weeks between the betrothal and the day following the wedding night. For example, she brought the bride's dowry to the groom's family, put the bride and groom to bed the night of the wedding, and so on.

Despite the importance of the matchmaker's work, after she had completed its final phase (overseeing the test of virginity the morning after the wedding), she was ritualistically insulted for having done a bad job. The "reason" for this was the sloppy housekeeping work required of the bride, which "proved" the matchmaker had made a poor marriage with an incompetent wife. As the bride swept improperly, "[t]hey put the matchmaker on a bench and begin to thrash her: 'Why did you make this match with such a one, she doesn't even know how to sweep a floor.'"[57] At another point, the guests beat the matchmaker again "for arranging a marriage with an idiot." Thus, the wedding ritual required women to work against each other, as the bride was compelled to feign stupidity, demeaning herself and making the matchmaker "look" incompetent. The wedding ritual publicly divided women against each other, undermining their capacity to build alliances among themselves that could function successfully in the community beyond the home. This ritual may seem gratuitous until we consider that men were never required to perform rituals which, jokingly or otherwise, humiliated them or pitted them or pitted individual men against the group.

During the "Finding Fault with the Matchmaker," the wedding guests sang songs which criticized the matchmaker's own capacity as a housekeeper.

Our matchmaker
Lives in a straw hut;
There's not a stick of fire wood in it,
There's dirt up to the knees.[58]

And

The matchmaker hurried to the wedding,
She dried her blouse on the churn-staff, . . .
On the threshold she ironed it,
And on the road she put it on.

While these songs were sung, the unmarried female guests danced, and the matchmaker "got annoyed" at them.[59] Thus, this ritual also set the matchmaker at odds with the unmarried women present. Meanwhile, the matchmaker's work was also defined as undermining the "womanly values" of tidiness and a well-functioning home. The matchmaker was so busy with her alliance-building, the songs claimed, she couldn't manage to keep her house clean or get fully dressed before running out the door to a wedding. Such a woman was clearly not to be emulated by other women in her community.

The Groom's Part in the Wedding

The groom's part in the wedding was less elaborate than the bride's in many ways. He was involved in almost no rituals. Throughout the entire period, his place was often taken by a substitute whom he delegated to carry out his part in the wedding, such as sending the matchmaker to propose marriage, and later to get the dowry[60] from the bride, as well as sending the bridal bed to the bride rather than delivering it himself.

The groom's parents helped to arrange his marriage; they inventoried the bride's dowry before the wedding; they hosted most of the postwedding festivities. The morning after the wedding night, the groom's father received the bride's bedclothes and interacted bawdily with the wedding guests regarding the first sexual encounter between his son and daughter-in-law. These events all had to do with the acceptance of the daughter-in-law into the groom's family, rather than with the groom's family separating themselves from their son. For when a man married, he gained a wife and eventually children, but these new people in no way replaced his earlier attachments, and in comparison with the bride's experience, did not substantially change his life.

The groom never underwent rituals or singing which prepared him to separate from his childhood protectors to cleave to his wife and children. This derived, of course, from patrilocality among the Russian peasantry, from which most workers had come within relatively few generations. Newly married Russian male workers would be responsible for maintaining the same *zemliak* ties as their fathers. But this also meant that young men entering marriage remained psychologically unprepared to develop a primary loyalty to their wives.

Although the groom's friends were extremely important in his life both before and after his marriage, and even though he spent most of his time over the course of his life with them, they did not have an important role during the weeks before the wedding. They therefore did not share the man's experience of his approaching wedding, empathizing and identifying with him as did the bride's girlfriends with her. The role of the women's friendship group during the wedding rituals, as well as their shared adolescent anticipations of their future role as wives, enabled women to understand the demands of one another's marriages and thus to yield priority to those demands when family and friendship bonds came into conflict.

This understanding of family needs was not developed among men. Each man's preparations for marriage took place almost behind his friends' backs, out of their sight. That the groom's friends were not, as a group, involved in excited anticipation or preparation—physical or psychological—for his wedding was a measure of how marginally the wedding was supposed to affect those friends. A man's wedding was the single, aberrant time in his life, when he concentrated much of his attention away from his friends and on his fiancée/wife. Thus, each man's friendship group was not asked to draw back to make room for an important new relationship in his life. And this situation held not only for his wedding, but for the rest of his life as well: his married life never became well integrated into his life with his friends.

In the weeks before his wedding, the man's sole responsibility was to pay social visits to his fiancée and her group of friends as they sewed the bride's trousseau. He brought one or two friends with him (not his entire group of friends), and ideally an accordion player to entertain those present.[61] This contrasts with the bride, who, accompanied by her group of girlfriends, sat sewing and singing day after day.

On the day of the wedding, male friends and relatives had an official role to play. The bride and groom were escorted to the church and shepherded through their various required actions by "best men" or "groomsmen." Among other things, the best men held the crowns on long poles over the heads of the bride and groom.[62] Sokolov has described the groomsman as "the master of ceremonies at the wedding."[63] The best men played a formal role in directing the mechanical aspects of official moments of the wedding events, but they had nothing to do with those events as they reverberated at the emotional level in either the bride or the groom.

Thus, the official moment of formation of the new family unit was directed by a group of men who placed the participants physically in the proper place at the proper time. Although women had accomplished the necessary long-term, deep psychological and other preparations for the wedding, a group of men took over at the last moment to carry out the formal deed. This gendered division of labor seems very much in keeping with the patriarchal structure of Russian working-class culture.

Some of the ritualistic actions taken by the groom vis-à-vis his fiancée (e.g., the interchange between them on their wedding night) established him as the patriarch of the new family; his wife was delegated to take care of this part of his life for him. It was the young man who initiated the marriage proceedings with the woman of his choice. Although a woman's parents permitted her to turn down a proposal,[64] she could not initiate a marriage proposal with the man of her choice.

During the two-week interval between the arrangement of the marriage and the wedding, while the bride adjusted her own psychological state for marriage, the groom brought her presents, such as cosmetics, hair ornaments, and clothing, including intimate items such as stockings. That is, while she worked on adapting her inward emotions to be a good wife, he gave her items of his choice to adapt her outward state to be appealing to him. The bride never made an equivalent gift by which she altered her future husband's appearance to suit her own tastes, nor was he encouraged to ready himself for her emotionally.

While the bride dressed in an elaborate outfit for the wedding ceremony, the groom did not wear special clothing; he wore a starched shirt with a tie and a "black suit or whatever there is, as long as it's a good suit. He doesn't wear a flower."[65]

There was no test during the wedding, public or otherwise, of the groom's fidelity to his wife. This, along with the different gender-specific adolescent activities, contributed to a very different sexual orientation in men and, ultimately, a very different attitude toward their children. In Russian working-class culture, men's sexual relationships with their wives were not necessarily considered unique. And for men, while their children might be especially dear to them as a result of their being biological offspring, they were not generally so, I believe, as a result of their being also the offspring of a beloved spouse, as was the case with a woman's attitude toward her husband and children. Perhaps partly as a result of this, men did not develop a highly responsible, constant parental attitude.

Each woman's wedding was the most significant turning point in her life, as her culture instructed her to give up her close reliance on girlfriends and family protectors. This cultural outgrowth of patrilocal tradition was perhaps the ultimate destroyer of women's preorganization, because it taught women that they could at best expect transitory loyalty from friends and family. Childhood ties should be broken at marriage. New networks formed after marriage should favor her husband's interests, not hers (just as the peasant husband's extended family and friends in his home village had favored his interests over those of his bride, the newcomer in their midst). A woman's close attachment to girlfriends was relegated by the culture to the premarital years. Adolescents watching their older sisters' marriages received this confirmation of the grim view of marriage previewed in their Semik rituals, and knew their reliance on close friendships should be set aside as a childish thing at their own marriages.

We might wonder whether the cultural prescription to leave girlhood ties behind was actually followed. Surely married women must have needed support networks to help them with all the new responsibilities of their families. Even women who moved to a different city or town at marriage must have formed new friendships after living there a while. Let us turn to the lives of married women to see how the cultural prescriptions played out in actual life.

TWELVE

Adult Women:
The Focus Narrowed

The married woman had lived through half a lifetime of preparation for her role as wife and mother, immersed in instruction regarding her expected bonding pattern. Did married women workers actually live according to this culturally prescribed bonding pattern? Did they focus their major commitment and loyalty on their nuclear family of marriage, inhibiting the formation of other bonds? Or did women act contrary to the cultural prescriptions, forming form ongoing ties with one another in accomplishing their daily life tasks, ties which could have served as the basis for ongoing political organization in 1917?

Daily Activities of Married Women

Working women's daily lives were consumed by providing and caring for their children. As one working woman put it, "Besides the factory and children, we knew only priests."[1] We saw above the intimate quality of the friendships of women active in October street fighting in Moscow. This intimacy in unmarried women's friendships, we might suspect, prepared women for the highly personal, intimate bonds with a small group (their children) their job as childrearers required. Since women were assigned the task of childrearing, they had to develop the skill of being attuned to human emotions and their vicissitudes. The relationship between a mother and her children was expected to be exquisitely unique, like no other relationship in their lives. While women may have had a generalized fondness for all children, their involvement with their own children stood in a separate category, so special that even a stepmother was not expected to love her adoptive children as profoundly.

Women's Networks and Child Care

My sources frequently noted routine daily child care being done by young girls, either sisters or other girls hired for this purpose. However, the one time child care was routinely done by adult women other than the biological mother was in the event of the mother's death or long-term absence (usually when she had to go away to another city to work). In this case, the relatives with whom the child lived were often country dwellers. Tat'iana Dontsova, for example, was taken care of by her grandmother in the country while her mother was away in Moscow working. Later, after her mother died, her aunt, who worked at the Trekhgorka factory, took her to live there.[2] Similarly, A. F. Golubevaia went to live with her grandmother after her father died and her mother left to work at the Prokhorovka factory.[3] It seems unlikely that the nature of this bond was such that it prepared women to take joint action in their own interests during the revolution, because these child care responsibilities were sequential rather than joint: one woman took over where the other left off. This may remind us of the women in breadlines who saved others' places in line so they could go home to sleep. These women helped each other to disperse, rather than cooperating on tasks in the same place at the same time.

Women's Networks in the Factory

There was another activity shared by women which at first glance might seem to have been a potential daily-life forerunner of organization among women during the revolution. When they began factory work, many girls were trained to do weaving or other jobs by their mothers or other female workers. Also, mothers were sometimes instrumental in obtaining first jobs for their daughters by being active in the hiring process. This seems to parallel some aspects of men's corporate workplace networks, which were an important basis of male solidarity in Russian working-class culture.

A report by factory doctors observed that in two large textile factories in Bogorodsk *uezd*, the predominantly female segment of the work force had the largest number of child workers, about two-thirds of whom were girls.[4] According to the Vladimir *guberniia* factory inspector, more than one-half of registered textile workers of both sexes had working children with them.[5] At

Morozov's textile factory in Orekhovo-Zuevo, in many cases, children worked alongside their parents.[6]

A. F. Golubevaia tells her own story of how factory hiring of adolescent daughters was arranged.

> I ended up at Prokhorovka [textile factory] too when I was still a girl. I remember, my mother and I went to the [hiring] office; there was a line there. We got in line. My mother came up to the director . . . and said, "Take my daughter to work."
>
> [The director] looked at me and answered curtly, "She's too small."
>
> . . . Then my mother got shrewd. She said, "Let's get in line again. When you get up to the window this time, stand on your toes. You'll seem taller then. He won't remember us from the first time."
>
> We did it this way [and she was hired].[7]

Mothers also intervened with other authorities, such as priests, to obtain necessary documents so their daughters could enter factory work. M. A. Khitrovaia recounted, "I also went into the factory when I was fourteen. My mother took a half bottle [of liquor, presumably] and carried it to the priest, who changed the year on my birth certificate" so she would appear old enough to work legally. Tiurina also described her mother's getting a birth certificate from a deacon so the daughter could begin factory work.[8] (At times, a girl's father might ask the priest for the document she needed to obtain work. A. S. Batovaia, neither of whose parents were factory workers, was sent to work in a textile factory about thirteen miles from her village. She was too young to work legally. "My father took the priest some eggs and a piece of meat—so in one day I was transformed from a fourteen-year-old to a sixteen-year-old."[9])

Girls rarely received professional training, "even in the textile industry . . . in which women often work their whole lives." Rather, job skills were transmitted to the children from their parents.[10] Valentina Petrova said,

> From the age of fourteen, I began to learn to be a weaver at the factory. I learned from my mother [who was also a weaver]. And my brother was a metalworker apprentice; he learned from my father. Among working people this was customary: if the mother is a weaver—so the daughter will be a weaver; if the father is a metalworker—the son will be a metalworker.[11]

Golubevaia said, "I learned from my mother, in order not to pay another woman weaver three rubles to teach me."[12] Klavdia Ukolova began work "when I was fourteen. I entered the factory and learned [to weave] from my mother."[13]

In cases where the mother was dead or absent, girls learned from other female relatives and friends. Sleptsovaia was taken to Moscow at age sixteen by her cousin, who worked as a weaver at the Prokhorovka factory. "I entered the weaving shop. In the beginning, my cousin taught me, and I paid her three rubles a month for this apprenticeship."[14] Tat'iana Dontsova, who had worked in a rural cigarette manufactory alongside her mother, was taken to work at the Trekhgorka factory by her aunt after her mother died. Having worked in the spinning shop for two years, she began "to run at lunchtime to the weaving shop to learn at the machines from a woman I knew"; she was later able to transfer to weaving with the help of another woman whom she had met there, who "negotiated with the timekeeper [in charge of hiring], and she promised that she would look after me."[15]

Some women either had no training (especially in the jobs less skilled than weaving), or received their training from women other than relatives and friends. One woman recalled the challenge of learning her job from a woman employed by the factory administration. "In the factory, they provided a (woman) teacher to show you what to do. One shift she would show you, the next shift she watched you. It would happen sometimes, when the end of the thread was at the head [part of the machine], she would say, 'Press it to the cylinder.' And you'd twist it on! When you'd twisted it on, then thank God!"[16] A. S. Batovaia, who went to work in a textile factory at age fourteen, was placed in the ribbon-fly frame shop. She complained, "They didn't teach us very well. I had to figure almost everything out myself."[17]

Although many women were aided in getting jobs by other women, and taught how to perform their work by other women, these networks were fundamentally different from men's workplace networks. Women did not construct a corporate sense of themselves based on a common profession or common employment in a particular workshop or factory as did men through various initiation and solidarity activities. Rather, women remained focused on their children: through short-term teaching arrangements, each taught her own offspring, or other individual girls, in order to serve her own nuclear family better.

The father who taught his job to his son introduced the boy, at the same time, into workshop-based activities after work, such as the massive, macho fistfights whose "teams" were based on a common job, workshop, or factory of employment, as well as large-group card-playing and tavern-hopping with *zemliaki.* Women did not have any similar large-group activities which recognized and emphasized workshop-based identity. Women's workplace interactions thus were a series of separate incidents which never received the institutional elaboration necessary to make them add up to an ongoing solidarity network.

Women's other interactions with the factory milieu were also results of their family commitments. Rodionova's mother, a weaver, desperately wanted her lame son to find work at the factory where she worked. But the factory did not hire disabled people ("one-eyed, lame, or hunchbacked persons").

My mother went and cried and begged for them to hire him somewhere, anywhere, in the factory. He was a healthy fellow, he just walked with a stick. Well, after that, after my mother's long tears, the director ordered her to bring [my brother] to the room where they hired people. My mother brought him . . . and they finally gave him a job in the laundry section, and he worked better than the others there.[18]

K. V. Petushkin recalled that when he began factory work as a carder at the age of eleven, "I had to work even at night. My mother used to pull me to work on a toboggan."[19]

Women interacted with factory administrators regarding their husbands. E. S. Goriacheva's alcoholic father, "was often fired from the factory for not going to work—and then mother prostrated herself before the old timekeeper, Osip Zakharovich Medvedev, begging him to take my father back to work again."[20] Rodionova, who had worked at the same factory as her husband, recalled, "My husband decided he didn't want to work [anymore], and so they fired me. I went day after day and begged. I said that I was not the same thing as my husband, I stood whole workdays at the director's desk, but he didn't even pay any attention. But after many such trips, he took me back to work."[21] Women's tenacity in all these individual appeals to factory owners prefigured their individual tenacity in food riots during 1917. Women's daily-life responsibility for their families had always required tremendous individual persistence against great obstacles.

Women also intervened at the factory pay office, hoping to get their husbands' pay before the latter did, since the husbands were likely to drink up the money. As one worker said, "Not one payday goes by without our daughters having to ask the [payroll] office not to give their fathers their pay. Wives go to intercept it."[22] All of these actions by women, while demanding,

211

were made by individual women to help their own families, not by groups of women. The differences between women's familially oriented interaction with factories and men's group-bonded pattern were so pervasive that they can be seen even in workers' thefts from the factories. Women often stole small amounts of thread, cloth, bobbins, and items they had woven, by hiding them in bags underneath their long skirts. Newspapers frequently reported cases of women being caught stealing during factory strip searches at the end of the work shift.[23] Kokushkina said:

> In confession you'd tell the priest that you'd taken a little cotton wool or laces [from the factory], and then after Easter [when all workers had to go through a rehiring process], they wouldn't hire you back at the factory. This happened to me. I told the priest in confession, then I arrived [at the factory] to be rehired, and the director said, "I'll rehire you, but from now on, don't take any more laces from the factory." I wondered how he'd found out, but that shaggy devil [the priest] had told him.[24]

Working women had little respect for the property rights of factory owners, at least when it came to getting small amounts of materials for their personal or family use. This may have been partly because many of these women were not far removed from the peasant milieu, where it was a major part of women's role to spin and weave, and where they had owned their raw materials, their tools, and the goods they produced. Thus, women's thefts from factories demonstrate a widespread attitude among working women before 1917 that they had a right to more of their produce and of the means of production than they were getting.

Women's thefts were carried out in isolation: they took only as much as they could fit under their skirts, and the small amounts and types of goods stolen suggest that they were primarily used for domestic purposes, or perhaps to sell in small quantities (just as peasant women traditionally sold eggs and milk) to get money needed for their children. This contrasts sharply with factory thefts perpetrated by men, which were usually done by two or more men working together on large-scale crimes involving extended planning. For example, three male workers committed "systematic theft" of linen worth 348 rubles; in another case, a worker "with the participation of three of his friends" took a piece of cable weighing seventy-two pounds; two other male workers stole forty sacks; two workers were caught lowering from the third floor over a hundred feet of drive belt, worth 120 rubles, cut from the mechanism of the spinning workshop. Men's robberies were more complex than women's, often necessitating a scheme to return to the factory at night, such as when two male workers entered through the windows by taking the glass out of the window frames.[25] The large quantities of goods stolen by men were clearly intended for sale, not for family use.

Women's Networks and Personal Grievances

From Annunciation and Semik rituals through wedding songs, Russian working women were socialized to accept many difficult and painful situations without ever talking to others about them.[26] That this cultural prescription to "endure grief silently" was followed by the average working woman is seen most poignantly in their inability to talk to one another about the abuses their husbands subjected them to. Tiurina said:

> My husband bullied me. Men were tormentors, they could even beat you. What were you going to do? Usually you'd keep quiet about it—*we were ashamed to talk to one another.* They [the men] did everything. He'd beat you unmercifully—and that was that. Where were you going to complain?
> . . . It would have been better if I hadn't gotten married. But it's too late to have regrets! *Many women don't talk about how they lived in their marriages, it's always, "I don't remember."*[27]

Tiurina reveals two classic (socially engineered) methods of maintaining artificial barriers between people who actually have interests in common: shame and repression. All women must have known that wife abuse was common. Crowded living conditions made direct evidence of other women being beaten unavoidable; it often occurred outdoors or in other public situations; and popular songs and proverbs dealt freely with the issue. Yet each woman who experienced this common situation felt ashamed, according to Tiurina. Shame derives from feeling that a disgraceful situation is the victim's fault; to maintain her dignity, she must keep the disgrace secret. This shame was culturally induced, and it prevented women from doing anything to alter the status quo. For talking about common grievances is the first prerequisite to creating change.

Tiurina said that women also intentionally "didn't remember" anything about their actual relationships with their husbands. Women had been brought up expecting wonderful things from their marriages. The disappointment of

213

those expectations was not something they cared to dwell on in conversations with one another. Thus, women more or less consciously repressed their awareness and memories of bad aspects of their life situations.

Another woman, Rodionova, also gave testimony as to how her natural outrage at being beaten was negated when she did have the temerity to share her feelings with other women:

> "I often had to withstand beatings if I didn't manage to hide somewhere. *But you go to complain about it and they say, 'You heard when you were married what they read in church: "a wife fears her husband." That means you have to put up with it!'* . . . It used to be that the husband had complete power over his wife, whatever he wanted, he did."[28]

Thus, Russian working-class culture inhibited women's ability to communicate spontaneously among themselves, using their own words about the outrage they felt at being abused. Rather, women were taught to substitute the church's words, which justified abuse.

Other evidence suggests that women were socialized not to take action to help one another, even when one of them was beaten in plain sight. (This real-life situation replicated exactly the courtship dances in which young women play-acted the cultural mandate not to aid another woman abused by a man.) In both of the following newspaper accounts, crowds of male and female passerby gathered to watch as a wife pleaded with her husband not to go out drinking. In the factory settlements in which these incidents took place, at least some of the woman onlookers were likely to have known the abused wife personally.

> "My dear, sweetheart, precious—let's go [home]," came a woman's imploring voice.
> [Her husband replied,] "Get lost! I'll smack you one! I said go away, so beat it!"
> Curious bystanders gathered around the woman and the man she was trying to persuade. There were children. The men chuckled condescendingly and the women sympathized.

As the woman continued to entreat her husband, he responded by pummeling her, then walking away without looking back. There is no indication that the women in the crowd moved to help their beleaguered friend. Another account was explicit about the crowd's not rendering any aid to a woman being beaten. This account too began with a woman pleading, "Kalistran Parfenych, come back home, what's wrong? Let's go. . . . I could get you some wine and you can drink at home." A crowd gathered as the argument heated up. The man hit his wife several times in the chest, causing her to fall. He walked off and the crowd began to disperse. "The unhappy woman turned to go home. Many [in the crowd] expressed sympathy with her, but no one approached her, and no one asked her about anything."[29]

That women were socialized not to communicate with one another about physical abuse, or to join together to defend themselves, contrasted strongly with men's socialization. Men were brought up to answer taunts and physical abuse from other men with group fights. That is, males were raised in an atmosphere of free and open communication about insults and threats from other solidarity groups, and they retaliated in a highly public, active way. Fistfights are not the ideal way to create change, but they did at least maintain parity among various male solidarity groups. Their highly public nature and their directing outward of hostilities prevented the shame and secrecy which inhibited collective action by women.

In addition to physical abuse, women typically endured men's tendency to squander the family's money in drinking and gambling.[30] Men not only spent the family money, they sometimes even resorted to pawning or selling family furniture and other household effects in order to keep themselves in liquor. Moneylenders did a flourishing business in working-class suburbs of Moscow; workers turned to them for two reasons: "extreme poverty or the aftereffects of drunkenness—the two eternal companions of the Russian worker."[31] Goriacheva remembered her father selling things from their home for this purpose, while her mother struggled to provide food for the family, sometimes resorting to borrowing. "We were often left without bread, if my mother couldn't borrow money from someone until payday. [My father] often even dragged things from home and sold them to get money for drinking."[32]

The system of credit at factory food shops gave men another opportunity to impair the family's economic position, adding to the might of these daily-life hunger tsars: even after a man had spent all his cash, he could obtain items on credit at the store and sell them for money or trade them for liquor. In so doing, he lessened the amount of credit available to his family for the food they needed. A letter to *Kineshemets*, signed "A Worker [male]" described conditions at the Tomna factory: "We don't look at the tears of our children, at their poverty and the hunger of the family. When there's no money—we go to the meal shop and get tea, sugar, or even a whole . . . *pud* [36 pounds] sack of wheat flour on credit, and we carry all this . . . to sell."[33] Another

215

letter described the system at the factory store and men's typical abuse of it. "On the first of every month, the worker takes his [credit] book, goes into the store, and gets the needed goods for provisioning and, meanwhile, he doesn't forget to take an extra half pound of tea or ten pounds of sugar [to sell for liquor]."[34]

Women and children suffered in another way from men's drinking. Many newspaper reports indicate a high rate of illness and death resulting from too much alcohol, from poisoning by impure liquor, and from wounds sustained in accidents and during drunken fights.[35] A medical report of the Bogorodsk *uezd* factory doctors reported twenty-six cases of poisoning by alcohol in one year at I. P. Abramov's textile factory and four cases of "acute and chronic poisoning by spirits" at the Brunovs' factory.[36] One man who died from drinking "leaves a daughter who is about to be married, two little children, and, from his second marriage, a wife who is in the last stage of pregnancy. The situation of the orphans is critical."[37]

Injuries resulted from fighting and accidents when men were drunk. During one Trinity celebration, for example, there were many drunks who sustained "bruised eyes, noses, cheeks, and even legs and arms," and as usual "many [men] don't show up for work after the holiday—they are in the hospital or hung-over."[38] Male workers also spent time away from their families in jail after being arrested for drunkenness.[39] Whether by accident, illness, arrest, or death, the effects of men's drinking frequently removed them, temporarily or permanently, from their families and prevented them from giving whatever support, emotional or financial, they ordinarily gave. Through all this tribulation, women followed the cultural prescription of struggling hard and relying on themselves, not friendship groups, to accomplish their difficult life tasks.

Women's Networks and Food

Women were responsible for the purchase and preparation of food for their families. Their daily behavior concerning this issue is particularly important because food became one of the main issues around which women rebelled in 1917.

Nutritious meals were beyond most workers' budgets.

. . . in many families, the workers' dinner consists only of tea with bread; for some, and such aren't rare, potatoes are almost a luxury item.

Even the simplest and most common cabbage soup is seen at workers' tables only beginning in autumn and the supplies of it run out after three or four months. . . .

It's true that meat sometimes appears on the worker's table, but in such a quantity that each member of the family gets not more than 10-15 *zolotniki* [1½-2½ ounces]. Milk and eggs are out of reach of the worker; their appearance in the workers' family always coincides with illness of some member of the family. . . .

Milk appears among those workers who have nursing children, but only to the age of six to nine months.[40]

Women's food preparation tasks must have been lightened by this meager fare. But those tasks were made more difficult by poor cooking facilities. At the Tomna factory, for example, while at first there had been two kitchens with ten ovens each for eighty or so families, the owner changed this to one kitchen with six ovens.[41]

Reports of theft from *kamorki* and outdoor barrack storage sheds give a sense of the type of food eaten by workers and the quantities in which it was prepared and stored, and suggest an element of the daily round of women's chores: trips to the backyard of the barracks to get the food needed by the family each day. One report, for example, recorded the theft from an outdoor storage shed of "three jars of jam weighing twenty pounds each . . . [and] twenty-five eggs."[42] Another listed "five pounds of meat . . . [and] a bottle of lamp oil weighing five pounds."[43]

Women were responsible, for the most part, for provisioning the family. They collected wages from family members who were working (in the factories, as *nian'ki*, and so on), often having to scheme to get their husbands' pay before the latter had wasted it. They made most of the purchases necessary for the family,[44] from street peddlers or in the shops which were plentiful around large factory centers. In Kostroma, the road leading to one of the factories was "a little trade city, with sixteen grocery shops, four tearooms, three beer halls, and a big general store. In each fourth building on this street there is a trade establishment."[45] Women who worked all day were often unable to get to the shops during regular business hours. So in Yaroslavl many shops remained open on Sundays, beyond the legal hours set by the city duma, trading out of their back doors. There were plenty of customers, and the shop owners "are ready to trade twenty-six hours in every twenty-four."[46] Shops could be less than clean. Inside one Moscow milk shop there is dirt everywhere, there's dust on the counters, and little piles of dead flies.

And the owner himself is no cleaner than a floor rag; his apron is filthy, his hands are green, his fingernails black![47]

Women had to contend with shop owners' frequent cheating and shortchanging. For example, customers paying before receiving their goods (the typical arrangement in Russian shops) sometimes found they had paid for more than they got. *Gazeta-Kopeika* reported on one shopkeeper who would sell kerosene only to those customers who also bought at least fifty kopeks worth of his fetid herring, rotting cabbage, or other goods.[48]

Women's group response to daily abuses by food merchants is an important issue because it was the escalation of such problems which drew many women into street activities in 1917. Did women support one another in dealings with merchants? Little evidence is available, but one newspaper description is informative. This article expressed surprise at the fact that such cheating took place openly, with many customers around, and yet the shoppers did not act to help one another. "Walking through Miusskii market, I see a crowd of people, workers; mostly women." One woman stood holding a supposedly smoked fish in her hand, which she had just paid for. The smoked appearance of the fish had turned out to derive mainly from a layer of dirt that covered it. "Trembling from the cold, [the woman] tearfully" complained to the merchant:

> "What did you give me, anti-Christ, for seventy kopeks? This is nothing but rot. It looks like it came from a garbage bin! And you can't get it near your nose—it stinks."
>
> But the merchant doesn't understand "evidence," and he doesn't pay the slightest attention to the tears of the poor old woman. As if nothing were going on . . . he hoarsely shouts, "Fresh fish! Smoked fish! Fish! . . ."
>
> The women who surround the crying shopper look blank and—don't say a word.
>
> Not one of them decides to throw a word of truth in the face of the trader who eats away at the people's hard-earned money. Not one.[49]

We see again the familiar pattern: the woman involved in the swindle protested loudly and persistently. But because Russian working women were socialized not to stand up for each other in public situations, she did so alone; she did not appeal for aid from her fellow shoppers, nor did the other women offer to help her. With this history of married women not helping each other with cheating merchants in daily life, there seems little wonder that women did not form ongoing ties to deal with the food crisis in 1917.

Married Woman's Role in Holiday Celebrations

At least in Yaroslavl, one holiday in the first year of marriage provided a short-lived honeymoon of husbandly attention to the new wife. Holidays over the subsequent years of marriage saw sex-segregated roles for women and men once again, the wife's role being far from festive.

The Yaroslavl holiday for newlyweds in their first year of marriage took place on Maslenitsa (the Russian Mardi Gras).

> In the city of Yaroslavl, there was a brass column, a monument to Demidov. On Maslenitsa Monday, the newlyweds, those in their first year of marriage, walked and rode on horses to carouse at this brass column. This outdoor fete was called "Columns." At this fete, the newlyweds showed off their . . . very best clothes. They walked around the brass column and bought . . . *"gromochki"* (little, blackish [cakes], six kopeks a pound). They bought *baranki* [ring-shaped rolls] and ate them; in one hand they held cakes, in the other hand a package of pears, dry or soaked, and tied to the hand, a bunch of knot-shaped biscuits, of *baranki*; this is how the newlyweds walked and feasted (they did this almost up to the revolution).[50]

These couples also made ritual visits to the wife's parents for pancakes, the characteristic Russian food associated with springtime and its renewal of life and fertility.

According to Sokolov, the Russian peasant celebration of Maslenitsa used gluttony in the expectation that it would magically encourage fruitful harvests and fertility.[51] The overarching symbol of sexual intercourse in the Yaroslavl observance—encircling a phallic object as the newlyweds walked around the brass column—and the endorsement of filling the body beyond satiation with delicacies, both seem to have represented and encouraged sensuality and sexuality among newlyweds, and hence fertility. The sexual character of Maslenitsa was also expressed through ribald songs, sayings, jokes, and probably sexualized conversation.[52]

After this holiday, there were no other celebrations at any point in the life cycle for husbands and wives together. Later holidays saw the resurgence of the more typical divisions between husbands and wives. The "From Factory

219

Life" column of *Kineshemets* described the local Trinity celebration. About twenty villages around the Tomna factory and the city of Kineshma observed the holiday together for two days, inviting relatives and close friends for the merrymaking. On the third day, each village celebrated by itself, pooling money to buy wine and food and "get drunk all together." *Kineshemets* contrasted the role of the husband and wife during Trinity:

> The . . . women await this holiday with a sinking of the heart. All the difficulty of the holiday falls to their lot. Before the holiday, the men have to buy provisions, above all wine; on the holiday, when the guests come, the male element will drink wine together with them. . . . The man does only this. The housewife, meanwhile, is up to her neck in work. For about three days before the holiday, she prepares for it; she makes home-brewed beer, she cleans, cooks, and minces meat jelly. . . . And when the holiday arrives . . . all the responsibility for preparing the table lies on her. In the morning, she must cook in large quantities and put everything in order. In the afternoon, she puts on the samovar, brings the dishes and food to the table, gets dinner together, cleans up, washes, and again puts food out, and so it goes all day. And her husband sits, drinking and yelling at his wife that she should act merrier. At the same time, the housewife must watch her little children. Some have older children who could look after the little ones, but you can't keep them home at this time, they themselves run out to have a good time [teenage daughters celebrated their Semik birch tree rituals during this holiday].
>
> [A]s a reward for all this, the woman receives the curses, and often the beatings of her drunken husband. The women also suffer from wandering guests, the so-called "rabbits," of whom there are many around the factory. These "rabbits" walk from village to village, . . . [hoping] that someone will invite them for the holiday. . . . [Sometimes a husband invites such "rabbits."] Often it is heard that Sidor beat his wife because she, feeding their infant baby, took a long time bringing food to where he was sitting in the garden with some strangers. . . .[53]

As celebrated by married adults, Trinity involved a ritual strengthening of group alliances: among nearby settlements on the first two days and within each settlement on the third day, while reaching out to create new contacts among the "rabbits." But because the women were largely tied up with providing food and drink for the guests and taking care of young children, the business of alliance strengthening was left to the men. This situation once again left each woman isolated. The woman who had been part of a group of friends during the holiday celebrations of her youth now struggled alone to serve hospitality to her husband and his contacts, just as she had been taught during the pancake and bathhouse rituals at her wedding. Women never seem to have joined together to brew beer or prepare food in large batches for several families together. Food preparation and clean-up was handled by each nuclear family individually.

Adult Women's Songs

Married women's folklore focused almost exclusively on their husbands and children. In folklore, female friends were portrayed as belonging to the relatively carefree premarital years. Whereas the folklore of single women often mentioned groups of girlfriends, married women's never did. Although married men's folklore dealt with issues beyond their spouses and nuclear families, almost no women's songs did.

Mother's Songs About Their Children

Many of these songs, such as lullabies, expressed the joys mothers found in their children, and enumerated deliciously all the things mothers wished to lavish on their offspring: soft, luxurious beds:

I'll sing a song for you . . . [about]
A golden cradle,
Gilded,
In it, a little bed is made . . .
A downy featherbed,
A pillow placed for your head.[54]

doves and peace:

Lullaby, hushabye,
Doves flew in
They began to coo, . . .
"Peace, take my daughter
Likewise Sleep and Drowsiness
All for my daughter at the head of her bed.[55]

nice clothes:

Lullaby, hushabye,

221

I'll buy Lenia some felt boots
They'll fit his feet perfectly
Pretty little boots . . .
To run down the road.[56]

food along with clothes:

I'll sew you a new fur coat, a new one I'll sew, . . .
Yes and then . . . I'll buy you a white kerchief
I'll give you a jug of milk, yes,
And a piece of pie.[57]

and justice:

The kitty walks on the counter
The kitty carries the biscuits
But mother takes the biscuits away
And gives them back to Vaniushka.[58]

In their songs, mothers' relationships with their children included qualities that we also associate with adult, romantic love: tenderness, cherishing, protectiveness, sensuality. As a result, when husbands failed to live up to wives' romantic expectations, wives could turn to their young children to meet some of their need to love and cherish.

In one lullaby, a mother neglected by her husband was ready for death. Only her son gave her reason to live.

Ah, lullaby, hushabye,
Sleep while you are little. . . .

When you are grown up,
You'll go into the factory. . . .

You'll have to work without end
Don't become, little son, like your father.

He beats a sledge-hammer day and night,
Whatever he earns, he drinks up.

Your father squanders money in drink
He comes home with songs.

He sings drunken songs,
He doesn't give us any peace.

If I try to soothe him
He begins to fight and harass me.

You see what kind of life I have,
Lay me living in my grave.

I'd be lain alive in my grave,
Only I'd be sorry to leave you.

[So] I work in the factory in the day
And at night I rock your cradle.[59]

Just as children could redeem their mother's lives when little, so too did mothers hope their children would grow up to understand their mother's plight as no one else would, providing a satisfying end to a mostly disappointing life.

Lullaby, hushabye,
Sleep, dear little son.
It's hard for your mother to live,
To bring you up without your father.
Little son, you'll grow up, . . .
You'll go to the city to work.
You'll experience need and grief.
When you are grown up,
You'll know my grief.[60]

Another lullaby was sung in the voice of a grandmother, who recounted the mother's tragic life and death, urging,

Sleep, my darling little one, sleep my dear
You'll grow up to pray for your mother.[61]

One striking point about these lullabies is that they were some of the only songs in which women mentioned their lives as workers in the factory, and described their husbands as on the balance oppressive figures who made their wives' lives miserable. In virtually all other songs in which women made negative comments about their husbands, they more than balanced out the negative with positive, romantic, and often sexual statements. Thus, her

223

sleeping child was the only culturally mandated confidant of the mother who had been brought up to remain silent about her griefs in marriage. This apparently placed an outsized burden on many children, one which most could not fulfil.[62] For daughters separated from their mothers at marriage and teenage sons shifted loyalty to street gangs and left for migrant labor and military service. The extreme pain felt by a mother in losing her grown children is expressed poignantly in a number of songs. The following song describes clearly the mother's expectation of salvation through her son, and her depression at the non-realization of this dream.

> Farewell to my son! You are going
> To another land—God be with you!
> Leaving your own dear mother
> With her miserable fate.
>
> You alone were my comfort
> I used to expect
> To find comfort and happiness
> In you on your life's path.
>
> I rocked you in your cradle
> Some sleepless nights
> I sat by your bed
> With hopes for your future.
>
> You grew up, and I dreamed
> That your strong youth
> Would bring me comfort in my old age
> My only true hope
>
> But you left for another land
> And I'm alone in our homeland
> I will suffer alone
> All because of you, my only son
>
> I'll catch sight of a nest on a branch
> My tears will flow involuntarily
> I'll say, akh! little birds, you have children
> But now I have none.
>
> I hear peals of thunder
> Far from our homeland
> Where, they ask, is your son? He's not at home

Now, perhaps, he's under threat

But for me there's not much more strength
To be worn out with my sorrows
You'll return and you'll see
Your mother's grave.[63]

This mother's devotion to her son during his childhood had not paid off for her; he did not respond in kind during her later years. When sons left for military service, their mothers sang ritual laments, grieving heartbreakingly. The following example dwells on the mother's sensual longing for the beloved body and hair of the drafted son.

You, my dear little child . . .
Where are you going, my darling?
They will take you, my dear little child,
To the high induction point
To the stern chief, . . .
Your ardent heart will be terrified . . .
And your swift legs, my dear little child,
. . . will be as if hacked from beneath you,
And your white hands will drop down.
But don't be frightened, my dear little child, . . .
They will make you undress,
And they will examine, my dear little child,
Your white body,
And they will shear your dear luxuriant head,
They will take off your light brown curls.
Gather them up in your handkerchief,
Tie them up tight-tightly,
And bring them, my dear little child,
To your own dear mother.
How sad I am at heart, how painfully I pine
Without you, my dear little child,
[So] I will get these light brown curls,
I will feast my eyes on them, I will admire them
To my heart's content.[64]

Sons apparently often left their mothers emotionally, even when they did not travel far away. A Kostroma newspaper observed the widespread phenomenon of sons' belligerent treatment of their mothers, angry and hostile with them at home, and often spending long periods of time in the streets or bars with their friends.[65] Maxim Gorky's portrait in *Mother* of the relationship between the mother and her sixteen-year-old son (prior to his becoming a revolutionary) contains the classic elements of this relationship. After the father's death, Pavel began drinking excessively and treating his mother as violently as his father had. Arriving home drunk one night, Pavel "was embarrassed by his mother's gentleness and touched by the grief in her eyes. He felt like crying and kept back the tears by pretending to be drunker than he really was."[66] Pavel suppressed his teary longing for his mother's gentleness because his culture demanded that a man be tough. His embarrassment at having forbidden "feminine" feelings fueled his exaggerated drunken behavior, as he sought to convince himself he was a real man.

Adult Women's Songs About Their Husbands

Aside from songs relating to their children, virtually all married women's songs were about their one true love in life, which was always insufficiently requited. A. M. Martynova told me that women probably sang most often when they were working in groups (perhaps doing laundry in bathhouses and cooking in communal kitchens); they also frequently sang when they were alone doing housework. They chose whatever songs felt particularly meaningful to them.[67] One working woman recalled, "Mama used to sit at her loom, weave, and sing. She would say, 'I'm not singing a song, I'm suffering grief.' "[68]

Ethnographers have noted that Russian women's songs were much more dominated by lyric songs (generally about the family) than were men's;[69] that is, their songs expressed intense personal emotion, from joy to anguish. Working women's songs voiced griefs plaintively and resignedly—a stance which did not encourage groups of women to unite actively to change their lives, but rather gave them renewed strength to accept the hardships of the status quo.

Many songs of married women were concerned with the vicissitudes of romantic love. Some historians have viewed romantic love as beginning among the upper classes,[70] and being essentially a "modern" phenomenon, a mutually satisfying, highly pleasurable relationship between a man and woman.[71] However, my work indicates that the most tender sentiments of romantic love were very well known among the Russian working class (and earlier among the peasantry as well). But although working-class boys and girls shared these sentiments during courtship, men rapidly turned away from this preoccupation after marriage, while women held to it—or rather to a distorted version of it—which served to keep them in relationships that had long since lost their mutuality. In short, romantic love served a purpose—to motivate women to keep nuclear families together—and was not a source of pleasure for both man and woman in a reciprocal and equal relationship. Romantic love was, in Russian working-class culture, not liberating, but binding.[72]

As for the songs themselves, a few of them were fairy-tale-like fantasies about a poor woman achieving wealth and luxury by marrying a prince, a serf-owner, or an army commander.[73] These songs perpetuated the fantasy of marriage as the means by which a woman's life could be dramatically improved.

The overwhelming majority of married women's songs, however, were lament-like. They alternately thrilled in recalling young love, and despaired over its loss. In these songs, married love had been lost in a number of ways, all resulting from the husband's behavior. Sometimes he was unfaithful with another woman; sometimes he simply stopped loving his wife; sometimes he was leaving her to work in a distant place. Some sample verses from various songs are:

The years went by, youth went by,
As if a wind roared past.
And what has happened
Now that my darling has forgotten me?

There was a time
When my darling loved me.
But now he has left
And ruined my whole life.[74]

And:

. . . On a winter's night
My ring came unsoldered from my hand
And suddenly this spring
My darling stopped loving me.[75]

And:

But I'll remember you all my life

You see, I can only love once
Oh, believe me, I'll never forget. . . .[76]

In some songs, the woman lost her love because her husband was leaving home to work elsewhere. These embodied the female perspective on the same situation men dealt with in their songs (examined below) about their lives as tramps, soldiers, and migrant workers in Siberia and other distant places. Whereas these men's songs contained brief, stereotypic asides about home and family, the women's songs wallowed in sighs, dreams, tears, and poetry about their beloveds, whose attractive aspects were tenderly enumerated. An example is:

Farewell, tender gazes,
Farewell, my dear darling
The valleys and mountains will separate us
We'll live apart now.
I won't hear your voice.
Your smile will vanish from your eyes;
Tears will overflow involuntarily
When the hour of parting sounds.
In this sad moment
With my tender simplicity
I will clasp your hand for the last time,
I will say farewell, my sweetheart . . .
When I am left without you; . . .
I will pray for you
God will hear my prayer
And we will see each other again.
Again we'll go on Sundays
To walk in the green garden.[77]

Would the beloved man return to his yearning woman? A few songs held out enticing hope:

My sweetheart has returned and is with me again
Happiness stirs again in my breast,
And there is much, much joy ahead. . . .

Forget that sad and depressing dream . . .
And . . . again sing of love to me, your darling
As in those former happy days.[78]

But in other songs, misery reigned when a sweetheart abandoned his love forever:

A poor girl like me
Listens to [a nightingale] in the night
Not closing my eyes,
Drowning in tears. . . .

Visit all countries
In the villages and cities
You won't find anywhere
A more miserable person than me.[79]

In another song, the poor woman died of grief before her man finally dragged himself back to her again.[80]

Thus, women's songs kept wives in an agony of suspense all their married lives—miserable, but ever hopeful that love would someday return to fill their lives with joy again. In the following song, the woman alternated between an optimistic and a pessimistic outlook as to whether love would return or not.

When, amidst sadness and grief,
Life becomes hard,
When death would be a blessing to me
. . . remembering your perfect face,
The fire of your wonderful eyes,
Suffering becomes bearable to me again,
Life becomes dear to me again
. . . my heart sings,
All my thoughts are busy with you
My heart stands still and moans,
These hopeless dreams torment me,
I'm thirsty for love, for sensual pleasures
But I see only grief.
The past is full of sorrow
The future seems dark.
Hope for a better lot
Suddenly revives me again.
And I want to be with you,
Love beckons me to life.
Throwing doubt aside again
I'm ready to struggle with life.
Say only one word to me
And I'll believe in love again.[81]

The vacillations between moods in this song are an extraordinary expression of the Russian working-class woman's continual inner debate between her wish that her darling's love would return and her awareness that the reality of her situation did not live up to her expectations.

This entire group of adult women's songs almost seems designed to paralyze women, to leave them ever hungering after love under the hold of another kind of hunger tsar. For the songs never say, "Your brute of a husband is never going to change as if by magic. You can't expect him to save you from unhappiness. Try some other strategy to improve your life." Rather, these songs kept alive the fantasy that husbands somehow would change, returning happiness and meaning to women's lives.

Russian working-class culture encouraged each woman's hope that her plight would be resolved individually, by her husband returning his love to her. Except for a few lullabies, married women's songs recognized only one source of their unhappiness: loss of their husband's love. No songs sung by groups of married women together named factory conditions, cheating merchants, or even husbands' physical abuse as sources of women's dissatisfaction with their lives. And even the one grievance all women were recognized as having—unloving husbands—was not to be resolved by women joining together to collectively change men's behavior, but by each woman passively waiting on her own for things to get better. Thus, the songs inhibited women's will to take some degree of control of their lives, leaving them eternally hungry for a better lot in life. As one song put it,

> I buy peace only as a victim
> Akh, I confess I suffer so
> And all the same I love you. . . .[82]

In short, all of these songs instilled in women a high expectation of married love as the most meaningful and joyous experience in their lives, preparing them to maintain this expectation despite its constant nonfulfillment in reality. The one purpose this may have served was to fuel each woman's commitment to taking care of her children, the only outgrowth of her marital love over which, for a time at least, she had some control.

Thus, it seems clear that women's lack of public peer-group solidarity—both in daily-life struggles with cheating merchants and husbands, and in political activism in 1917—was prescribed and inculcated by their culture. Throughout their lives, girls and women were taught to narrow their commitments to focus only on husbands and children, not to broaden them to strengthen peer solidarity. The peer group was taught to stand back from each woman's private struggles, and let her suffer alone.

Women did not typically accept difficulty passively in daily life. They frequently stood up individually, for example to factory owners who had fired or would not hire them or members of their families. The methods women used in such situations—arguing, demanding, pleading, crying, and above all phenomenal persistence—were sometimes eventually successful. But women typically approached their foes—factory owners, shopkeepers, or their own husbands—as individuals, not in groups. In contrast, men's leisure activities consisted of constant repetition and playing out of each man's right to lay claim to his friends' support, whatever scrapes he got himself into.

THIRTEEN

Adult Men:
Focus on Solidarity Groups

To understand the situation of married Russian working women, an examination of the male bonding of their husbands is useful, both because the contrasts highlight women's particular bonding pattern, and also because men's activities had a major impact on women's lives.

Daily-Life Activities of Married Men

After marriage, men for the most part continued to take part in the same after-factory-shift male bonding activities they had been engaging in most of their lives: card-playing, lotto, fistfights, drinking, and, for some, soccer.[1]

Men's Group Meeting Places

Russian working men had group meeting places where they typically headed immediately after work, to see one another and immerse themselves in common relaxations. Such meeting places have often been seen by historians as important precursors to political activism, because people who are already in the habit of gathering and acting together prior to revolutionary times will be more easily able to shift to acting together politically during a revolution. Women's lack of such large group meeting places has often been seen as a hindrance to their activism.

In Moscow in the wintertime, fights between the Trekhgorka workers and workers from other factories routinely took place on the frozen Moscow river; in the summertime they were held in a vacant lot near the dump.[2] Factory yards were one of the most common after-work lotto- and card-playing areas.

Factory administrations at some Kostroma textile plants, fed up with the arguments, swearing, and fighting that accompanied lotto, forbade play in factory yards under penalty of fines, so workers moved their games to other locations: "beyond the factory gates, in a grove belonging to [another] factory owner," or to peasant-owned land nearby.[3] Sevriugov workers habituated a nearby forest, where they played lotto and cards; workers from Terskaia gathered on the road near the factory barracks;[4] and Kineshma textile workers gathered on the bank of the Volga. "On Saturday, at the end of work, tens of workers sit on the bank of the Volga, and laugh and talk peacefully. Some of them have already been to the bath house; the rest are getting ready to go there. . . . Everyone, if not completely drunk, is half 'under the fly.' "[5]

In addition to these outdoor meeting places, there were taverns and other drinking establishments at almost every turn near most factories. In Moscow, "The Prokhorovka [factory] was surrounded by a dense network of . . . taverns, beer halls, and state wine stores."[6] In Vichuga, where ten or so factories employing 20,000 to 25,000 workers were crowded together within two miles, "local merchants, especially tavern owners, live happily." In the two-thirds of a mile between the railroad station and Konovalov's factory, there were about twenty establishments selling alcoholic drinks.[7]

The corridors and even the rooms of factory housing also at times served as meeting places for groups of men: "In the [barrack] kitchens and corridors everywhere," wrote Ermilov, "card games flourish."[8] Another source, describing factory barracks around Kineshma, said, "On holidays and Sundays, circles of card players sit in the corners of corridors"; their singing (often obscene), accordion playing, and swearing "hangs in the air, heard by children and adults."[9]

Forging Male Bonding

In addition to having meeting places where each worker knew he could find his friends, male workers forged bonds in other ways. Drinking was used to bind members of groups together and to integrate new members into the group. One article singled out the entrance of apprentices into work and their finishing training as alcoholic celebrations "honored almost as a sacred thing. The whole workshop participates in them."[10] The beginning and ending of apprenticeships were important because they involved new people entering the workshop solidarity group, first as apprentices and then as full-fledged workers.

The same solemnity and ritual occurred when adult male workers entered the workshop through being hired on. "Drinking companies" occurred in large numbers when many new workers were hired at one time, and "by custom the notorious 'contribution' is taken from them, which is used to buy vodka [for the whole workshop]. This extortion is called 'from the newcomer,' and [the amount of] it differs for the various jobs, depending on wages."[11] These "contributions" were the equivalent of initiation dues paid to an organization, set high enough to compel each newcomer to take a serious stake in the group.

The pooling of contributions from each worker in a workshop was a common way of raising money for group drinking in other situations as well; this supported group solidarity much more than if each worker had bought his own refreshments. One of the best-known working-class holidays took place on the first day of work after the Easter vacation (and sometimes after Christmas also). After the workers had gotten their machines set up and adjusted, the steam was stopped, and the factory administration gave about ten kopeks to each worker to "congratulate them on an easy running [of the machines]." The men typically pooled this money to buy liquor, "adding to it their last ruble."[12] Similarly, when a new director took over the running of the Tomna factory in Kineshma, the factory administration gave a ten-kopek coin to each of the four thousand workers. "Instantly, delegates were found to go for vodka. By twelve noon, we were sitting peacefully around the factory in drunken circles. . . . But after about two hours, the attack of one artel on another began." Bloody fights ensued.[13]

In the large-group fistfights so common among male Russian workers, men fought in solidarity groups: workers of one factory, workshop, or trade against those of another; factory workers against town dwellers. In Kineshma, for example, "Fights occur mostly between the workers of the Vetka factory and the Annenskaia textile mill," each of whom blamed the other as a pretext for the battles.[14] The positive attitude men held toward fighting is seen in the macho delight of the worker describing the drunken battle above.

We had a heated battle that day. More than one bottle was broken as a result of energetic contact with the foreheads of the contenders. We suffered from vodka and beer bottles alike.

Unfortunately, no medical orderlies were to be found among us this time, and there was no one to set the broken bones of those who had fallen on the field of battle. Our four doctors' assistants were busy with bandaging.[15]

Injuries obtained in these fights were often seen as badges of valor. While men's massive fistfights at first seem gratuitous, they undoubtedly strengthened male solidarity, perhaps by establishing dominance over rights to scarce resources. Beyond this, they probably served an important role in channelling aggression and personal dislikes outward, rather than inward toward members of the solidarity group. We saw that during the Moscow street fighting of 1917, women chose small groups of friends based on personal compatibility, while men worked in larger groups based not on compatibility, but on common employment or residence. It may be that when men of a given solidarity group disliked or became angry with one of their own number, rather than allowing rifts within their group, they preserved their cohesion by turning the negative affect outward toward workers of another factory instead. Eternally holding up the spectre of a common foe (the factory, workshop, or neighborhood next door), workers of a given solidarity group suppressed their internal differences by being constantly mobilized against the supposedly greater threat of the outsiders. Ever vigilant to the need to avenge offenses committed by the "heinous" enemy next door, they were distracted from confronting tensions within their group. These attitudes formed the *tsekhovshchina* which William Rosenberg has noted undermined trade union leaders' efforts to forge bonds among workers of entire industries.

Fights began when a member of one solidarity group insulted or physically attacked a member of another. Often workers called each other names to stir up a battle.

Fights began roughly as follows: the Prokhorovtsi [workers of the Prokhorov factory] beat up a worker from Mamontov's factory; or sometimes the other way around. The one [man] beaten appealed to his friends for help. Armed with whatever came their way, the latter went to Gulian'e [a tavern] and beat up the first Prokhorov worker they found. [Then] the bloody battle began. On holidays in Gulian'e there were tens of such fights. Often the slaughter occurred between workers of various shops of the Prokhorov factory, most of all between the *"mamiia"* ([insulting nickname for] the dyers) and the *"rogali"* ([insulting nickname for] the weavers).[16]

Individual workers from other workshops or factories were considered targets purely by virtue of their working in the other place; that is, by being a member of a different solidarity group. Retribution was taken against *any* worker of the other solidarity group, whether or not that man had taken part in the initial attack. He was seen not as an individual, but as a member of a group wherein each person was held responsible for the actions of the entire group. And each individual who was attacked could count on support from all of his fellow workers to avenge the insult against him, support which ultimately resulted in large-scale fights of entire workshops, factories, or neighborhoods against other entire workshops, factories, or neighborhoods.[17]

Men's solidarity can be seen in arenas other than the "battlefield" as well. For example, a man who, brought to trial for setting up an illegal gambling operation in his home, was supported by petitions from coworkers who did not want him to be convicted.[18] Even a man who got in trouble with the law could expect his friends and coworkers to close ranks behind him.

The cohesiveness of men's groups was also fostered through lotto and card playing. Remarking on the popularity of lotto, a reporter wrote, "Whenever you see a group of workers—you almost automatically know this game is going on [unless they're playing 21 instead]. . . . They play with passion. They win and they lose, sometimes by very large amounts." These games also offered opportunities for workers of one factory (or other solidarity group) to gang up against those of another. A *Kineshemets* article described cheating at lotto, often directed by workers of a local factory against workers from other factories and inexperienced players, especially when the outsiders started winning.[19]

In a less contentious vein, imaginative workers might come up with an entertaining spectacle for the whole group to watch and cheer on. At Tikhomirov's factory in Kostroma:

> Recently . . . two of the workers . . . declared during an argument that they would eat a pound and a half of boiled sausage each. A third worker, taking on the "pair," bought 3 5/8 pounds of sausage on the condition that if they didn't eat it, they must buy him four bottles of vodka.
>
> Many curious onlookers gathered around. To the astonishment of all, the sausage was all eaten within fifteen minutes; the third worker was out eighty-four kopeks. One of the eaters lay around more than an hour with his mouth wide open, and the other said he could eat another half pound.[20]

Such public contests gave vent to the participants' competitive and exhibitionistic impulses. They also provided focal points for the entire solidarity group, to root for during the contest itself and to provide a conversation-worthy common experience to be remembered, shared, and exclaimed and laughed over by the group for a long time afterward. Such activities form a strong contrast with married women workers' behavior, which had no similar spectacles or public contests to help strengthen group cohesion.

These patterns of male solidarity behavior contrasted with working women's in another important way. Men elaborated and thus sustained and strengthened workplace-based networks. For example, both female and male workers trained newcomers to their professions. But I found no evidence that women forged newcomers into ongoing female workshop solidarity groups, as men did by making apprentices pay a monetary contribution and share a celebration by the entire workshop. In fact, women did not have any counterpart to the large-group activities, ranging from lotto to fighting, that men used to strengthen their sense of being part of an ongoing group of peers.

Rejecting Claims by Wives

Wives who attempted to get their husbands to leave the male group to come home were typically verbally abused by their husbands to the approving laughter and jeers of their companions. In addition, a more violent form of rejection of wifely intrusion into the male group was often expected by a man's peers. "In Berezin's tearoom I have often observed the following scene. A woman comes in with tears in her eyes and asks her drunken husband to come home, to which he answers with a hard blow of his fist on her head. The others sitting around all laugh and suggest that he 'tip' her with yet another good hit."[21] In this context, violence toward wives can be seen as similar to the violence directed by men toward workers not of their factory or shop.[22] In both cases, the high level of aggression was used to strengthen the cohesiveness of the male bonding group, by attempting to destroy the capacity of an outsider to impinge on the group.

One difference between male violence toward wives and that toward workers outside the solidarity group was that each man was responsible for the physical force used to keep his own wife in line, while the group as a whole took responsibility for fighting any male outsider's attacks. The following portrays a group of men affirming their view of what real manhood entailed, in face of one of their number who was acting aberrantly.

A young worker walked along, his wife following after him, begging:
"Mitia, let's go to our room."
"No, Dasha, I'll just stay out for another hour. . . ."
"Let's go, Mitia, and we'll drink a little tea, or those men will be calling you to play cards. . . . Let's go. It would be better to take half a bottle and drink it at home. And I with you."
"Well, all right."

An older worker, overhearing this conversation, commented scornfully to the other men standing around nearby.

"Is this really a man? His wife comes up to him and suddenly his friends aren't good enough for him, he dumps us. He listens to a broad! Mark my words, she'll twist him around her little finger. You can't deal with women that way. When I got married, my Dun'ka came after me too. I told her, go away—but she didn't go. So I stood up and whacked her one on the ear—she rolled head over heels. And I gave her a few more after she'd fallen down. Since then, she's changed completely. I come home drunk and she doesn't say a word, she just howls. And I've even begun to break her of that habit now. So what's with Mitia? Tffu!"
"You're right, that's true," several voices were heard at once.[23]

In short, a man's attitude toward his wife, as well as his conception of what it meant to be a man, was shaped by the mores of male solidarity.

Men's Singing

Men's singing helped forge peer bonding in the public sphere as women's did not. Men sang in public in groups, wherever they were drinking or hanging around in the streets. One newspaper article complained about groups of men singing indecent songs in Yarloslavl's streets; another protested that the groups of men who played cards in Kineshma barrack corridors on Sundays loudly swore and sang songs with accordions, disturbing everyone who lived in the building.[24] Another article described the holiday which took place after the Easter break from work. After pooling money for liquor, "The whole drunken company sprawled out on the hill opposite the factory gates. . . . Everyone enjoyed themselves . . ., singing songs filled with vulgar [sexual] expressions."[25]

If a man had a good voice, he might sing for the others. Goriacheva remembered of her father, "he had a good voice, and when he was drunk, he sang in the tavern at Napol'nyi—people thronged in from all the streets to hear his songs."[26] And in Yarloslavl's

> Sennaia Square, . . . in the evening hours always can be seen a tight ring of workers.
> Accordions wail, to which some "virtuoso" performs a ditty, and a tambourine rattles loudly.[27]

Men's singing strengthened male bonding above all through the content of their songs, which differed strikingly from women's. Some men's songs were ballads about male heroism during military battles. Many others, like women's songs, were about love and sexuality. But in sharp contrast to women's songs, men's songs warned of the dangers of caring too deeply for one's beloved. Instead, men's sexual, and even their tender, loving feelings were directed away from their wives and toward public sex symbols (female entertainers in taverns, ballerinas, fiery gypsy dancers). For doting on individual wives had the potential to fragment men's loyalty, while lusting as a group after popular sex symbols provided men with yet another shared emotional experience to strengthen male bonding.

In men's songs, the female dancer or singer was the most common focus of sexual interest. In one song, Joe fell passionately in love with Klo, a tango dancer "In far-away, hot Argentina,/ Where the southern sky is so blue." Klo was beautiful:

> Her face a classic cameo
> Her figure stylish
> Everyone knew her and loved her. . . .
>
> Klo, bending her lissome waist
> And scattering a smile to all,
> Goes to dance the tango.[28]

Klo was the embodiment of wealth and sexuality, and she beckoned the Russian male worker away from his mundane home and wife. Applying her lissome body to the exotic tango, not to factory work; reclining on luxurious divans and drinking champagne, Klo was the antithesis of the Russian working man's wife. Most importantly, Klo was desired by all men. Hence she was in a sense shared by all men, increasing their sense of having common passions and interests. Real-life wives, on the other hand, belonged to individual workers. Romance and sexuality could be experienced with one's wife only in private, not by men as a group. Passion for one's wife thus undermined male bonding. As a result, each man's passion had to be deflected away from his wife and onto a shared fantasy figure such as an entertainer.

Another song, addressed to a tavern singer, expressed some of the most tender love sentiments of the entire body of male working-class folklore I found, sentiments almost never directed in songs toward men's wives:

Oh, why did you kiss me [?]
Crazy ardor cherished in my chest
You called me darling
And I vowed to be yours, yours.

In this hour of our entrancing meeting
Only the moon shone, through the window
And I endlessly kissed, kissed
Your wonderful shoulders.

Alone, I don't know joys
You sing on the cafe stage
For flowers, jewels, and rings
You sell yourself to carousers.

But maybe you'll have a downfall
And not once will you remember me,
How you called me darling
And vowed, "I am yours, I am yours."[29]

The protagonist of this song could never have the singer as his own, because her job was to arouse the unrequited passions of all the men in her audience, not to enter a real relationship with any one of them.

A last example of this type of song was about Columbine, a ballerina who "danced with fire on the stage."

. . . Columbine
Flowered as in springtime
She fell in love with a harlequin
With all her ardent soul.

Harlequins don't know how to love
This harlequin was only infatuated

241

Columbine suffers, falls ill. . . .

On stage, the curtains were closed
They called to Columbine, "Dance!"
And she danced for her sated admirers.
She respected dancing and put her whole heart into it

Don't judge anyone ever
There are countless such Columbines in the world
You'd do better to look into her soul
Besides laughter there are tears there.[30]

This song is notable for its protective stance toward the ballerina who, though unhappy, nonetheless came through on the stage for her audience of admirers. Interestingly, Columbine's plight was the same as male workers' wives—they languished for lack of dependable love from the men they loved. The statement, "Harlequins don't know how to love/ This harlequin was only infatuated," described male workers as well, with their inability to maintain a tender relationship after their first infatuation during courtship. This song demonstrates that men were capable of compassion for a woman whose faithful love was not requited. Men probably often felt badly about the real-life suffering they caused their wives. But the culture did not permit them to express those feelings toward their wives, providing them with songs which instead encouraged them to displace those feelings from their wives to a public entertainer.

Men also seem to have directed their protective feelings toward the real-life singers who entertained them in taverns. One newspaper report described a tavern full of men protecting a singer against the insults of a couple of drunks. The men willingly paid to hear the woman sing old Russian lyric songs that moved them to tears.[31]

The only type of song which permitted men's expression of longing for their families was a specific genre in which the male protagonists were hopelessly separated from home by being in the army, by their jobs (coach driver in the far steppe, conductor on a Siberian train, etc.), or because they were tramps (usually in Siberia). For example, a coachman, freezing to death in the steppe, suddenly remembered his family as he

. . . gave instructions to his friend:
"Friend, . . .
Bury me

Here in the remote steppe.
Take my horses to my father,
Bow to my mother for me,
And to my wife, say a sad word,
Take her my betrothal ring
And tell her, so that she won't grieve,
That she should marry another
About me, say that I froze in the steppe
But I took her love with me
It's not my fate to live
With my young wife,
It's my fate to lie here
In the remote steppe."[32]

These songs expressed an emotional truth in the lives of Russian men: even if they loved their wives, it was "not their fate to live with" them, but to lie buried in emotional remoteness. Thus were men's emotions again subject to social engineering: they were permitted expression of their usually suppressed love for their families, but only within the context of hopeless obstacles (death and great distances) placed in the way of that love.

Another type of song common among men was the prisoner song, in which a man was in prison for life because he killed another man in a fight over a beloved woman.

"Tell me, prisoner, what are you in jail for?
Why are you gazing sadly at freedom through that bitter lattice? . . ."

The prisoner explained he ruined his life for

". . . a beautiful maiden.
She swore to me, she vowed she'd be
    true til the grave,
And my heart was agitated, like
    a wave at sea.
It used to be, as soon as I finished work,
    I'd be on my way to see her,
I'd strike up a tune on the accordion,
    I'd sing a happy song. . . .
For a long time already, my darling would
    have been waiting for me . . .
One time I went and saw the beauty
    hadn't been faithful to me.

243

The beauty had betrayed me—she
   was kissing another.
I began to tremble with jealousy. . . .
I had a sharp dagger with me. And
   then the bloodied maiden
Fell like a cut leaf
In the light of the moon I saw that
   my rival was my own brother. . . .
He fell to his knees and begged for mercy. . . .
That I wouldn't destroy his young life
   in its blossoming years.
But I didn't give my brother mercy:
   The sharp knife glittered in my hands
And I killed my own brother, I laid both
   of them down on the spot.
Then I went to the country and told
   all the men. . . .
The police ran in then, they took me then and there. . . ."
The prisoner finished his story and
   fell on his bed
Tears rolled from his eyes, and he
   began to sob like a child.[33]

Many other prisoner songs followed this basic plot, with a few variations. Sometimes the rival in love was a friend or a rich merchant who could offer the beautiful maiden many luxuries. One constant was the profound love the protagonist felt for his beloved. The message of these songs was clear: if a man loved a woman dearly, he would be subject to jealousy and its deadly rage against other men: "One glance from a black-haired, shy woman/ Arouses murderous blood."[34] The end result, in the prisoners' songs, was always life imprisonment. These songs were cautionary tales, teaching men that to love a woman deeply would lead him—and other men close to him—to a terrible end. Best, then, to take his accordion and songs not to his beloved's after work, but instead to his male friends at the tavern or card game.

    Thus was men's capacity to love and care for their families distorted and engineered to serve male bonding rather than the daily needs of their wives and children. The emotional deadening caused by men's need to distort and suppress their true feelings is expressed in a men's song reminiscent of the teenage boys' *chastushki* above about their sense of emotional emptiness:

It's all the same to me: to suffer or take pleasure
I grew accustomed to suffering long ago. . . .

It's all the same to me to love or hate
Love was forgotten by me long ago,
I'm prepared to caress and to offend,
It's all the same to me, it's all the same to me![35]

While men had power over women, they did not always feel triumphant. Apparently, the high price exacted by the need for male bonding often left men feeling meaningless. The need to avoid awareness of such feelings of emptiness was probably a contributing factor in men's alcoholism. For although men did not recognize their craving for intimate connectedness as clearly as women did, men too starved under the rule of their own particular kind of hunger tsar.

The Need for Male Bonding in Russian Working-Class Communities

Male bonding tends to be strong in communities where close, cooperative activity among the men is required to accomplish important tasks. Working-class Russia may have constituted such a community, in its precarious conditions of life and work: the difficulty of finding jobs, arbitrary firing, high fines, the high rate of job-related injuries, problematic relationships with landlords, and so on. The precariousness of life is illustrated, for example, in the endless numbers of mutilating injuries received by workers in the factories. Workers had hands crushed in machinery, they slipped on wet floors near dangerous equipment, they received burns from fires and chemicals. In a very common kind of accident, one Ivanovo man's right hand was torn off in a machine and had to be amputated at the elbow. Another had all five fingers of his left hand crushed in a textile sizing machine. Another was heavily burned over his entire body by steam from a vat in which calico was soaked. The rate of such accidents was very high,[36] as was that of other catastrophes in workers' lives. Thus, the paucity of government or other public institutions protecting workers necessitated a strong commitment to mutual aid across families. In the long run, male bonding may have served family needs, despite its detrimental effect on the family in the short run.

This is not the place for such issues to be addressed definitively. But our understanding of women workers' situation will be enhanced by a quick speculative review of the possible social efficacy of male bonding.

Taverns as Labor Exchanges and Sources of Legal Aid

One possible way that men's collectively oriented behavior was advantageous to men and their families is suggested by the following newspaper article. The article began by describing how the "simple person" went about obtaining legal aid when he needed it.

> [S]ay he's been unjustly fired from the factory or he's had a misunderstanding with his landlord, etc. Where can he go to find [legal] help? He goes to the tavern. "I come into the tavern," he says, "and already there's a lawyer sitting at the table . . . and he will write me a petition for ten kopeks."
>
> We have too few labor exchanges, so that in order to find work, in order to make inquiries about whether there's a job available in a factory or plant, again he has to go to the tavern. Here it's possible to meet *zemliaki* and even to easily make contacts with strangers, and maybe find out about an available job. Thus, in the absence of the aforementioned institutions among us, the tavern acts as a substitute for them. In the meantime, it is an extraordinarily important link in our social life. Among us, the tavern is the bureau for the dissemination of legal help, it performs tasks in finding work, it even acts as a popular club, and so on.[37]

Another source stated that in the tavern "the unemployed found out about available jobs in one factory or another, and helped one another."[38] In many factories, workers were frequently hired only if recommended by a friend or relative already employed there.[39] In Ivanovo-Voznesensk, hiring of even unskilled workers was done only by recommendation—"without one, you can't get a job anywhere." The result was that "among the local factory population, a peculiar new business has been born: the trade in recommendations. The lower factory 'authorities' and old workers do business in recommendations, levying 3-5 rubles each for a recommendation in the name of relatives, grandfathers, aunts, brothers-in-law, etc."[40] Long-standing *zemliak* ties were thus apparently not always sacred to workers. What we see in this description is the formation of a new kind of tie, perhaps equally strong, among workers dependent on other workers for obtaining factory work.

The types of legal problems for which workers turned to lawyers who set up office in taverns often involved grievances against their employers. For example, one man entered lengthy legal proceedings against the factory where his young son had received an injury on the job; another turned to a lawyer for help in writing a petition asking to be rehired at the factory where he had been fired after working forty years.[41] We saw above the case of a father dealing with the police to try to ensure punishment of a youth who had attacked his daughter sexually.

Male Group Defense of Family Interests in the Public Sphere

The men of working-class communities, acting together, may have performed other tasks important to the family. For example, groups of workers frequently approached the factory management to request changes in factory or barrack routines. Although it is rarely stated whether these workers were male or female, it is likely that they were men because newspapers seem to have generally made special mention of gender when women were involved. A male weaver wrote to *Kineshemets* that, at the Annenskaia factory, workers were having trouble figuring out why the material they wove was suddenly turning out in very bad quality. "[W]e weavers . . . finally came to the conclusion that the reason was either the poor quality of the thread or the incorrect sizing of the warp." So the workers went to the director of the factory to see if corrections could be made.[42] In another case, the steam engine in the weaving section was breaking down continuously, causing the workers to remain idle for long periods of time. This was reducing their wages, so they went in a group to the factory owner to ask for a bonus to cover the down time. Workers injured on the job had to petition the factory for the small payment allotted to them. For example, a twenty-year-old working woman lost the fingers of her left hand in a machine and was granted five rubles in compensation.[43] Workers also made requests to factory administrations regarding long hours and low wages.[44]

In addition, there were many problems in barracks living about which workers turned to the factory administration. When the cost of firewood skyrocketed around Yaroslavl, "the workers in the factories and plants asked their employers to sell them firewood at the factory price, with deductions for delivery."[45] At the Tomna factory, copper and metal workshops in the basement of one barrack filled the entire living area with a stench from acid and carbon monoxide. "The workers went to the [factory] office with the request that the workshops be located elsewhere." When the factory administration stopped heating the barracks after March, the workers protested and the heat was turned on again.[46] The inhabitants of a newly built workers' settlement near the Tomna factory were forced to walk a roundabout route to and from the factory because the factory owners prohibited them from walking across factory land. "The settlement inhabitants entered negotiations with the [factory] office which finally agreed . . . to arrange a path for them on their land."[47] Workers also wrote letters to the local newspaper complaining about difficulties their wives faced when the factory owners changed bathhouse rules, making laundry washing more difficult.[48]

Requests to factory administrations were apparently successful in only a fraction of cases. But when they were successful, they—like the legal and "labor exchange" functions of taverns—resulted in important improvements in the lives of the whole family. Thus, if male bonding aided in producing these results, it may have been the case that, however destructive much of male behavior was to wives and children in the short run, it was helpful to them over the long run. It is possible that the very infrequency of successful outcomes—due to the great power of factory owners, backed by the tsarist autocracy—meant that, in order to keep men together in groups, able to respond with joint petitions and requests as problems arose, they had to give themselves incentive to stay together. Friendship, game-playing, alcohol, and rowdiness may have been those incentives.

There were other types of neighborhood problems to which men also responded as a group. For example, workers of a Moscow factory "arranged a collection of money for the benefit of some friends who were literally starving because they were unemployed."[49] Workers at the Tomna factory became involved as a group in trying to catch a thief who had been stealing from many of them.[50] The road in another textile settlement was impassable, so "the inhabitants . . ., collecting many signatures, made an appeal to the city government requesting the speedy repair of the road to their settlement . . ., and the digging of gutters for sewage."[51] In Navoloki, workers called a village assembly to plan how to deal with a frightening noise emanating from the bathhouse, which some in the community thought was the devil.[52]

In short, male bonding maintained cross-family ties that were called upon to solve problems as need arose, from collecting money for aid to unemployed friends to protecting the community from mysterious threats. The sense of common interest among the men involved was sealed with vodka.

Male Bonding and Military Service

Beyond the daily needs of the family and local community, another important imperative in men's lives affected male bonding: military service.[53] The length of the peacetime draft was reduced from twenty years to four years after 1888 (and to three years after the Russo-Japanese war). However, once drafted, a man was subject to mobilization during wartime for indefinite service up to the age of thirty-nine, no matter what his family obligations. This occurred during both the Russo-Japanese and the First World wars. Thus, during wartime, "the system resembled a lottery little different from the pre-reform system."[54]

The following newspaper report makes connections among army service, male bonding, and drinking.

> On Oct. 15, the call-up of young people to do their military service began, and along with it the drinking also began.
>
> Every recruit considers it necessary to have a good time during the year they are drafted; that is, to drink. The good time begins in the villages long before the call-up, almost a year before. But it appears in its greatest degree, of course, during the days of the call-up. Then, fathers' pockets are emptied, and the fathers themselves, using this as an opportunity to drink, don't lag behind their dear sons. For this, they sell everything they can possibly sell . . . go into debt, and approach total impoverishment.[55]

In order for a man to weather the hardships of three to potentially eighteen years at the bottom rung of the tsarist army, far from the physical and emotional comforts of home, certain personal qualities were desirable. These included the capacity to turn one's back on loved ones to seek satisfaction among all-male company in distant lands, to be ready to fight, and to identify strongly with the solidarity group, the army, against the common foe. Whatever the causal links here, these personal qualities were strikingly common among working-class men.

Men working in factories were aware of military events that might affect their lives. For example, "The Balkan events," noted an October 1912 newspaper story, "called forth many different conversations among the workers at our factory." The interplay between this awareness of international belligerence and male workers' everyday belligerence and provocations is suggested by a newspaper report of a group of men who got into a fistfight resulting from their discussion of the international hostilities. Although it is impossible to make definitive statements based on this evidence alone, it does suggest that men's belligerence and solidarity may have been in part a preparation for the rigors of army service. As one of the brawling workers put it, "The Turks are at war and we are at war."[56]

Outside Groups' Encouragement of Male Bonding Behavior

The needs of the military raise the issue of the state's impact on male workers. From the point of view of the Russian government, good army material was needed: men able to fight shoulder to shoulder with other men and not handicapped by a constant longing to return home to their families. Thus it may be that the state in some way encouraged everyday male behavior, which shaped men's personalities to its needs. For example, government-owned liquor shops were plentiful around at least some factories.[57]

In addition to the government, some sources stated that factory owners encouraged fighting among workers in order to divert their hostility away from their employers. One worker at the Trekhgorka factory described the workers' violent fights and then said, "The [factory] administration encouraged such fights—they tried to distract us from politics."[58] Employers' actual practices support this view insofar as factory owners often gave workers bonuses at the traditional celebration of starting work after the Christmas and Easter breaks and for such events as the arrival of a new factory director, even though they knew that the workers always used this money for drink.[59] Another source argued that the brewers of moonshine and the purveyors of prostitution in and around working-class communities encouraged workers' fighting with the hope of thus encouraging the demand for their merchandise.[60]

Government, industry, and the community all had a great deal at stake in keeping men and women in their culturally assigned places. And, as we have seen, even when the Russian people began to rebel against the first two, they remained in thrall to the third.

FOURTEEN

Conclusion

One of the most confusing things about oppressed people is that they behave like oppressed people. This simple fact complicates almost any investigation into gender-related issues. On the one hand, the rediscovery of women's history demands that achievements be given their due and viewed as the remarkable victories over the odds they so often are. On the other hand, a clear-eyed view of occasions when women do not soar above their culture is critical if we are to understand the forces that have shaped their lives.

As we have seen, before and during the October Revolution, women were actively involved in food actions, demonstrations, and "spontaneous" searches of the homes and shops of suspected hoarders and speculators. During Moscow street fighting, they served as reconnaissance agents, first aid workers, food suppliers, and support troops. Individual women became active in revolutionary organizations and rose in the ranks to attain positions of leadership. However, the vast majority of working women did not participate in ongoing organizations to further women's liberation.

The Russian Revolution gave women's history a great many achievements to respect and celebrate. It also seems to provide yet more evidence that men and women who are molded from childhood to fit certain roles more often than not play out those roles—even when the mold itself is thrown away.

Among working-class men and women in Russia during the early years of this century, socialization was intense and strongly focused. Women were prepared—by custom, ritual, family influence, and peer pressure—to invest their emotional energy and their hopes of fulfillment in a husband and nuclear family. All other bonds were discouraged or minimized. Men were trained to direct their energies toward other men in their community, and to hold in contempt feelings of love and affection for their own families. Thus, women were expected to willingly sacrifice anything for their children, while men were expected to willingly sacrifice anything for each other.

During the revolution, women and men continued to act according to these scripts, internalized during nonrevolutionary times. Men joined and supported the revolution based in their daily life solidarity groups. Women fought to improve their lives, not unified in large groups which might have affected real change, but as individuals, or at best as groups coming together momentarily before dispersing once again.

If human beings always decided their life strategies based on rational assessments of their changing needs and assets, we would probably have seen a very different pattern of activism among Russian working women during the window of opportunity for a new way of life opened briefly between the February and October Revolutions of 1917. Instead of spending hours waiting in breadlines, women might have used this time to organize to affect the root causes of the food shortage. Instead of accepting workers' organizations' evaluations of women's family problems as irrelevant, women might have joined together to collectively assert alcoholism and wife-beating as issues whose amelioration was central to the reorganization of society into a more just order. Instead of accepting the fragmentation of women's networks mandated by patrilocal tradition, women might have formed sisterly bonds in struggle with their peers. Women were already abused physically and neglected financially. A rational assessment of their situation would say they had nowhere to go but up.

But human beings do not always behave according to rational assessments of new opportunities in their environment. For, as anthropologists have helped us realize, emotional bonding is a centrally important element of the organization of human communities. Individuals' internalization of the bonding pattern appropriate to the work they do in daily life is as important to their successful accomplishment of that work over the long haul—through easy times and hard times—as is acquisition of the appropriate job skills.

Emotional bonding is important because it makes human beings feel committed to carrying out their assigned roles even when the going gets almost impossible. Russian working women were socialized to bond above all to their nuclear families. As a result, they remained committed to their husbands even when those husbands beat them. They remained committed to their families of marriage even when they longed to return to childhood protectors. They remained committed to obtaining pure food for their children even when it meant confrontation with armed authority.

But while emotional bonding keeps men and women committed to their assigned roles through difficult times, it also fossilizes that commitment when social, political, or economic conditions change, presenting the possibility of redoing social organization in a more equitable way. The old saw "You can't teach an old dog new tricks" can be reframed in a social context: Groups of human beings have a hard time teaching themselves new ways of thinking about their deepest human ties, even under—perhaps especially under—radically new historical conditions.

The issue of women's isolation in the home versus their access to collective meeting places in barracks is illuminating because it highlights the roles of two types of factors—material resources and cultural prescriptions—in influencing collective action. As we have seen, the spaces where Russian factory women typically spent much of their time together happened to be large, communal areas later used as locations for revolutionary meetings. Women gathered in these spaces each day, carrying out work which they all had in common. Yet they did not form the type of ongoing, institutionalized peer bonding that men did in their taverns and other meeting places. It becomes clear, then, that the real issue for women's organizing was not access to communal meeting places, or even whether women regularly gathered together, but whether their culture permitted them to utilize these opportunities to forge strong bonds, as did male workers.

Some historians have supposed that one obstacle to women's organization into trade unions was that union halls were often located in or above taverns, which were defined as men's spaces. However, the fact that the most obvious communal spaces in Russian working-class communities (barracks kitchens and laundry facilities) were defined as *women's* territory did not in the least undermine *men's* capacity to forge collective bonds. Men's culturally assigned need for gathering places made them willing to devote large chunks of their wages to pay for meeting spaces, as tavern after tavern opened near factories to meet the demand. When taverns were not sufficient, men simply met outdoors, in factory yards, forests, roadways, meadows, river banks, and even on frozen rivers themselves in wintertime.

In short, the theory that isolation at home and lack of group meeting places has historically fragmented women's ties to each other seems to have the real relationship backwards. More correctly, it could be argued that where people's prescribed daily-life responsibilities required group solidarity, they found and/or created a demand and paid for spaces adapted to group meeting, even if they had to go outdoors. And where daily-life child care and other family responsibilities required narrowing one's focus to a commitment to the nuclear family only, they ignored the communal group meeting places and other resources readily available to them.

Because women were raised to ignore opportunities for collective organization in everyday life, they continued to ignore opportunities for collective action during the revolution. They did not take advantage of the new resources which came into being in their environment: breadlines as possible meeting places, potential alliances with the soldiers standing next to them in lines, factory organizations, food provisioning committees, and so on. Although the open political situation between the revolutions of 1917 briefly raised the possibility of a new and better order, women continued, as in daily life, to ignore the potentiality for group effort to improve their lives.

Historians have tended to assume that women's friendship and support networks were as suited to support collective action in the public sphere as were men's. However, among Russian working women, women's group activities and rituals strengthened their ties, not to each other, but to their husbands and children. Dance songs and wedding rituals did not merely prepare each individual woman to accept a married life of abuse. They prepared *groups* of women not to come to each other's aid when some of their number were being abused. Thus, women's rituals seem designed more to inhibit the tendency for a natural interest group to act in concert than to encourage its solidarity, as do many of the group rituals studied by anthropologists. And if women were raised not to help each other when they were being beaten, how can we expect them to have been able to organize around other grievances?

In short, to answer the question raised in the introduction to Part Two, Pelegeia's women friends were not with her in her moment of need because they had been taught, at the deepest level of the human psyche, to *stay away* when she was in trouble.

I believe that part of the reason women (and men) remained so committed to their culturally prescribed bonding patterns was that sex role socialization occurred not through rational appraisal of their situation, but at a deep emotional level, through rituals and folklore which engaged the unconscious recesses of the psyche, of women's and men's most profound senses of identity. To act counter to the cultural prescriptions for each gender was to go against the very core of one's sense of self.

The cultural prescriptions transmitted through folklore remained unquestioned partly because they were usually conveyed during holidays, parties, and celebrations, in an atmosphere which stressed not rational consideration, but pleasure. Even the most painful cultural messages were conveyed not through lectures, but during times of merriment, joking, beauty, good food, flirtation, and sexual titillation. As a result, even the most painful aspects of ones life role became unconsciously associated with pleasure. On the surface, everyone was having fun during rituals and celebrations. Underneath, unnoticed, each man's and woman's most profound sense of self was being shaped.

Does this mean culture is the ultimate determinant of human behavior? Are Marxist and other historians wrong to look to the organization of work as the ultimate necessity which forges culture and human behavior? I would answer that they are *not* wrong—with two caveats. First, work must be defined more broadly than the production of subsistence. Both men and women in Russia worked their entire lives in factories, and yet their behavior differed radically. In order for us to understand their very different gendered activity patterns, we must define work as including the myriad responsibilities of childrearing, as well as the many activities beyond wage earning needed to maintain life (e.g., whatever one must do to get back a job from which one has been fired, get an impassable road repaired, or be able to survive in the event an industrial accident destroys one's capacity to earn a living).

Secondly, historians must recognize that psychological commitments—one's sense of self as inextricably bound by emotional ties to particular people in one's environment—are as much job requirements of particular forms of work as are work skills. To accomplish their work, women had not only to learn to weave or spin in the factory. Within the Russian patrilocal tradition, they also had to bind intimately to their husbands and children, and to inhibit ties to other women. Each was a prerequisite of their work as assigned by their culture. And emotional bonds, once programmed, in turn become almost as powerful as the hard wiring of economic necessity in effecting human behavior.

It is important to note that, while men's solidarity provided more of a basis for collective action during 1917 than did women's daily life bonding, male workers were ultimately also very oppressed in Soviet society. The particular shape of men's prerevolutionary solidarity was their downfall as well as their achievement, because it created solidarity only by setting up each group of men against other groups (men of other factories or other trades)—who were in reality very much like themselves. As trade union leaders observed, *tsekhovshchina* divided the working class because it forged solidarity within its subunits but not between them. Perhaps this lack of overall unity facilitated the rise of the central Soviet dictatorship.

At any rate, under the Soviet system, male workers gained the wage and job security their *zemliak* groups had long striven to provide before the revolution. But after the new regime had consolidated itself, they completely lost their right to organize in any kind of self-governed group. Men's jobs and wages may have been more secure after the revolution, but they paid for this by accepting atomization of even the degree of solidarity they had had before the revolution.

Women in prerevolutionary Russia often fought tenaciously and sometimes successfully against factory owners who fired them or merchants who cheated them. But they did so as lone individuals. Each woman formed bonds of hope for a better life only with her children. Her bonding tools were lullabies, caresses, and nurturance. But nurturance alone cannot hold together the mass movements which, in the absence of any other source of power, have always been the strength of poverty-stricken people fighting for a better life.

At the same time, men's method of creating solidarity by diverting anger aroused within the group onto other "outside" groups during massive fistfights could not unite a large enough movement to prevent the rise of dictatorship. Clearly, we must devise ways of combining women's and men's strengths in bonding, while overcoming the weaknesses of each. We must be able to work together with people with whom we have disagreements, without blaming some other outside group for the negative emotions thus raised. We might speculate that, if genuine concern for the nurturance of others' ideas and well-being could be applied on a mass scale, individual differences and disagreements might be more easily integrated, or at least tolerated. Undoubtedly, liberation will be achieved only when we manage to devise and carry out some combination of men's ability to form impersonal solidarity together with women's capacity for nurturance and intimacy.

Notes

EDITOR'S INTRODUCTION

1. Edward T. James, Janet Wilson James, and Paul S. Boyer. eds. *Notable American Women, 1607-1950: A Biographical Dictionary*, 3 vols. (Cambridge: Harvard University Press, 1971); Barbara Sicherman and Carol Hurd Green, eds., *Notable American Women, the Modern Period: A Biographical Dictionary* (Cambridge: Harvard University Press, 1980).
2. New York: R.R. Bowker, 1979.

CHAPTER ONE

1. #335, p. 3.
2. Gail Lapidus, *Women in Soviet Society: Equality, Development, and Social Change* (Berkeley: University of California Press, 1978); Michael Paul Sacks, *Women's Work in Soviet Russia: Continuity in the Midst of Change* (New York: Praeger, 1976).
3. Tsentral'nyi Gosudarstvennyi Arkhiv Literatury i Iskusstva (TsGALI), fond 1455, opis' 1, edinitsa khranenii 52, list 44.
4. "Where are the Organized Women Workers?" *Feminist Studies* III (Fall 1975), p. 92.
5. Other obstacles to women workers' organization have been noted as well. Kessler-Harris's article, for example, argued that the main problem for women was men's reluctance to allow women to organize.
6. The decline of activism among the immigrant operatives who succeeded them in the Lowell mills in later years has correspondingly been attributed in part to the latters' more dispersed living situations within individual families, rather than in dormitories. Hannah Josephson, *The Golden Threads* (New York: Russell and Russell, 1967); Gerda Lerner, "The Lady and the Mill Girl: Changes in the Status of Women in the Age of Jackson," *MidContinent American Studies Journal* 10 (Spring 1969); Thomas Dublin, "Women, Work, and the Family: Female Operatives in the Lowell Mills, 1830-1860," *Feminist Studies* 3 (Fall 1975); and his *Women at Work: The Transformation of Work and Community in Lowell, Massachusetts, 1826-1860* (New York: Columbia University Press, 1979); and Anne Bobroff,

"Maximum Hour and Minimum Wage Legislation for Women, 1840-1940" (undergraduate seminar paper, 1971), pp. 48-56. The conceptual division between "public" and "private" has been critiqued by Michelle Rosaldo, "Thoughts on Domestic/Public" (paper prepared for Rockefeller Foundation conference, "Women, Family, and Work," New York City, September 1978); Joan Kelly, "The Doubled Vision of Feminist Theory: A Postscript to the 'Women and Power' Conference," *Feminist Studies* 5 (Spring 1979); Rayna Rapp Reiter, "Household and Family," *Feminist Studies* 5 (Spring 1979). The observation that women in scattered housing have more difficulty organizing than do men who meet together after work probably ultimately derives from Marx's observation that workers grouped in factories can organize more easily than can peasants dispersed in small settlements throughout the countryside.

7. Dormitory or barracks living was dictated by the same conditions in the Russian textile industry as it was in early New England: these factories were often built in semi-rural or rural areas where there was not enough housing for the large, newly gathered work force. To attract workers, factory owners had to supply them with a place to live.

8. *Za vlast' sovetov* (Moscow: Moskovskii rabochii, 1957), p. 18. See also O. N. Chaadaeva, *Rabotnitsa na sotsialisticheskoi stroike, Sbornik avtobiografii rabotnits* (Moscow: Partiinoe Izdatel'stvo, 1932), p. 140, describing kitchen meetings, and *Na putiakh k Oktiabr'iu, Vospominaniia starykh Bol'shevikov o revoliutsionnykh sobytiakh vo Vladimirskoi gubernii* (Vladimir: Vladimirskoe Knizhnoe Izdatel'stvo, 1957), p. 33, for a meeting held in a factory communal dining room.

9. *Kur'er*, March 24, 1917, #64, p. 3.

10. M. I. Petrakov, "Vospominaniia," in *Istoriko-Kraevedcheskii sbornik*, ed. by Orekhovo-Zuevskii Pedagogicheskii Institut (Moscow, 1959), p. 211.

11. Carroll Smith-Rosenberg, "The Female World of Love and Ritual: Relationships between Women in Nineteenth-Century America," *Signs* 1 (Autumn 1975), pp. 1-29; Johnny Faragher and Christine Stansell, "Women and their Families on the Overland Trail to California and Oregon, 1842-1867," *Feminist Studies* 2 (Winter 1975), pp. 150-66; Nancy F. Cott, *The Bonds of Womanhood: "Women's Sphere" in New England, 1780-1835* (New Haven: Yale University Press, 1977); Carol B. Stack, *All Our Kin: Strategies for Survival in a Black Community* (New York: Harper and Row, 1974). This trend has also utilized the classic earlier study by Michael Young and Peter Willmott, *Family and Kinship in East London* (Glencoe, Illinois: The Free Press, 1957).

12. Jane Abray, "Feminism in the French Revolution," *American Historical Review* 80 (February 1975); Dorothy Thompson, "Women and Nineteenth-Century Radical Politics: A Lost Dimension," in *The Rights and Wrongs of Women*, ed. by Juliet Mitchell and Ann Oakley (New York: Penguin Books, 1976), pp. 112-38; Barbara Taylor, " 'The Men are as Bad as their Masters

. . .': Socialism, Feminism, and Sexual Antagonism in the London Tailoring Trade in the Early 1830s," *Feminist Studies* 5 (Spring 1979), pp. 7-40; Darline Gay Levy, Harriet Branson Applewhite, Mary Durham Johnson, eds., *Women in Revolutionary Paris, 1789-1795, Selected Documents* (Urbana: University of Illinois Press, 1979); Jill Liddington, "Rediscovering Suffrage History," *History Workshop* (Autumn 1977), pp. 192-202; Olwen Hufton, "Women in Revolution, 1789-1796," *Past and Present* 53 (November 1971), pp. 90-108; Elizabeth Racz, "The Women's Rights Movement in the French Revolution," *Science and Society* 16 (Spring 1952), pp. 151-74; Smith-Rosenberg, "Beauty, the Beast, and the Militant Woman: A Case Study in Sex Roles and Social Stress in Jacksonian America," *American Quarterly* 23 (October 1971), pp. 562-84.

13. Ryan, "The Power of Women's Networks: A Case Study of Female Moral Reform in Antebellum America," *Feminist Studies* 5 (Spring 1979), pp. 66-85. Barbara Berg makes a similar argument about the origins of American feminism in *The Remembered Gate: Origins of American Feminism* (New York: Oxford University Press, 1978).

14. Ross contribution to Rayna Rapp, Ross, and Renate Bridenthal, "Examining Family History," *Feminist Studies* 5 (Spring 1979), p. 186. This issue, recently raised for working women in particular, has been studied in some detail for male workers. For Russian workers, for example, Robert Eugene Johnson has examined the impact of *zemliak* ties on the political activism of Moscow workers in the late nineteenth century, *Peasant and Proletarian*, pp. 75-79, 159-60.

15. Thompson, "Women," is an example of this. Other historians have noted the very short-lived character of women's organizational activity, Ryan, "The Power of Women's Networks," pp. 81-83; Taylor, "Socialism, Feminism, and Sexual Antagonism," p. 19. Liddington also notes that, although working women signed petitions and attended meetings, "it seems highly probable that even the radical suffragists, with their strong local contacts, found it virtually impossible to involve the majority of local working women in a political campaign," i.e., in ongoing participation in the suffrage movement, "Rediscovering," p. 200.

16. Ethnographic material, including oral histories, from textile workers of Tver was later included. These materials are located in Rukopisnyi Otdel Instituta Russkoi Literatury (Pushkinskii Dom), Rasriad V, kollektsiia 53.

17. The Yaroslavskaia Bol'shaia textile mill, established in 1722, employed 10,615 workers in 1917; the Norskoe textile factory had 1,398 workers (R. V. Balashov, *Ustanovlenie rabochego kontrol' Iarosl.* [avtoreferat], p. 6). For further information on the size of work forces in Yaroslavl factories, see *Iaroslavets*, November 8, 1912, #131, pp. 3-4.

18. A. G. Rashin's statistics for all factory workers of Moscow guberniia in the 1880s revealed similar proportions: the age group 17-39 years accounted for 61.8% of the male workers and 61.2% of the female workers, p. 278.

Rashin also provides 1896-1900 statistics for the Glukhovskaia factory and for all of Bogorodsk uezd. *Formirovanie*, p. 83.

19. Riazanova, *Zhenskii trud*, pp. 93, 156-57, 278.
20. S. P. Tolstov, *Narodny mira. Etnograficheskie ocherki* (Moscow: Izdatel'stvo Akademiia Nauk, 1958), p. 474.
21. Johnson, *Peasant and Proletarian*, p. 52.
22. Ts. S. Bobrovskaia, *Twenty Years in Underground Russia: Memoirs of a Rank and File Bolshevik* (New York: International Publishers, 1934), p. 165.

CHAPTER TWO

1. *Gazeta-Kopeika*, March 15, 1917, #226, p. 3.
2. Ibid.
3. My sources for this chapter are primarily local newspapers of a political hue sympathetic to the working class but not tied very closely to any one party's agitational work. The highly political press which I examined for the CIR in 1917, Soviet as well as Bolshevik, rarely reported on workers' spontaneous activity. The probable reason for this was that these groups were deeply engaged in the effort to generate new institutions and relatively disciplined political organizations; they therefore saw urban street actions, not focused by any overarching group, as potentially destructive to the revolution and certainly not worthy of in-depth coverage. The local political press, Bolshevik, Soviet, and other, of the Moscow textile region often reads like a bulletin board of official notices, recording resolutions taken by factory meetings (but not descriptions of the meetings themselves), measures resolved by newly established revolutionary institutions (but not the street actions which were sometimes the forerunners of those institutions' concerns). The memoirs (most published by Soviet publishing houses), which I rely on heavily later, are also almost devoid of information on the least organized aspects of the revolution. Only those newspapers whose editorial boards and reporters were less concerned with *making* the revolution had the time to spend in the streets *observing* the action and reporting it in all its myriad detail. The scale of detail was very fine, reporters often recording conversations among those in the streets. The journalistic style was frequently satirical, the stories written with the biting, dark humor through which many of these reporters expressed their sympathy toward the plight of the lower classes.
4. In this spirit, see E. P. Thompson on food riots, "The English Crowd in the Eighteenth Century," *Past and Present* 50 (February 1971).
5. *Povolzhskii vestnik*, June 6, 1917, #3163, p. 1; July 4, #3186, p. 3. Three days after the women's food riots in St. Petersburg that began the February Revolution, an Ivanovo-Voznesensk merchant, president of a trading house, wrote a letter to the editor of the local newspaper denying rumors

circulating "among the worker population of the city" that he was hoarding enough flour to "feed the whole city for the rest of the year." *Ivanovskii listok*, February 26, 1917, #45, p. 1.

6. *Gazeta-Kopeika*, January 27, 1917, #183, p. 2.
7. *Golos*, August 15, 1917, #180, p. 4.
8. Ibid., September 16, 1917, #203, p. 3. See also August 6, #174, p. 4, and September 28, #212, p. 3, for articles on the food shortage among workers.
9. Ibid., October 13, 1917, #224, p. 4.
10. Ibid., January 19, 1917, #175, p. 3.
11. *Ivanovskii listok*, January 28, 1917, #23, p. 2; February 4, #28, p. 2; February 18, #38, p. 2. The newspaper recommended that bakers make an announcement to the waiting lines when one lot of bread was sold out, specifying by what time the next batch would be baked. "We recommend this so that the poor folk will not stand in line in the freezing cold for unnecessary hours, waiting in vain to get bread when it is all sold." The newspaper pointed out that some bakers were already posting their shop doors with written notices about when the next bread would be ready, "not realizing the fact that not everyone knows how to read."
12. Ibid., January 28, 1917, p. 1.
13. *Ivanovskii listok*, March 2, 1917, #48, p. 1.
14. *Gazeta-Kopeika*, January 7, 1917, #26/163, p. 3.
15. Ibid., March 16, 1917, #227, p. 4.
16. *Izvestiia Ivanovo-Voznesenskago Soveta Rabochikh i Soldatskikh Deputatov*, June 14, 1917, #20, p. 1.
17. *Gazeta-Kopeika*, January 7, 1917, #26/163, p. 3; February 12, #199, p. 3; February 20, #207, p. 3. Some of the children in lines had been sent by their employers to fetch bread for them (ibid., January 24, #180, p. 3). Some others of the shivering children were parentless street urchins, who always made their meager living by various devices. The queues were a boon for them, for they offered to stand in line for anyone with a few extra kopeks to spare for the luxury of having someone else do his or her legwork (ibid., February 20, #207, p. 3).

Despite the presence of children and elderly women in the breadlines, they were infrequently reported as being present during food actions. This may have been because moving around in the streets, from shop to shop, from merchant's cart to city council to offices of the local provisioning committee, and so on, was so strenuous that children and elderly people simply could not keep up the pace. Additionally, many of these people may have quit the lines before the action really got started by mid-March. The composition of breadlines which generated food actions was overwhelmingly adult women, sometimes accompanied by hungry soldiers from local garrisons.

Various other types of people appeared in the *khvosty* in smaller numbers. For example, "Among the elderly women and children were mixed in a pair of young housemaids and four depressed students" (ibid., February 20, 1917, #207, p. 3). However, while students and others undoubtedly continued their presence in the queues throughout the year, they did not play a major role in food actions, nor do I have any indication that women attempted to get such groups to join in their actions as allies.

18. Ibid., January 14, 1917, #170, p. 3. This article was actually written during a brief moment of plentiful bread and described women's attempts to overbuy bread against the expected shortages ahead. But undoubtedly the strategizing was the same during the more common periods of shortage.

19. *Povolzhskii vestnik*, September 19, 1917, #3245, p. 3.

20. Ibid., September 24, 1917, #3250, p. 3; *Gazeta-Kopeika*, July 28, 1917, #337, p. 3.

21. *Gazeta-Kopeika*, August 20, 1917, #356, p. 3.

22. *Povolzhskii vestnik*, July 4, 1917, #3186, p. 3. On the milk shortage in Moscow, its effect on infant mortality, and the introduction of special milk ration cards for small children, see *Gazeta-Kopeika*, August 20, #356, p. 3; September 10, #373, p. 3; September 21, #381, p. 2. On a proposal for a special flour rationing system for children under ten years of age, see *Vlast' naroda*, May 19, #18, p. 5. On the effects of the bread shortage in Kovrov on the children of the poor, see *Kovrovskiia vesti*, May 16, #10, p. 2. Women's concern for their children's well-being was such that one political group in Serpukhov lured the local factory women to an election meeting by promising that "in addition to the elections, the question of sugar and milk for their children would be discussed." E. Popova, *Moskovskaia provintsiia v semnadtsatom gody: Sbornik* (Moscow: Moskovskii Istpart, 1927), p. 143.

23. September 1, #366, p. 4.

24. *Gazeta-Kopeika*, July 26, 1917, #335, p. 4.

25. *Povolzhskii vestnik*, July 4, 1917, #3186, p. 3.

26. *Golos*, October 7, 1917, #219, p. 3.

27. By 1917, close to 37 percent (roughly 15 million) of Russia's men had been called into the army. This did not have as drastic an impact on food production and availability as might be expected. There had been a surplus of labor in the countryside prior to the outbreak of war. Struve et al. estimated this number as somewhere between 3.6 to 4.7 million men. Thus, the removal of this number of men from the countryside into the army did not have a significant impact on the productivity of agriculture. Second, Russia's tremendous peacetime exports of grain fell during the war to virtually nothing. This gained Russia somewhat more grain that was lost by the decrease in harvest levels during the war. The average grain harvest in 1909-13 was 3,633 million *pudy*; average grain exports during this period were 686 million *pudy* each year, leaving Russia with 2,947 million *pudy* per year for domestic use in the prewar period. The grain harvest of 1917 was 3,185 million *pudy*, most of which was available for domestic use, a larger domestic availability than in the prewar years. B. P. Struve, K. I. Zaitsev, N.

V. Dolinsky, and S. S. Demosthenov, *Food Supply in Russia during the World War* (New Haven: Yale University Press, 1930), pp. 297-98, 308, 329.

28. Ibid., pp. xiv, 309.

29. Leon Trotsky, *The History of the Russian Revolution*, Vol. I, *The Overthrow of Tsarism* (New York: Simon and Schuster, 1937), p. 411.

30. This policy was begun by the tsarist government and was continued, with some reluctance, by the Provisional Government after the February Revolution. Struve, *Food Supply*, pp. 97, 103.

31. Ibid., pp. 228-29, 401.

32. Ibid., p. 448.

33. Ibid., pp. 330-31.

34. *Gazeta-Kopeika*, July 12, 1917, #323, p. 4.

35. When the Moscow city council established a rationing card system, it stated that it believed that there was enough bread in the city for everyone, but that the rich were managing to seize far more than their share of it. The rationing card system was meant to limit each individual to his or her rightful portion. *Gazeta-Kopeika*, February 18, 1917, #205, p. 3; February 23, #210, p. 3.

36. Struve, *Food Supply*, pp. 24, 26.

37. Women often called the police when they found carters transporting food for speculation (see *Vlast' naroda*, August 23, 1917, #99, p. 3; *Golos*, August 17, #181, p. 3).

38. On dual power, see Trotsky, *History*, pp. 206-15.

39. Hoarding by consumers can be seen as the single method by which women attempted to affect the long-term availability of food. Like many of women's strategies during 1917, this was a privatized solution, one carried out by each *family* in its own interests. Yet looking beyond the boundaries of the individual family, this strategy was the opposite of a rational solution to the problem, for in the aggregate it was one of the factors which contributed to the food crisis by increasing demand beyond actual consumption need and hence increasing merchants' opportunity for speculating.

40. *Povolzhskii vestnik*, May 5, 1917, #3139, p. 3.

41. Ibid., June 13, 1917, #3196, pp. 1-2.

42. *Golos*, July 15, 1917, #156, p. 3.

43. Ibid., July 19, 1917, #159, p. 2; July 18, #158, p. 2; July 19, #159, p. 2; August 4, #172, p. 2.

44. *Povolzhskii vestnik*, August 6, 1917, #3214, pp. 2-3.

45. *Vlast' naroda*, August 9, 1917, #88, p. 4; August 29, #104, p. 4.

46. Ibid., September 2, 1917, #108, p. 3.

47. Ibid., September 8, 1917, #113, p. 5.

48. *Golos*, August 6, 1917, #174, p. 4.

49. Ibid., September 17, 1917, #204, p. 3; September 21, #207, p. 3; September 26, #211, p. 3; September 28, #212, p. 3; October 22, #232, p. 3. *Yaroslavskaia mysl'* provides some information about food availability

in the guberniia and the actions of the guberniia provisioning committee, September 30, #37, p. 3; October 27, #60, p. 2.

50. Soldiers may have begun waiting in food lines earlier than this, but if they did, the newspapers were not reporting it.
51. *Gazeta-Kopeika*, July 14, 1917, #325, p. 3.
52. Ibid., August 22, 1917, #357, p. 3.
53. *Povolzhskii vestnik*, September 10, 1917, #3239, p. 3.
54. *Golos*, August 5, 1917, #173, p. 3.
55. Ibid., August 18, 1917, #183, p. 3.
56. Ibid., August 17, 1917, #181, p. 3.
57. Ibid., September 10, 1917, #199, p. 3.
58. Ibid., May 4, 1917, #98, p. 3.
59. Ibid., July 26, 1917, #164, p. 3.
60. *Iaroslavskaia mysl'*, September 22, 1917, #31, pp. 3, 4; September 23, #32, pp. 3, 4; *Golos*, September 22, 1917, #208, pp. 2, 3, 4; September 23, #209, pp. 2, 5; September 24, #210, pp. 2-3; September 26, #211, p. 3; September 30, 1917, #214, p. 3.
61. *Iaroslavskaia mysl'*, September 22, 1917, #31, p. 4.
62. *Golos*, September 22, 1917, #208, p. 4. *Iaroslavskaia mysl'* also observed the rumors rampant throughout the city about exactly what had been found during the searches, September 22, 1917, #31, p. 3.
63. *Golos*, September 26, 1917, #211, p. 3.
64. Ibid., September 24, 1917, #210, p. 2; September 26, #211, p. 3.
65. *Iaroslavskaia mysl'*, September 23, 1917, #32, p. 3; *Golos*, September 24, 1917, #210, pp. 2-3.
66. N. P. Paialin, *Volzhskie tkachi (1722-1917 gg.)* (Moscow: Gosudarstvennoe Izdatel'stvo "Istoriia Zavodov," 1936), p. 369.
67. *Povolzhskii vestnik*, August 20, 1917, #3223, p. 3; August 22, #3224, p. 3; August 23, #3225, p. 3.
68. Ibid., September 10, 1917, #3239, p. 3.
69. *Golos*, September 30, 1917, #214, p. 4.
70. The newspaper report gave no information about exactly who initiated and carried out these searches. *Gazeta-Kopeika*, August 24, 1917, #359, p. 3.
71. Two reports of nonsearch activity in Iurevets regarding the ongoing issue of flour being sent out of the city from the local flour mill to be consumed elsewhere may manifest the same contrast between female and male worker activity. In one large meeting attended mainly by the poorest women of the city, the unruly participants' main demand was for the arrest of the local provisioning commissioner, whom they accused of ordering flour to be sent out of Iurevets. The women were impervious to the orators, who pointed out that the commissioner was not the responsible party but was acting on orders from the guberniia provisioning committee. Discovering that the commissioner was out of town, however, the women instead arrested the former president of the zemstvo board and provisioning conference, who apparently no longer had any power over food matters. No other plans were

developed by which these women might have had an organized impact on the food supply situation. *Novaia zhizn', Iurevetskaia narodnaia gazeta*, May 13, 1917, #4, pp. 2-3.

Meanwhile, workers, apparently all men, from the local Mindovskii linen factory carried on a campaign to prevent barges carrying flour from the Iurevets mill from leaving the city. Headed by the president of the factory committee, they appeared in a group at the uezd revolutionary committee, which had taken over the mill, on July 3. They demanded its arrest and that of the provisioning board, demonstrated before a city committee representative, reproached some members of the soviet for deceiving them, and finally the Mindovskii factory committee worked against the election to the city duma of people who had opposed them on this issue. Women apparently took no significant part in all this activity. *Novaia zhizn'*, July 13, 1917, #16, pp. 3-4; July 16, #17, pp. 3-4; *Grozovye gody, vospominaniia starykh kommunistov* (Ivanovo, 1961) pp. 206-7.

72. The workers also turned violent toward a merchant who had lowered the sugar ration on his own authority. *Povolzhskii vestnik*, June 13, 1917, #3169, p. 2.

73. *Ivanovskii listok*, February 25, 1917, #44, p. 1.

74. *Povolzhskii vestnik*, June 23, 1917, #3178, p. 3.

75. No women were mentioned as having taken part in these events, with the single exception of one woman who incited "to pogrom." *Nasha zvezda; Organ Ivanovo-Voznesenskago Goroda i Ivanovo-Kineshemskago Okruzhnogo Komiteta RSDRP (b)*, October 17, 1917, #13, p. 3.

76. *Golos*, August 17, 1917, #181, p. 4.

77. *Gazeta-Kopeika*, August 26, #361, p. 3.

78. *Vlast' naroda*, September 7, 1917, #112, p. 4.

79. *Nasha zvezda*, October 12, 1917, #12, p. 4.

80. *Grozovye gody*, p. 114.

CHAPTER THREE

1. *Gazeta-Kopeika*, October 4, #392, p. 4.

2. *Vlast' naroda*, May 16, 1917, #15, p. 6.

3. *Gazeta-Kopeika*, October 11, 1917, #398, p. 3.

4. *Za vlast' Sovetov*, pp. 47-48.

5. *Gazeta-Kopeika*, September 6, 1917, #370, p. 3.

6. Ancharova wrote that the shape of the breadline tended to distort communication and generate rumors as, telephone-game-like, information passed from one end of the *khvost* to the other. *Vlast' naroda*, May 16, 1917, #15, p. 6. Obviously this problem could have been solved by looping the line around into a circle, or by assigning numbers so shoppers could move temporarily out of line without losing their places.

7. By "Vanka Pustomeia" in *Gazeta Kopeika*, July 5, 1917, #317, p. 4.

8. Ibid., July 6, 1917, #318, p. 3.

9. Ibid., July 19, 1917, #329, p. 3.

10. Ibid., January 26, 1917, #182, p. 3.

11. Ibid., July 5, 1917, #317, p. 4.

12. Ibid., March 5, 1917, #217, p. 3 (my emphasis).

13. Ibid., September 23, 1917, #383, p. 4; *Nasha zvezda*, September 2, 1917, #3, pp. 2-3; Petrakov, "Vospominaniia," p. 206.

14. *Gazeta Kopeika*, August 1, 1917, #340, p. 3.

15. Trotsky, *The History of the Russian Revolution*, p. 109.

16. During the French Revolution, political leaders also often assigned women to propagandizing troops, because of their skill in influencing soldiers' political behavior. Racz, "The Women's Rights Movement in the French Revolution," p. 173.

17. Petrakov, "Vospominaniia," pp. 208-10 (see also p. 207); *Za vlast'*, pp. 412-14; *Grozovye gody*, p. 62.

18. The fact that women workers were active in food actions beginning in the streets rather than in the factories creates problems in the historical evidence, for when lower-class women were observed in the *streets*, there was virtually nothing about their appearance or behavior by which to determine what type of work they did, or indeed whether they worked at all. Most urban working-class women looked very much alike no matter what their occupation. Only rarely were food activists clearly identified in newspaper reports as factory working women.

A newspaper reporter's main clue as to the class position of women in the streets was their headgear: kerchiefs (*platki*) were the well-known attire of lower-class women, while elegant hats (*shliapy*) were generally worn by upper-class women. However, all lower-class women wore kerchiefs: domestic servants, workers in service occupations (for example, laundresses), and nonworking wives of male factory laborers, as well as female factory workers.

In addition to the few clearly identified cases of factory working women participating in specific food actions, there are, however, some other ways by which it can be determined that factory working women were among the activists. We know that many food actions took place in predominantly working-class communities where many women were employed in factories. Factory workers suffered greatly from food shortages, probably disproportionately to their share of the population. This resulted in their having to endure long waits in food lines, the spawning ground of most women's food actions. Loss of factory work time when women were stuck waiting in lines seems to have become a large-scale social problem.

If the major organizational framework of women's food actions had been the social networks of the factory, the participants would have been more easily identifiable as workers because many actions would likely have begun with women throwing down their work and/or gathering at the factory before moving into the streets. The citywide searches of the stores and homes of suspected hoarders, undertaken by male workers, *were* organized through factory networks, and their participants were *always* identified in newspaper accounts as workers: the participants could readily be recognized because they organized themselves during meetings held at their factories.

19. Some information on the workers' cooperative movement in the 1910-14 period is located in *Staraia Kostromskaia zhizn'*, January 3, 1912, #2, p. 2; February 23, #42, p. 4; March 22, #65, p. 3; *Gazeta-Kopeika*, May 21, 1911, #155/681, p. 3; *Kineshemets*, June 27, 1912, #78, p. 3; July 8, #82, p. 4; September 19, 1912, #111, p. 3; September 30, #116, pp. 3-4; December 9, #143, p. 3; December 23, #149, p. 4; February 6, 1913, #164, p. 3; February 8, #165, p. 3; March 31, #186, p. 3; April 3, #187, p. 3; April 7, p. 3; April 24, #192, p. 3; August 28, #12, pp. 3-4; May 7, 1914, #46, p. 2; N. Vladimirskii, *Nostromskaia oblast', istoriko-ekonomicheskii ocherk* (Kostroma: Kostromskoe Knizhnoe Izdatel'stvo, 1959), p. 143. The August 12, 1913, issue of *Kineshemets* gave in passing some information about women's nonparticipation in cooperatives. Insufficient publicity for a recent meeting of the workers' cooperative society had led to less than a quorum in attendance. Notification of the meeting had been posted only in the food shop itself. This was not sufficient notification because "the majority of the society's members are men, but in the majority of the cases, women and children go to make the purchases. . . . But female curiosity is nowhere near as aroused by matters of the society as it is by clothes and other such things. It is natural, therefore, that they did not communicate to the head of the family [about the meeting notification]; in addition, the greater part of the working women are illiterate," and hence could not have read the sign anyway. This indicates the separateness of men's and women's involvement with issues of food: although women took responsibility for food on a daily basis, they had no involvement in the cooperative society.

20. *Grozovye gody*, p. 180.

21. Especially as women became more and more antiwar, they probably felt that the military did not have prior right to the transport capacities of the country.

22. *Gazeta-Kopeika*, August 19, 1917, #355, p. 3.

23. Women's militance, often noticeably greater than men's, has been observed in various time periods for various countries. See, for example, E. P. Thompson, "The English Crowd," pp. 115-16 ("in all public tumults [women] are foremost in violence and ferocity"); D. Thompson, "Women and Nineteenth-Century Radical Politics," p. 119; Hufton, "Women in Revolution," p. 101 ("In every outward manifestation in 1793 women were more frenzied, more intense, . . . doubly vindictive"); Trotsky, *History* I, p. 109 (Women "go up to the cordons [of soldiers] more boldly than men").

24. "The Other Side of the Paycheck: Monopoly Capital and the Structure of Consumption," in *Capitalist Patriarchy and the Case for Socialist Feminism*, ed. Zillah R. Eisenstein (New York: Monthly Review Press, 1979), pp. 193, 199, 201.

25. *Primitive Rebels: Studies in Archaic Forms of Social Movement in the Nineteenth and Twentieth Centuries* (New York: Norton, 1959), pp. 106-7.

CHAPTER FOUR

1. Diane Koenker, *Moscow Workers and the 1917 Revolution* (Princeton: Princeton University Press, 1981), pp. 335, 338. Most histories of the Russian Revolution focus on the capital of St. Petersburg, mentioning the rest of the country at best only in passing. This has produced a distorted understanding of the revolutionary process, which Koenker's work has taken a major step in correcting.

2. See specific references below and *Za vlast' Sovetov*, pp. 242, 306-10.

3. John L. H. Keep, *The Russian Revolution: A Study in Mass Mobilization* (New York: Norton, 1976), p. 283; Koenker, *Moscow Workers*, pp. 335-43.

4. See Koenker's description of the social life which, in addition to political conviction, drew young people into politics. She also talks specifically about romantic ties among the activists, "Urban Families, Working Class Youth Groups, and the 1917 Revolution in Moscow," in *The Family in Imperial Russia: New Lines of Historical Research*, ed. David Ransel (Urbana: University of Illinois Press, 1978), pp. 296-99.

5. Women's Battalions, volunteer units in the regular Russian army under the Provisional Government, do not come within my scope because they contained almost no working women. While they became famous due to the sensation caused by women in combat, their numbers (around 5,000) were tiny in comparison to the total female population in Russia and to the numbers of men in the army (15,000,000). Their activities were not typical outgrowths of women's culture in Russia. For a description of the Women's Battalions, see Richard Stites, *The Women's Liberation Movement in Russia* (Princeton: Princeton University Press, 1978), pp. 280, 289, 295-300, 305, 318.

6. *Za vlast'*, p. 231.

7. Ibid., p. 268.

8. Ibid., pp. 250-51.

9. Ibid., p. 178. There was also a dining room near the Guzhon plant, p. 298.

10. The possibility that such traditionally women's tasks might have developed into female solidarity is raised by such historians as Thompson, in "Women and Nineteenth-Century Radical Politics," pp. 112-38. Thompson describes a melange of Chartist women's activities, ranging from cooking suppers of "potato pie and home-brewed ale" and decorating halls for meetings, to

women's political organizations. The possibility that women's traditional tasks may sometimes have led to political organization is also raised by those historians who have begun to speculate that "women's culture" formed the basis for political activism.

11. *Oktiabr'skie dni*, p. 54.
12. *Za vlast'*, p. 222. Sometimes males, primarily teenage boys, were included in the first aid detachments when there were not enough arms to send them all into battle. Ibid., pp. 102, 222-24.
13. *Oktiabr' v Zamoskvorech'e*, p. 62. For mentions of the establishment of first aid units in other raions, see p. 88; *Oktiabr'skie dni*, pp. 98, 174.
14. *Za vlast'*, p. 265.
15. *Oktiabr'skie dni*, p. 61.
16. *Za vlast'*, p. 222.
17. *Oktiabr' v Zamoskvorech'e*, p. 281.
18. *Za vlast'*, p. 272.
19. *Oktiabr' v Zamoskvorech'e*, p. 282.
20. *Oktiabr'skie dni*, p. 139.
21. Ibid. See also p. 152.
22. Peche, *V boiakh*, p. 67.
23. *Oktiabr'skie dni*, p. 105.
24. *Za vlast'*, pp. 229-30.
25. Peche, *V boiakh*, pp. 66-67. See also p. 23; *Za vlast'*, p. 265; *Oktiabr' v Zamoskvorech'e*, pp. 88, 129; *Oktiabr'skie dni*, pp. 98, 112.
26. *Za vlast'*, p. 239.
27. Ibid., p. 180.
28. *Oktiabr' v Zamoskvorech'e*, p. 130.
29. The single striking exception was the memoir of a working woman of the Brokar perfume factory, who described her warm feelings toward the "many friends" she made among the working women when she began working at this factory. "Gradually my girlfriends attracted me to revolutionary work." During October 1917, she fulfilled "various tasks," including first aid and delivering medical supplies, ibid., pp. 128-30. Several memoirs from Rogozhskii raion gave brief observers' testimony that working women from Ostroumov's perfume and soap factory, Keller's chemical and soap plant, and Sumin's came to the raion headquarters in groups to sign up for first aid units, *Za vlast'*, p. 294; *Oktiabr'skie dni*, p. 162. But most women's memoirs give no sense that such groupings were long-standing rather than an ephemeral by-product of the immediate circumstances, nor that they were maintained after the women arrived at headquarters and were assigned to first aid positions.
30. A. V. Shipulina, "Uchastie Ivanovo-Voznesenskikh rabochikh v stroitel'stve sovetskogo gos. apparata (1917-1918 gg.)" in *Iz istorii rabochego klassa SSSR, Sbornik*, ed. M. M. Viziaev (Ivanovo: Ivanovskii Gosudarstvennyi Pedagogicheskii Institut, 1967), pp. 67-83.

31. *Za vlast'*, p. 179.
32. *Oktiabr'skie dni*, p. 112.
33. Ibid., pp. 177-78.
34. *Oktiabr' v Zamoskvorech'e*, pp. 278, 281.
35. Koenker, *Moscow Workers*, p. 337.
36. William Rosenberg, "Workers and Workers' Control in the Russian Revolution," *History Workshop* (Spring 1978), pp. 93-94.
37. Gubernskoe Biuro Komissii po Istorii Oktiabr'skoi Revoliutsii i R.K.P. (bol'sh.), *Oktiabr'skie dni v Moskve i raionakh (po vospominaniiam uchastnikov)* (Moscow: Moskovskii rabochii, 1922), pp. 172-73.
38. *Oktiabr' v Zamoskvorech'e*, p. 280.
39. *Oktiabr'skie dni*, p. 69.
40. Ian Peche, *V boiakh za Oktiabr' (Vospominaniia ob Oktiabr'skoi revolutsii v Moskve)* (Moscow: Molodaia gvardiia, 1933), p. 64.
41. *Oktiabr'skie dni*, p. 162.
42. "Institut Istorii Partii MKi MGK/KPSS, *Za vlast' Sovetov!* (Moscow, 1957), p. 294.
43. *Za vlast'*, p. 246.
44. Ibid., p. 228.
45. See, for example, *Oktiabr'skie dni*, pp. 65, 67-68.
46. William Rosenberg speculates intriguingly on the tension between localism and centralization, "Workers and Workers' Control," pp. 93-96.
47. Ibid., p. 163. For another example of a worker memoirist identifying a group of fighters by the region in which they lived, see p. 174, in which the writer described the tasks accomplished by the Lefortovtsy, that is, the workers from the Lefortovskii raion.
48. Ibid., pp. 177-78.
49. Popova, *Moskovskaia provintsiia*, p. 97.
50. M. I. Petrakov, "Vospominaniia," in *Istoriko-kraevedcheskii sbornik*, ed. Orekhovo-Zuevskii Pedagogicheskii Institut (Moscow, 1959), pp. 213-14.
51. *Za vlast'*, pp. 379-80. For other examples from the Orekhovo-Zuevo area, see pp. 392-410.
52. Peche, *V boiakh*, p. 9.
53. *Oktiabr'skie dni*, p. 173.
54. *Za vlast'*, p. 245.
55. Peche, *V boiakh*, p. 9. Another memoirist gave an account of similar relations between soldiers of the 55th regiment and the Mikhelson mechanical plant, an alliance that began during the February Revolution, *Oktiabr' v Zamoskvorech'e*, pp. 84-85.
56. Institut Istorii Partii Mk i MGK KPSS, *Slovo starykh Bol'shevikov (Iz revoliutsionnogo proshlogo)* (Moscow: Moskovskii rabochii, 1965), p. 247.
57. *Oktiabr'skie dni*, p. 60.
58. Popova, *Moskovskaia provintsiia*, p. 99.
59. Koenker, *Moscow Workers*, p. 339.

60. Ibid., p. 338.
61. *Vlast' naroda*, May 3, 1917, #5, p. 5.
62. Women's attitudes toward participation in combat can also be examined via their stance toward fighting against the Germans in World War I. In a letter from a working woman to the editor of *Golos*, July 8, 1917, #150, p. 3, the writer states that women did not fear combat: "We never decline [to go to] the trenches, but [then someone else must] feed our nursing infants, who are left behind here." Two descriptions of the small number of working women who did join detachments to fight the Germans are in July 19, #159, p. 3; August 3, #171, p. 4.
63. *Oktiabr'skie dni*, p. 101.
64. *Za vlast'*, p. 239.
65. Ibid., p. 245.
66. Ibid., p. 404. Another memoirist wrote that in Moscow's Sokol'nicheskii raion, most women freely chose first aid detachment assignment: "the majority of those . . . were women, who by their free choice wanted to be in this detachment, in order to give what help they could," *Oktiabr'skie dni*, p. 139.
67. *Za vlast'*, p. 416.

CHAPTER FIVE

1. *Oktiabr' v Zamoskvorech'e*, pp. 277-78 (my emphasis).
2. Petrov's case happened to come up in court in 1913, the three hundredth anniversary of founding of the Romanov dynasty, in honor of which many "criminals" were pardoned.
3. Chaadaeva, *Rabotnitsa*, pp. 40, 45-58 (my emphasis).
4. Ibid., pp. 47-48.
5. Another memoirist recalled that six of the working women who helped run a Red Guard dining room during the Moscow revolution told her they were nonparty; their revolutionary sympathies were born "both under the influence of those speeches which they had heard in meetings, *and also in connection with the fact that their husbands and sons participated in strikes and insurgency.*" Institut Istorii Partii, *Slovo starykh Bol'shevikov*, p. 247 (my emphasis).
6. Kor, *Kak my zhili*, pp. 31-34. Sleptsovaia's description of her activity during 1905—"I gave help, however I could, to the people on the barricades"—is strikingly similar to the helping hand, Jill-of-all-trades activity of many working women who participated in 1917 Moscow street fighting.
7. *Grozovye gody*, pp. 87-88 (my emphasis).
8. *Slovo starykh*, pp. 84-85 (my emphasis).
9. Goriacheva, "Vospominaniia," pp. 218-19 (my emphasis).

10. Richard Pipes, *Social Democracy and the St. Petersburg Labor Movement, 1885-1897* (Cambridge: Harvard University Press, 1963), pp. 6-15, 41, 61; Allan K. Wildman, *The Making of a Workers' Revolution* (Chicago: University of Chicago Press, 1967), pp. 31, 52.
11. Goriacheva, "Vospominaniia," p. 244.
12. Sokolov, *Chastushki*, pp. 13-15.

CHAPTER SIX

1. For a general article about the variety of types of factory committees, see *Vlast' naroda*, May 10, 1917, #11, p. 4.
2. *Za vlast'*, p. 417. Given the Soviet government's claim to have liberated women, bringing them into important positions in the economy and government, it is in the interests of Soviet memoirists to claim great, sustained activity on the part of working women. Thus, vague claims as to women's extensive activism must be accompanied by detailed material describing exactly what that activity consisted of before we can trust the accuracy of such statements.
3. In addition to memoirs a few scattered newspaper accounts contain some relevant information, but never enough to indicate clearly that groups of women took part in ongoing organizations. For example, the woodworkers' trade union in Kostroma adopted a constitution and then later amended it to include a statement about the establishment of "special places in the factories and plants for women to feed their children," *Povolzhskii vestnik*, May 25, 1917, #3153, p. 3. This must have happened under pressure by some women, but who these women were, how active, and whether they formed an organizational base was not discussed.

   At the factory of Gratri, Zherar, and Mikhin, a currier accused of informing to the police was judged by and pardoned in a comrade court by "twenty factory women." Whether these women sat at any other trials beyond this one or became part of a legal institution was not mentioned in the article. *Povolzhskii vestnik*, June 13, 1917, #3169, p. 1.

   Workers' clubs and trade unions also apparently did not draw many female members. A long, detailed article about a lecture and social evening in one workers' club in Moscow noted that among the four hundred, mostly young, workers present, there was not even one woman, *Svobodnoe slovo*, July 24, 1917, #15, p. 2. A newspaper of the Ivanovo-Kineshma area noted the apathy of workers toward the textile trade union: "workers will not go to meetings, will not carry out the monthly collection of membership dues." The article contrasted this with the very active life of workers' clubs during the 1905-6 revolutionary period, and attributed the 1917 decline mainly to the absence of young men resulting from the wartime army draft, *Nasha zvezda*, October 17, 1917, #13, pp. 2-3.

4. *Za vlast'*, p. 417.
5. Mariia A. Shustova, "Soiuz soldatskikh zhen," p. 144.
6. This entire account is taken from ibid., pp. 139-51.
7. *Na putiakh k Oktiabr'iu*, p. 31.
8. Moskovskii Komitet RKP(b), *Oktiabr'skie dni v Moskve i raionakh (Po vospominaniiam uchastnikov)* (Moscow: Moskovskii Rabochii, 1922), p. 135.
9. Popova, *Moskovskaia provintsiia*, p. 131. *Golos* recorded a case in which the committee of workers' deputies of the Norskoe textile factory took up a problem many local women were experiencing: soldiers from a reserve regiment located in Yaroslavl had been arriving in Norskoe in rowdy groups, walking around town singing "obscene songs and they insolently approach young girls and women. On Wednesday, August 16, around 70 of them came here. Many were drunk, many . . . were without belts, and with their collars unbuttoned." On the following day, the Norskoe factory committee resolved to arrest the soldiers "for their escapades and outrages, and to transport them back to their units," *Golos*, August 20, 1917, #184, p. 3. The article did not say whether the women involved had appealed to the committee, or whether the committee acted on its own. A similar problem was raised in Kostroma during a meeting between factory deputies and soldiers' representatives. "One of the woman deputies of the factory workers pointed out the improper attitude of some of the local soldiers, who permitted themselves to press up against women in the evenings. The deputy from the soldiers asked that the soldiers be excused for these rude pranks, since they were called forth by the backwardness and unenlightenment of the soldiers," *Kur'er*, April 17, 1917, #78, p. 3. Here, again, no information was given about the relationship between the female deputy from the workers and the factory working women as a whole.
10. Popova, *Moskovskaia provintsiia*, pp. 24, 111.
11. *Gazeta-Kopeika*, January 1, 1917, #157, p. 3.
12. *Golos*, April 15, 1917, #82, p. 3.
13. *Povolzhskii vestnik*, May 5, 1917, #3139, p. 3; May 7, #3141, p. 3.
14. *Golos*, March 25, 1917, #68, p. 4.
15. Ibid., April 11, 1917, #78, p. 3; April 12, #79, p. 3; April 15, #82, p. 3. In April, the Society of Mutual Help for Women also held a benefit concert, together with the soviet, for the benefit of children of the war troops. The audience was primarily the local factory workers and their families, and the Iaroslavskaia Bol'shaia textile factory committee sent a letter of thanks afterward, ibid., April 17, #84, p. 3.
16. Ibid., May 4, 1917, #98, p. 3.
17. Ibid., May 6, 1917, #100, p. 3; July 12, #153, p. 3; July 14, #155, p. 3.
18. *Povolzhskii vestnik*, May 19, 1917, #3249, p. 2; May 23, #3152, p. 3; October 1, #3255, p. 3; October 12, #3262, p. 3. For more general information on the demand for literacy during 1917, see *Iaroslavskaia mysl'*, August 12, 1917, #1, p. 4; August 29, #14, p. 3; September 1, #16, p. 4; September 5, #18, p. 4; September 10, #22, p. 4; September 13, #24, p.

3; *Golos*, June 16, 1917, #132, p. 3; September 10, #199, p. 3; *Povolzhskii vestnik*, April 18, 1917, #3125, p. 4; *Vlast' naroda*, August 26, 1917, #102, p. 4.

19. *Vlast' naroda*, June 29, 1917, #53, p. 4; July 1, #55, p. 3.

20. In Iurevets, a women's union of upper-class "lady patronesses" opened several creches accommodating 615 children (age ten months to seven years) of working women. No women workers were involved in setting up or running the child care centers. Like the Moscow and Kostroma organizations, this one also appealed to the city government for funds, which were granted, *Novaia zhizn' Iurevetskaia narodnaia gazeta*, July 16, 1917, #17, p. 3; July 20, #18, p. 4.

21. *Za vlast'*, p. 101.

22. Popova, *Moskovskaia provintsiia*, pp. 150-51.

23. Sources describing demonstrations, in addition to those cited below, are *Novaia zhizn'*, April 22, 1917, #1, p. 3; *Golos*, March 9, 1917, #55, p. 2; April 20, #86, p. 31; July 1, #144, p. 4; *Kur'er*, March 12, 1917, #55, p. 3; April 20, #77, p. 3; *Povolzhskii vestnik*, May 16, 1917, #3146, p. 3; *Nasha zvezda*, October 2, 1917, #11, p. 4; *Grozovye gody*, pp. 98-105, 156-57; *Za vlast'*, pp. 58, 68; *Oktiabr' v Zamoskvorech'e*, pp. 58, 84; Vladimirskii, *Kostromskaia oblast'*, p. 151. Not all of these mentioned women specifically, but they took place around factories where large numbers of women were employed. Given women's general record of frequent participation in demonstrations, their presence may not have caused particular comment by the observers.

Very little material is available relating to 1917 strikes in which women participated. Surprisingly, all newspapers of the CIR, whatever their political perspective, contain relatively little description of strikes, and only insignificant tidbits on women in strikes. Memoirs proved similarly unenlightening on this score. At the time I was doing research in the Soviet Union, archival holdings regarding workers' activity during 1917 were generally not made available to Westerners. Even for the earlier periods, newspapers, including local newspapers, remained for the most part silent about strikes taking place in their own localities, presumably because censorship, factory owners, and police did not permit investigation and reporting of these "disorders." Newspapers cited had virtually no reportage of strikes, with the exception of *Kineshemets*, which had substantial coverage in June-July 1914, and *Kostromskie novosti*, which had two short articles: July 6, 1912, #41, p. 3; July 13, #44, p. 3. Now that Soviet archives have been more widely opened to Westerners, they may prove a rich source for future investigation of women in strikes

24. *Vlast' naroda*, May 16, 1917, #15, p. 5.

25. *Izvestiia Ivanovo-Voznesenskago soveta*, May 19, 1917, #10, p. 2.

26. *Golos*, April 20, 1917, #86, p. 4.

27. *Za vlast'*, pp. 421-22. The language of the working woman who gave the speech is interesting both in its use of familial analogies and also because, in translating familial concepts into the sphere of public aid, they became completely male: "younger brother," "brotherly hand," "brotherly help."
28. Ibid.
29. Petrakov, "Vospominaniia," p. 206.
30. *Za vlast'*, p. 61.
31. Louise Bryant, *Six Red Months in Russia: An Observer's Account of Russia Before and During the Proletarian Dictatorship* (New York: Doran Co., 1918), pp. 187-88.
32. John Reed, *Ten Days that Shook the World* (New York: Modern Library, 1935), p. 222.
33. The possibility that women did not attend all general meetings in their factories is raised by the large number of newspaper descriptions of factory meetings (for the purposes of being informed about rapidly breaking events, discussing political developments, forming and electing factory committees and elections to soviets, collecting contributions for various causes, and discussing issues relating to factory work) which did not mention the presence of women, *Golos*, March 28, 1917, #69, p. 3; *Rabochii gorod*, November 5, 1917, #2, p. 3; *Kur'er*, March 16, 1917, #57, p. 2; March 21, #61, p. 2; March 28, #66, p. 2; *Povolzhskii vestnik*, June 24, 1917, #3179, p. 3; October 24, #3273, p. 2. This evidence is not conclusive, and is mentioned only because the presence of women at meetings was often novel enough that it was noted by newspaper reporters when it occurred.
34. This situation became so common that the Ministry of Labor issued a directive that meetings must take place during nonworking time, because under the present system, "the normal course of work" was being "destroyed," *Vlast' naroda*, September 5, 1917, #110, p. 6.
35. See, for example, *Izvestiia Ivanovo-Voznesenskago Soveta*, May 17, 1917, p. 2; *Kur'er*, March 24, 1917, #64, p. 3; April 15, #76, p. 2.
36. *Gazeta-Kopeika*, March 14, 1917, #225, p. 4. Another two articles described a preelection meeting of about a thousand women of all classes, "about nine-tenths of whom were of the democratic layers of the population," to select and put forth their candidates for the city duma. The meeting "went badly," the candidates were not chosen, and "there was division instead of unity." The articles blamed the dissension on the attempt to unite women of all classes, *Novaia zhizn'*, May 27, 1917, #6, p. 3; July 2, #15, p. 4.
37. Petrakov, "Vospominaniia," pp. 206-7, 212. A *Golos* article also described a working woman inciting a street crowd to pogroms against Jews, August 18, 1917, #182, p. 3; another description of the amorphous street crowd meeting was October 19, #229, p. 3.
38. *Golos*, July 8, 1917, #150, p. 4.
39. *Kur'er*, February 10, 1917, #33, p. 2.
40. *Nasha zvezda*, September 2, 1917, #3, pp. 2-3.

41. *Kur'er*, April 13, 1917, #74, p. 2.

CHAPTER SEVEN

1. Otdel Rukopisei i Redkikh Knig Gosudarstvennoi Publichnoi Biblioteki im. Saltykova-Shchedrina (OR RK GPB), fond 1027, post. 1967.72, tetrad' 1, Sbornik narodnoi tvorchestva Ivanovskoi oblasti sost. Speranskoi Veroi Nikolaevnoi, gorod Shuiia, Iv. oblast', Zapiski 1905-1967 gg., list 121.
2. *Vlast' naroda*, September 1, 1917, #107, p. 3; September 30, #130, p. 4.
3. *Gazeta-Kopeika*, September 21, 1917, #381, p. 4.
4. Of course, people who are involved in ongoing organizations usually go home to sleep at night as well. But they also work in and identify with an entity whose express purpose is to exist and develop over time. And frequently such an organization, especially during moments of crisis (such as all-night contract negotiations for a labor union, or a street battle for the Red Guard), claims the total, undivided loyalties of its active members, who then neglect their other responsibilities (including their families) and needs (including sleep).
5. *Golos*, September 28, 1917, #212, p. 3.
6. *Kineshemets*, March 9, 1914, p. 3 (my emphasis).
7. *Iaroslavskie novosti*, July 22, 1913, #29, p. 2 (my emphasis).
8. Jessica Tovrov, "Mother-Child Relationships among the Russian Nobility," in David Ransel, ed., *The Family in Imperial Russia: New Lines of Historical Research* (Urbana: University of Illinois Press, 1978); Robert Eugene Johnson, *Peasant and Proletarian: The Working Class of Moscow in the Late Nineteenth Century* (New Brunswick: Rutgers University Press, 1979), pp. 51-65, 74-75.

   Scholars studying Western Europe have looked at some of the working-class behaviors that I found for the Russian working class: Nancy Tomes, "A 'Torrent of Abuse': Crimes of Violence between Working-Class Men and Women in London, 1840-1875," *Journal of Social History* 2 (Spring 1978); A. E. Dingle, "Drink and Working-Class Living Standards in Britain, 1870-1914," *Economic History Review* 25 (November 1972); Laura Owen, "The Welfare of Women in Laboring Families: England, 1860-1950," *Feminist Studies* 1 (Winter-Spring 1973); and William Reddy, "Family and Factory: French Linen Weavers in the Belle Epoque," *Journal of Social History* 8 (Winter 1975).

   "Women's culture" has been studied by American historians, though not specifically for working women: Carroll Smith-Rosenberg, "The Female World of Love and Ritual: Relations between Women in Nineteenth-Century America," *Signs* 1 (Autumn 1975); Johnny Faragher and Christine Stansell, "Women and their Families on the Overland Trail to California and Oregon, 1842-1867," *Feminist Studies* 2 (Winter 1975).

American historians have also engaged in lively debate over the relationship between middle-class women's home life and political activism: Carroll Smith-Rosenberg, "Beauty, the Beast, and the Militant Woman: A Case Study in Sex Roles and Social Stress in Jacksonian America," *American Quarterly* 23 (October 1971); Mary P. Ryan, "The Power of Women's Networks: A Case Study of Female Moral Reform in Antebellum America," *Feminist Studies* 5 (Spring 1979); Ellen Dubois, "The Radicalism of the Woman Suffrage Movement: Notes Toward the Reconstruction of Nineteenth-Century Feminism," *Feminist Studies* 3 (Fall 1975); Nancy Cott, *The Bonds of Womanhood: "Woman's Sphere" in New England, 1780-1835* (New Haven: Yale University Press, 1977); the series of articles by Ellen DuBois, Mari Jo Buhle, Gerda Lerner, and Carroll Smith-Rosenberg entitled "Politics and Culture in Women's History," *Feminist Studies* 6 (Spring 1980).

9. Katie Stewart has formulated these issues for contemporary U.S. working-class culture in a way very similar to my analysis.

Men's peer groups . . . recognize marriage as an institution which divides men. In marriage and fatherhood each man attains adult status as an individual; he frees himself from his natal family to become the father of *his* children, the breadwinner of *his* household, and the sole sexual partner of *his* wife. But in so doing he also breaks or weakens bonds with his father, brothers, and peers. Men say they are "caught," "tamed," and "henpecked" in marriage. Brothers and peers throw ritual bachelors' parties for the groom in which they reassert their solidarity as a group of men and express hostility toward the women who drive wedges between them. Peer groups are maintained, even after marriage . . .; in these, men are drawn out of their families against the protests of their wives.

"The Marriage of Capitalism and Patriarchal Ideologies: Meanings of Male Bonding and Male Ranking in U.S. Culture," in Lydia Sargent, ed., *Women and Revolution: A Discussion of the Unhappy Marriage of Marxism and Feminism* (Boston: South End Press, 1981), pp. 293-94.

10. For male bonding and the rituals that structure it, see: Robert H. Lowie, *Primitive Society* (New York: Liveright, 1920), chapters 10 and 11; George Murdock, *Social Structure* (New York: Macmillan, 1960); S. N. Eisenstadt, *From Generation to Generation: Age Groups and Social Structure* (London: Collier-Macmillan, 1956); Yehudi A. Cohen, *Childhood to Adolescence: Legal Systems and Incest Taboos* (Chicago: Aldine, 1964), pp. 60-68, 102-13; Judith K. Brown, "Adolescent Initiation Rites Among Preliterate Peoples," in Robert E. Grinder, ed., *Studies in Adolescence* (New York: Macmillan, 1963), pp. 75-85; Ruth Benedict, "Continuities and

Discontinuities in Cultural Conditioning," in Patrick Mullahy, ed., *A Study of Interpersonal Relations* (New York: Heritage, 1949), pp. 297-308.

11. Lionel Tiger, *Men in Groups* (Bristol, England: Thomas Nelson, 1969).

12. Frank Young, *Initiation Ceremonies: A Cross-Cultural Study of Status Dramatization* (Indianapolis: Bobbs-Merrill, 1965), chapters 2, 4, 5. See also Robert F. Murphy, "Social Structure and Sex Antagonism," *Southwestern Journal of Anthropology* 15 (1959), pp. 89-98. John M. Whiting, Richard Kluckhohn, and Albert Anthony have raised an alternative, psychological explanation for initiation rites, which Young counterposed to his own position. The two theories are not actually irreconcilable. However, the method that Whiting, Kluckhohn, and Anthony chose to test their hypothesis is inadequate, suffering from an incomplete choice of measures (mother and infant sleeping in the same bed and postpartum sex taboo) and from the authors' not having sought an explanation of why such child-rearing practices vary from culture to culture. See their "The Function of Male Initiation Ceremonies at Puberty," in E. E. Maccoby, T. M. Newcomb, and E. L. Hartley, eds., *Readings in Social Psychology* (New York: Henry Holt, 1958), pp. 359-70.

13. Johnson, *Peasant and Proletarian*, pp. 67-79, 87-91; Diane Koenker, *Moscow Workers and the 1917 Revolution* (Princeton: Princeton University Press, 1981), pp. 48-50.

14. Young took his work on male solidarity one step further, showing that the types of subsistence and warfare patterns that usually give rise to male bonding tend to occur in communities that are in a particular relationship to a larger, dominant national organization, a relationship that is in effect

> an uneasy truce between full participation in the urbanized world and the relative autonomy of the folk. When this marginal position is interpreted [by the local community] . . . male solidarity results: the men draw together for security, and they do not defect because there is no place to go (*Initiation Ceremonies*, p. 104).

Murphy earlier made a similar observation, but he did not provide the extensive survey of cultures that Young used to prove the point. See "Social Structure and Sex Antagonism," p. 102.

While Young included no working-class communities in his sampling, it seems likely that the Russian working class in the late nineteenth and early twentieth centuries in fact fit the essential elements of his description. The tenuous economic position that Russian workers were forced into vis-á-vis powerful factory owners backed by the tsarist state made it crucial for workers to aid one another by sharing access to resources, employment information, etc. Upward mobility was extremely limited for most of them, while a permanent return to the peasant village was also impossible: they had moved from the countryside to the factory because of their need for earnings that could not be met by the rural sector.

The Russian working class also seems similar to Young's category of an ethnic or racial group condemned to second-class status within a larger society. "Under such conditions, the men are in a situation not unlike that brought about by intercommunity warfare or collective hunting. If they are to avoid total disorganization, they have no recourse but to maintain a high level of cooperation and solidarity." (p. 103)

15. Young, *Initiation Ceremonies*, chapters 6 and 7; Tiger, *Men in Groups*, p. 51; Rayna Rapp Reiter, "Men and Women in the South of France: Public and Private Domains," in her *Toward an Anthropology of Women* (New York: Monthly Review Press, 1975).

16. The feminist movement has raised the question of why such *sharp* division of labor occurs: why don't men and women share both child rearing and the maintenance of social bonds? Dorothy Dinnerstein, for example, has dealt with this question in *The Mermaid and the Minotaur: Sexual Arrangements and Human Malaise* (New York: Harper, 1977).

17. Edward Shorter, *The Making of the Modern Family* (New York: Basic Books, 1977), p. 168. As David Hunt has pointed out in his excellent critique of Ariès (*Parents and Children in History: The Psychology of Family Life in Early Modern France* [New York: Harper, 1970], pp. 44-49), Ariès seems to have been confused as to whether he was referring to infants and young children as well as to children over the age of seven, an age group for which Ariès's hypothesis is much more tenable. Shorter, on the other hand, stated that he is referring to both infants and young children. Thus, Shorter deals with an age group for which this whole trend in historical thinking is questionable.

18. Joan Wallach Scott, *The Glassworkers of Carmaux: French Craftsmen and Political Action in a Nineteenth-Century City* (Cambridge, Mass.: Harvard University Press, 1974), chapter 19; Michael Hanagan, *The Logic of Solidarity: Artisans and Industrial Workers in Three French Towns, 1871-1914* (Urbana: University of Illinois Press, 1980), pp. 93-94, 96-98, 129-35, 142-44, 178-81, 194-98.

19. A number of scholars have already turned to various branches of psychology and psychoanalysis to help generate a theory explaining women's subordinate position. Juliet Mitchell was among the first, with *Psychoanalysis and Feminism* (New York: Pantheon, 1974); critiqued by Sherry Ortner in "Oedipal Father, Mother's Brother and the Penis," *Feminist Studies* 2 (Winter 1975). Gail Rubin also made use of Freudian theory in "The Traffic in Women: Notes on the Political Economy of Sex," in Reiter, *Toward an Anthropology of Women*, pp. 157-210. More recently, others have turned to object relations theory, which focuses on pre-Oedipal issues of the relationship between mother and child: Nancy Chodorow, *The Reproduction of Mothering: Psychoanalysis and the Sociology of Gender* (Berkeley: University of California Press, 1978); Jessica Benjamin, "Authority and the Family Revisited: or, A World Without Fathers?" *New German Critique* 13 (Winter 1978), pp. 35-57, and "The Bonds of Love: Rational Violence and

Erotic Domination," *Feminist Studies* 6 (Spring 1980), pp. 144-74; Ethel Spector Person, "Sexuality as the Mainstay of Identity: Psychoanalytic Perspectives," in Catharine R. Stimpson and Ethel Spector Person, eds., *Women: Sex and Sexuality* (Chicago: University of Chicago Press, 1980). Dinnerstein's *The Mermaid and the Minotaur* is another important study using psychoanalysis to create a theory of women's subordination.

20. For example, Jerome Kagan, "The Child in the Family," *Daedalus* 106 (Spring 1977), pp. 42-44, sees the bestowal or withdrawal of this positive emotional state as the incentive by which modern parents induce their children to achieve, particularly in their work. However, the infant and very young child is not yet dealing with his or her future work. The infant is above all a biological, not a social, being and is making the transition from biological to social functioning.

21. For a review of this literature, see Anne Bobroff, "Working Women, Bonding Patterns, and the Politics of Daily Life: Russia at the End of the Old Regime," Vols. 1 and 2 (Ph.D. dissertation, University of Michigan, 1982) Chapter 2, available through University Microfilm International, Ann Arbor, Michigan. David Hunt assumed general scholarly acceptance of the notion that infants and young children require parental caring. However, recent trends in historical work make clear that many historians do not accept this notion.

22. Rene Spitz utilized data from a Latin American Indian village in *The First Year of Life: A Psychoanalytic Study of Normal and Deviant Development of Object Relations* (New York: International Universities Press, 1965). For Jamaica: M. Curti, F. Marshall, and M. Steggerda, "The Gesell Schedule Applied to One-, Two-, and Three-Year-Old Negro Children of Jamaica, BWI," *Journal of Comparative Psychology* 20 (1935), pp. 125-56. For Africa: Mary Salter Ainsworth, *Infancy in Uganda: Infant Care and the Growth of Love* (Baltimore: Johns Hopkins Press, 1967); Diane Lusk and M. Lewis, "Mother-Infant Interaction and Infant Development among the Wolof of Senegal," *Human Development* 15 (1972), pp. 58-69; Marcelle Geber, "The Psycho-Motor Development of African Children in the First Year, and the Influence of Maternal Behavior," *The Journal of Social Psychology* 67 (1958), pp. 185-95; Janet E. Kilbride, Michael C. Robbins, and Philip L. Kilbride, "The Comparative Motor Development of Baganda, American White, and American Black Infants," *American Anthropologist* 72 (1970), pp. 1422-28; Liddicoat and Koza, "Language Development in African Infants," *Psychologica Africana* 10 (1963), pp. 108-16; N. Warren, "African Infant Precocity," *Psychological Bulletin* 78 (1972), pp. 353-67.

One of the major findings of the African studies is that African children go through the same developmental stages more precociously than do Western infants. The psychologists speculate that this results from the much greater amount of social stimulation which African infants receive through being carried around constantly in slings on their mothers' hip or back, sleeping in the same bed as the mother, and being continually in the company of older children and other adults. So much for the neglected, emotionally impoverished infants of Shorter's picture of premodern societies! In fact, in comparison with African societies, children in the West today, isolated from constant contact with people beyond the nuclear family, often physically isolated in playpens and cribs, rather than being carried in slings by day and slept with at night, sometimes with only inanimate mobiles and toys to play with, can just as legitimately be viewed as being sorely neglected by their parents.

The African data also call into question Ariès's assumption that bringing children into contact with people of all ages in the public sphere resulted from a lack of awareness of children's special needs during the alleged period of maternal indifference. The African data suggest that children thrive on being routinely integrated into social situations with people of all ages, because they provide children with more attention and stimulation than occurs in the isolated life-style of middle-class nuclear families in the modernized West, where children have many fewer human sources of stimulation in their immediate environment. In fact, it has been argued that the increasing incidence of "narcissistic personality disorder" in the United States in recent decades has resulted from the increasing isolation of children in the nuclear family in modern society. See Heinz Kohut, *The Restoration of the Self* (New York: International Universities Press, 1977), especially pp. 269-73.

23. Sylvia Bell, "The Development of the Concept of Object as Related to the Infant-Mother Attachment," *Child Development* 41 (1970), p. 309; H. Rudolf Shaffer and Peggy Emerson, "The Development of Social Attachment in Infancy," *Monographs of the Society for Research in Child Development* 29, 3 (1964), p. 11; Spitz also used cross-class data in *First Year of Life*.

24. Under more propitious circumstances, responsibility for child care in and of itself does not preclude collective action in the public sphere.

25. Among the Russian peasantry, women did not share in the communal land and other property held by their husbands' families, but did hold their own "private property": their dowries and the small earnings they made by selling such produce as eggs and mushrooms. This "private property" was inherited by daughters from their mothers, separately from the land inheritance which came through the husband's family. Here we find another example of the tradition of communal behavior by the husband's family alongside individualistic behavior by the wife.

Working-class mothers' financial support of their children had a precedent in the peasant mother's use of her earnings from selling items she had produced to buy clothing for her children and for household needs. Ethel and Stephen Dunn, *The Peasants of Central Russia*, p. 56; Sula Benet, trans., *The Village of Viriatino, An Ethnographic Study of a Russian Village from before the Revolution to the Present* (New York: Doubleday, 1970), pp. 102-3; Zelnik, p. 329.

26. GLM, f. 263, p. 9v, 1.72-74.
27. These collections are located in Tsentral'nyi Gosudarstvennyi Arkhiv Literatury i Iskusstva (TsGALI) and Gosudarstvennyi Literaturnyi Musei (GLM) in Moscow; and in the folklore division of the Institut Russkoi Literatury (Pushkinskii Dom), and Otdel Rukopisei i Redkikh Knig Gosudarstvennoi Publichnoi Biblioteki im. Saltykova-Shchedrina (OR RK GPB) in St. Petersburg.
28. Iu. M. Sokolov, *Russkii fol'klor*, vyp. IV *Chastushki meshchanskie i blatnye pesni fabrichno-zavodskii i kolkhoznyi fol'klor* (Moscow: Narkompros, 1932), p. 4. Soviet ethnographer S. P. Tolstov wrote that "in the city workers' midst . . . popular peasant customs were preserved to one degree or another." Tolstov explained that as peasants moved from the countryside to become workers, they abandoned those rituals that had to do with agricultural labor, the peasant commune, and the extended family. But they maintained, at least until the 1917 revolution, the rituals related to the nuclear family. Indeed, Russian workers were criticized for their high rate of absenteeism due to their many holidays. Tolstov, *Narody mira*, pp. 476, 478. Another type of song attributed to the city was the *romans*. Soviet scholars have typically claimed that workers did not sing *romansy*, because they wished to paint the working class as concerned only with songs about revolution, capitalists, and bad conditions at work. However, my research indicates clearly that *romansy*—with their themes of cruelty, lust, passion, and other less than ideal proletarian concerns—was one of the most widespread and important types of songs sung by adult workers.
29. Anne Bobroff, "Working Women," passim.
30. *Kineshemets* reported on the reading habits of the local workers, noting the popularity of "both *Kopeiki*" (presumably *Gazeta-Kopeika* and *Ivanovskaia Kopeika*), but claiming that *Kineshemets* itself sold the greatest number of copies, March 6, 1913, #175, p. 3. Another issue gave specific numbers of copies sold of many dailies and other newspapers and journals, in an article entitled "What does Kineshma read?" March 13, 1913, #178, p. 2. In an article on what workers were reading prior to the elections to the Fourth Duma, the reporter singled out *Gazeta-Kopeika* as having "great success" among the local workers. *Kineshemets*, March 2, 1912, #33, p. 3. A Bolshevik source noted that around 1912-13, many Moscow trade unions relied on *Gazeta-Kopeika* for information. With the increased politicization of trade unions, they opposed the political stance of *Kopeika* and called workers to boycott it. But workers were devoted to the newspaper; the boycott was not successful. N. Ovsiannikov, ed., *Nakanune revoliutsii, Sbornik statei, zametok i vospominanii* (Moscow: Gosudarstvennoe Izdatel'stvo, 1922), p. 146. *Kineshemets* also noted *Kopeika*'s "huge circulation in the cities," May 29, 1914, #52, p. 4. For statements of *Gazeta-Kopeika*'s own policy regarding its close ties with its lower-class readership, see *Gazeta-Kopeika*, February 27, 1917, #214, p. 4; March 21,

1917, #231, p. 3. A woman worker described her reading habits in her memoir, saying that although she did not read well, she read books and, "Of the newspapers, I read *Kopeika*; I was interested in current events," O. N. Chaadaeva, *Rabotnitsa na sotsialisticheskoi stroike* (Moscow: Partiinoe Izdatel'stvo, 1932), p. 98.

31. "Looking over the tens of reports from the factory," wrote a newspaper editor, "written in the majority of cases by the workers themselves, you see with surprise that their entire existence outside the factory is absorbed by very few interests: wine, cards, lotto, fights, etc." *Kineshemets*, May 1, 1913, #195, p. 3. See also August 1, 1912, #92, p. 2; November 25, 1912, #138, p. 3.

32. Ibid., May 13, 1912, #59, p. 3.

CHAPTER EIGHT

1. Some workers did have a rural upbringing before they entered the factory, either because they were first-generation workers, because a factory was located near their peasant village where the workers continued to live while employed at the factory, or because their worker-parents sent them to relatives in the countryside. The last situation usually occurred when parents felt the children could be better cared for in the rural environment than near the factory. However, with regard to the issues examined in this chapter, the experience of children brought up in the countryside did not differ substantially from that of those brought up near factories. See, for example, Chaadaeva, *Rabotnitsa*, pp. 97-98, 115-16, 127-28, 137-38, 153; I. Kor, *Kak my zhili pri tsare i kak zhivem teper'* (Moscow: Moskovskii rabochii, 1934), p. 14; S. P. Tolstov, *Narody mira*, pp. 463-73; N. Vladimirskii, *Kostromskaia oblast'* (Kostroma: Kostromskoe Knizhnoe Izdatel'stvo, 1959), p. 97.

2. B. V. Tikhonov, "Migratsiia fabrichno-zavodskikh rabochikh v Shuiskom uezde Vladimirskoi gubernii (po materialam podvornoi perepisi 1899 g.)," in L. G. Beskrovnyi, ed., *Istoricheskaia geografiia Rossii, XII-nachalo XX v.* (Moscow: Nauka, 1975), p. 116.

3. *Kineshemets*, March 31, 1913, #186, p. 3.

4. E. M. Kabo, *Ocherki rabochego byta* (Moscow, 1928), p. 23.

5. M. S. Kamneva, "Vrachebnaia pomoshch' rabochim na nekotorykh fabrikakh Vladimirskoi gubernii v 1896-1989 gg.," *Vrach'*, 1901, #7, pp. 201-2.

6. *Kineshemets*, March 13, 1913, #178, p. 2 and *Golos*, October 12, 1917, #223, p. 3.

7. Vladimir Ermilov, *Byt rabochei kazarmy* (Moscow, 1930), p. 9. See also Bogorodskaia Uezdnaia Zemskaia Uprava, *Ob'iasnitel'nyia zapiski uchastovykh i fabrichnykh vrachei Bogorodskago uezda (Mosk. gub.) po*

meditsinskoi deiatel'nosti za 1902 god (Moscow: Pechatnia S. P. Iakovleva, 1903).

8. D. L. Kasitskaia and Z. P. Popova, "Polozhenie i byt rabochikh-tekstil'shchikov Prokhorovskoi Trekhgornoi manufaktury v Moskve (Materialy ekspeditsii 1950 g.)," in A. M. Pankratova, ed., *Istoriko-bytovye ekspeditsii 1949-1950 gg.* (Moscow: Gosudarstvennoe Izdatel'stvo Kul'tur'no-Prosvetitel'noi Literatury, 1953), p. 176.

9. Ermilov, *Byt rabochei*, p. 9; M. N. Levinson-Nechaeva, "Polozhenie i byt rabochikh tekstil'noi promyshlennosti Moskovskoi gubernii vo vtoroi polovine XIX veka (Materialy ekspeditsii 1949 goda v g. Orekhovo-Zueva)," in Pankratova, *Istoriko-bytovye*, p. 160.

10. Kasitskaia and Popova, "Polozhenie i byt," p. 178. See also P. A. Peskov, *Fabrichnyi byt Vladimirskoi gubernii; Otchet 1882-1883 g. Fabrichnago Inspektora nad Maloletnykh Rabochikh Vladimirskago Okruga* (St. Petersburg: V. Kirshbaum, 1884), p. 86; *Kineshemets*, January 13, 1913, #155, p. 3; Vladimirskii, *Kostromskaia oblast'*, p. 89; and E. Popova, *Moskovskaia provintsiia v semnadtsatom godu* (Moscow: Moskovskii Istpart, 1927), p. 73.

11. Kor, *Kak my zhili*, p. 33.

12. Levinson-Nechaeva, "Polozhenie i byt," pp. 161-62. See also Kasitskaia and Popova, "Polozhenie i byt," p. 178, for a similar description of the barrack *kamorki* in another factory of the Central Industrial Region.

13. Peskov, *Fabrichnyi byt*, p. 87.

14. Levinson-Nechaeva, "Polozhenie i byt," p. 160, and Vladimirskii, *Kostromskaia oblast'*, p. 89.

15. Ermilov, *Byt rabochei*, p. 11. See also Kor, *Kak my zhili*, p. 33, on the "eternal fights" that took place in workers' *kamorki* before the revolution.

16. *Kineshemets*, January 13, 1913, #155, p. 3.

17. Most descriptions of *kamorki* note these curtains. See, among others, Vladimirskii, *Kostromskaia oblast'*, p. 89, and TsGALI, fond 1479, opis' 1, edinitsa khranenii 3, 1. 23.

18. Kasitskaia and Popova, "Polozhenie i byt," p. 178. See also Kor, *Kak my zhili*, p. 33.

19. *Kineshemets*, March 22, 1913, #182, pp. 2-3.

20. See, for example, Peskov, *Fabrichnyi byt*, p. 87, and Kasitskaia and Popova, "Polozhenie i byt," p. 178.

21. On the existence of large outdoor storage areas, see reports of thefts from them, for example, *Iaroslavets*, September 4, 1912, #66, p. 5; September 25, 1912, #87, p. 3.

22. Peskov, *Fabrichnyi byt*, p. 86; Kasitskaia and Popova, "Polozhenie i byt," pp. 178, 181. The Morozov barracks kitchens in Orekhovo-Zuevo were similar. See Levinson-Nechaeva, "Polozhenie i byt," p. 160.

23. Ermilov, *Byt rabochei*, p. 5. Men frequently left the barracks altogether to engage in these same activities in taverns or other all-male meeting places. On factory kitchens, see also *Gazeta-Kopeika*, January 10, 1917, #166, p. 3.
24. Peskov, *Fabrichnyi byt*, p. 98.
25. S. M. Lapitskaia, *Byt rabochikh Trekhgornoi manufaktury* (Moscow: Gosudarstvennoe Izdatel'stvo "Istoriia Zavodov," 1935), p. 64.
26. *Kineshemets*, February 8, 1913, #165, p. 3.
27. Ibid., June 9, 1913, #209, p. 4.
28. *Golos*, September 5, 1917, #196, p. 3.
29. Bobrovskaia, *Twenty Years in Underground Russia*, p. 165. See also P. N. Shchennikov, *Preobrazhennoi gorod* (Ivanovo: Ivanovskoe Knizhnoe Izdatel'stvo, 1961), p. 5.
30. Quoted in A. V. Shipulina, "Ivanovo-Voznesenskie rabochie nakanune pervoi russkoi revoliutsii. Uslovii ikh truda i byta," *Doklady i soobshcheniia Instituta Istorii* 8 (1955), 53.
31. Levinson-Nechaeva, "Polozhenie i byt," p. 162.
32. *Gazeta-Kopeika*, January 16, 1911, #12/578, p. 5.
33. Ibid., February 6, 1917, #32/193, p. 4.
34. Ibid., January 5, 1911, #3/569, p. 4. See also E. S. Goriacheva, "Vospominaniia," in *Istoriko-kraevedcheskii sbornik*, vyp. 2, ed. Orekhovo-Zuevskii Pedagogicheskii Institut (Moscow, 1959), p. 217.
35. *Iaroslavets*, August 20, 1912, #51, p. 3.
36. Massachusetts Bureau of Statistics of Labor, "Early Factory Labor in New England," Part IV, *Fourteenth Annual Report* (Boston: Wright and Potter Printing Co., 1883), pp. 384-85.

CHAPTER NINE

1. GLM, fond 263, papka 24d, list 4; Kor, *Kak my zhili*, p. 8.
2. Lapitskaia, *Byt rabochikh*, p. 67.
3. GLM, f. 263, p. 24d, l. 4.
4. N. Pismennyi, "O vliianii fabrichnykh uslovii raboty i zhizni materei na smertnost' detei," *Zhurnal Pirogovskago obshchestva* 1-2 (1904): 42.
5. Tolstov, *Narody mira*, p. 475.
6. Quoted in Lapitskaia, *Byt rabochikh*, p. 67.
7. *Gazeta-kopeika*, January 5, 1911, #3/569, p. 5.
8. Kor, *Kak my zhili*, p. 8; Lapitskaia, *Byt rabochikh*, p. 68; Tolstov, *Narody mira*, p. 475.
9. Goriacheva, "Vospominaniia," p. 217.
10. Chaadaeva, *Rabotnitsa*, p. 60.
11. Pismennyi, "O vliianii fabrichnykh," p. 43.
12. *Kineshemets*, December 12, 1912, #144, p. 3.
13. *Rabochee delo*, quoted in Lapitskaia, *Byt rabochikh*, p. 68.

14. Lapitskaia, *Byt rabochikh*, p. 68.
15. See Pismennyi, "O vliianii fabrichnykh," p. 43; I. Ianzhul, *Ocherki i issledovaniia* (Moscow, 1884), p. 392; and *Kineshemets*, June 26, 1913, #217, p. 3.
16. Institut Istorii Partii, *Slova starykh bol'shevikov (Iz revoliutsionnogo proshlogo)* (Moscow: Moskovskii rabochii, 1965), p. 20.
17. *Nasha Kostromskaia zhizn'*, April 6, 1912, #74, p. 3.
18. *Kineshemets*, March 31, 1913, #186, p. 3.
19. Pismennyi, "O vliianii fabrichnykh"; Ianzhul, *Ocherki*, p. 392; Bogorodsk, *Ob"iasnitel'nyia zapiski*, p. 62; *Nasha Kostromskaia zhizn'*, April 6, 1912, #74, p. 3.
20. Even the number of conceptions was apparently affected by women's factory work: if we divide the number of pregnancies by the number of mothers, we derive figures of 4.7 pregnancies per mother who had worked in the factory more than half her married life, 5.4 pregnancies per woman who worked in the factory less than half her married life, 6.1 pregnancies for nonworking wives of workers, and 7.5 for peasant mothers. Dr. Veger provided similar statistics for Kostroma guberniia. Ivanovo-Voznesenskoe Gubernskoe Nauchnoe Obshchestvo Kraevedeniia, *Ivanovo-Voznesenskaia guberniia: Kratkii obzor prirody, naseleniia, ekonomiki i istorii* (Ivanovo-Voznesensk: Osnova, 1929), p. 49, and *Nasha Kostromskaia zhizn'*, April 6, 1912, #74, p. 3.
21. Goriacheva, "Vospominaniia," p. 217.
22. Lapitskaia, *Byt rabochikh*, p. 68.
23. Kabo, *Ocherki rabochego byta*, p. 24.
24. See, for example, Levinson-Nechaeva, "Polozhenie i byt," pp. 160, 161; GLM, f. 263, p. 24d, l. 10.
25. *Kineshemets*, March 6, 1913, #175, p. 3.
26. GLM, f. 263, p. 21n, l. 1.
27. Ibid., p. 1a, l. 1.
28. Kor, *Kak my zhili*, p. 35.
29. *Iaroslavets*, July 24, 1912, #24, p. 3.
30. Chaadaeva, *Rabotnitsa*, pp. 137-38.
31. *Rabochii gorod*, November 15, 1917, #10, p. 3.
32. *Nasha Kostromskaia zhizn'*, March 9, 1912, #55, p. 3.
33. Goriacheva, "Vospominaniia," p. 217.
34. Chaadaeva, *Rabotnitsa*, pp. 42-43.
35. GLM, f. 263, p. 1a, l. 5.
36. Chaadaeva, *Rabotnitsa*, p. 60.
37. Ibid., pp. 127-28.
38. Ibid., p. 138.
39. Shorter, *Making of the Modern Family*.
40. *Iaroslavets*, September 5, 1912, #67, p. 4.

41. *Kineshemets*, April 24, 1913, #192, p. 2. For specific cases of abandonment, see for example *Ivanovskii listok*, August 8, 1910, #168, p. 2, and August 11, 1910, #170, p. 3; *Kineshemets*, December 8, 1911, #3, p. 3, June 27, 1912, #78, p. 3; *Iaroslavets*, October 21, 1912, #113, p. 3.

42. Spitz, *The First Year of Life*; Sally Provence and Rose C. Lipton, *Infants in Institutions: A Comparison of Their Development with Family-Reared Infants During the First Year of Life* (New York: International Universities Press, 1962); and William Goldfarb, "The Effects of Early Institutional Care on Adolescent Personality," *Journal of Experimental Education* 12, 2 (1943).

43. A 1911 study of infanticide concluded that the overwhelming majority (74 percent) of Russian women who committed this crime between 1897 and 1906 were unmarried girls, and that poverty of the mother was also an important contributing factor. M. N. Gernet, *Detoubiistvo. Sotsiologicheskoe i sravnitel'no-iuridicheskoe izsledovanie* (Moscow: Tipografiia Imperatorskago Moskovskago Universiteta, 1911), pp. 120, 126, 138-39. It seems likely that similar factors would have influenced child abandonment.

44. David Ransel has examined some aspects of the foundling home system in "Abandonment and Fosterage of Unwanted Children: The Women of the Foundling System," in *The Family in Imperial Russia: New Lines of Historical Research* (Urbana: University of Illinois Press, 1978), pp. 189-217.

45. Kor, *Kak my zhili*, pp. 23-24.

46. These include Lawrence Stone, *The Family, Sex, and Marriage in England, 1500-1800* (New York: Harper, 1977); Louise A. Tilly and Joan W. Scott, *Women, Work, and Family* (New York: Holt, 1978); William Reddy, "Some Comments on the History of the Family," (unpublished paper), pp. 4-10. Virginia Tufte and Barbara Myerhoff provide a short critical summary of this viewpoint, along with citations to the anthropological literature on the issue of how high infant mortality rates affect parental attitudes toward children. Anthropological research indicates that, "Sometimes infants are fiercely loved and protected precisely because they may not survive without this." *Changing Images of the Family* (New Haven: Yale University Press, 1979), p. 3.

47. Lapitskaia, *Byt rabochikh*, p. 68.

48. *Kineshemets*, January 18, 1913, #157, p. 2.

49. "Roditeli i deti v narodnykh poslovitsakh i pogovorkakh," *Vladimirskie gubernskie vedomosti*, October 28, 1911, #44, pp. 10-11. Lullabies and other songs sung by working-class mothers to their children were identical to peasant lullabies (A. M. Martynova, personal communication, October 1977). That lullabies and other songs changed perhaps less than any other genre during the transition from countryside to city suggests that the relationship between mother and young children—including the loving sentiments expressed in many lullabies—changed the least of all human relationships during that transition.

50. For content analysis regarding sex roles in songs sung by mothers to children, see my "Working Women," pp. 143-55 (This type of analysis has

already been done for Soviet children's books by Mollie Schwartz Rosenhan, "Images of Male and Female in Children's Readers," in Dorothy Atkinson, Alexander Dallin, and Gail Warshofsky Lapidus, eds., *Women in Russia* [Stanford: Stanford University Press, 1977], pp. 293-306); for a fuller discussion of lullabies as a form of communication between mother and child, see pp. 155-75; for a discussion of violence and negative emotions in lullabies, see pp. 164-71.

51. GLM, f. 263, p. 44g, l. 6.
52. Ibid., l. 7.
53. Ibid.
54. RO IRLI, k. 53, p. 1, l. 20.
55. GLM, f. 263, p. 44g, l. 9.
56. Ibid., f. 263, p. 44g, l. 5. Professor Shishkoff identified this type of song among the folklore collected.

CHAPTER TEN

1. Tolstov, *Narody mira*, p. 475.
2. Goriacheva, "Vospominaniia," p. 217. See also *Rabochii gorod*, November 29/December 12, 1917, #21, p. 2, and *Povolzhskii vestnik*, July 4, 1917, #3186, p. 3.
3. GLM, fond 263, papka 1a, list 1-2.
4. Kor, *Kak my zhili*, p. 28. T. Ia. Lobova became a nian'ka at the age of nine. GLM, f. 263, p. 21m, l. 1.
5. Kor, *Kak my zhili*, p. 39.
6. M. I. Smirnov, *Pereslavl'-zalesskii uezdnyi kratkii kraevedcheskii ocherk* (Pereslavl'-Zalesski: Pereslavl'-Zalesskoe Nauchnoe Prosvetitel'noe Obshchestvo, 1922), p. 36.
7. GLM, f. 263, p. 1a, l. 1.
8. Kor, *Kak my zhili*, p. 45.
9. Chaadaeva, *Rabotnitsa*, p. 40.
10. GLM, f. 263, p. 24g, l. 12.
11. Chaadaeva, *Rabotnitsa*, p. 60. For additional information on the ages when women and men began factory work, including memoirists' and informants' descriptions of the beginning of their own work experience, see Rashin, *Formirovanie*, pp. 271-73, 278-79, 283, 533; Bogorodskaia Uezdnaia Zemskaia Uprava, *Ob"iasnitel'nyia zapiski uchastovykh i fabrichnykh vrachei Bogorodskago uezda*, pp. 105-7; Vladimirskii, *Kostromskaia oblast'*, p. 86; Ianzhul, *Ocherki i issledovaniia*, pp. 365-66; Levinson-Nechaeva, "Polozhenie i byt," p. 169; *Izvestiia Ivanovo-Voznesenskago Soveta Rabochikh i Soldatskikh Deputatov*, May 18, 1917, #5, p. 2; *Iaroslavets*, November 8, 1912, #131, p. 3; I. Kor, *Kak my zhili*, pp. 6, 22, 36, 39-41,

45-46; GLM, f. 263, p. 24d, l. 1; p. 26, l. 1, 8; TsGALI, fond 1479, opis' 1, edinitsa khranenii 3, l. 23, 26, 42.

12. See *Vladimirskie gubernskie vedomosti*, June 10, 1911, #24, pp. 2-3, for a comment by a contemporary observer that the most boisterously celebrated holidays were those observed by only one subsection of the population, that is, by women alone, men alone, youth alone, and so on.

13. Ermilov, *Byt rabochei kazarmy*, p. 14. See also P. M. Ekzempliarskii, *Istoriia goroda Ivanova* (Ivanovo-Voznesensk: Ivanovskoe Knizhnoe Izdatel'stvo, 1958), p. 113. One folklore collector noted the continued existence of fortune-telling through 1967. Rukopisnyi Otdel Gosudarstvennoi Publichnoi Biblioteki im. Saltykova-Shchedrina, fond 1027, post. 1967.72, tetrad' 1, Sbornik narodnoi tvorchestva Ivanovskoi oblasti sost. Speranskoi Veroi Nikolaevnoi, gorod Shuiia, Iv. oblast', Zapiski 1905-1967 gg., list 27.

14. Three working women's accounts of various methods of fortune-telling are GLM, f. 263, p. 28v, l. 1-3; p. 1d, l. 101-3; and p. 242, l. 1.

15. Ibid., p. 24z, l. 1.

16. Ibid., p. 1d, l. 101.

17. For a discussion of sexual socialization in Russian working-class communities, see my "Russian Working Women: Sexuality in Bonding Patterns and the Politics of Everyday Life," in Ann Snitow, Christine Stansell, and Sharon Thompson, eds., *Powers of Desire: The Politics of Sexuality* (New York: Monthly Review Press, 1983). The following newspaper story describes young women's sexual behavior.

One young person from Sevriugov's factory writes us, "If you look attentively at the young women of Sevriugov's, you'll see . . . in the daytime they are proud and inaccessible, but at night they are sweet and obliging. If you pay attention to their proud walk during the day, [it's as if you're confronted with the admonition] inscribed for sinners on the gates of hell, 'Abandon hope forever.' But this pride is characteristic of them only in the daytime because they have two personalities—one in the moonlight and the other in the sun. The moon personality is quite fine and appealing. . . . But the one in the sun is no good at all."

Kineshemets, May 25, 1912, #64, p. 3. This report gives evidence of young women's eagerness to express their sexuality and of their capacity for repression of their sexual responsiveness during the daytime. The young men, meanwhile, were apparently more consistent in their diurnal rhythm of interest in sexuality.

18. GLM, f. 263, p. 1d, l. 106.

19. Ibid., p. 28v, l. 5. Tiurina gave a similar, brief account, p. 24e, l. 3. *Gazeta-Kopeika* observed, "Today is the holiday of Annunciation. The traditional trade in birds is taking place on Trubnaia Square. Each year on this day, the bird-prisoners are freed from their cages" May 25, 1917, #235, p. 3.

20. Given the fact that males were permitted more freedom than were females, one might interpret that, in psychoanalytic terms, the single braid may have been a phallic object representing freedom, and the parting of the hair a representation of the female genitals, which in that culture brought relative unfreedom, especially for married women. This seems both plausible and complementary to my analysis.

21. A. N. Sobolev, *Detskiia igry i pesni, Trudy Vladimirskoi Uchenoi Arkhivnoi Kommissii* (Vladimir: Tipografiia Gubernskago Pravleniia, 1914), pp. 41-42; Smirnov, *Kraevedcheskii ocherk*, p. 40; and GLM, f. 263, p. 1d, l. 107-8, 116, 121; p. 2, l. 12; p. 21v, l. 10; p. 24e, l. 1; p. 28v, l. 5. On little girls' celebration in a factory settlement, see GLM, f. 263, p. 24e, l. 1.

22. Ibid., f. 263, p. 1d, l. 110.

23. Ibid., p. 24g, l. 1. See also p. 2, l. 12. This was perhaps the only time women used the more typically male method of buying refreshments by pooling money from each participant; they also brewed beer for themselves, another male-associated tradition.

24. I. V. Dal', in his exhaustive nineteenth-century dictionary of Russian folkloric language, gave the saying, "Hops seek a support-pole [like] a girl [seeks] a young fellow," *Tolkovyi slovar' zhivogo velikorusskago iazyka* (St. Petersburg: M. O. Vol'f, 1909), p. 886.

25. GLM, f. 263, p. 21v, l. 4, l. 1.

26. Ibid., p. 21v, l. 2.

27. Ibid., p. 21v, l. 8-10. The word used here for "bride" is *mlada*, a word used frequently in young women's folklore. It is a dialect word derived from *molodaia*, which means either young woman or bride. Some of the repetitions of words and syllables I have cut to make this song easier to read convey a sense that the singer is weeping while singing it.

28. Ibid., p. 21v, l. 6; p. 1d, l. 109-10.

29. A. A. Potebnia, *Pereprava cherez vody kak predstavlenie braka* (Moscow, 1867); Potebnia, *O nekotorykh simvolakh v slavianskoi narodnoi poezii* (Kharkov: Universitetskaia Tipografiia, 1860), p. 73; Kostomarov, *Sobranie sochinenii*, p. 487.

30. E. V. Pomerantseva, ed., *Pesni i skazki Yaroslavskoi oblasti* (Yaroslavl: Iaroslavskoe Knizhnoe Izdatel'stvo, 1958), p. 17.

31. Aleksei Smirnov, "Fabrichnye pesni," *Vladimirskaia gazeta*, May 25, 1903, #117, p. 2. The *chastushka* was one of the few folkloric genres whose origins lay in the city rather than among the peasantry.

32. Sokolov, *Chastushki*, p. 6. Sokolov identified *chastushki* as a genre in which performers strove to outdo each other in demonstrating mastery of rhyme, rhythm, dance steps, and new repertoire. I have built my argument on his, speculating that the performers were also demonstrating mastery of individualized integration of cultural mores.

33. Ibid., p. 10.

34. Ia. Korobov, "Derevenskaia pripevka i fabrichnaia chastushki," *Staryi vladimirets*, December 14, 1914, #275, p. 3.

35. Sokolov, *Chastushki*, pp. 6-7.
36. *Kineshemets*, April 14, 1913, #191, p. 2.
37. TsGALI, f. 1470, op. 1, ed. khr. 2, l. 7.
38. *Trudy*, pp. 17-18, #82. There is another variant on p. 68, #405.
39. Tovrov deals with similar issues for the nobility in "Mother-Child Relationships among the Russian Nobility," pp. 15-43.
40. *Kineshemets*, May 2, 1912, #55, p. 3.
41. Ibid., June 8, 1912, #70, pp. 2-3 (my emphasis).
42. Lapitskaia, *Byt rabochikh*, p. 70.
43. "Roditeli i deti v narodnykh poslovitsakh i pogovorkakh," p. 9.
44. *Kineshemets*, February 12, 1912, #26, p. 3.
45. For working women-informants' descriptions of the burning of the Maslenitsa bonfires, see GLM, f. 263, p. 28v, l. 3, and p. 1d, l. 105. Rodionova reported the Maslenitsa was burned in Yaroslavl as late as 1925. Lobova also noted the burning of bonfires, p. 21i, l. 2. In 1913, an article with the byline "A Weaver" reported that the Annenskaia textile factory administration had finally conceded to the workers' demands that they be given a day off during Maslenitsa. This was apparently only a formality, for absenteeism was typically very high on that day anyway. *Kineshemets*, February 22, 1913, #171, p. 3.
46. *Kineshemets*, February 10, 1912, #25, p. 3.
47. Sokolov, *Russian Folklore*, pp. 188, 189.
48. GLM, f. 263, p. 28v, l. 3. Unfortunately, I found only one example of this type of song from among Central Industrial Region workers. This does not mean that there were not many others, for it may well have been that female informants were reluctant to sing for ethnographers the ribald songs that had been reserved for performance by young males during the Maslenitsa celebration.
49. Sokolov, *Russian Folklore*, pp. 188-89.
50. GLM, f. 263, p. 1d, l. 118. The occasion for this holiday was the church's August 29 commemoration of the "day of the cutting off of the head" of John the Baptist. V. I. Dal', *Tolkovyi slovar' zhivogo velikorusskago iazyka* (St. Petersburg, Moscow: M. O. Vol'f, 1905-1907), 2: 3, 3: 1015. August 30 was referred to by the workers as the day of Alexander Nevskii, perhaps because this military figure symbolized the combative, fighting spirit of the men during the celebration.
51. GLM, f. 263, p. 1d, l. 118.
52. In many cities, the factory district was on the outskirts of town. Factory workers rarely ventured into the center of the city, and there was tension between factory workers and the lower-class urban dwellers. *Iaroslavets*, August 30, 1912, #61, p. 5.
53. Natalie Davis examines the phenomenon of youth bands in sixteenth-century France in her "The Reasons of Misrule: Youth Groups and Charivaris in Sixteenth-Century France," *Past and Present* 50 (February 1971): 41-75.
54. Ermilov, *Byt rabochei kazarmy*, pp. 15-16.

55. *Ivanovskii listok*, July 16, 1910, #150, p. 3. The slang words for fistfight (*stenka*), teams (*stenki*), and one large group of people facing off against another (*stena stenoi*) are all derived from the Russian word for "wall," *stena*. "*Stena stenoi*" is an expression typically used to describe a "wall" of Tatar warriors bearing down in an attack. It is interesting that these highly colloquial early-twentieth-century expressions again emphasized the notion of solidarity groups fighting against each other: a group of individuals as solid and united as a wall facing off against another similar group. Also, the allusion to warriors from Russia's military history was part of a general phenomenon among the youth groups, who referred to themselves and the other youth bands as Cossacks, Tatar khans, and so on.

56. TsGALI, f. 1479, op. 1, ed. khr. 3, l. 26-27. Mamai was a particularly brutal Tatar khan, whose name was a universal insult throughout Russian culture. *Rogali* is a dialect word whose meaning is unclear here. It may make some reference to cursing or to being cuckolded.

57. This is not to say that political views played no part in marshaling men's political commitments. Rather, the existence of solidarity groups in daily life facilitated the transmission of revolutionary ideas among workers, the development of trust among those engaging in illegal and dangerous activities, and so on. Robert Johnson deals with some of these issues in raising the question of how *zemliak* ties encouraged political activity among *zemliaki*. He speculates that daily-life grapevines of communication among *zemliaki* gave them information about strikes occurring in distant places; he also observes that the everyday loyalties among *zemliaki* caused even nonactive *zemliaki* to aid their politically active fellows when the latter were in need (e.g., running from the police, in need of shelter, etc.), Johnson, *Peasant and Proletarian*, pp. 76-79.

58. *Trudy Vladimirskoi Arkhivnoi Kommissii* 16 (Vladimir: Tipografiia Gubernskago Pravlenii, 1914), #440, p. 73. Sokolov also recorded a variant many years later, *Chastushki*, p. 28.

59. *Trudy*, p. 72, #427.

60. Sokolov, *Chastushki*, p. 28.

61. *Kineshemets*, April 14, 1913, #191, p. 2.

62. TsGALI, f. 1480, op. 1, ed. khr. 2, ll. 113-14; Kor, *Kak my zhili*, p. 16. Boys' songs boasting about their drinking are *Kostromskie novosti*, June 8, 1912, #30, p. 3. and *Trudy*, p. 47, #273.

63. *Kineshemets*, April 14, 1913, #191, p. 2.

64. Ibid., May 2, 1912, #55, p. 3.

65. *Iaroslavets*, September 17, 1912, #79, p. 3; September 18, 1912, #80, p. 4. See also August 24, 1912, #55, p. 3 (men harassing women with sexual comments); and *Kostromskaia zhizn'*, January 8, 1912, #6, p. 3.

66. *Iaroslavets*, September 13, 1912, #75, p. 3; September 7, 1912, #69, p. 4; *Kineshemets*, July 4, 1912, #80, p. 4.

67. *Iaroslavets*, December 28, 1912, #179, p. 3. See also November 7, 1912, #130, p. 3, for a similar case that occurred at a dance put on by the volunteer fire *druzhina*; and *Kineshemets*, April 14, 1913, #191, p. 2.

68. *Kineshemets*, July 8, 1912, #82, p. 3. See also May 11, 1912, #58, p. 3, on a rape by two young men of a seventeen-year-old woman. For further information on youthful hooliganism, including the influence of the factories on the countryside in this regard, see August 1, 1912, #92, p. 2, and another article, p. 3; June 7, 1913, #208, p. 3; and *Vladimirskie gubernskie vedomosti*, August 13, 1910, #33, p. 1.

69. For more on youth bands, see *Gazeta-Kopeika*, February 4, 1917, #191, p. 2, and *Iaroslavets*, September 17, 1912, #79, p. 3.

70. Sokolov, *Chastushki*, p. 28; *Trudy*, p. 72, #435; p. 73, #440; Smirnov, "Fabrichnye pesni," p. 2. Some male youths' songs seem to blame their mothers for not rescuing them from their despair. Perhaps because, as small children, their mothers did rescue them from life's hurts, they resented having to move beyond the protection of childhood. For example,

> My bold head,
> Will I carry you for long?
> . . . my hard fate,
> . . . ruined me, a fine fellow. . . .
> For what did my mother give birth to me?
> For what—to sit in this cell
> And curse prison life? . . .
> Look what's become of me,
> Where have my good looks gone?
> Where has that former glow gone?
> Those ringlets of black curly hair?
> It seems that I'll die on a prison pillow,
> They'll bury me any which way.
> And for this, for my death
> My own dear mother won't mourn!

Ibid., p. 2.

71. For a discussion of sports and male bonding, see Stewart, "The Marriage of Capitalist and Patriarchal Ideologies," pp. 288-90.

72. There was a great increase during 1917 of reports in newspapers about a general phenomenon of working-class youths hanging around in the streets, behaving destructively and harassing women. As early as January, a Moscow newspaper complained that drunken "hooligans" spent their evenings in public squares, singing "naughty songs" and behaving outrageously. "Not one woman is allowed to pass without being insulted with vile words or having her sleeve jerked." *Gazeta-Kopeika*, January 28, 1917, #184, p. 3. Factory youth at the Prokhorovka textile plant were especially implicated. Ibid., January 17, 1917, #173, p. 3. In Kostroma, "at the factory,

hooliganism takes on a serious character"; the newspaper called for measures "to protect the working women leaving the factory, especially in the evening." *Kur'er*, March 28, 1917, #66, p. 2. Norskoe reported a similar problem around the same date, *Golos*, April 12(25), 1917, #79. By October, Yaroslavl's working-class outskirts reported a great increase in drunks in the city streets. "They conduct themselves extremely obscenely. . . . Here, women fear to appear outdoors in the evening, risking encountering great trouble." *Yaroslavskaia mysl'*, October 10, 1917, #45, p. 3. "Hooligans work everywhere, and women passing them must move with greatest speed, in order to escape in time the too-intimate appeals of various 'night-time cavaliers.' . . . The dark night and the hooligan 'pals' and the apprehensively running young women—all this strikes the mind with something sharp and painful." Ibid., October 25, 1917, #58, p. 3. An interesting insight was provided by a Kostroma reporter soon after the February Revolution, when both "worker youth" and soldiers went around the city's squares and boulevards, breaking trees, bushes, and fences. "To the protests of other citizens, they answer 'Now we have freedom.' This certainly is true, but freedom isn't to break trees. . . . We have already several times been asked to report about this and also about the fact that in the evening . . . women cannot go alone in the streets, in order not to encounter outrages." *Kur'er*, April 14, 1917, #75, p. 2. One wonders to what degree these young men viewed their behavior not as reactionary, but rather as a "freedom" provided by the revolution.

73. *Kineshemets*, June 21, 1913, #215, pp. 3-4.
74. *Novyi Kineshemets*, July 31, 1913, #2, p. 3.
75. *Kineshemets*, June 21, 1913, #215, p. 4.
76. Ibid., June 2, 1913, #207, p. 2.
77. *Novyi Kineshemets*, August 18, 1913, #8, p. 2.
78. Ibid., August 21, 1913, #9, pp. 2-3; *Kineshemets*, June 2, 1913, #207, p. 2, and June 14, 1913, #211, p. 4.
79. *Novyi Kineshemets*, July 27, 1913, #1, p. 3; and May 11, 1914, #47, p. 3. The phenomenon of theater groups based in factories is an important one, which unfortunately I was unable to pursue. My sense is that these groups were made up mostly or entirely of male workers and employees. If these groups were widespread, they would be another example of the type of highly organized men's group activity, based on differentiated functioning and concerted action, and having institutionalized and regularized contact with members of other classes as peers. Ekzempliarskii, for example, gives some brief information about local theater in Ivanovo-Voznesensk in *Istoriia goroda Ivanova*, pp. 113-14, 168-69, 290-91. Theater groups also contributed money to other causes. For example, as reported by a Yaroslavl newspaper, on Sunday, July 22, 1914, a performance of "Avodotia's Life" was staged in the Romanovskaia linen manufactory by the local amateur music and drama group, the proceeds of which were donated to the Romanovo-Borisoglebsk city public library. *Iaroslavets*, July 22, 1912, #22,

p. 4. GLM's f. 263 has substantial material from men involved with these theater groups.

80. *Kineshemets*, June 21, 1913, #215, pp. 3-4; *Novyi Kineshemets*, August 18, 1913, #8, pp. 3-4; June 11, 1914, #57, p. 3.

81. Ibid., June 4, 1914, #54, p. 3. *Gigany* is probably a pole with ropes to swing on; *prokhozhdenie* is probably an obstacle course. On the growth of interest in sports and sport societies, see May 25, 1914, #51, p. 3.

82. Ibid., May 7, 1914, #46, p. 3, and May 18, 1914, #49, p. 2.

83. *Iaroslavskie novosti*, November 11, 1913, #45, p. 3; *Iaroslavets*, October 22, 1912, #114, p. 3. Both of these articles complained of disorganization and other problems within the society; unfortunately, I have no further information on its development after 1913.

84. "Men and Women in the South of France: Public and Private Domains," in *Toward an Anthropology of Women*, p. 266.

85. *Golos*, July 16 (29), 1917, #157, p. 3; *Nasha Kostromskaia zhizn'*, April 24, 1912, #89, p. 3.

86. A further element of the "team's" cover was their uniform: "We had *futbol* shirts with black and white stripes to symbolize 'Thunderstorm.' " M. N. Petrakov, "Vospominaniia," in *Istoriko-kraevedcheskii sbornik*, Orekhovo-Zuevskii Pedagogicheskii Institut (Moscow, 1959), 2: 200-201.

87. *Kineshemets*, June 21, 1913, #214, pp. 3-4.

88. *Novyi Kineshemets*, July 31, 1913, #2, p. 3.

89. *Kineshemets*, June 21, 1913, #215, pp. 3-4.

90. I found very little information on the character and composition of audiences at soccer games and other sports, aside from the fact that they were often large and enthusiastic. See, for example, *Kineshemets*, August 1, 1912, #92, p. 3; June 14, 1913, #211, p. 4; and *Novyi Kineshemets*, August 18, 1913, #8, p. 2; August 28, 1913, #12, p. 2; June 27, 1914, #63, p. 2. This is regrettable, since it seems likely that young working women were among the spectators. However, it also seems likely that even if women did attend, they did so with the same stance as in their rituals: all-female groups participating together in an activity in which they focused their attention more on young men (in this case, on the players they were watching) than on their all-female friendship networks.

CHAPTER ELEVEN

1. Other dances included the *lantse* (like a square dance but with "three opposite three"), the simple waltz, and the swinging waltz. See GLM, f. 263, p. 28g, l. 1.

2. Otdel Rukopisei i Redkikh Knig Gosudarstvennoi Publichnoi Biblioteki im. Saltykova-Shchedrina (OR RK GPB), f. 1027, post 1959.114, Russkii fol'klor, Ivanovskaia oblast', Zapisi narodnogo tvorchestva s 1906 g.-1958

god, Speranskoi, Very Nikolaevny, l. 19. See also TsGALI, fond 1455, opis' 1, edinitsa khranenii 76, list 1-12, passim, for information on *gulian'ia* and other dances in rural areas of the CIR.

3. A. P. Golitsynskii, *Ocherki fabrichnoi zhizni* (St. Petersburg, 1886), p. 56. Finder-bal'zanchik may have been an aromatic substance derived from a balsam or other plant. See pp. 5-6 for Golitsynskii's methodology.

4. GLM, fond 263, papka 28g, list 1.

5. *Kineshemets*, January 18, 1913, #157, p. 3; N. I. Savushkina, *Russkii narodnyi teatr* (Moscow: Nauka, 1976), pp. 130-33; and Lapitskaia, *Byt rabochikh*, p. 76. The working woman Rodionova described such entertainments as taking place in Yaroslavl during the great yearly fair in March. GLM, f. 263, p. 1d, l. 106.

6. F. Samoilov, ed., *Fabrika 'Krasnyi Perekor,' Iaroslavskaia Bol'shaia Manufaktura, 1722-1933*, I, *Volzhskie tkachi* (Moscow: Gosudarstvennoe Izdatel'stvo "Istoriia Zavodov," 1936), p. 276. Samoilov said that the workers attributed the Bol'shaia factory owner's 1906 temporary termination of the *gulian'ia* to the 1905 revolution. *Iaroslavets* later reported a rumor circulating among workers that the fetes were to be stopped by the factory administration because the workers had gone on strike in June of 1912. See the July 3 issue, p. 3.

7. *Iaroslavets*, July 3, 1912, #3, p. 4; July 10, #10, p. 5; July 17, #17, p. 5; July 31, 1912, #31, p. 3; August 9, 1912, #40, p. 4; August 17, 1912, #48, p. 5; August 21, 1912, #52, p. 3; August 30, 1912, #61, p. 4.

8. *Novaia zhizn'; Iurevetskaia narodnaia gazeta*, August 26, 1917, #25, p. 2. Another *gulian'e* was held in Kostroma on Sunday, April 9, 1917, for the benefit of "the worker-soldiers in the trenches as a gift on May Day." The event enjoyed a large attendance. *Povolzhskii vestnik*, April 12, 1917, #3119, p. 2.

9. GLM, f. 263, p. 28v, l. 4.

10. Petrakov, "Vospominaniia," p. 200.

11. *Iaroslavets*, November 7, 1912, #130, p. 3. The teenage working-class boy, Pavel, in Maxim Gorky's *Mother* "did all that was expected of a young man: he bought himself an accordion, a shirt with a starched front, a bright necktie, galoshes [the height of working-class youth fashion], and a cane. In this way, he became like all other boys of his age. He went to parties in the evening, learned to dance quadriiles and the polka, and came home drunk on Sundays." (Moscow: Progress Publishers, 1976), p. 21.

12. GLM, f. 263, p. 1d, l. 116 and p. 28v, l. 3. For a description of one such celebration, see l. 121.

13. Ibid., p. 21n. l. 1.

14. Ibid., p. 9a, l. 113.

15. Ibid., p. 21m, l. 1-3. See also p. 1d, l. 117.

16. Ibid., p. 6d, l. 208-10 contains Petrova's oral history, which describes her experiences as a singer.

17. The indecisiveness of the cat-youth and his escape from the eager girl at the end of the song is an example of the ambivalence of Russian working-class men's stance toward women.

18. GLM, f. 263, p. 9v, l. 91. In all songs, I have eliminated repetitions of phrases, lines, and refrains.

19. Vorob'eva learned this song "from my aunt Nastasiia in childhood." GLM, f. 263, p. 9v, l. 91-92.

20. Premarital sexual intercourse was not condoned for women. The shame and approbation resulting from premarital pregnancies can be seen in the case of A. F. Golubevaia, the only memoirist I found who had become pregnant before marriage. Although she had had a close relationship with her mother up until then, the latter threw her "into the street" after she became pregnant, having first refused to give her any food to eat and beaten her. The impossible situation of women pregnant out of wedlock is also seen in the incidence of child abandonment and infanticide when unmarried women did become pregnant. M. N. Gernet, *Detoubiistvo. Sotsiologicheskoe i sravitel'no-iuridicheskoe issledovanie* (Moscow: Tipografiia Imperatorskago Moskovskago Universiteta, 1911), pp. 120, 126, 138-39. There was a very widely sung song about the plight of a girl who cut ties with her family in order to sleep with her boyfriend out of wedlock; he later abandoned her to her terrible fate. One variant is located in OR RK GPB, f. 1027, post. 1967.72, Tetrad' 1, Sbornik narodnoi tvorchestva Ivanovskoi oblasti sost. Speranskoi, Veroi Nikolaevnoi, gorod Shuiia, Iv. oblast', Zapisi 1905-1967gg., l. 118.

21. OR RK GPB, f. 1027, post. 1967.72, Tetrad' 1, l. 119.

22. The first song quoted is GLM, p. 28a, l. 3. It is a dance version of a song sung during the Semik-Trinity ritual by teenage girls; the Semik version focused entirely on the girls' friendship group, while the dance version shifts to focus on the relationship between one woman and one man. See Bobroff, "Russian Working Women," pp. 317-22. The second song quoted is in ibid., p. 24a, l. 4-6.

23. Another popular song was about a factory woman hospitalized and refusing to take life-saving medicine because her boyfriend had left her, so her life was meaningless: "Save me or don't save me/ Life isn't dear to me." The young woman died. TsGALI, f. 1413, op. 2, ed. khr. 53, l. 35. Another variant is located in Rukopisnyi Otdel Instituta Russkoi Literatury (Pushkinskii Dom), Razriad V, kollektsiia 53, papka 4, list 6.

24. GLM, f. 263, p. 28a, l. 1. The maternal cast of this woman's behavior as she put her transgressing husband to bed occurred in other songs as well. I suspect that this maternal quality attributed to romance helped identify the beloved man with their future children, to establish women's responsibility for the emotional support of her family. And, just as the beloved man took on some of the qualities of a troublesome but beloved child in the courtship dance songs, so too would the emotional energy generated by romantic

excitement help instill in women the commitment to care, day in and day out, for often troublesome but beloved children.

25. Ibid., p. 21b, l. 6-9. The Russian word used for "fell" in describing the star also means "degenerate."

26. Ibid., p. 9v, l. 72-74.

27. One folklore collector, for example, described "dance songs, which accompany the quadrille. . . . All the girls dancing move and sing to the accompaniment of an accompanist, one couplet several times, until the figure is completed." Aleksei Smirnov, "Fabrichnye pesni," *Vladimirskaia gazeta*, May 25, 1903, #117, p. 2. A folklore collector in Kostroma guberniia noted that among the peasantry "Each song had its own figures, dances." TsGALI, f. 1455, ed. khr. 76, l. 1.

28. GLM, f. 263, p. 24d, l. 3-4.

29. N. I. Kostomarov, *Sobranie sochinenii*, VIII (St. Petersburg: Tipografiia M. M. Stasiulevicha, 1905), p. 629. This imagery appeared very often; for example, a song from the wedding ritual described the groom as having "Bright falcon's eyes." GLM, f. 263, p. 24a, l. 2.

30. Another very common form of sexualized abuse of Russian working women was that by foremen and other men in positions of authority at the factory. That this was a widespread phenomenon is attested to in many of the sources on Russian working women. Some relevant newspaper reports are *Kineshemets*, January 24, 1914, #9, p. 3; March 9, 1914, #27, pp. 2-3; *Gazeta-Kopeika*, February 8, 1911, #30/569, p. 3.

31. GLM, f. 263, p. 1b, l. 10.

32. My description of the working-class wedding is based on two detailed accounts, one from Norskoe, a large textile factory town ten miles up the Volga from Yaroslavl, and the other from Sed'maia Tysiach', inhabited by descendants of some of Iaroslavskaia Bol'shaia textile mill's earliest working-serfs of the late eighteenth and early nineteenth centuries, who apparently continued to live in a discrete district of Yaroslavl through the early twentieth century. GLM, fond 263, papka 1d, list 117; Samoilov, *Fabrika 'Krasnyi Perekop'*, p. 89. Also utilized were a number of fragmentary archival accounts and songs transmitted to ethnographers by various informants, newspaper stories, and other general sources. On the connection between the peasant and worker weddings, see Tolstov, *Narody mira* p. 476.

33. Descriptions of the Russian peasant wedding rituals abound. See, for example, Mary Matossian, "The Peasant Way of Life," in Wayne Vucinich, ed., *The Peasant in Nineteenth-Century Russia* (Stanford: Stanford University Press, 1968).

34. *Sbornik statisticheskii svedenii po Moskovskoi gubernii. Otdel sanitarnoi statistiki*, T. IV, ch. 1 (Moscow, 1890), p. 273, quoted in Tolstov, *Narody mira*, p. 476.

35. The Soviet ethnographer S. P. Tolstov write, "worker youth, for the most part, married by their own choice." Even though a matchmaker was involved in the wedding process, "the youth retained the right of the final decision.

Youth of both sexes met and got to know each other at work, at parties, and especially at the popular *gulian'ia* which were so characteristic of city life." *Narody mira*, p. 476. Kokushkina, however, claimed that many fathers went ahead with weddings over their wives' and daughters' objections, GLM, f. 263, p. 28b, l. 1-2. Another working woman informant told ethnographers how she had allowed both her son and her daughter to make their own choice of marriage partner, RO IRLI, k. 53, p. 1, l. 77-78. The transition from peasant marriages arranged by fathers to marriage partners being chosen by the young people involved was probably gradual; in the 1850s in Ivanovo-Voznesensk, neither the bride nor the groom had any part in choosing his or her spouse. Ekzempliarskii, *Istoriia goroda Ivanova*, p. 113.

36. Tolstov gave this time period as one and a half weeks among Moscow textile workers. *Narody mira*, p. 476.

37. See, for example, Sokolov's chapter, "Wedding Ceremonials and Chants," especially pp. 212, 214-16 in *Russian Folklore*. Z. R. Skvortsova has written about the similarities between peasant ritual wedding laments and funeral laments. "O prichitaniia v svadebnom obriade," in B. I. Putilov, *Fol'klor i etnografiia. Obriady i obriadny fol'klor* (Leningrad: Nauka, 1974). Skvortsova's findings suggest that for the peasant bride, marriage was almost the equivalent of death (in the sense of completely losing her previous life), followed by a far-removed "after"-life.

38. Although I do not know what proportion of women workers married men living in another city or factory settlement, the fact that many methods of working-class girls' fortune-telling were efforts to find out how far away a bride would go at marriage, and from which direction her husband would come, indicates that factory women were concerned about actual physical distance as well as psychological distance. For example, young women slid down the corridor in factory barracks and counted the number of floorboards "traveled." This was supposedly the number of versts (a verst is 3,500 feet) each would travel to be married. A tub of water would be placed at a crossroads, and each girl would stir it vigorously. Whichever way the water splashed was the direction each would go to be married. Each girl would throw her shoe over a fence. The direction it pointed when it landed was the direction her husband would come from. GLM, f. 263, p. 28v, l. 1-3; p. 1d, l. 101-3; and p. 24z, l. 1.

39. Ibid., p. 9v, l. 94-96. Some of the repetitions of words and syllables I have cut out to make this song easier to read convey the impression of weeping during the singing.

40. Tolstov, *Narody mira*, p. 476; GLM, f. 263, p. 1d, ll. 124-25; p. 28b, l. 3.

41. Some of these songs are located in GLM, f. 263, p. 24a, l. 1-2.

42. Ibid., p. 24a, l. 1-2.

43. Ibid., l. 1.

44. Ibid., p. 1e-2h, l. 2; p. 28b, l. 3; and Lapitskaia, *Byt rabochikh*, p. 73.

45. Tolstov also noted the dressing of the hair in the married woman's style, *Narody mira*, pp. 476-77.
46. RO IRLI, koll. 53, p. 4, l. 11.
47. GLM, f. 263, p. 1d, l. 126-27. The bride's wedding dress was decorated with cheap lace and flowers when it could not be made of more costly materials. Levinson-Nechaeva, "Polozhenie i byt," pp. 165-66, and Kasitskaia and Popova, "Polozhenie i byt," p. 176.
48. GLM, f. 263, p. 1d, l. 128.
49. GLM, f. 263, p. 1e-zh, l. 1.
50. Tolstov, *Narody mira*, p. 477.
51. GLM, f. 263, p. 28b, l. 4.
52. Ibid., l. 4-5. It may be difficult to imagine how all of this postwedding feasting and merry-making could have taken place in factory barracks, with their tiny *kamorki*. But the fact that weddings did occur in barracks is evidenced by such newspaper items as a police report in which a worker declared that his silver watch had been stolen out of his pocket while he was at a wedding in "room #21, 10th factory building." *Yaroslavets*, September 6, 1912, #68, p. 3. Another article reported on a type of hooligan "extortion" to which wedding parties in the Tomna factory area were subjected; it gave a specific case in which the victims were a groom and his wedding procession, who were held up for an hour at the factory barrack where they had come for the bride to bring her to the church. *Kineshemets*, February 6, 1913, #164, p. 3.
53. *Kineshemets*, February 8, 1912, #24, p. 4. *Kostromskaia zhizn'* also sniffed disapprovingly,

> *Miasoed* [the period between Christmas and Shrovetide] has arrived, and with it the opening of the wedding season. In the course of these weeks, wedding guests perform their wedding processions all over the streets of the village of Sereda and its factory district.
> This whole wedding procession . . . [proceeds] with cries, dancing, clanging on copper basins and iron covers, and the singing of various types of songs, sometimes even of obscene content. (January 13, 1912, #10, p. 3.)

54. GLM, f. 263, p. 28b, l. 4.
55. Ibid., p. 1d, l. 129-30. The fact that the bride was always "blamed" for the "bad marriage," but never the groom, established her as the outsider (in patrilocal tradition) who could easily be blamed for difficulties.
56. Tolstov, *Narody mira*, p. 476.
57. GLM, f. 263, p. 1d, l. 129-30.
58. Ibid., p. 1e-zh, l. 1.
59. Ibid., p. 24a, l. 3.

60. Dowries of blankets, pillows, sheets, tablecloths, curtains, and clothing continued at least into the late 1920s. TsGALI, f. 1455, op. 1, ed. khr. 52, ll. 144-45.
61. GLM, f. 263, p. 1d, l. 125.
62. Ibid., l. 127-29 and p. 28b, l. 3; Tolstov, *Narody mira*, p. 477.
63. Sokolov, *Russian Folklore*, p. 218.
64. GLM, f. 263, p. 24a, l. 1; p. 1d, l. 124.
65. Ibid., l. 128.

CHAPTER TWELVE

1. Kor, *Kak my zhili*, p. 8. Unfortunately, my sources revealed little about women's involvement with religion; this is an area that merits further investigation. Working women also made use of fortune-tellers and wise woman (*znakharki*). One source, a compilation of information from working women's oral histories, said that working women were very superstitious and went to fortune-tellers to find out whether their husbands still loved them, what the sex of an expected baby would be, what to do about family problems. Lapitskaia, *Byt rabochikh*, pp. 73-74. One working woman who lived in Yaroslavl factory barracks was poisoned by a *znakharka*'s medication. *Iaroslavets*, December 30, 1912, #181, p. 3.
2. Chaadaeva, *Rabotnitsa*, pp. 115-16.
3. Kor, *Kak my zhili*, pp. 21, 39.
4. Bogorodskaia uezdnaia, *Ob"iasnitel'nyia zapiski*, p. 57.
5. Riazanova, *Zhenskii trud*, p. 93. Data from the Tsindel' factory in Moscow indicated that in 1899, a few families, especially some from one settlement, worked in the factory as entire families. V. Kurakhtanov, *Pervaia sittsenabivnaia* (Moscow: Izdatel'stvo Sotsial'no-ekonomicheskoi Literatury, 1960), p. 7.
6. Levinson-Nechaeva, "Polozhenie i byt," pp. 157-58.
7. Kor, *Kak my zhili*, p. 22.
8. Ibid., p. 36; GLM, f. 263, p. 24d, l. 3.
9. Kor, *Kak my zhili*, p. 6.
10. 1897 report of the Vladimir guberniia factory inspector, quoted in Riazanova, *Zhenskii trud*, p. 93.
11. Chaadaeva, *Rabotnitsa*, p. 41. Weaving was the most skilled women's job in textiles, and hence more frequently required training than did other jobs. Riazanova, *Zhenskii trud*, p. 309. An unusual case was that of M. I. Baliasova, who began work in the same workshop as her mother, as a *s"emshchitsa* on a spinning jenny (her mother was a fly frame operator). She later became a weaver, which was her father's job, and her two daughters also became weavers. Levinson-Nechaeva, "Polozhenie i byt," p. 158.
12. Kor, *Kak my zhili*, p. 23.

13. Chaadaeva, *Rabotnitsa*, p. 60
14. Ibid., p. 29.
15. As it turned out, this friend was not close enough to her in the shop to help when she made a mistake; fortunately the foreman was kind, and he showed her how to correct her error. Chaadaeva, *Rabotnitsa*, pp. 116-19. See also p. 40 for the story of Valentina Petrova, who at first learned to spin and weave from girls in the factory, in secrecy from her parents.
16. GLM, f. 263, p. 24d, l. 4.
17. Kor, *Kak my zhili*, p. 6. However, in the factory where Tiurina worked, "The foreman taught us." GLM, f. 263, p. 24d, l. 2.
18. Ibid., p. 1a, l. 1, 4.
19. Ibid., p. 30g, l. 1.
20. Goriacheva, "Vospominaniia," p. 217.
21. GLM, f. 263, p. 1a, l. 5.
22. *Kineshemets*, May 13, 1912, #59, p. 3.
23. Ibid., January 29, 1912, #22, p. 3; February 29, 1912, #32, p. 3; March 7, 1912, #35, p. 3; *(Nasha) Kostromskaia zhizn'*, April 24, 1912, #89, p. 3; *Iaroslavets*, August 15, 1912, #46, p. 5; *Izvestiia Ivanovo-Voznesenskago Soveta Rabochikh i Soldatskikh Deputatov*, June 7 (20), 1917, #17, p. 2; June 9 (22), 1917, #18, p. 2.
24. Kokushkina went on to recall how the factory director had "shamed me" in front of a large group of people: "in front of all these upright people he said that I had taken the laces. So I said, 'Mr. Director, I didn't dare ask for them.' " GLM, f. 263, p. 28g, l. 2.
25. *Nasha Kostromskaia zhizn'*, February 12, 1912, #33, p. 2; *Ivanovskii listok*, February 10, 1917, #33, p. 1; *Iaroslavets*, September 1, 1912, #63, p. 5; *Kineshemets*, March 21, 1912, #41, p. 3; July 6, 1912, #81, p. 4; August 1, 1912, #92, p. 4. *Iaroslavets* also reported two small-scale thefts by individual male workers, September 29, 1912, #91, p. 4; October 6, 1912, #98, p. 4.
26. Many popular songs, for example, supported a man's right—indeed his obligation—to beat his wife. See GLM, f. 263, p. 9v, l. 63, 72-74.
27. GLM, f. 263, p. 24d, l. 17 (my emphasis). This oral history, and the others in this collection, were collected by ethnographers when the working woman-informants were in their advanced old age. This undoubtedly explains the perspective Tiurina was able to bring to bear on her life, as well as her capacity to speak freely and honestly about it.
28. Ibid., p. 1a, l. 4 (my emphasis).
29. *Kineshemets*, August 5, 1912, #94, p. 2; March 1, 1913, #173, pp. 3-4.
30. Ibid., April 10, 1913, #190, p. 3; November 10, 1913, #41, p. 3.
31. *Gazeta-Kopeika*, January 26, 1911, #20/586, p. 5.
32. Goriacheva, "Vospominaniia," pp. 216-17. *Kineshemets* also recorded a case of a husband who had pawned his wife's dowry fur coat, to her great sadness, March 1, 1913, #173, pp. 3-4.
33. *Kineshemets*, January 18, 1913, #157, p. 3.

34. Ibid., March 21, 1912, #41, p. 5. The same phenomenon, of paying the *shinkar* with goods instead of money, was noted in another article, December 16, 1911, #6, p. 3.
35. Ibid., December 16, 1911, #6, p. 2; January 11, 1912, #14, pp. 3-4; March 9, 1912, #36, p. 3; January 29, 1914, #11, p. 3; *Iaroslavets*, December 29, 1912, #180, p. 3; October 31, 1912, #123, p. 4.
36. Bogorodskaia Uezdnaia, *Ob"iasnitel'nyia zapiski*, pp. 89, 91.
37. *Kineshemets*, September 8, 1913, #16, p. 3.
38. Ibid., June 12, 1913, #210, p. 2. For more on injuries, see *Ivanovskii listok*, July 24, 1910, #156, p. 4. Another example is the *Iaroslavets* account of a man who had been drinking with his brother in the factory barrack. On his way home, in a drunken state, he fell off a third-floor stairway, injuring his head, "with damage to the skull, and broke two ribs." September 11, 1912, #73, p. 3. For injuries during fights, see *Kineshemets*, February 27, 1913, #172, p. 4. In another example during a drunken card game, one worker who suspected another of cheating began to hit him over the head with a beer bottle. The injured man, "all bloody," was taken to the factory hospital. December 5, 1912, #142, p. 3. Another man ended up in the hospital with a deep knife wound in the back after drunken holiday fights. *Iaroslavets*, September 11, 1912, #73, p. 3.
39. See, for example, *Golos*, August 19 (September 2), 1917, #183, p. 3; *Ivanovskii listok*, 1910, passim. Almost every daily issue has an item on the arrest of at least twelve drunks.
40. *Kineshemets*, March 31, 1913, #186, p. 3.
41. Ibid., September 4, 1913, #14, p. 3.
42. *Iaroslavets*, September 4, 1912, #66, p. 5.
43. Ibid., September 25, 1912, #87, p. 4. For similar reports, see October 3, 1912, #95, p. 6; October 4, 1912, #96, p. 4; October 25, 1912, #117, p. 3; October 28, 1912, #120, p. 3.
44. Tolstov, *Narody mira*, p. 474.
45. *Nasha Kostromskaia zhizn'*, February 26, 1912, #45, p. 2.
46. *Iaroslavets*, August 30, 1912, #61, p. 5.
47. *Gazeta-Kopeika*, July 19, 1917, #329, p. 3.
48. *Iaroslavets*, September 30, 1912, #192, p. 5.
49. *Gazeta-Kopeika*, January 4, 1917, #160, p. 3.
50. GLM, f. 263, p. 1d, l. 104. T. Ia. Lobova also gave a brief description of some of newlyweds' activities during Maslenitsa, p. 21i, l. 1.
51. Sokolov, *Russian Folklore*, pp. 187-88.
52. Ethnographers and their informants modestly avoided giving many specific examples of these sexualized songs and jokes. Maslenitsa permitted a license of sexual expression that was considered taboo at all other times; this taboo may have affected informants' willingness to recall Maslenitsa songs and jokes for ethnographers. The scholars' own modesty also interfered with a full account: Sokolov, for example, nervously evaded such "songs, ribald sayings

and jests" by saying that their eroticism amounted "to a license which cannot be reproduced in print," ibid., p. 188.

53. *Kineshemets*, June 12, 1913, #210, p. 2.
54. "Kolybel'nyia i detskiia pesni," p. 121
55. Ibid., p. 125. For other variants, see p. 121; RO IRLI, k. 53, p. 1, l. 49; p. 3, l. 40; and GLM, f. 263, p. 44g, l. 9.
56. RO IRLI, k. 53, p. 3, l. 40.
57. GLM, f. 263, p. 44g, l. 8.
58. "Kolybel'nyia i detskiia pesni," p. 122.
59. RO IRLI, k. 53, p. 3, l. 45.
60. Ibid., p. 3, l. 46.
61. TsGALI, f. 1432, op. 2, ed. khr. 53, l. 44.
62. Jessica Tovrov describes strikingly similar patterns among families of the Russian nobility in "Mother-Child Relationships," pp. 15-43.
63. TsGALI, f. 1432, op. 2, ed. khr. 53, l. 9. Two half-lines, missing due to a torn archival manuscript, were supplied by Serge Shishkoff. This song was the other side of the coin of men's soldier, tramp, and distant-worker songs (examined in Chapter 13), so it is not surprising that the last line had to do with the mother's death, just as in the men's songs, the long-absent man returned only to find members of his family long dead.
64. RO IRLI, k. 53, p. 3, l. 11. Another variant is given, l. 10.
65. Problems were most frequent, said the article,

> in those families where, after the death of the husband-breadwinner, the entire burden of supporting the family lies on the mother.
> Often sick and weak-willed, she endures all sorts of humiliations from her adult sons, who partake of all the "delights" of the free life of the streets.

Nasha Kostromskaia zhizn', March 3, 1912, #50, p. 2.
66. Moscow: Progress Publishers, 1976, p. 21.
67. Personal communication, May 1978. Sokolov noted that peasant women sang together when they gathered to spin in the evenings and during other kinds of work, giving "vent to their feelings . . . in songs which were traditional, but always adapted to their own case. . . ." *Russian Folklore*, p. 515.
68. GLM, f. 263, p. 21sh, l. 1.
69. N. M. Lopatin and V. P. Prokunin, *Russkie narodnye liricheskie pesni* (Moscow: Gosudarstvennoe Muzykal'noe Izdatel'stvo, 1956), p. 186.
70. Barbara J. Harris, "Recent Work on the History of the Family: A Review Article," *Feminist Studies* 3 (Winter-Spring 1976): 167.
71. Shorter defines romantic love as "the capacity for spontaneity and empathy in an erotic relationship." Spontaneity, he says, "involves substituting extemporaneous dialogue for traditional scripts," and empathy "beats down the sex roles, the entire sexual division of labor that had customarily

separated the lives and emotions of men and women," *Making of the Modern Family*, pp. 15, 148-49. We may applaud Shorter's definition of healthy romantic love, but it was not accurate for Russian workers, among whom romantic love was not spontaneous, nor did it break down inequality and sexual division between women and men.

72. For a discussion of social engineering of sexual orientation in Russian working-class communities, see my "Russian Working Women."

73. TsGALI, f. 483, op. 1, ed. khr. 478, l. 27 and a variant in OR RK GPB, fond 1027, post. 1967.72, Tetrad'1, l. 116; TsGALI, f. 1413, op. 2, ed. khr. 53, l. 35 and a variant in RO IRLI, k. 53, p. 4, l. 6; OR RK GPB, f. 1027, post. 1967.72, l. 125.

74. Ibid., l. 121. Another similar song is l. 126.

75. TsGALI, f. 1432, op. 2, ed. khr. 53, l. 32. Sokolov gives a peasant women's song which uses the same image of a ring coming unsoldered symbolizing lost love, *Russian Folklore*, p. 516.

76. TsGALI, f. 1432, op. 2, ed. khr. 53, l. 15. Other songs with these same themes are l. 14, 16, 38, 39.

77. Ibid., f. 483, op. 1, ed. khr. 518, l. 9.

78. Ibid., f. 1432, op. 2, ed. khr. 53, l. 18. See also l. 19.

79. Ibid., l. 32.

80. Ibid., l. 20.

81. Ibid., l. 64.

82. Ibid., l. 37.

CHAPTER THIRTEEN

1. In addition to references cited elsewhere, see *Novaia zhizn', Iurevetskaia narodnaia gazeta*, June 15, 1917, #10, p. 3; *Golos*, September 13 (26), 1917, #201, p. 3; *Rabochii gorod. Organ Ivanovo-Voznesenskago Gorodskago Obshchestvennago Samoupravleniia*, November 15 (28), 1917, p. 3; *Povolzhskii vestnik*, May 21, 1917, #3151, p. 3; Tolstov, *Narody mira*, p. 474 (Tolstov said that alcoholism was widespread and had deep social roots); *Kostromskie novosti*, June 3, 1912, #28, p. 5; TsGALI, f. 1479, op. 1, ed. khr. 3, l. 36; Chaadaeva, *Rabotnitsa*, p. 128. A zemstvo exhibition in Kineshma in 1912 had a display showing that, while American workers spent 2 percent of their income on alcohol, Russian workers spent 12 percent of theirs on drink. *Kineshemets*, September 11, 1913, #17, p. 2.

2. S. Lapitskaia, *Byt rabochikh*, p. 76.

3. *Kineshemets*, March 14, 1912, #38, p. 3; May 3, 1913, #196, p. 3.

4. Ibid., April 18, 1912, #49, p. 3.

5. Ibid., May 1, 1913, #195, p. 3.

6. Lapitskaia, *Byt rabochikh*, p. 74. One newspaper gave a description of a tavern in the factory area of Romanovo-Borisoglebsk, near Yaroslavl.

In our taverns . . . are tables covered with dirt, napkins often full of holes and wet with spilled tea and wine. . . .

The other decorations of the salon: a scratch in the throat from the tobacco stench, and rumors emphasized with foul language. . . .

On the plates there are . . . the standard snacks: a little piece of black bread, the size of a boot-heel tap; and a piece of sausage as small as an aspen leaf—when fish, it's of uncertain species; when meat, it's boiled to death [having earlier been boiled to make soup three times]. In addition, there's a jar with some sort of dregs, designated as "the very best" mustard. . . .

The tavern owner is a seventy-year-old man, Ivan Nikolaevich, who has lived his whole life in a dirty corner, all his life eating only cabbage soup and porridge, wine never having been in his mouth. (*Iaroslavets*, September 1, 1912, #63, p. 5.)

For a similar brief description of Ivanovo-Voznesensk taverns, see a contemporary observer's account quoted in P. N. Shchennikov, *Preobrazhennyi gorod* (Ivanovo: Ivanovskoe Knizhnoe Izdatel'stvo, 1961), p. 4, which refers to the "invariable tavern with a monster-bellied samovar on the signboard."

7. *Kineshemets*, December 16, 1911, #6, p. 3. This article observed the "remarkable" beer in Vichuga: "nasty, turbid, and smelly."
8. Ermilov, *Byt rabochei kazarmy*, p. 11; *Kineshemets*, December 16, 1911, #6, p. 11.
9. Ibid., March 22, 1913, #182, pp. 2-3.
10. Ibid., September 5, 1912, #106, p. 4.
11. The article gave the amounts for various textile jobs: sorters, yard workers, and others paid 50-60 kopeks per day must contribute 1 ruble, 5 kopeks (roughly two days' pay); workers paid 70-80 kopeks must contribute 3-5 rubles (4½-6 days' pay); and "weaving apprentices, the moving spirits of drunkenness, must actually squander the appalling sum of twenty-five rubles on drink, almost an entire month's wages." Ibid., May 15, 1913, #200, p. 3.
12. For descriptions of this holiday in Moscow, Kokhma, and Kineshma, see Lapitskaia, *Byt rabochikh*, p. 74; *Gazeta-Kopeika*, April 30, 1911, #98/664, p. 5; *Kineshemets*, May 1, 1913, #195, p. 3; May 22, 1913, #203, p. 3.
13. *Kineshemets*, June 2, 1913, #207, p. 3.
14. Ibid., May 17, 1913, #201, p. 3.
15. Ibid., June 2, 1913, #207, p. 3.
16. Lapitskaia, *Byt rabochikh*, p. 76. An account of the typical genesis of holiday fights among the peasantry of the Kovrov area is:

If the fellows from one village are mad at the fellows from some other village, and if there are few friends for them from other villages, then they buy beer or vodka and offer it to the (male) peasants of their village, but only on the day when there will be a *gul'bina* [dialect for unruly holiday carousing]. For example: on Trinity Day in Iazviny [village], or Whit Monday in Krutye [village], or on Petrov Day in Kliuchy [village], when they are sure that their enemies will be at the *gul'bina*. They . . . walk around the village, shout, sing, swear, and try to somehow knock against some one from their foes. That's when there is a scuffle. The men all come running to the defense of one or the other side, and rarely does anyone leave such a fight uninjured. Everything goes flying: gloves, rubbers, daggers, stakes, stones. In general in our region, an offense is rarely forgotten.

This source went on to say that the most frequent type of offense among youth occurred when a boy liked a girl who liked someone else better. In order to preserve his honor from becoming the brunt of his friends' jokes, the scorned lad had to get the youth of his village drunk and lead them into battle somewhere on the next holiday. Tsentral'nyi Gosudarstvennyi Arkhiv Literatury i Iskusstva, fond 1455, opis' 1, edinitsa khranenii 76, list 10-11. Thus, unlike the girl who was supposed to be incapacitated by unrequited love for a particular boy, boys were supposed to take action, with the support of their male friends, to redeem their dignity. The peasant male solidarity group, based on residence in a particular village, is apparent in this description.

17. Many violent fights between individual male workers were reported in the newspapers, for example *Kineshemets*, December 30, 1911, #10, pp. 3-4; June 12, 1913, #210, p. 4; *Iaroslavets*, July 21, 1912, #21, p. 3; August 23, 1912, #54, p. 3; October 30, 1912, #122, pp. 3-4. In light of the description provided by the Prokhorov workers, it is interesting to wonder whether such fights were really purely individual quarrels, or whether they actually fit into a larger scheme of competition and rivalry between workshops, factories, and other solidarity groups.

18. *Iaroslavets*, July 27, 1912, #27, p. 4.

19. *Kineshemets*, March 14, 1912, #38, p. 3; May 3, 1913, #196, p. 3.

20. Ibid., September 21, 1912, #112, p. 4.

21. *Kineshemets*, May 13, 1912, #59, p. 3.

22. The difference between the two cases was of course that women did not have an institutionalized method of fighting back against such attacks.

23. *Kineshemets*, August 5, 1912, #94, p. 2. A working-class song justified men's beating their wives by claiming wives would not love their husbands otherwise. In this song, a man who bought beautiful presents for his wife, didn't drink, and only had eyes for her, was unloved by his angry wife. He turned to his neighbors for advice, and learned he must instead buy her a lash as a present, and must stay away from home drinking and carousing. After this, his wife fell in love with him, "such a good husband, . . . a dear, comely husband." GLM, f. 263, p. 9v, l. 63.

24. *Golos*, October 1(14), 1917, #215; and *Kineshemets*, March 22, 1913, #182, p. 3.

25. *Kineshemets*, May 22, 1913, #203, p. 3.
26. E. S. Goriacheva, "Vospominaniia," p. 217.
27. *Iaroslavets*, September 6, 1912, #68, p. 3.
28. TsGALI, f. 1432, op. 2, ed. khr. 35, l. 10. A similar song about a gypsy woman who won men's hearts is l. 58.
29. Ibid., l. 49.
30. Ibid., op. 1, ed. khr. 53, l. 63.
31. *Gazeta-Kopeika*, February 8, 1917, #195, p. 2.
32. TsGALI, f. 483, ed. khr. 494, l. 22.
33. OR RK GPB, f. 1027, post. 1959.114, l. 147-48.
34. TsGALI, f. 1432, op. 2, ed. khr. 53, l. 21.
35. Ibid., l. 25.
36. Workers' factory accidents were described and discussed in many sources, among them Bogorodskii uezd, *Ob"iasnitel'nyia zapiski*, pp. 76-7, 80, 83, 94, 103, 110; Smirnov, "Neskol'ko dannykh," pp. 308, 312, 313, 317; *Ivanovskii listok*, July 17, 1910, #151, p. 3 and August 14, 1910, #173, p. 2. So many accidents were reported in *Kineshemets* that I stopped making note of them. A few are: January 25, 1912, #20, p. 3; March 7, 1912, #35, p. 3; March 21, 1912, #41, p. 3.
37. *Kostromskie novosti*, June 8, 1912, #30, p. 3.
38. *Slovo starykh Bol'shevikov (Iz revoliutsionnogo proshlogo)* (Moscow: Moskovskii Rabochii, 1965), p. 92.
39. One example is V. S. Liadyshev, who wrote a petition to the factory administration asking that his two daughters, aged five and fifteen, be hired at the same factory as their parents. He strengthened his position by saying that he had worked at Morozov's for nineteen years. "My wife and I have been your constant servants, and our children were born and grew up in the Morozov factory . . . so where are we to find them work besides [the same factory]?" Quoted in Levinson-Nechaeva, "Polozhenie i byt," pp. 157-58.
40. *Kineshemets*, April 20, 1912, #50, p. 4.
41. Ibid., April 13, 1912, #47, p. 3; *Nasha Kostromskaia zhizn'*, January 20, 1912, #16, p. 3.
42. *Kineshemets*, February 10, 1913, #166, p. 3.
43. Ibid., March 16, 1912, #39, p. 3 and March 21, 1912, #41, p. 5, and Levinson-Nechaeva, "Polozhenie i byt," p. 158.
44. See, for example, ibid., January 29, 1912, #22, p. 3.
45. *Iaroslavets*, September 18, 1912, #80, p. 5.
46. *Kineshemets*, December 12, 1912, #144, p. 3. Another case occurred when the factory administration refused to heat the barracks after March 1. The workers protested, and the heat was turned on again, ibid., April 15, 1913, p. 3.
47. Ibid., November 6, 1913, #39, p. 3.
48. Ibid., February 8, 1913, #165, p. 3, and June 9, 1913, #209, p. 4. Demands for better laundry facilities were common in Russian workers' strikes.

49. *Gazeta-Kopeika*, January 4, 1911, #2/568, p. 5.

50. *Kineshemets*, November 21, 1912, #136, p. 3; November 28, 1912, #139, p. 3.

51. *Iaroslavets*, July 7, 1912, #7, p. 4. Male workers were also well enough organized that when the city council began considering closing all the alcoholic establishments in town, they banded together and presented a petition against it. *Iaroslavskie novosti*, July 22, 1913, #29, p. 2. Working women also wrote petitions as individuals, to the courts and to factory inspectors. This seems to have occurred most often in cases where a woman did not have a husband, for example in the case of one woman who was attempting to get financial compensation from the factory in which her husband had burned to death in an industrial accident. *Kineshemets*, March 7, 1912, #35, p. 4. See also *Rabochee dvizhenie vo Vladimirskoi gubernii, 1910-1914 gg.* (Vladimir: Vladmirskoe Knizhnoe Izdatel'stvo, 1957), pp. 50, 53-54, which includes one case from a married woman.

52. Ibid., January 30, 1913, #162, p. 3 provides a detailed account of this episode. Another incident occurred later when the community was faced with a mysterious, loud noise emanating for over a week from a pond near the factory. Ibid., May 31, 1913, p. 3; June 7, 1913, #208, p. 3.

53. Ibid., November 16, 1917, #134, p. 2.

54. Allen K. Wildman, *The End of the Russian Imperial Army: The Old Army and the Soldiers' Revolt (March-April 1917)* (Princeton: Princeton University Press, 1980), pp. 26-27.

55. *Iaroslavets*, October 20, 1912, #112, p. 3.

56. *Kineshemets*, October 26, 1912, #125, p. 3 provides some of the workers' conversation, including the eventual teasing which precipitated a fight.

57. *Kineshemets*, December 16, 1911, #6, p. 3.

58. TsGALI, f. 1497, op. 1, ed. khr. 3, l. 26. Lapitskaia, *Byt rabochikh*, p. 74, also argued this position.

59. *Gazeta-Kopeika*, April 30, 1911, #98/664, p. 5; *Kineshemets*, May 1, 1913, #203, p. 3; June 2, 1913, #207, p. 3; and Lapitskaia, *Byt rabochikh*, p. 74. Another piece of evidence for this position may be a newspaper story describing the efforts of some workers in the Tomna factory to establish "sobriety circles" among themselves by which the workers themselves tried to stop drinking. The workers had appealed to the factory owners to create "a sobriety society in the factory, but the administration refused this application." *Kineshemets*, August 28, 1913, #12, p. 3.

60. *Kineshemets*, May 17, 1913, #201, p. 3. The church, on the other hand, mounted at least one campaign against alcoholism. *Vladimirskie gubernskie vedomosti*, September 23, 1911, p. 39; June 17, 1911, #25, p. 3.

Bibliography

PRIMARY SOURCES

Archives

Gosudarstvennyi Literaturnyi Musei, fond 263.
Otdel Rukopisei i Redkikh Knig Gosudarstvennoi Publichnoi Biblioteki im. Saltykova-Shchedrina, fond 1027.
Rukopisnyi Otdel Instituta Russkoi Literatury (Pushkinskii Dom), Razriad V, kollektsiia 53.
Tsentral'nyi Gosudarstvennyi Arkhiv Literatury i Iskusstva, fondy 483, 1413, 1432, 1455, 1470, 1479, 1497, 1480.

Newspapers

Gazeta-Kopeika, 1911-12, 1917.
Golos, 1917.
Iaroslavets, 1912-13.
Iaroslavskaia mysl', 1917.
Iaroslavskie gubernskie vedomosti, 1911-12.
Iaroslavskie novosti, 1912-14.
Ivanovskaia kopeika, 1913-14.
Ivanovskii listok, 1917.
Izvestiia Ivanovo-Voznesenskago Soveta Rabochikh i Soldatskikh Deputatov, 1917.
Izvestiia Kineshemskago Revoliutsionnago Komiteta Obshchestvennoi Bezopasnosti, 1917.
Izvestiia Orekhovo-Zuevskago Soveta Rabochikh Deputatov, 1917.
Kineshemets, 1911-14.
Kostromskaia zhizn', 1913.
Kostromskie novosti, 1912.
Kovrovskiia vesti, 1917.
Kur'er, 1917.
Nasha zvezda; Organ Ivanovo-Voznesenskago Goroda i Ivanovo-Kineshemskago Okruzhnogo Komiteta RSDRP (b), 1917.
Nasha Kostromskaia zhizn', 1912.

Novaia zhizn'; Iurevetskaia narodnaia gazeta, 1917.
Novyi Kineshemets, 1913.
Povolzhskii vestnik, 1917.
Rabochii gorod. Organ Ivanovo-Voznesenskago Gorodskogo Obshchestvennago Samoupravleniia, 1917.
Sotsial-demokrat, Organ Moskovskago Biuro Tsentral'nago Komiteta i Moskovskago Komiteta, 1917.
Svobodnoe slovo, gazeta obshchestvenno-politicheskaia i literaturnaia, 1917.
Vladimirskie gubernskie vedomosti, 1911.
Vlast' naroda, gazeta demokraticheskaia i sotsialisticheskaia, 1917.

Other Primary Sources

Bobrovskaia, Ts. S. *Twenty Years in Underground Russia: Memoirs of a Rank and File Bolshevik*. New York: International Publishers, 1934.
Bogorodskaia Uezdnaia Zemskaia Uprava. *Ob "iasnitel'nyia zapiski uchastovykh i fabrichnykh vrachei Bogorodskago uezda (Mosk. gub.) po meditsinskoi deiatel'nosti za 1902 god*. Moscow: Pechatnia S. P. Iakovleva, 1903.
Chaadaeva, O. N. *Rabotnitsa na sotsialisticheskoi stroike: Sbornik avtobiografii rabotnits*. Moscow: Partiinoe Izdatel'stvo, 1932.
Goriacheva, E. S. "Vospominaniia." *Istoriko-kraevedcheskii sbornik*. Vyp. 2. Edited by Orekhovo-Zuevskii Pedagogicheskii Institut. Moscow, 1959.
Grozovye gody, vospominaniia starykh kommunistov. Ivanovo, 1961.
Gubernskoe Biuro Komissii po Istorii Oktiabr'skoi Revoliutsii i R.K.P. (bol'sh). *Oktiabr'skie dni v Moskve i raionakh (po vospominaniiam uchastnikov)*. Moscow: Moskovskii rabochii, 1922.
Ianzhul, I. *Ocherki i issledovaniia*. Moscow, 1884.
Institut Istorii Partii. *Slova starykh bol'shevikov (Iz revoliutsionnogo proshlogo)*. Moscow: Moskovskii rabochii, 1965.
Kollontai, Alexandra. *The Autobiography of a Sexually Emancipated Communist Woman*. New York: Schocken, 1975.
Kor, I. *Kak my zhili pri tsare i kak zhivem teper'*. Moscow: Moskovskii rabochii, 1934.
Korobov, Ia. "Derevenskaia pripevka i fabrichnaia chastushka." *Staryi Vladimirets*, December 14, 1914.
Krupskaia, N. K. *Reminiscences of Lenin*. New York: International, 1960.
Na putiakh k Oktiabr'iu, Vospominaniia starykh Bol'shevikov o revoliutsionnykh sobytiakh vo Vladimirskoi gubernii. Vladimir: Vladimirskoe Knizhnoe Izdatel'stvo, 1957.
Oktiabr' v Zamoskvorech'e. Moscow: Goslesbumizdat, 1957.
Ovsiannikov, N., ed. *Nakanune revoliutsii. Sbornik statei, zametok i vospominanii*. Moscow: Gosudarstvennoe Izdatel'stvo, 1922.
Peche, Ian. *V boiakh za Oktiabr' (Vospominaniia ob Oktiabr'skoi revolutsii v Moskve)*. Moscow: Molodaia gvardiia, 1933.

Peskov, P. A. *Fabrichnyi byt Vladimirskoi gubernii; Otchet 1882-1883 g. fabrichnago inspektora nad maloletnykh rabochikh Vladimirskago okruga*. St. Petersburg: V. Kirshbaum, 1884.

Petrakov, M. N. "Vospominaniia." *Istoriko-kraevedcheskii sbornik*. Vyp. 2. Edited by Orekhovo-Zuevskii Pedagogicheskii Institut. Moscow, 1959.

Popova, E. *Moskovskaia provintsiia v semnadtsatom gody: Sbornik*. Moscow: Moskovskii Istpart, 1927.

Rabochee dvizhenie vo Vladimirskoi gubernii, 1910-1914 gg. Vladimir: Vladimirskoe Knizhnoe Izdatel'stvo, 1957.

Trudy Vladimirskoi Arkhivnoi Kommissii. 16. Vladimir: Tipografiia Gubernskago Pravlenii, 1914.

Za vlast' sovetov. Moscow: Moskovskii rabochii, 1957.

SECONDARY SOURCES

Abray, Jane. "Feminism in the French Revolution." *American Historical Review* 80 (February 1975).

Alekseeva, O. B. *Ustnaia poeziia russkikh rabochikh. Dorevoliutsionnyi period*. Leningrad: Izdatel'stvo Nauka, 1971.

Aliavdina, P. "K voprosy o pitanii i zabolevaemosti rabochikh na sittsepechatnykh fabrikakh v gorode Ivanovo-Voznesenske." *Vestnik obshchestvennoi gigieny, sudebnoi i prakticheskoi meditsiny* (1900).

Atkinson, Dorothy, Alexander Dallin, and Gail Warshofsky Lapidus, eds., *Women in Russia*. Stanford: Stanford University Press, 1977.

Baranov, E. Z. *Moskovskie legendy*. Vol. I. Moscow: Staraia Moskva, 1928.

Bell, Sylvia. "The Development of the Concept of Object as Related to the Infant-Mother Attachment." *Child Development* 41 (1970).

Benedict, Ruth. "Continuities and Discontinuities in Cultural Conditioning." *A Study of Interpersonal Relations*. Edited by Patrick Mullahy. New York: Heritage, 1949.

Benjamin, Jessica. "Authority and the Family Revisited: or, A World Without Fathers?" *New German Critique* 13 (Winter 1978).

_____. "The Bonds of Love: Rational Violence and Erotic Domination." *Feminist Studies* 6 (Spring 1980).

Bettelheim, Bruno. *The Uses of Enchantment: The Meaning and Importance of Fairy Tales*. New York: Knopf, 1976.

Blank, A. S. "Bol'shevistskie organizatsii v Ivanovo-Voznesenskom raione v 1912-1914 godakh." *Voprosy istorii* III (1956).

Bobroff, Anne. "The Bolsheviks and Working Women, 1905-20." *Soviet Studies* (October 1974).

_____. "Alexandra Kollontai: Feminism, Workers' Democracy, and Internationalism." *Radical America* 13 (November-December 1979).

_____. "Working Women, Bonding Patterns, and the Politics of Daily Life: Russia at the End of the Old Regime." Doctoral dissertation, University of Michigan, 1982 (available through University Microfilm International, Ann Arbor, Michigan).

_____. "Russian Working Women: Sexuality in Bonding Patterns and the Politics of Daily Life." *Powers of Desire, The Politics of Sexuality.* Edited by Ann Snitow, Christine Stansell, and Sharon Thompson. New York: Monthly Review Press, 1983.

Brown, Bruce. *Marx, Freud, and the Critique of Everyday Life. Toward a Permanent Cultural Revolution.* New York: Monthly Review Press.

Brown, Donald, ed. *The Role and Status of Women in the Soviet Union.* New York: Columbia Teachers College Press, 1968.

Brown, Judith K. "Adolescent Initiation Rites Among Preliterate Peoples." *Studies in Adolescence.* Edited by Robert E. Grinder. New York: Macmillan, 1963.

Bryant, Louise. *Six Red Months in Russia: An Observer's Account of Russia Before and During the Proletarian Dictatorship.* New York: Doran Co., 1918.

Chodorow, Nancy. *The Reproduction of Mothering: Psychoanalysis and the Sociology of Gender.* Berkeley: University of California Press, 1978.

Clements, Barbara Evans. "Kollontai's Contribution to the Workers' Opposition." *Russian History* 2 (1975).

Cohen, Yehudi A. *Childhood to Adolescence: Legal Systems and Incest Taboos.* Chicago: Aldine, 1964.

Coser, Lewis. "Some Aspects of Soviet Family Policy." *American Journal of Sociology* 56 (March 1951).

Cott, Nancy. *The Bonds of Womanhood: "Woman's Sphere" in New England, 1780-1835.* New Haven: Yale University Press, 1977.

Dal', I. V. *Tolkovyi slovar' zhivogo velikorusskago iazyka.* St. Petersburg, Moscow: M. O. Vol'f, 1905-9.

Davis, Natalie. "The Reasons of Misrule: Youth Groups and Charivaris in Sixteenth-Century France." *Past and Present* 50 (February 1971): 41-75.

Dianova, Mariia Konstantinova. *1917 god v Ivanovo-Voznesenskom raione.* Ivanovo-Voznesensk: Osnova, 1927.

Dingle, A. E. "Drink and Working Class Living Standards in Britain, 1870-1914." *Economic History Review* 25 (November 1972).

Dinnerstein, Dorothy. *The Mermaid and the Minotaur: Sexual Arrangements and Human Malaise.* New York: Harper, 1977.

Dodge, Norton. *Women in the Soviet Economy: Their Role in Economic, Scientific, and Technological Development.* Baltimore: Johns Hopkins Press, 1966.

Dublin, Thomas. "Women, Work, and the Family: Female Operatives in the Lowell Mills, 1830-1860," *Feminist Studies* 3 (Fall 1975).

DuBois, Ellen. "The Radicalism of the Woman Suffrage Movement: Notes Toward the Reconstruction of Nineteenth-Century Feminism." *Feminist Studies* 3 (Fall 1975).

DuBois, Ellen, Mari Jo Buhle, Gerda Lerner, and Carroll Smith-Rosenberg. "Politics and Culture in Women's History." *Feminist Studies* 6 (Spring 1980).

Dundes, Alan. *The Study of Folklore.* Englewood Cliffs, N.J.: Prentice-Hall, 1965.

Dunn, Stephen and Ethel. "The Great Russian Peasant: Culture Change or Cultural Development." *Ethnology* 2 (July 1963).

Dye, Nancy Schrom. "Feminism or Unionism? The New York Women's Trade Union League and the Labor Movement." *Feminist Studies* 3 (Fall 1975).

Eisenstadt, S. N. *From Generation to Generation: Age Groups and Social Structure.* London: Collier-Macmillan, 1956.

Ekzempliarskii, P. M. *Istoriia goroda Ivanova.* Ivanovo-Voznesensk: Ivanovskoe Knizhnoe Izdatel'stvo, 1958.

Ermilov, Vladimir. *Byt rabochei kazarmy.* Moscow, 1930.

Faragher, Johnny, and Christine Stansell. "Women and their Families on the Overland Trail to California and Oregon, 1842-1867." *Feminist Studies* 2 (Winter 1975).

Field, Mark G. "Alcoholism, Crime, and Delinquency in Soviet Society." *Social Problems* 3 (October 1955).

_____. "The Relegalization of Abortion in Soviet Russia." *New England Journal of Medicine* 42 (August 1956).

Filipovic, Milenko. *Forms and Functions of Ritual Kinship among the South Slavs.* Paris: VI Congres International des Sciences Anthropologiques et Ethnologiques, 1963.

Galkina, P. I. "Voobshchaia stachka Ivanovo-Voznesenskikh tekstil'shchikov letom 1905 g." *Voprosy istorii* 6 (1955).

Geiger, Kent. "Deprivation and Solidarity in the Soviet Urban Family." *American Sociological Review* 20 (February 1955).

_____. *The Family in Soviet Russia.* Cambridge: Harvard University Press, 1968.

Gernet, M. N. *Detoubiistvo. Sotsiologicheskoe i sravnitel'no-iuridicheskoe izsledovanie.* Moscow: Tipografiia Imperatorskago Moskovskago Universiteta, 1911.

Golitsynskii, A. P. *Ocherki fabrichnoi zhizni.* St. Petersburg, 1886.

Gosudarstvennaia Konservatoriia. *Kabinet narodnoi muzyki.* Moscow: Izdatel'stvo muzyka, 1966.

Grigor'ev, B. N. *Predmetnyi ukazatel' materialov v zemsko-statisticheskikh trudakh c 1860-kh godov po 1917 g.* Moscow: Tsentral'noi Statisticheskoe Upravlenie Soiuza SSR, 1926-27.

Halpern, Joel Martin. *Bibliography of Anthropological and Sociological Publications on Eastern Europe and the USSR.* Los Angeles: Russian and Eastern European Studies Center, UCLA, 1961.

Harris, Barbara J. "Recent Work on the History of the Family: A Review Article." *Feminist Studies* 3 (Winter-Spring 1976).

Hayden, Carol Eubanks. "The Zhenotdel and The Bolshevik Party." *Russian History* 2 (1976).

Hufton, Olwen. "Women in Revolution, 1789-1796." *Past and Present* 53 (November 1971).

Hunt, David. *Parents and Children in History: The Psychology of Family Life in Early Modern France.* New York: Harper, 1970.

Ivanovo-Voznesenskoe Gubernskoe Nauchnoe Obshchestvo Kraevedeniia. *Ivanovo-Voznesenskaia guberniia: Kratkii obzor prirody, naseleniia, ekonomiki i istorii.* Ivanovo-Voznesensk: Osnova, 1929.

Jay, Martin. *The Dialectical Imagination: A History of the Frankfort School and the Institute of Social Research, 1923-50.* Boston: Little, Brown, 1973.

Johnson, Robert Eugene. *Peasant and Proletarian: The Working Class of Moscow in the Late Nineteenth Century.* New Brunswick: Rutgers University Press, 1979.

Kabo, E. M. *Ocherki rabochego byta.* Moscow, 1928.

Kagan, Jerome. "The Child in the Family." *Daedalus* 106 (Spring 1977).

Kamneva, M. S. "Vrachebnaia pomoshch' rabochim na nekotorykh fabrikakh Vladimirskoi gubernii v 1896-1898 gg." *Vrach'* 7 (1901).

Kasitskaia, D. L., and Z. P. Popova. "Polozhenie i byt rabochikh-tekstil'shchikov Prokhorovskoi Trekhgornoi manufaktury v Moskve (Materialy ekspeditsii 1950 g.)" *Istoriko-bytovye ekspeditsii 1949-1950gg.* Edited by A. M. Pankratova. Moscow: Gosudarstvennoe Izdatel'stvo Kul'tur'no-Prosvetitel'noi Literatury, 1953.

Kazantsev, B. N. "Ar'ergardnye boi rabochikh-tekstil'shchikov tsentral'nogo promyshlennogo raiona Rossii v ianvare-iiule 1907 g." *Istoricheskie zapiski* 17 (1965).

Kelly, Joan. "The Doubled Vision of Feminist Theory: A Postscript to the 'Women and Power' Conference." *Feminist Studies* 5 (Spring 1979).

Kessler-Harris, Alice. "Where are the Organized Women Workers?" *Feminist Studies* 3 (Fall 1975).

Kharuzina, V. N. "Ob uchastii detei v religiozno-obriadovoi zhizni." *Etnograficheskoe obozrenie.* 1-2 (1911).

Kingsbury, Susan M. and Mildred Fairchild. *Factory, Family, and Woman in the Soviet Union.* New York: Putnam's, 1935.

Koenker, Diane. *Moscow Workers and the 1917 Revolution.* Princeton: Princeton University Press, 1981.

_____. "Urban Families, Working Class Youth Groups, and the 1917 Revolution in Moscow." *The Family in Imperial Russia: New Lines of Historical Research.* Edited by David Ransel. Urbana: University of Illinois Press, 1978.

Kolpakova, N. P. "Fol'klor'nye obrazy v Bogorodskoi igrushke." *Fol'klor i etnografiia.* Edited by Boris N. Putilov. Leningrad: Nauka, 1970.

"Kolybel'nyia i detskiia pesni i detskiia igry y krestian Vladimirskoi gubernii." *Etnograficheskoe obozrenie* 1-2 (1915).

Kondrat'ev, V. A., and B. I. Nevzorov, eds. *Iz istorii fabrik i zavodov Moskvy i Moskovskoi gubernii (Konets khush.-nachalo XX v.). Obzor dokumentov.* Moscow: Arkhivnyi otdel Mosgorispolkoma, 1968.

Kostolovskii, I. V. "Iz svadebnykh i drugikh poverii Yaroslavskoi gubernii." *Etnograficheskoe obozrenie* 1-2 (1911).

Kostomarov, N. I. *Sobranie sochinenii.* VIII. St. Petersburg: Tipografiia M. M. Stasiulevicha, 1905.

Kovalevskaia, Maxine. *Modern Customs and Ancient Laws of Russia.* St. Petersburg, 1891.

Kozhanyi, P. M. *Rabotnitsa i byt.* 1926.

Krupianskaia, V. Iu., ed. *Etnograficheskoe izuchenie byta rabochikh. Po materialam otdel'nykh promyshlennykh raionov SSSR.* Moscow: Institut Etnografii, 1968.

Kurakhtanov, V. *Pervaia sittsenabivnaia.* Moscow: Izdatel'stvo Sotsial'no-ekonomicheskoi Literatury, 1960.

Lapitskaia, S. M. *Byt rabochikh Trekhgornoi manufaktury.* Moscow: Gosudarstvennoe Izdatel'stvo "Istoriia Zavodov," 1935.

Laverychev, V. Ia. *Rabochee dvizhenie v Ivanovo-Voznesenske v gody pervoi mirovoi voiny (1914-fevr. 1917 g.)* Moscow: Izdatel'stvo Moskovskogo Universiteta, 1957.

Levinson-Nechaeva, M. N. "Polozhenie i byt rabochikh tekstil'noi promyshlennosti Moskovskoi gubernii vo vtoroi polovine XIX veka (Materialy ekspeditsii 1949 goda v g. Orekhovo-Zueva)." *Istoriko-bytovye ekspeditsii 1949-1950 gg.* Edited by A. M. Pankratova. Moscow: Gosudarstvennoe Izdatel'stvo Kul'tur'no Prosvetitel'noi Literatury, 1953.

Liddington, Jill. "Rediscovering Suffrage History." *History Workshop* (Autumn 1977).

Lineff, Eugenie. *Russian Folk-Songs as Sung by the People and Peasant Wedding Ceremonies Customary in Northern and Central Russia.* Chicago: Summy, 1893.

Lowie, Robert H. *Primitive Society.* New York: Liveright, 1920.

Marcuse, Herbert. *Counter-Revolution and Revolt.* Boston: Beacon, 1972.

_____. *Five Lectures, Psychoanalysis, Politics, and Utopia.* Boston: Beacon, 1970.

Martynova, A. N. "Life of the Pre-Revolutionary Village as Reflected in Popular Lullabies." *The Family in Imperial Russia: New Lines in Historical Research.* Edited by David Ransel. Urbana: University of Illinois Press, 1978.

_____. "Sotsial'nyi protest v narodnoi poezii." *Russkii fol'klor* 15 (1975).

_____. "Opyt klassifikatsii Russkikh kolybel'nykh pesen." *Sovetskaia etnografiia* (1974).

Masson, Margaret. "The Typology of the Female as a Model for the Regenerate: Puritan Preaching, 1690-1730." *Signs* 2 (Winter 1976).

Matossian, Mary. "The Peasant Way of Life." *The Peasant in Nineteenth-Century Russia.* Edited by Wayne Vucinich. Stanford: Stanford University Press, 1968.

McNeal, Robert. "Women in the Russian Radical Movement." *Journal of Social History* (Winter 1971-2).

Mel'ts, Mikaela Iakovlevna, comp. *Russkii fol'klor; bibliograficheskii ukazatel', 1917-1944.* Leningrad: Akademiia nauk, 1966.

Mints, S. I. "Fol'klornyi Arkhiv Gosudarstvennogo Literaturnogo Museia." *Sovetskaia etnografiia* 3 (1963).

Mosely, Philip. "The Russian Family: Old Style and New." *The Family: Its Function and Destiny.* Edited by Ruth Nanda Anshen. New York, 1959.

Murdock, George. *Social Structure.* New York: Macmillan, 1960.

Murphy, Robert F. "Social Structure and Sex Antagonism." *Southwestern Journal of Anthropology* 15 (1959).

Nettl, J.P. *Rosa Luxemburg.* London: Oxford University Press, 1966.

Nosova, G. A. "A Preliminary Ethnographic Study of Habitual Orthodoxy (Based on Data from Vladimir Oblast')." *Soviet Sociology* 8 (1963).

Owen, Laura. "The Welfare of Women in Laboring Families: England, 1860-1950." *Feminist Studies* 1 (Winter-Spring 1973).

Paredes, Americo, and Richard Bauman, eds. *Toward New Perspectives in Folklore*. Austin, Texas: American Folklore Society, 1972.

Pereslavl-Zalesskii Istoriko-khudozhestvennyi i Kraevedcheskii Musei. *Programma po obsledovaniiu religiozno-bytovoi zhizni mestnogo naseleniia*. Pereslavl-Zaleskii: Gosudarstvennaia Tipografiia, 1930.

Person, Ethel Spector. "Sexuality as the Mainstay of Identity: Psychoanalytic Perspectives." *Women: Sex and Sexuality*. Edited by Catharine R. Stimpson and Ethel Spector Person. Chicago: University of Chicago Press, 1980.

Pismennyi, N. "O vliianii fabrichnykh uslovii raboty i zhizni materei na smertnost' detei." *Zhurnal Pirogovskago obshchestva* 1-2 (1904).

Pomerantseva, E. V., ed. *Pesni i skazki Yaroslavskoi oblasti*. Yaroslavl: Iaroslavskoe Knizhnoe Izdatel'stvo, 1958.

Potebnia, A. A. *O nekotorykh simvolakh v slavianskoi narodnoi poezii*. Kharkov: Universitetskaia Tipografiia, 1860.

_____. *Pereprava cherez vody kak predstavlenie braka*. Moscow, 1867.

Putilov, B. I. *Fol'klor i etnografiia. Obriady i obriadnyi fol'klor*. Leningrad: Nauka, 1974.

Racz, Elizabeth. "The Women's Rights Movement in the French Revolution." *Science and Society* 16 (Spring 1952).

Ransel, David. "Abandonment and Fosterage of Unwanted Children: The Women of the Foundling System." *The Family in Imperial Russia: New Lines of Historical Research*. Urbana: University of Illinois Press, 1978.

Rashin, Adol'f G. *Formirovanie rabochego klassa rossii; istoriko-ekonomicheskie ocherki*. Moscow: Izdatel'stvo Sotsial'no-ekonomicheskoi Literatury, 1958.

Reddy, William. "Family and Factory: French Linen Weavers in the Belle Epoque." *Journal of Social History* 8 (Winter 1975).

Reed, John. *Ten Days that Shook the World*. New York: Modern Library, 1935.

Reiter, Rayna Rapp. "Household and Family." *Feminist Studies* 5 (Spring 1979).

Reiter, Rayna Rapp, ed. *Toward an Anthropology of Women*. New York: Monthly Review Press, 1975.

Riazanova, A. *Zhenskii trud*. Moscow: Moskovskii rabochii, 1926.

"Roditeli i deti v narodnykh poslovitsakh i pogovorkakh." *Vladimirskie gubernskie vedomosti*, October 28, 1911.

Rosaldo, Michelle. "Thoughts on Domestic/Public." Paper prepared for Rockefeller Foundation conference on "Women, Family, and Work," New York City, September 1978.

Rosenberg, William. "Workers and Workers' Control in the Russian Revolution." *History Workshop* (Spring 1978).

Rowbotham, Sheila. *Women, Resistance, and Revolution, A History of Women and Revolution in the Modern World*. New York: Pantheon, 1972.

Ryan, Mary P. "The Power of Women's Networks: A Case Study of Female Moral Reform in Antebellum America." *Feminist Studies* 5 (Spring 1979).

Samoilov, F. *Pervyi Sovet rabochikh deputatov*. Moscow: Molodaia gvardiia, 1931.
Samoilov, F., ed. *Fabrika 'Krasnyi Perekop,' Iaroslavskaia Bol'shaia Manufaktura, 1722-1933. I. Volzhskie tkachi*. Moscow: Gosudarstvennoe Izdatel'stvo "Istoriia Zavodov," 1936.
Savushkina, N. I. *Russkii narodnyi teatr*. Moscow: Nauka, 1976.
Schmeidler, Gertrude, and George Windholz. "Sex Roles and the Subjective: A Cross-Cultural Test." *Signs* (Autumn 1976).
Schurer, H. "Some Reflections on Rosa Luxemburg and the Bolshevik Revolution." *Slavonic and East European Review* 40 (June 1962).
Shchennikov, P. N. *Preobrazhennoi gorod*. Ivanovo: Ivanovskoe Knizhnoe Izdatel'stvo, 1961.
Shimkin, D. B., and Pedro Sanjuan. "Culture and World View: A Method of Analysis Applied to Rural Russia." *American Anthropologist* 55 (1953).
Shipulina, A. V. "Ivanovo-Voznesenskie rabochie nakanune pervoi russkoi revoliutsii. Uslovii ikh truda i byta." *Doklady i soobshcheniia Instituta Istorii* 8 (1955).
_____. "Uchastie Ivanovo-Voznesenskikh rabochikh v stroitel'stve sovetskogo gos. apparat (1917-1918gg)." *Iz istorii rabochego klassa SSSR. Sbornik*. Edited by M. M. Viziaev. Ivanovo: Ivanovskii Gosudarstvennyi Pedagogicheskii Institut, 1967.
Shorter, Edward. *The Making of the Modern Family*. New York: Basic Books, 1977.
Sigal, B. S. *Zabota o detiakh v rabochei sem'e*. Moscow: Izdatel'stvo okhrana materinstva i mladenchestva, 1927.
Simpson, J. "After 'The Great Days' of the Revolution: Impressions from a Recent Visit to Russia." *Nineteenth Century* 82 (July 1917).
Skibnevskago, A. I. "Sanitarnoe sostoianie zhilishch fabrichno-zavodskikh rabochikh Bogorodskago uezda (Moskovsk. gub.) v 1884-1899 g.g." *Vestnik obshchestvennoi gigieny, sudebnoi i prakticheskoi meditsiny* 1 (1901).
Smirnov, A. V. "Neskol'ko dannykh dlia kharakteristiki zabolevaemosti fabrichnago naseleniia." *Trudy Shestiago Gubernskago S"ezda Vladimirskago Zemstva* 6 (1890).
Smirnov, Aleksei. "Fabrichnye pesni." *Vladimirskaia gazeta*, May 25, 1903.
Smirnov, M. I. *Pereslavl'-zalesskii uezdnyi kratkii kraevedcheskii ocherk*. Pereslavl'-Zalesski: Pereslavl'-Zalesskoe Nauchnoe Prosvetitel'noe Obshchestvo, 1922.
Smirnov-Kuticheskii, A. M. "Fol'klor-etnograficheskaia rabota v g. Iaroslavle." *Etnografiia* 1 (1927).
Smith, Jessica. *Women in Soviet Russia*. New York: Vanguard, 1928.
Smith-Rosenberg, Carroll. "Beauty, the Beast, and the Militant Woman: A Case Study in Sex Roles and Social Stress in Jacksonian America." *American Quarterly* 23 (October 1971).
_____. "The Female World of Love and Ritual: Relations between Women in Nineteenth-Century America." *Signs* 1 (Autumn 1975).
Sobolev, A. N. *Detskiia igry i pesni, Trudy Vladimirskoi Uchenoi Arkhivnoi Kommissii*. Vladimir: Tipografiia Gubernskago Pravleniia, 1914.
Sobolev, P. M., and V. I. Murav'ev, eds. *Fol'klor fabrichno-zavodskikh rabochikh. Stat'i i teksty*. Smolensk: Izdatel'stvo ZONI, 1934.
Sokolov, Iu. M. *Russian Folklore*. New York: Macmillan, 1950.

_____. *Russkii fol'klor*, vyp. IV *Chastushki meshchanskie i blatnye pesni fabrichno-zavodskii i kolkhoznyi fol'klor*. Moscow: Narkompros, 1932.

Stankiewicz, Edward. "Slavic Kinship and Perils of the Soul." *Journal of American Folklore* 71 (1958).

Stewart, Katie. "The Marriage of Capitalism and Patriarchal Ideologies: Meanings of Male Bonding and Male Ranking in U.S. Culture." *Women and Revolution: A Discussion of the Unhappy Marriage of Marxism and Feminism*. Edited by Lydia Sargent. Boston: South End Press, 1981.

Stites, Richard. *The Women's Liberation Movement in Russia: Feminism, Nihilism, and Bolshevism, 1860-1930*. Princeton: Princeton Univeristy Press, 1978.

_____. "Zhenotdel: Bolshevism and Russian Women, 1917-1930." *Russian History* 2 (1977).

Struve, B. P., K. I. Zaitsev, N. V. Dolinsky, and S. S. Demosthenov. *Food Supply in Russia during the World War*. New Haven: Yale University Press, 1930.

Taylor, Barbara. " 'The Men are as Bad as their Masters . . .': Socialism, Feminism, and Sexual Antagonism in the London Tailoring Trade in the Early 1830s." *Feminist Studies* 5 (Spring 1979).

Teitelbaum, Saloman. "Parental Authority in the Soviet Union." *American Slavic and East European Review* 4 (1945).

Thompson, Dorothy. "Women and Nineteenth-Century Radical Politics: A Lost Dimension." *The Rights and Wrongs of Women*. Edited by Juliet Mitchell and Ann Oakley (New York: Penguin, 1976).

Thompson, E. P. "The English Crowd in the Eighteenth Century." *Past and Present* 50 (February 1971).

Tiger, Lionel. *Men in Groups*. Bristol, England: Thomas Nelson, 1969.

Tikhonov, B. V. "Migratsii fabrichno-zavodskikh rabochikh v Shuiskom uezde Vladimirskoi gubernii (po materialam podvornoi perepisi 1899 g.)." *Istoricheskaia geografiia Rossii, XII-nachalo XX v*. Moscow: Nauka, 1975.

Tilly, Louise. "The Food Riot as a Form of Political Conflict in France." *Journal of Interdisciplinary History* 2 (Summer 1971).

Tilly, Louise A., and Joan W. Scott. *Women, Work, and Family*. New York: Holt, 1978.

Tolstov, S. P., ed. *Narody mira. Etnograficheskie ocherki*. Moscow: Izdatel'stvo Akademiia Nauk, 1958).

Tomes, Nancy. "A 'Torrent of Abuse': Crimes of Violence between Working Class Men and Women in London, 1840-1875." *Journal of Social History* 2 (Spring 1978).

Tovrov, Jessica. "Mother-Child Relationships among the Russian Nobility." *The Family in Imperial Russia: New Lines of Historical Research*. Edited by David Ransel. Urbana: University of Illinois Press, 1978.

Trotsky, Leon. *The History of the Russian Revolution*. New York: Simon and Schuster, 1937.

Tyrkova, A. "Zhenskii trud i prostitutsiia." *Russkaia mysl'* 6 (1910).

Vladimirskii, N. *Kostromskaia oblast'*. Kostroma: Kostromskoe Knizhnoe Izdatel'stvo, 1959.

Vohn, B. M., ed. *Poeziia rabochikh professii*. Moscow: Novaia Moskva, 1924.

Von Wahl, Rita. "A Personal Record." *Atlantic Monthly*, 126 (July 1920).

Weinbaum, Batya, and Amy Bridges. "The Other Side of the Paycheck: Monopoly Capital and the Structure of Consumption." *Capitalist Patriarchy and the Case for Socialist Feminism*. Edited by Zillah R. Eisenstein.

Whiting, Bernice, and John Whiting. *Children of Six Cultures: A Psycho-Cultural Analysis*. Cambridge: Harvard University Press, 1975.

Wilbur, George, and Warner Muensterberger. *Psychoanalysis and Culture: Essays in Honor of Geza Roheim*. New York: International Universities Press, 1951.

Young, Frank. *Initiation Ceremonies: A Cross-Cultural Study of Status Dramatization*. Indianapolis: Bobbs-Merrill, 1965.

Zelenin, D. K., comp. *Bibliograficheskii ukazatel' russkoi etnograficheskoi literatury o vneshnem byte narodov rossii, 1700-1910 g*. St. Petersburg: Tipgrafiia A. B. Orlova, 1913.

Zhegalova, S. K. "Tekstil'naia razdatochnaia kontora Moskovskoi gubernii." *Istoriko-bytovyi ekspeditsii 1949-1950 gg*. Edited by A. M. Pankratova. Moscow: Gosudarstvennoe Izdatel'stvo, 1953.

Index